CHINA

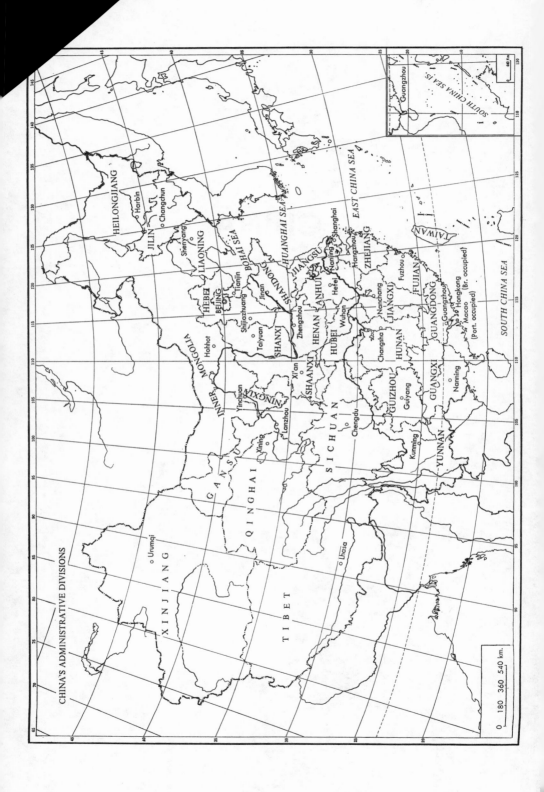

CHINA'S ADMINISTRATIVE DIVISIONS

China

A Concise History

Second Edition, Revised

Milton W. Meyer

Littlefield Adams Quality Paperbacks

LITTLEFIELD ADAMS QUALITY PAPERBACKS

a division of Rowman & Littlefield Publishers, Inc.
4720 Boston Way, Lanham, Maryland 20706
3 Henrietta Street
London, WC2E 8LU, England

Copyright © 1994 by Rowman & Littlefield Publishers, Inc.

Published in the United States of America

British Cataloging in Publication Information Available

Published simultaneously in a cloth edition
by Rowman & Littlefield Publishers, Inc.
ISBN 0-8476-7953-5

Library of Congress Cataloging-in-Publication Data

Meyer, Milton Walter.
China : a concise history / Milton W. Meyer. —2nd ed., rev.
p.   cm.
Includes bibliographical references and index.
I. China—History.   I. Title.
DS736.M44   1994   954—dc20   94-2239   CIP

ISBN 0-8226-3033-8 (pbk. : alk. paper)

Printed in the United States of America

∞™ The paper used in this publication meets the minimum requirements of
American National Standard for Information Sciences—Permanence of
Paper for Printed Library Materials, ANSI Z39.48–1984.

To the memory of
Kenneth Scott Latourette

CONTENTS

PREFACE

The purpose of this book is to provide an introduction to the history of China over the course of some four millennia. The first part introduces the land and the people, traces briefly the history of China, and outlines the traditional way of life. Parts Two through Six relate the ancient traditional eras before 221 B.C. and the history of imperial China, 221 B.C. to A.D. 1912, with its cycles of several dozen dynasties (ruling families) of varying duration. The final part charts the path of modern China since 1912 through periods of political ferment and change that culminated in the establishment of the People's Republic of China. A bibliography is appended.

I have had long-time interest in China and the Chinese. As a pre-World War II resident in the Philippines, I formed early friendships with overseas Chinese in the archipelago. During World War II, I experienced military duty in Kunming and Xi'an. My postwar Foreign Service duty with the Department of State in Jakarta and Hong Kong, as well as extensive subsequent travels throughout China and neighboring lands, kept me in contact with its peoples.

In academic courses I was privileged to study as an undergraduate at Yale, in the fourth generation of Chinese studies there, with Kenneth Scott Latourette, whose professor, in turn, was the son of S. Wells Williams, the first American sinologue in China (*Middle Kingdom*, 1848), and who introduced at Yale the first American college curricula relating to that country. At Columbia, as part of a master's degree that included intensified courses in the language, I studied with L. Carrington Goodrich. When I was at Stanford, my doctoral adviser, Arthur Wright, with his erudition, sparked a special interest in Buddhistic themes.

Over the years, students at California State University, Los Angeles, in lecture courses relating to Chinese history, have helped to focus the organization and presentation of the material. Thanks are due sinologist Hugh O'Neill, as well as colleagues Philip Leung and Teresa Sun, for reviewing, with suggestions, Part One of the text. The late Professor Goodrich graciously offered corrections on passages relating to the Yuan and Ming dynasties. It is my hope that through this introductory history I may share my appreciation of the complex but wonderfully human world of China and the Chinese.

Milton Walter Meyer

INTRODUCING CHINA

There are compelling reasons to study China. The first is demographic: the Chinese themselves probably have always constituted the largest single mass of human beings in the world to live in one country at any given period of time. Now more than one billion in number, they account for one-fourth of the human race. Estimates project future growth, a phenomenon the government is trying to contain with the model one-child family policy, among other measures. In past eras, China could sufficiently sustain its inhabitants within natural boundaries on existing food supplies. In modern times, with only limited additional arable land for agricultural development, as well as little possibility of increasing yields on existing acreages, China has faced problems that result from ever-growing population pressures on available food and natural resources.

A second reason to study China is its impressive geographic size. After the Russian Federation and Canada, it is third in total land area. (China is slightly larger than the United States.) It forms one-fourth of the Asian landmass and one-tenth of the total world land area, excluding the Antarctic. East to west, it ranges over 3,000 miles, a distance comparable in the United States to that between San Francisco and New York. North to south, it stretches over 2,000 miles, approximating an equal distance between Winnipeg in Canada and Mexico City. The sheer magnitude of the country lends itself to topographical variety that includes alpine heights, forbidding deserts, lush valleys, dusty plains, lengthy rivers, and a continental climate of weather extremes. The geographic immensity contributes to a historical heritage that embraces numerous regional cultural variations. Its penetrable mountain ranges, although some are quite high, have permitted a pattern of historic mobility and movement through internal migrations, as well as the conquest by, or absorption of, nomadic invaders, from chiefly northern and western frontier areas.

1

China, moreover, enjoys the oldest and most continuously recorded civilization in the world. Its cultural and written heritage is approximately 4,000 years old. Evolving out of legendary periods and archaic times into recorded history, the Chinese, long before the Christian era in the Western world, had initiated the ideological basis for a political state that has endured over several millennia. They learned, through doctrine and practice, how to accommodate themselves to each other in an impacted society, and how to achieve a pattern of harmony between man and his natural environment. Proud of their accomplishments and ethnocentric in their outlook, they coursed their own unique way. Through conquest or cultural example, they embraced peripheral states into their mode of life. Japan, Korea, Central Asia, Tibet, and North Vietnam came into the Chinese sphere of influence. The term East Asia, in this broad cultural context, encompasses all these political units, for it designates the far-ranging geographic area that has been materially inspired by Chinese civilization.

Over time, the Chinese developed great empires and recorded the reigns of their outstanding rulers. They reckoned some two dozen traditional dynasties, which were a succession of royal families, who dated in origin back to the second millennium B.C. Throughout their history, they exhibited periods of military and territorial expansion that took them, despite geographic obstacles, east into Korea, north into Mongolia, west into Central Asia, and south into India and Southeast Asia. In turn, China was periodically conquered by foreigners, who ruled first over part of the land (the north and west) and then, by the thirteenth century, over the whole country. Through later cycles of domestic and alien rule, the Chinese, when not occupied by others, utilized a variety of tactics in dealing with their neighbors, whom they invariably characterized as cultural barbarians from lesser lands. The Chinese, as a means to contain enemies, variously forged alliances with them, bought them off, intermarried with them, or played them off against each other.

The Chinese perennially maintained that everything good came from China and that the civilized world, in fact, was China. This attitude was revealed in the names they gave their country, which they termed from ancient times as the Middle Kingdom (*Zhongguo*) or (Everything) under Heaven (*Tianxia*). A third descriptive connotation, *Hua*, meaning something flowery or elegant, is incorporated into the formal political names of both the Republic of China (on Taiwan) and the People's Republic of China (centered in Beijing). Proud of their heritage, they also called themselves men of Han or men of Tang, two of their most illustrious imperial dynasties. The term *China*, which Westerners and Chinese use alike, is derived from a short-lived third-century B.C. dynasty called *Qin* whose first emperor escalated, in terminology, the political state from kingdom to empire.

Yet despite China's importance in Asia, and now world history, there have been several basic problems in understanding the country and people. In the past, great time and geographic distances separated China from the Occident. The Middle Kingdom lay thousands of miles distant from Europe and the United States. Until American West Coast ports opened up in the mid-nineteenth century, ships from eastern coastal cities in the Middle Atlantic and New England states took months to reach China via the long circuitous routes around the tips of South America or Africa. The distance between Europe and China seemed as far. Prior to the opening of the Suez Canal in 1869, ships took some three months to sail from London to Chinese coastal ports in the Far East. China was remote to the West, and Westerners in China were far from home.

China was also semiisolated from its Asian neighbors. Vast inhospitable deserts sprawled to the north and west. The towering Himalayan mountain range bordered the south. To the southeast lay jungles. In the east, seas restricted the movement of Chinese, who did not take readily to overseas navigation. The long perilous land routes to border countries, which were reached principally by skirting the deserts in Central Asia, or by traversing mountain passes into Burma (officially known as Myanmar after 1990) and India, discouraged all but the most hardy. Yet despite these physical obstacles, the Chinese as well as foreigners were able to break through the geographic barriers. Over the past fifteen centuries, fascinating accounts of peregrinations across sea and land routes to and from the Middle Kingdom have been detailed by Chinese, other Asian travelers, and Westerners.

In addition to the issue of relative Chinese self-containment, the problem of assessing continuity and change within the country tends to complicate any long-term analysis of Chinese history. What characteristics have basically remained the same through the millennia in China? What features have fundamentally changed? The generalization often advanced, that China was an unchanging country, is inaccurate, because China, both prior to the impact of the West and subsequent to it, did manifest internal change and growth. The concept of "change within tradition" might be a more appropriate phrase for describing the historical process in China: borrowing from abroad but yet retaining recognizable indigenous traits.

Much that is traditional seems to have survived even into Communist China, especially the written language with its time-honored characters. Village life continues as the predominant social and economic factor of everyday affairs. The agricultural basis for society still embraces a vast network of grain fields. Human labor continues to be used extensively. Social solidarity is emphasized, and a paternalistic hand directs political and economic life. But within these persisting aspects of Chinese society, modernization and industrialization have been in evidence, especially during the past century in urban areas. Revolutions, implying basic changes suddenly introduced, in Chinese society, politics, and economics, have advanced more sketchily and unevenly. The Chinese, although relative newcomers to the concept of political nationalism, are as nationalistic as any other peoples. Results and evidences of these upheavals are easier to ascertain in the material sphere; psychological adjustments to modernization and change, probably the more important, are harder to gauge and penetrate by the outsider.

Despite a certain amount of modernization and cross-cultural assimilation, gaps of understanding between China and the West continue to exist. Some have been difficult to bridge. The Occidental finds traditional Chinese philosophies puzzling and present communist ideology incompatible with the Western liberal tradition. The written language, with its multitude of odd-looking characters, seems to be forbidding. Chinese dialects, with their several tonal inflexions, sound strange to the unaccustomed ear. Family names appear in reversed order, with patronyms placed first and personal appellations following. Cultural connotations and implications of similar words or terminology often differ. For instance, would the simple but basic word *family* mean the same to a Chinese as to an American? The traditional and idealized Chinese concept of the term involves not only a nuclear one but a family in the extended form, one that embraced all members of several generations who lived under one roof in closely knit and precisely defined ties and roles.

Linguistic problems are particularly complex, for they involve a knowledge not only of one culture and language but appropriate equivalents to, and translations in, the host country. Foreigners in China have been perennially faced with this phenomenon. Early Indian Buddhist pilgrims, as well as later American Christian missionaries, met with similar perplexities in trying to express their complex theological beliefs in the Chinese language and its thought patterns that might not have embraced similar concepts. The role of the ideological transmitter, native or foreign, was crucial in bridging cultural and linguistic chasms.

China's world may be divided into three geographical areas: China proper, its border regions, and certain outlying lands and overseas countries. The first, China proper, is the cultural and political heartland; it has been where the greater proportion of the Chinese population has resided. Traditionally, it has consisted of eighteen provinces, an administrative feature that dates from the nineteenth and early twentieth centuries. The border regions ring this heartland on land and sea. In these, the Chinese until recently were in the minority, although the distinction between Chinese and non-Chinese has been fading with the incorporation of most of these areas into the Chinese political fold. Finally, some outlying lands, such as Japan and most of Southeast Asia, although never under directly political control of the Chinese, have been subjected periodically to Chinese racial or cultural presence.

China Proper

China proper constitutes only one-third of the total area of China, but it contains 95 percent of the population. By comparison, it is, in this shrunken form, a third the geographic size of the United States, but it has about four times the population. (The size and population analogy to the United States would be as if most Americans lived east of the Mississippi River.) Despite the fact that China proper possesses a variety of subordinate topographical features and a continental climate of extremes, the Chinese people succeeded in forming a unified country because of the existence of a common written script and a uniform political philosophy. Naturally, regionalism exists in such a large country, but obstacles were never so great that they divided the Chinese culturally to the extent that, say, Europeans have been divided by the Alps. Physical features, such as mountain ranges and large rivers, have helped to define the internal boundaries of China proper, which might be divided into three subparts: north, central, and south. All three are based on riverine systems.

North China is watered by the Yellow River (Huang He) which flows from the Tibetan plateau through the North China plain to the Yellow Sea. This river and its plain represent the source of livelihood for one-fourth of China's people. But throughout history, because of alternating droughts and floods, the river has represented death, as well as life, to them. An early nineteenth-century emperor appropriately termed it as "China's Sorrow." Some 2,900 miles long, the sixth longest in the world (it vies with two Siberian rivers of equal length), it initially courses through mountain gorges at 14,000 feet, and then drops precipitously to 5,800 feet after the first 700 miles. It next gradually flattens out at an average of a few feet per mile in great bends through western and northern China. A wide but relatively shallow river, it is not navigable by deep-draft vessels. Along the banks of the Yellow River there is a great problem of siltage. In the Ordos region, bounded by the great turns of the river, the current cuts away the loess, a friable soil, and carries it off to the sea in muddy swirls: hence the name of the river. In the course of centuries, through this extensive siltage, the river has risen from 10 to 40 feet above the surrounding plains. Consequently dikes have had to be erected to contain its course. When the river bursts the dikes, its mouth changes, emptying into the sea at variant points. The Yellow River has few tributaries, and because of the flood dangers involved, no sizable communities were ever built directly on its banks. However, the Chinese Communists have constructed multipurpose dams along the middle and lower reaches of the river to control the floods and to develop irrigation, navigation, and electric power.

Ancient sites of the North China plain record the earliest known centers of Chinese civilization, as well as some of the later great capitals of China's dynasties. In the North China plain today, there are a number of big cities, notably Beijing and Tianjin (Tientsin), which, because of their large sizes, are administered directly by the central government organs of the People's Republic of China. These urban centers, located along the thirty-eighth parallel, are comparable in latitude to Washington, D.C. or San Francisco. But despite this coincidence, the northern Chinese cities experience more extreme variations in climate, with cold dry winters and hot humid summers. As the average yearly rainfall is only 20 to 30 inches, the one-crop agricultural period is short. The main harvests include such dry-land grains as wheat, legumes, millet, and kaoliang, a form of millet. The mineral resources of the area include some oil in the northwest and 85 percent of all of the country's coal reserves.

North China's provinces, some of whose names derive from geographic descriptions, include Hebei (north of the river), Henan (south of the river), Shandong (east of the mountains), Shanxi (west of the mountains), Shaanxi, Gansu, and recently Qinghai, carved out of other areas, mainly Tibet, Also in the central Ordos reaches of the Yellow River is the Ningxia Hui Autonomous Region, so designated by the Chinese Communists after the Hui, an indigenous group defined as a minority since it is mainly Muslims who reside there.

Central China has as its backbone the Yangtze River, known to the Chinese as the Chang Jiang (Long River), similarly rising in the Tibetan plateau and breaking through the mountains into the vast central plain. The region is a transitional zone in terms of geography, culture, wealth, and crops. In its upper reaches, the Yangtze is also called the Jinsha Jiang (Golden River). Some 3,900 miles long, the third longest river in the world (after the Nile in Africa and the Amazon in South America), it is navigable only in its lower reaches below the gorges.

Unlike the Yellow River, extensive silting does not occur along the deeper Yangtze, although much soil is carried into the sea. And it does not have the flooding problems that the Yellow River has because there are several natural catchment lakes in the central plain to siphon off the excess water. The Chinese Communists have constructed a dam at the point where the gorges end and the river spills out into the valley. Other ambitious projects are planned to harness the great volume of water carried off to its mouth.

Although Central China is not the traditional political focus of the country, it is the economic heartland. Some national capitals were located in the lower Yangtze, but the middle region of China proper has generally been less important historically than the northern. There are several big cities on or near the river, particularly in the lower reaches. Near the river mouth on a tributary channel is Shanghai, also administered directly from Beijing. With more than twelve million people (the largest, most industrialized, commercial, and dynamic city in China), it is a relative newcomer to the Chinese urban scene, having been developed by Western countries initially from the mid-nineteenth century. In the delta area of the river are the historical and cultural centers of Hangzhou, Suzhou, and Wuzi. Some hundred miles upstream, Nanjing has, on occasion, been a capital of China. The industrialized three-city Wuhan complex (Wuchang, Hankow, and Hanyang) is situated on the central reaches of the river. Hills and mountains are more in abundance on the fringes of Central China than they are in North China. And because rains from the South China Sea drench the central coastal area, giving it an average annual rainfall of 40 inches, the climate is wetter than that of North China. The growing season is longer than in the north. The important crops of the area are wheat, rice, and tea. The mountains contain some mineral deposits, and there are iron reserves around Wuhan.

Central China is populous. Three regions each have approximately a hundred million people. The provinces that make up Central China include Jiangsu, Zhejiang, Anhui, Jiangxi, Hubei, Hunan, Guizhou, and Sichuan.

South China, with its numerous mountain ranges, has an abundance of small valleys and short rivers, of which the most important is the West River (Xi Jiang). At 1,200 miles, it is comparable in length to the Ohio River. It empties into the South China Sea near Guangzhou (formerly Canton), at which point it is popularly known as the Pearl River (Zhu Jiang). There are other short rivers in the south that flow into the West River, or directly into the sea. South China was never important as a political center, but because it was far from the central and northern capitals, it was often a center of revolt. The climate is wet, and hurricanes strike with terrifying force in the summer. Hong Kong, the British crown colony near Guangzhou, registers 80 inches of rain per year. For an area that is in the latitude of Calcutta and Havana, the winters are quite cool. Rice and tea are the chief crops of South China, and, since the growing season may extend from six to all twelve months, up to three rice crops a year are possible. Some of the mineral resources of the area are bauxite, antimony, mercury, and tungsten.

The provinces of South China include coastal Fujian, Guangdong, Hainan (island), and inland Yunnan. Guangxi, formerly a province, has been designated as Guangxi Zhuang Autonomous Region by the Chinese Communists to indicate there the presence of the minority Zhuang people. Most of the Chinese who have emigrated abroad have come from these southern coastal provinces.

China's Border Regions

Beyond China proper, as a second geographic and historical entity, are continental and insular border areas that have periodically been incorporated into Chinese empires. These include Tibet, Xinjiang, Mongolia, Manchuria, Taiwan, and the Ryukyu archipelago, of which some now are in, some out, of the People's Republic of China's territorial control. The first four, extensive in size, are each comparable in geographic scope to the state of Alaska.

Tibet, known to the Chinese as Xizang (Western Land) Autonomous Region, from time to time came within the Chinese political orbit. The name *Tibet* is a term that had been used in thirteenth-century Europe from Marco Polo's time. It is derived from an English transliteration of the Chinese representation of the Mongolian designation. A mountainous area, Tibet covers about half a million square miles; much of it is a plateau, the most extensive the world, of over 15,000 feet in altitude. The source of main Chinese and some Asian rivers, this large area is occupied by a population of about two million. Agricultural and mineral resources are minimal.

Chinese interest in Tibet dated from A.D. 650, when a princess from the Chinese court arrived in Lhasa, the capital, to marry the monarch to cement Sino-Tibetan relations. Tibetans, in turn, later expanded their area and captured temporarily the eighth-century Chinese capital located at what is now Xi'an. Receiving also Buddhistic impulses from North India and China, Tibet sent out monks and pilgrims into neighboring Himalayan lands, including present-day Bhutan, northwestern India, and northern Pakistan. In the thirteenth century, the Mongols incorporated Tibet into their empire, and Kublai Khan, the greatest of their line in China, set up the rule of priest-kings. In time, a type of dyarchy arose, with the Dalai Lama as the chief spiritual and temporal ruler at Lhasa and the Panchen Lama in a secondary position of leadership at Xigaze (Shigatse) in the west.

After the Mongols, China's rulers periodically attempted to reincorporate the territory into their domains. In the early decades of the twentieth century, the Nationalist Chinese interfered in internal Tibetan politics. In 1950, the Chinese Communists invaded Tibet and later incorporated the area into China. Because of the political vicissitudes of Tibet over time, the term is defined in several senses. Now geographically contracted, it has included more expansive racial and cultural boundaries.

Xinjiang (New Territory) has also been a part of the Chinese empire on and off throughout history. With an area of 635,000 square miles, it embraces a population of only some five million, the majority of whom are Turkish-speaking Islamic peoples, mainly Uygur, related to similar tribes in neighboring Central Russian Asia. Xinjiang is divided into two parts by the traversing Tian Shan range, with the Dzungarian Plain to the north and the Tarim Basin, encompassing the forbidding Taklamakhan desert (an extension of the Gobi, which means desert), to the south. The main areas of the settlement are the oases fringing the northern and southern borders of the Tarim Basin, through which passes the silk and trade routes to India and the West. These routes were also used by the Buddhist pilgrims en route between China and India or in the reverse direction.

The dry desert air of Xinjiang has preserved many ancient artifacts. From Dunhuang, one Buddhist cave complex at the eastern end of the Taklamakhan desert, has come, among other treasures, the world's oldest extant printed book (by the wood-block method), dated the equivalent of A.D. 868. As the last of the major outlying districts to be brought into the Chinese political realm within the past century, Xinjiang was created in 1884. In the early 1900s local warlords arose who, depending on the shifting political winds, alternated their allegiance between the Russians and the Chinese. When the Chinese Communists acquired control after 1949, they created the Xinjiang Uygur Autonomous Region. Because of the ties between the Uygur and their counterparts in neighboring Kazakhstan, there have been border problems. In the great open desert areas of Xinjiang, the Chinese Communists have conducted nuclear experiments.

Mongolia, both Inner and Outer, was an intermediary zone between the Chinese and the culturally designated barbarian ways of life. Inner Mongolia (Nei Mongol to Chinese), south of the forbidding desert expanses of the Gobi, was more oriented to China. Of its some ten million inhabitants, most are Chinese. The area is now an autonomous region in the Chinese Communist political structure. Across the Gobi to the north and northwest is the independent state of (Outer) Mongolia, formerly the Mongolian People's Republic, with two million inhabitants in 604,000 square miles. Claimed by Chinese rulers as part of their domains, it was a principal source of invasions by nomadic tribes. From it came, among other invaders, the Mongols, who established in thirteenth-century Eurasia the largest land empire in world history up to that time. With the downfall in 1912 in China of the Manchu dynasty, which also ruled over Mongolia, and the concurrent rise of the Soviet Union, Mongolia entered the Russian orbit after World War I. In 1921, Soviet troops moved into the area as part of their eastward thrust through Siberia. Three years later, the Mongolian People's Republic was established as the first Communist state outside Russia. Nationalist China after 1912 continued to press its interests there, as did the Chinese Communists after 1949. But geography, politics, race, and ideology into the early 1990s bound Mongolia more closely to the former Soviet Union than to either of the two successive Chinas on the mainland.

Manchuria is known to the Chinese as the Dongbei (Northeast).The border land has more than fifty million people living in half a million square miles, Manchuria is especially well endowed in coal, iron, oil, and timber, as well as in agricultural resources. Chinese colonies existed in the south of Manchuria from the second century B.C., and throughout history expansionist Chinese emperors periodically reasserted control. Manchuria (the origin of the name is unclear) was also the source of numerous invasions into China. The last thrust was that of the Manchu, who, like the earlier Mongols, conquered all of China in the seventeenth century. Into the twentieth century, Manchuria was a pawn in international power politics. Nominally ruled by Chinese warlords after 1912, first the Russians, and then the Japanese, intervened in the political and economic life of the rich border land.

At the turn of the century the Russians were moving Manchuria into their sphere of influence, but in 1905, the Japanese succeeded in acquiring Russian economic rights in the southern half. In 1931-1932, they appropriated all of Manchuria, after which they created the puppet state of Manchukuo. The Japanese developed an extended network of railways and exploited the area economically. After World War II, the Soviets, by international agreement, occupied Manchuria, where they stayed for almost a year. Upon their withdrawal, both Chinese Nationalists and Communists competed for the rich territory. By late

1948, the Communists won the race to assimilate Manchuria, an event that presaged shortly thereafter the takeover of all of mainland China. The Communists divided up the area into the three provinces of Heilongjiang, Jilin, and Liaoning.

Taiwan (Terraced Bay), which foreigners used to call Formosa, lies a hundred miles off the coast of China across the strait that bears its name. It also has experienced a checkered historical background. As early as 605, the Chinese claimed the territory, but colonization was slow. Although the island officially became a protectorate of the Chinese empire in 1206, only tenuous control was established. In the sixteenth century, Westerners, particularly the Dutch and Portuguese, tried unsuccessfully to establish trading colonies there. During the Manchu conquest of China in the mid-seventeenth century, large numbers of refugees fled to Taiwan. Eventually incorporated into the Manchu empire, the island attracted more Chinese emigrants. In 1886, the island, which previously had been administered as part of Fujian province across the strait, was designated as a separate province. In 1895, as a result of the Chinese defeat in the Sino-Japanese War, title went to the Japanese, who colonized it for half a century. In 1945, after the Japanese surrender ended World War II, Chiang Kai-shek's troops occupied Taiwan, which four years later became the home of his refugee Nationalist government, the Republic of China. Although the Nationalists held the island, the People's Republic of China staked out Taiwan as one of its legitimate provinces. As the two Chinese antagonists laid claims to the island, the native Taiwanese themselves have been relegated the a secondary political role on their homeland. A fertile island, Taiwan grows a variety of crops, including rice, sugarcane, fruit, and forest products. Taipei is the chief and capital city.

Northeast of Taiwan, the Ryukyu Islands string out in an extended arc. The archipelago consists of three principal groups, of which Okinawa, with its capital of Naha, is the most important. In the seventh century A.D., the Chinese invaded the islands and began to extract tribute. By the 1600s, the Japanese also received tribute. In 1854, Commodore Matthew Perry concluded a treaty with the independently acting ruling house. The anomalous international status was resolved by the Japanese, who in 1879 annexed the islands into their empire over Chinese protests. After World War II, for strategic considerations, the islands were placed under the administration of the United States, while the Japanese retained residual sovereignty. This arrangement, confirmed by the 1951 Japanese peace treaty, lasted for two decades, after which administrative control also reverted to the Japanese.

Outlying Lands

In a third geographical dimension, Chinese territorial as well as cultural boundaries have also spread into outlying countries, such as neighboring Korea. That country, a mountainous peninsular land, is 600 miles long and 135 miles wide. Wedged among more powerful states, because of its location, Korea has compromised more than once its political sovereignty. Chinese colonies were founded in northern Korea in the second century B.C. when the land, along with southern Manchuria, was effectively annexed to China. In the first decades of the third century A.D., as Korea divided itself into the three main states of Koguryo, Paekche, and Silla, Chinese influence declined. Warfare was endemic in the peninsula until Silla, in the seventh century, united the warring factions with requested Chinese military assistance.

About this time, Buddhism entered Korea from China, and Koreans in turn assumed a major role in exporting the faith to Japan. In the tenth century, as Chinese ties weakened, Silla fell. A rebel established the Koryu dynasty (from which the name *Korea* derives), but it continued as a vassal of China under the Mongols into the fourteenth century. The successor Yi dynasty also acknowledged Chinese suzerainty (indirect rule as an alternative to direct subjugation). After the mid-nineteenth century, the Japanese in new moves of expansionism reasserted historic interests in Korea, where they also had enjoyed periodic political ties. After expelling first the Chinese, and subsequently the Russians, the Japanese assimilated Korea as a colony (1910-1945). In the post-World War II era, Korea continued to reflect international power struggles, with the Democratic People's Republic of Korea in the north under a communist regime and the Republic of Korea in the south with an anti-Communist stance. The Chinese role in the Korean War (1950-1953) revealed dramatically that the neighboring country continued to have more than a passing academic interest in the vital and strategically located peninsula.

As a peripheral insular country, Japan itself came within the cultural, but not the territorial, sphere of Chinese interest. As early as A.D. 400, Chinese and Koreans emigrated to Japan, where they helped to establish the first historic Japanese state of Yamato in the Kyoto-Nara-Osaka area at the eastern end of the Inland Sea. The Japanese, emerging from a relatively primitive society, at this time began to adopt much of Chinese culture, including the written script, the Buddhist religion, and concepts of centralized economic and political power. The particular grandeur of the Chinese dynasties of the sixth to ninth centuries left their imprint on the Japanese ruling class, who wanted to transplant more sophisticated Chinese ideas wholesale into Japanese life in order to create a cohesive national unity centered on the Japanese imperial line. Augmenting expedient political and economic policies, the oligarchy also embraced printing, architecture, dances, and literary forms from the mainland. In the ninth century, after achieving a degree of cultural sophistication themselves, and with the decline of the Chinese political order at home, Japanese ardor for things Chinese cooled off. Relations were revived sporadically in the fifteenth century, but they were not to last. In the early twentieth century, Japan returned to the Asian mainland, but this time it began a decades-long attempt at conquest.

Another region that experienced Chinese expansion was Southeast Asia. Chinese interest there has been particularly directed toward a geographically contiguous North Vietnam. Troops of the first great Chinese emperor, in the late third century B.C., temporarily conquered the area to a distance some 250 miles north of present-day Ho Chi Minh City (formerly Saigon). After the emperor's death, a Chinese general established the independent southern kingdom of Nam Viet (Southern Viet, an ethnic term, inverted in modern usage), with its capital at Guangzhou, to include North Vietnam and some southern Chinese provinces. In 196 B.C., Nam Viet became a vassal of the Chinese empire, and in 110 B.C. it was annexed and divided into seven counties.

Despite native rebellions, this incorporation of Vietnamese territory into the Chinese empire lasted until A.D. 939. By this time, the Chinese had designated the southern region as Annam (Pacified South), a term persisting into the contemporary usage to designate the central third of Vietnam. To the northern half of Vietnam in this millennium of rule, the Chinese imprinted their system of writing, law, codes, administrative structures, and bureaucracy. Although Vietnam is now Communist dominated, its leaders read their history well, and they have long considered the hazards involved in living as a neighbor to a strong China of whatever ideology. A common adage in Vietnam, as well as in other countries of the Indochinese peninsula, has been that "when China sneezes, we catch cold."

In other areas of mainland and insular Southeast Asia where early native kingdoms had come under Indian influences through Hindu or Buddhist ties, the Chinese set up merchant enclaves. Chinese artifacts have been discovered in wide-ranging areas of Southeast Asia, including the Philippines. In the thirteenth century, the Mongols sent land expeditions into Burma and Vietnam and sea expeditions as far as Java. In the early fifteenth century, the Chinese emperors sporadically dispatched naval expeditions into southern and western waters as far as the Persian Gulf. These intrusions brought no lasting results, and as the

European powers commenced their expansion in Asia, China withdrew into its shell.

The peace and prosperity of colonial rule in Southeast Asia by the nineteenth century attracted the Chinese once again, particularly those from the economically hard-pressed provinces of South China. They flocked into the southern countries, which they called Nanyang (Lands of the Southern Sea). Despite sporadic persecution, they remained in the adopted lands, some of them for several generations. By the 1990s, 20 million Chinese had established themselves in Southeast Asia. Singapore, the largest Chinese-populated city outside of China itself, has a Chinese majority of 80 percent. Almost half of the population on the Malay peninsula to the north is also Chinese. Cholon, the twin city of Saigon, is mainly Chinese. Before World War II, the Chinese residents in these colonies were able to achieve certain material benefits and economic advantages. However, after Southeast Asian countries achieved their independence, Chinese were subjected to rigid nationalization laws that discriminated against them and their livelihoods.

Although the Chinese were less numerous in more distant lands, a large number of them did emigrate to the United States in the mid-nineteenth century as part of the gold rush or to provide labor on the transcontinental railroads. Upon completion of the projects and the end of the gold rush, they settled down in West Coast communities, where they were kept aloof from local affairs or were excluded from them. Later immigration laws kept the Chinese quota to a minimum. Fewer Chinese went to other countries in the western Hemisphere, although Canada, Mexico, Cuba, and Peru did attract sizable Chinese minorities. Some Chinese settled in the Pacific islands, Europe, Africa, and the Middle East. Wherever they went, they left a definite imprint of their distinctive race and culture.

China's Provincial Level Administrative Units

Municipalities under central control (3): Beijing, Shanghai, Tianjin. Autonomous regions, with capitals indicated (5): Guangxi Zhuang (Nanjing); Inner Mongolia (Hohhot); Ningxia Hui (Yinchuan); Tibet (Lhasa); Xinjiang Uygur (Urumqi).

Provinces (23): Anhui (Hefei); Fujian (Fuzhou); Gansu (Lanzhou); Guangdong (Guangzhou or Canton); Guizhou (Guiyang); Hainan (Haikou); Hebei (Shijiazhuang); Heilongjiang (Harbin); Henan (Zhengzhou); Hubei (Wuhan); Hunan (Changsha); Jiangsu (Nanjing); Jiangxi (Nanchang); Jilin (Changchun); Liaoning (Shenyang, formerly Mukden); Qinghai (Xining); Shaanxi (Xi'an); Shandong (Jinan); Shanxi (Taiyuan); Sichaun (Chengdu); Taiwan (Taipei) claimed; Yunnan (Kunming); Zhejiang (Hangzhou).

Part One

THE CHINESE WAY OF LIFE

The Chinese way of life in its formative stages dated back to archaic eras. Early on, the Chinese began to define the basic outlines of their concerns. Ancient thought included the political visions of a well-ordered state with rulers as philosopher-kings presiding over their contented subjects, all playing clearly defined roles. Concerned with the here-and-now, and with the ceaseless search for human utopias, later philosophers and historians elaborated and encapsulated these relations and goals into structured forms of etiquette and behavior, precisely defined in time-honored classics and works of history. Orthodox literature wove these themes into a historical scroll depicting a continued evolution over time into the twentieth century of some two dozen dynasties, or royal families, of varying duration and territorial size.

Monarchs came and went, but a centralized bureaucracy, recruited principally from examinations based on a common core of knowledge, managed quite efficiently the affairs of state in times of both peace and adversity. The mass of people were kept in bonds not so much through the direct exercise of authority but by a universal and supplementary subscription to shared unwritten goals of common law and acts in their Middle Kingdom, the center of the known world. Other indigenous philosophies lent a balance to the intellectual scene; imported Buddhism, Islam, Christianity, and Communism later added layers to Chinese thought.

The great majority of Chinese were farmers. Agriculture loomed large in the economic sector, where some 80 to 90 percent of the populace was concerned with agrarian affairs. They planted and harvested grain crops, notably that of rice, but they supplemented their diet with an extraordinary range of food stuffs. Although living lives of drudgery, they managed to engage in time-honored communal festivals and to note family anniversaries. Spread over such a large geographic area, they spoke varying dialects, but those who were literate all wrote in a common script. It was the educated elite in the cities and countryside, in or out of office, who augmented official literature with more informal forms. They also experimented in practical science. Chinese were credited with numerous inventions, including the manufacture of paper and the printing medium, pyrotechnics (later gunpowder), and the compass.

The Chinese literati also enjoyed a rich culture. In decorative arts, they produced textiles, of which silk was justly famous. They valued jade, and they utilized household items, including lacquer. In the performing arts, they enjoyed music and drama. In the plastic arts, their artisans wrought works of bronze, sculpted animals and human figures, and fashioned exquisite ceramic forms which achieved such international fame that the term china came to be equated with the country. They painted, executed calligraphy, and wrote poems—all termed as arts of the brush. They designed tranquil garden oases. Their architecture embraced many forms, from humble dwellings to monumental palaces and the Great Wall. The multifaceted Chinese genius was expressed in rich and varying forms, highlights of which are outlined here.

HISTORICAL LITERATURE

The Chinese have written much about their country. In copious historical records and numerous chronicles transmitted over thousands of years, they have documented their progress. The traditional Chinese interpretation of their history argues a succession of some two dozen dynasties that commenced in the second millennium B.C. and persisted into the early twentieth century. Dynasties were simply imperial families, analogous to those that existed in Western monarchies (such as the Hapsburgs, Bourbons, or the contemporary Windsors in England). Dynastic histories, compiled by court bureaucrats, constituted the ongoing source material of Chinese political life. These works drew upon a plethora of imperial records, monographic material, numerous biographies of important people, official annals, and essays on selected topics. In addition to the dynastic histories, the Chinese compiled miscellaneous histories of lesser scope and time, such as regional political entities and specific, short-time historical eras.

The Dynasties

Early Chinese historical theories held that the ancient past had been a golden age, one in which all men lived in peace and harmony. In time, unity gave way to division, war, and strife. Among later chroniclers of historic times, however, a pattern of dynasties appeared as the central idea in history. Through analogy to the life cycle, a repetitious pattern of rise and fall, of growth and decline, good founders initiated dynasties and evil rulers terminated them. History became a continuous succession of dynasties, one replacing the next. The two dozen orthodox dynasties varied greatly in length, from between four years (with one short-lived ruler) to nine centuries, with many monarchs.

The dynasties themselves were established by men who conquered rivals in recurring battles for succession to the throne. The victors were elevated to kingship by their men, or in cases of competing kingdoms, received an arbitrary imprint of orthodoxy from later historians. Dynastic names generally derived from geographic regions or, as in later dynasties, from abstract concepts, such as Bright (Ming) or Pure (Qing). In the formation of dynasties, the border areas, with non-Chinese tribes, were sometimes important, for they interacted with the Chinese to fashion new ruling families. Some 234 kings and emperors presided over the dozens of historic dynastic families, but only a few rulers were of great ability. (All were men; only one woman actually occupied the throne of China as a reigning monarch, in the eighth century.) Despite the mass of writing on imperial personages, most rulers seem to be nonentities in the endless chronicles of Chinese history.

Consistent with the great-man approach, traditional historians emphasized personal factors in explaining the dynastic cycle. The founder and his immediate successor might be portrayed as super-human, having received the mandate of heaven, or right to rule the country by virtue of his wisdom and good works that pleased the gods, but which meant, in reality, the feat of subduing all imperial contestants. Later rulers, having become debauched and weakened, lost the throne and the right to rule by alienating the deities on whose goodwill depended the well-being of the country. Within each dynasty of some length, the imperial line in its later decades seemed to degenerate. Sometimes, a revival by later rulers would temporarily stay or reinvigorate the ruling line, but this was not often the case. Strong or weak, kings and emperors remained the center of the state, but the people around them, such as the imperial families, empresses, concubines or secondary wives, eunuchs, advisers, and bureaucrats, were also important.

Undergirding traditional dynasties, modern interpretations of Chinese history, stressing less the imperial personal qualities, have analyzed and interpreted economic and administrative factors, which also played their appropriate roles in accounting for the rise and fall of dynasties. New rule commenced with a period of prosperity, wealth, peace, and population growth. Consolidation at home and expansion abroad were some of the indices of early dynastic years. But as time went on and the expenses of government grew, as well as the population, the spread of tax-free estates enjoying fiscal immunity resulted in the ever-increasing shrinkage of revenue, imperial prestige, and territorial boundaries. Additional hardships were heaped on the peasants to produce more. Public works fell into disrepair, crop failures become noticeable, and natural calamities, which might previously have gone unreported by bureaucrats to a strong monarch, were now brought to imperial attention. Countrywide rebellions broke out; in the free-for-all succession struggles, a single new leader would finally emerge. As victor, he ascended the throne and established a new family dynasty in accordance with the will of heaven. The less successful contenders lost their heads.

The origins of the Chinese people are still conjectural, but historical China rose in the North China plain along the banks of the Yellow River. The first of the traditional dynasties, for which archaeology has yet to find proof, is the Xia (Hsia), 2205-1766 B.C. or 1994-1523 B.C., according to two different ancient sources. Founded and ruled by legendary demigods, it was described in histories as a small state in north-central China. Its supposedly cruel last ruler was overthrown by a virtuous man, who established the Shang dynasty, 1766-1122 B.C. or 1523-1027 B.C., also centered in the North China plain. An authenticated period through archaeological discoveries, the Shang practiced agriculture, worshiped ancestors, developed early forms of Chinese written characters, invented the calendar, and shaped beautiful bronze vessels. In these early times, great social gaps existed between the authoritarian aristocratic leaders and the mass of the people.

Then followed the feudal age of the Zhou (Chou), 1122 or 1027 to 221 B.C., divided into two political subperiods. This, the longest dynasty in Chinese history, in its later centuries was a chaotic period of warring states. The early kingdom, which covered most of the North China plain, was governed from an administrative center near the present-day city of Xi'an, close by the last great bend of the Yellow River. In the eighth century B.C., under the pressures of foreign incursions and civil disorder, the Zhou were forced out of their homeland. In 771 B.C., they moved east to safer regions and ruled over a constricted area from a city now called Luoyang. In the course of the Earlier (or Western) and Later (or Eastern) Zhou periods, Chinese society became increasingly feudalistic and fragmented. Central power tended to break down, and semiautonomous city states arose. Yet despite political divisiveness, China in this overall era registered economic gains, as evidenced by its entry into the Iron Age and the establishment of a flourishing merchant class. It was also a golden age for Chinese philosophy and literature. A "hundred schools" of political thought contended for popular support and kingly sanction, while a "hundred flowers" blossomed in the cultural garden. Confucius, who flourished around 500 B.C., and who later became China's most respected philosopher, was in his lifetime only one of many thinkers seeking to be heard and to be accepted.

This earliest triad of political periods, known in Chinese histories as the Three Dynasties (*San Chao*), was headed by kings. When Zhou division was replaced by Qin unity (251-206 B.C.), its founder upgraded the position of king to emperor by title and initiated an imperial structure that provided the political framework for the Chinese state until 1912. He centralized the government, developed a professional bureaucracy, standardized writing, consolidated the Great Wall, and brooked no opposition. Essentially a one-man dynasty, the Qin, because of rebellions and weak successors, fell under the Han (206 B.C.-A.D. 220). Contemporaneous with the Roman Empire, the Han was one of the most expansive Chinese dynasties. In the course of four centuries of its existence, the classics of Confucius were defined as the basis of state orthodoxy; bureaucratic examinations based on those ideals were initiated. The Han, like the Zhou, was divided into two periods: an earlier or Western (206 B.C.-A.D. 9) and a later or Eastern (A.D. 23-220), separated by a brief interregnum of a usurper. The Han expanded into southern Manchuria, northern Korea, Central Asia, and North Vietnam.

Because no one man was strong enough to reunite China after the end of the dynasty, the Han was followed by three and a half centuries of political division, termed the period of the Six Dynasties (*Liu Chao*), 220-589. Alien rulers, fanning out from Manchuria and Mongolia, presided over the northern provinces, while the Chinese, who had been migrating southward through the centuries maintained rule over the central and southern areas. Despite the political turmoil, China's population increased and culture broadened. Buddhism, principally via Central Asia, made its entry from India. As the most important foreign institution imported into the country until modern times, it contributed variety and depth to Chinese life.

The next cycle of imperial unity, growth, and decline began with the short-lived Sui dynasty (589-618), which, like the Qin, reunified the country. Another imperialistic phase emerged as Chinese missions were dispatched to Korea, Taiwan, and the East Indies. It was also during this period that the early rulers in Japan began voluntarily to adopt Chinese customs and laws. As successor to the Sui, the Tang empire (618-907) was contemporaneous with that of Charlemagne's in Europe and was, like the Han, another high-water mark in Chinese history. Despite the earlier challenge from Buddhism that made inroads into the orthodox Confucian faith, this reemerged strengthened, and the civil service examinations dating from Han times became systematized. Chang'an, the great Tang capital, was located again near present-day Xi'an in the same area as had been the capitals of the Earlier Zhou, Qin, Earlier Han, and Sui. The Tang ruled an empire that extended into Central Asia, Tibet, Korea, and North Vietnam. Imperial achievements were matched by those in the cultural sphere; some of China's greatest poets, painters, and writers flourished in these centuries. The end of the Tang was followed by the Five Dynasties (*Wu Chao*), 907-960, another, but briefer, period of political division.

Much of the country was reunified under the Song (960-1279), but growing Chinese nomadic pressures from the north and west eventually forced the Chinese political center, south this time (not east), into a more militarily tenable area. With capitals first located in Kaifeng, and then after 1127 in the coastal city of Hangzhou, the Song presided over continually shrinking territory. Despite the political and military weakness of the period, culture again flourished in what has been termed the golden age of China. Neo-Confucianism, endowed with a more metaphysical outlook than the original version, emerged as the orthodox political doctrine. The scholar-gentry, as the result over centuries of the examination system, administered China. Outstanding painters and essayists created works of note. China underwent a commercial revolution, and what has been characterized as early modern China began to emerge with sizable commercial cities, increased trade, and the growth of a money economy.

Then the Mongols, who had been pressing down for decades from the north, managed to sustain sufficient strength to conquer the Chinese. With the establishment of the Mongol or Yuan (First or Original) dynasty (1279-1368), all China fell entirely under a foreign yoke for the first time in its history. However, the Mongols found the conquest slow. It took several more decades to absorb North China and an additional half-century to end Song rule in the south. The greatest of the Mongol leaders was Kublai Khan, whose capital was at what is now Beijing. Far from being a stereotyped Chinese image of a culturally deprived barbarian, he was a tolerant and understanding ruler. A pragmatic emperor, he utilized the administrative skills of foreigners, Asian and Western alike—including Marco Polo, who arrived in the country during his reign.

The Mongol emperors who followed Kublai Khan were weak men, unable to hold onto his empire. With the establishment of the Ming (Bright) dynasty (1368-1644), a Chinese house reemerged. As the paradigm of Chinese dynasties, the rulers presided over a prosperous and stable country. During the era, because of the continued alien military presence to the north and the west, the Chinese became once again inward-looking and self-centered, although the early rulers sent out sporadic sea expeditions and temporarily renewed contacts with South and Southeast Asia. The nativistic, comfortable Ming empire was eventually conquered by another foreign power, that of the Manchu, who, in Chinese political fashion, adopted the dynastic name of Qing (Pure).

As the last of the imperial dynasties, the Qing (1644-1912) brought China to renewed heights. The non-Chinese emperors not only conquered all of the country, but they reestablished roughly the boundaries as they had been defined in the earlier Tang. Governing first from Manchuria and then from Beijing, their most illustrious rulers lived in the first half of the dynasty; the last great emperor sat on the throne (1736-1796) as the infant American republic commenced its national life. The latter half of Manchu rule was plagued by the arrival and presence of ever-growing numbers of Westerners, who desired extensive trading rights in the country and were willing to resort to hostilities to obtain them. The first war of China with the west, the so-called Opium War, broke out between 1839 and 1842, with the English as the adversary. The defeated Manchu and Chinese were forced to open up selected coastal areas of their country, first to the English, and then to other alien powers. Now ensconced in China, Western rights and privileges increased in the course of the latter half of the nineteenth century. At last, by 1912, through a combination of complex forces that included Western might, Manchu decline, and Chinese restiveness, the imperial structure collapsed. In the initial decades of the twentieth century, the Chinese embarked on the quest for successor political institutions that could survive into the modern world.

The search for political viability in the period between 1912 and 1949 under the Republic of China was variously described as revolutionary, republican, and nationalistic. These were years of ferment, revolution, and unrest in which a multitude of ideologies found adherents among the Chinese. Eventually, the political spectrum coalesced into two antagonistic philosophies, the rightist Nationalist camp under Chiang Kai-shek, and the leftist Communist under Mao Zedong. By 1949, the civil war, held in abeyance by World War II, resulted in the defeat of the Nationalists, their evacuation to Taiwan, and the establishment of the People's Republic of China at Beijing.

Indigenous Histories

Myriad indigenous texts have chronicled the rise and fall of dynasties. Works of history have always held an important place in man-oriented Chinese society. The earliest Chinese histories were records of diviners and ritualists, genealogies of important families, and chronicles of princely states. Into these accounts were interwoven fact and fiction, history and legend. A basic predynastic work, whose editing has been traditionally attributed to Confucius, although it actually predated him, is the *Classic of History* (*Shujing*). This book, which constitutes the

---

China's Dynasties

Xia (unsubstantiated): 2205-1766 B.C. or 1994-1523 B.C.

Shang: 1766-1122 B.C. or 1523-1027 B.C.

Zhou: 1122 or 1027-221 B.C. (Earlier or Western, to 771 B.C.; Later or Eastern, after)

Qin: 221-206 B.C.

Han: 206 B.C.-A.D. 220 (Earlier or Western, to A.D. 9; Later or Eastern, after A.D. 23)

Six Dynasties: 220-589

Sui: 589-618

Tang: 618-907

Five Dynasties: 907-960

Song: 960-1279 (Northern, to 1127; Southern, after)

Mongol or Yuan: 1279-1368

Ming: 1368-1644

Manchu or Qing: 1644-1912

---

first major history of China, is a compilation of historical miscellany by mostly anonymous authors. Another classic, the *Spring and Autumn Annals (Chunqiu)*, records events in the home state of Confucius in North China during the Later Zhou period.

Around 100 B.C., histories authored by individuals, compiled either officially or privately, began to be composed. Emphasizing men and politics, the works include annals of imperial events, essays, genealogies of the imperial family, and biographies of prominent persons. The father of Chinese history is Sima Qian (Ssu-ma Ch'ien), 145?-90? B.C., who wrote a general history of his country known as the *Historical Records (Shiji)*. It was an unofficial work that had been initiated by his father, who was both a court historian and an astrologer. (To Chinese there was no incongruity between the two occupations.) In style, content, and organization, it set the pattern for most of the later Chinese historical works. Drawing upon the most accessible and reliable sources, Sima Qian compiled a history of China from earliest times to his own day.

Some two centuries later, Ban Gu (Pan Ku), A.D. 32-92, picked up where his predecessor left off. Coming also from a distinguished family that included his historian father, Ban Gu limited his efforts to chronicling events only in the first half (206 B.C.–9 A.D.) of the Han dynasty. This was the beginning of the dynastic histories; his *History of the Earlier Han* (*Qian Hanshu*) served as a prototype for the later official dynastic histories that focused on one period rather than on the extended and universal treatment of history.

The tradition of writing and compiling dynastic histories by official court historians subsequently developed. Groups of historians worked under governmental direction. The state appropriated the function of historical writing, which utilized as primary sources varying official documents that included the so-called "diaries of activity and repose," accounts of imperial audiences, and contemporaneous discussions between emperors and ministers. These basic sources were worked into the daily records, which toward the end of the imperial reign were again reworked into the "veritable records." Out of all this continually reshaped mass of material a dynastic history would eventually emerge. Official historians spent lifetimes in collating these annals. The Tang dynasty set a precedent by compiling the standard history of the preceding dynasty as well as that of its own. Eventually, some two dozen standard dynasty histories were compiled; the last one, relating to the Manchu, is awaiting formalization by the Nationalist regime on Taiwan.

Traditional Chinese historiography, or the art of writing history, had its strengths and weaknesses. The numerous documents helped to preserve the Chinese written language as well as to provide a contemporary record of events. They emphasized a succession of dynasties that lent continuity to the historical process. They gave insight to the Chinese about themselves and their country. But the drawbacks to their historical writing were limiting and serious. In general, Chinese historiography was culture-bound; it was thoroughly steeped in the Confucian milieu, and that tradition had to be penetrated in order to comprehend the written works. In particular, by assuming political continuity and an orderly succession of dynasties, the historians were sometimes more arbitrary than accurate, for China was, as noted, periodically divided among various warring kingdoms, of which only one was later chosen by historians as orthodox. Histories were overwhelmingly great-man centered and political in emphasis. They relegated analytical and interpretive material to secondary importance. Causation was not stressed, and there was little critical spirit in analyzing material. The terse and abrupt official style of writing lacked any feeling of intimacy and personality. It tended to employ a didactic, moralistic tone with its praise-and-blame approach to men and problems. Written by Confucian bureaucrats principally for their own group, Chinese historical works revealed deep-set prejudices, circumscribed values, and predictable orientations.

Despite the traditional emphasis on dynastic cycles in historical writing, some Chinese writers advanced a nondynastic approach to history. Hints of this type of linear interpretation were present in the ancient *Classic of History* and Sima Qian's *Historical Records*. Later writers advanced similar concepts. A Tang historian suggested a four-period division of Chinese history; some later Chinese writers of the nineteenth and twentieth centuries followed a like approach. The philosopher-reformer Kang Youwei (K'ang Yu-wei), 1898-1927, suggested that world society, including China, moved toward utopia through three evolutionary ages. A student of his, Liang Qichao (Liang Chi-ch'ao), 1873-1929, also posited a three-period approach, which included the first age of China as China, then China in the Asian context, and finally China in world affairs. Others categorized China into ancient, medieval, and modern times, or alternatively into preempire, imperial, and modern eras.

Chinese Communists advanced their own linear but doctrinaire concept of history, Borrowing from Karl Marx, they posited five stages of history as based on the prevailing modes of production and wealth: primitive, slave, feudal, capitalist, and socialist. Accepting the validity of the dynasties, but bound to a thesis that emphasized economic determinism and scientific socialism with deterministic laws, they periodized Chinese history according to prearranged and inflexible dogma. The Communists considered pre-Xia times as primitive. Subsequently, from the Xia to the mid-Zhou (roughly between 2000 and 475 B.C.), when slaveowners existed in North China, the country passed through the slave period of history. Having developed iron tools, but utilizing land as the main source of wealth, the slave society gradually transferred itself into feudal society. This third period of history was the longest, for it lasted more than two millennia (approximately 475 B.C. to A.D. 1840). During the feudal period, China enjoyed a rich culture, but according to communist theory, it was dependent on exploitation of the peasant, which resulted in the numerous uprisings and rebellions that communist doctrine interpreted as class struggles.

The century that the Chinese Communists considered as capitalistic (1840-1949) was more ideologically imprecise. It was explained as a semicolonial and semifeudal era imposed on China by Western capitalist and military presence. According to the theory, foreign imperialism did not permit native capitalism to develop as fully as it had in the West. However, as a result of the successive and increasingly successful revolutions, the socialist state in Chinese society was finally achieved in 1949. The resulting Communist nation was simply a more refined type of socialism.

In endeavoring to reconcile Marxist creed and historical fact, Chi-

nese Communists have been faced with problems. Ideological peri-
odizations caused doctrinal debates in Beijing, since all five periods
had to be accounted for; none could be eliminated. Peasant rebellions,
commonplace in Chinese history, were stressed as a recurring theme
for social and ideological significance. The origins and nature of capitalism in China, which embraced notions of commerce, incentive,
profits, and incipient industry, resulted in drawn-out arguments among
party members. Another major problem was how to reconcile the predominantly agrarian Chinese society with a doctrine that emphasized
industry and the role of the urban proletariat in establishing the revolution. To party spokesmen, the fusion of history and ideology was
imperative.

Foreign Histories

For their part, foreigners have presented their own interpretations of
Chinese history, however imperfect. Most early works on China were
composed by aliens living there: Jesuits in the sixteenth, seventeenth,
and eighteenth centuries; other Catholic and Protestant missionaries,
diplomats, and university professors in the nineteenth and early twentieth centuries. Many of their works transcended the bounds of history.
As compendiums of encompassing knowledge they included related
topics such as geography, sociology, literature, language, and the arts.
These were in the early tradition of sinology, or the study of China.
Modern writers attempted to interpret Chinese political upheavals and
other epochal events of the day and to project as well their possible
repercussions on Western relations.

Works on China by non-Chinese authors over time generally have
been controversial and contradictory. They have ranged between the
extremes of those praising the enlightened Chinese and these derogat-
ing the heathen hordes. Over the centuries, alien authors such as Indian
Buddhist pilgrims, Arab travelers, European traders, Jesuit missionaries, and American residents in the country all have had their differing
firsthand versions of the story of China. Because of the complexity of
interpreting the country as a whole, the works variously have advanced
themes, some polarized, that ranged between respect for and fear of,
or friendship for, and hostility toward, the Chinese.

During the past century and a half of contacts between Chinese and
Westerners, while most Chinese consistently viewed foreigners as
cultural barbarians, in the same period impressions of that country and
its people varied in the United States. The sixty-year period between
the earliest direct Chinese-American contact in 1784 and the first

Chinese-American treaty in 1844 might be characterized as one of friendship and appreciation. Local traders in South China, where international trade had been confined, registered a favorable impression on their Yankee counterparts. Friendly trading ties were enhanced by Occidental philosophy of the time that gave approval to Confucianism. In a Western age characterized by reason, enlightenment, and the Platonic concept of philosopher-kings, it was natural for American political leaders, such as Thomas Jefferson and Benjamin Franklin, to idealize China as the state wherein the wise man ruled over a prosperous realm. Moreover, the physiocratic school in the West, with its emphasis on agricultural virtues and the ideal of a happy peasant life, conferred approval on China because it imputed similar values to Chinese society. And Confucianism, with its impersonal concept of heaven and creation, was taken to be somewhat like Deism, a doctrine then in vogue that viewed the universe as similar to a watch created by a supreme being, who wound up the universe and left it to operate on its own will. In America, as in Europe, there developed a desire to utilize Chinese-inspired artifacts, such as pagodas, landscape gardens, pavilions, sedan chairs, lacquered objects, incense, and *chinoiserie*, or Chinese-type decorative arts.

In the second half of the nineteenth century, American friendship and appreciation for the Chinese were overtaken by disdain. Critical outlooks replaced the earlier favorable ones. Because of the inequality of the first treaties imposed on China in the 1840s, the defeated Chinese were now transformed in imagery from a delightful people into an inferior one. Easily vanquished, initially by the English, they subsequently lost wars in the nineteenth century to Westerners as well as to an expanding modern Japan. The Chinese were forced to cede more territory and to extend greater privileges to foreigners. The treaties gave more and more rights to aliens, including American traders and missionaries, who initially had been confined to coastal treaty ports, but who came to reside throughout most of China. In their protected havens, many adopted patronizing or condescending attitudes toward their hosts, who were transformed into a faceless mass characterized as mysterious and inscrutable. The unfavorable image in China was buttressed by Chinese presence in the United States, for in these decades Chinese immigrants flooded into the western United States as indentured labor performing jobs on railway projects. They were initially welcomed as a source of cheap labor, but as the projects were completed and the Chinese stayed on, hostility against them began to erupt on the West Coast.

In the first half of the twentieth century, American disdain toward China and the Chinese was replaced once again by renewed friendship,

partly because of international political considerations. This new attitude had been influenced by the failure of the Boxer Uprising of 1899-
1900 in North China to oust the Western intruders. As a result, the
Chinese had been forced to cede once again additional rights to foreigners. In 1905, when Japan was successful in containing Russia and
thus gained the status of a world power, and in official American eyes
a menacing one, the Chinese, as a friendly people and an ally, were
needed to reshape the balance of power in Asia. Yet in the politically
fluid times after 1912, most Americans abstained from overt interference in the turmoil involving China.

The first half of the twentieth century also witnessed a growing
number of Americans born in China who wrote sympathetically of
Chinese life and customs. One of the most widely read of these authors
was Pearl Buck, whose *The Good Earth* was published in 1931, when
the Japanese were overrunning Manchuria. The novel, which individ-
ualized its characters and chronicled the ordinary lives of a Chinese
peasant family, had a universal appeal; its broad humanity was understandable to almost any reader in any country. Simultaneously, West-
ern-educated Chinese as well were interpreting their country to Americans. Into World War II, Americans continued to praise the Chinese,
who were perceived as sacrificial allies fighting on a common cause
against Japan. But at the war's end, and during the Chinese civil war
(1945-1949), many in the United States became increasingly disen-
chanted. Subsequent to 1949, American interpretations of the complex
Chinese political scene that included the presence of both Nationalists
and Communists have been varied and subjected to antipodal points of
view.

Whatever the foreign impressions, information on China abounds
from both indigenous Nationalist and Communist sources. Direct official and communications channels with Taiwan have rendered easy
access to material there. Travel to mainland China facilitates firsthand
information and knowledge. Chinese government publications themselves are numerous and translated into other languages; many of them
are available abroad from both Taipei and Beijing sources.

From Beijing, the official mouthpiece *Renmin Ribao* (*People's Daily*)
is widely circulated on the mainland. The New China News Agency
(NCNA) issues daily bulletins from domestic and foreign posts. Beijing issues voluminous translations of works by Communist leaders,
present and past, particularly those by the late Party Chairman Mao
Zedong. Of the mainland Chinese magazines and periodicals exported
abroad, the more widely read in English are the monthly *China Today*
(formerly *China Reconstructs*) and *China Pictorial*, as well as the

weekly *Beijing Review*, the authoritative ideological journal intended for foreign consumption.

In the United States, to the student seeking information on China, a plethora of material is also available for study. The Library of Congress possesses the largest collection of Chinese-language materials on Communist China and Taiwan in the United States, and possibly in the non-Communist world. It receives on a regular basis several hundred periodicals relating to the People's Republic of China, and it has catalogued tens of thousands of books and pamphlets about the Beijing government. Not only do congressional committees in Washington publish reports about the People's Republic of China, but the Department of State through its consulate-general in Hong Kong provides press translation services for a tremendous volume of Chinese newspapers and periodicals. The Foreign Broadcast Information Service monitors the air waves. A wide-ranging geographical array of academic institutions in the United States have centers for the study of China and the Chinese; private research organizations supplement knowledge, open to all. Because of the many domestic and foreign publications relating to modern-day China and its ideological factions, the problem confronting the reader is not one of their availability, but rather one of selectivity and judicious use.

2

POLITICS

Over the millennia, Chinese civilization fashioned itself with broadly identifiable historic bases. In the interrelated fields of politics, economics, society, culture, art, and architecture, the Chinese revealed basic though varied traits of behavior and accomplishment. They created, experimented, and lived with institutions and traditions that have persisted in recognizable forms from early times into the present. As a result, the Chinese today have inherited a remarkably complex and multifaceted way of life.

Offices and Officials

The Chinese manifested genius in the shaping of their political system. This feature was never considered to be an isolated, separated sphere of human endeavor; it permeated all aspects of life. It is remarkable that so many people in such a large country could have registered the political achievements that they did and could still live together in comparative harmony over an extended period of time. The road to political unity and centralization commenced early. Several basic Chinese political traits were involved in this developing cohesiveness. One of the most important aspects was that the Chinese adhered to a family concept of the state, with the emperor as the head of the national family (*guojia*). Aiding him and providing political continuity to the state, as emperors came and went, was a relatively small elite of educated bureaucrats. The governmental system that they fashioned was imperial, bureaucratic, hierarchical, and paternalistic. Emperors and officials, if effective, asserted an unchallenged right to govern and to regulate wide-ranging social, economic, moral, and behavioral aspects of society. The ruled, never consulted, gave tacit consent to the conduct of life as formulated by the rulers, who were overthrown only in

31

times of deep distress. Yet into the twentieth century, only individuals, not systems, were then replaced,

Contributing to overall ongoing stability was the equilibrium of complementing, political theories. On the one hand, emperors advocated a policy of authority, force, and centralization. On the other, they also posited a middle road of ethical and responsible government. Through this blend, the religious sanction of the state was accepted; official regulation of, and interference in, personal life was taken for granted. The main concern of the ruling class was with the here-and-now, the smooth functioning of the organs of state. Politically oriented and ruling by example, officials believed that society could flourish only if men practiced prescribed correct relations with each other. This pattern of managed behavior was inculcated into bureaucrats as role models. A uniform system of state education, buttressed by the examination system based on accepted orthodox canon, provided a common core of beliefs and practice.

Moreover, the idea of the family state manifested itself in international relations; what was considered valid for China was also rated good for the known world. The Chinese felt that all men in the Middle Kingdom, including those in the peripheral states, were indeed Confucian brethren. Because they predominated in numbers and influence in East Asia, the Chinese, as elder brothers in the system, defined the terms of conduct in foreign affairs. And because of their transcendent position that precluded a give-and-take approach in dealing with foreigners, the Chinese remained inexperienced in flexible multilateral power arrangements well into modern times.

At the apex of the Chinese governmental structure was the emperor, father of his people, ruler of all mankind. He held a position initially achieved by force but morally cloaked in the mandate or approval of heaven. In theory, he ruled by virtue in a government operated by ethics; in reality, his dynasty was supported by military strength and authoritarian measures. Once a dynasty was established, its ruling family sought to perpetuate itself in familial lines, visibly centered at the capital in grandiose imperial structures.

After assuming power, because of the power of his person, the emperor was not addressed by any previously used personal names. While on the throne, he was showered by his fellow men with high-sounding honorifics, such as the Son of Heaven (*Tianzi*) or the Lord of Ten Thousand Years (*Wansuiye*). About 140 B.C., court histories began the precedent of giving year designations or reign names (*Nian Hao*) to the emperor, hopefully to characterize descriptively subperiods of his rule (such as Great Military Power or Union through Strength). Long reigns usually had several such subdesignations, which were often changed in times of natural or political crises. (One emperor, in the seventh century A.D., within a period of 33 years had fourteen such designated successive reign names.) After the inception of the Ming dynasty in 1386, with only one notable exception, it became custom to assign only a single reign name to one imperial rule. Traditional Chinese political dates are reckoned through these reign eras. There were, additionally, temple or posthumous names (*miao hao*) bestowed by later historians upon the deceased rulers, with similarly high-sounding titles, such as Grand Ancestor or Martial Emperor. These names were generally used to designate the monarchs themselves in Chinese histories, at least until the fourteenth century, after which single reign names superseded posthumous imperial titles in official annals.

The emperor himself was a complex figure embracing many functions. As the embodiment of the Chinese way of life, he radiated cultural power out from the capital. In a predominantly agricultural country, he was the first farmer of the empire, and, as one related duty, he went through ceremonial plowing rites every spring. His ritualistic duties were abundant for he, as supreme priest as well, performed all types of involved and mandatory rites that included prescribed salutations to revered mountains, important rivers, and heavenly gods. In a family state, he held the position as supreme father, or benevolent paternal head of all subjects. The emperor was also assigned the job of top scholar; theoretically, he graded the highest civil service examinations in the palace. Once or twice a year, usually from ghost-written notes, he gathered scholars together to lecture them on the classics. Additionally, he was both supreme military officer and top civil bureaucrat, commanding and appointing officials. Since the Chinese did not separate governmental branches or functions, the emperor administered the judicial, executive, and legislative affairs of state. His position forced him to concern himself with much onerous paperwork, to endure numerous audiences that began at dawn, to listen to unending memorials, and because he was the court of last appeal, to review all capital punishments. Finally, the emperor attempted to maintain political equilibrium as the arbiter among the numerous rival cliques in government.

Although imperial powers were great, they were circumscribed. The mandate of heaven could be forcibly taken from the emperor for loss of his virtue, a quality essential to perform correctly the manifold duties of state. Since an evil, debauched ruler could not properly execute rites to the demanding gods, the Chinese maintained their right to revolt and to replace him with a new leader who could command more favorable attention from above. Less drastic restraints could also be imposed on the emperor. Technically, he could initiate no political measures, for such matters had to emanate from his ministers of state, who memorialized the monarch on various issues. When the occupant of the throne was weak or vacillating, other factions asserted or reasserted influence. Ambitious family members in the imperial household could gain sway. The heavy hand of orthodox bureaucracy was always omnipresent. And there was always the threat of rebellions in the capital or in the countryside that might presage the downfall of the dynasty.

Imperial succession was not always automatically smooth, since male primogeniture was not assumed in the selective process of the heir. Traditionally, the emperor had only one legal, recognized wife, the empress, but the monarch took additional, secondary wives or concubines of varying rank. If the empress bore several sons, the eldest did not necessarily assume the throne; the emperor could chose any male offspring he considered as the strongest candidate as his heir. If a chosen heir died prematurely, a male offspring of any of the female consorts, backed by political factions, could then be advanced as the next in line since all children were considered to be legitimate. It is a wonder that over the centuries there were not more openly divisive succession disputes, a perennial problem that sometimes resulted in civil war.

For the efficient operation of the imperial structure, the emperor relied on officials (*guan*) as the functioning central bureaucracy (as distinct from the extended imperial family, also centered in the capital), appointed by him and responsible to him. It was a nonelective body. Admission to membership was achieved principally through examination on the classics, although it could also be obtained through purchase, patronage, appointment, or imperial ties. Parliaments did not exist in China; an independent judiciary was unknown; financial accountability was not practiced. There was no intricate interlocking system of governmental checks and balances. Officialdom had its roots in a top-heavy executive branch, a tendency that continued into the twentieth century in the political complexion of both Nationalist and Communist China.

By the eighteenth century, when Westerners began to arrive in China with ambitious trade delegations, several top policy-making groups existed at the capital. A Grand Secretariat (*Nei Ge*), dating from Ming times, helped emperors in routine matters of state. About 1730 the Manchu superimposed another body, the Grand Council, or the Council of State (*Jun Ji Ghu*), as the political center at Beijing. Consisting of some four to five highest ranking officials of both Manchu and Chinese extractions, it met almost daily to discuss the important affairs of the country. The heads of yet other chief administrative boards formed a third type of cabinet that reported to the emperor. This drew from the six chief boards, dating in origin to Qin and Han times but finalized in the Tang: Civil Affairs (*Li Bu*), Revenue (*Hu Bu*), Rites (also *Li Bu*, but with a character *li* different from that of Civil Affairs), War (*Bing Bu*), Punishments (*Xing Bu*), and Public Works (*Gong Bu*). Presiding over the boards in Manchu times were two presidents and two vice presidents, each with one Manchu and the other Chinese.

The Censorate (*Du Cha Yuan*), dating from the Qin, checked on bureaucrats in the capital and the countryside. Its earliest task was that of open investigation of official injustice, corruption, or mismanagement in central or local ranks. (Secret police were not the norm in traditional Chinese political thought.) Because of any possible conflict of interest, censors were not assigned to their home regions. Moreover, drawn from the regular ranks of bureaucracy, they held only temporary office. The possibility existed that when they returned to their regular posts, new censors, who might have received poor marks from earlier incumbents, could in turn, in newfound authority, match the earlier displeasure that they had received.

The Office of Transmission (*Tong Zheng Si*) handled the routine and endless flow of documents. Memorials, petitions, decrees, and edicts streamed from the capital, and all had to be couched in proper terminology and correct address, depending on the ranks of the officials involved. The Grand Court of Revision (*Da Li Si*) administered criminal law, and the Colonial Office (*Li Fan Yuan*) concerned itself with relations as they affected the border states of Mongolia, Tibet, and Xinjiang. The Imperial Academy (*Hanlin Yuan*) included the top-ranking scholars of the land; it dealt with functions of literature and history and issued the imperial gazette (*jing bao*). Since China did not create a Western-style foreign affairs office until late in the nineteenth century, and then only because of the insistent demands of the European powers, the Board of Rites traditionally handled foreign relations. Imperial ranks, from top to bottom, comprised nine ranks, each divided into upper and lower grades, and all were designated with prescribed titles and costumes.

Augmenting the central operations were other bureaucrats in the lower echelons of government throughout China, all of whom were appointed from the capital. Usually they served from three to six years in any given assignment. In order to minimize opportunities for graft, corruption, and nepotism, through the law of avoidance, they were not to serve any official time in their home provinces. Imperial commissioners, such as censors, visited local posts regularly. There were some language problems. All Chinese characters are written the same and have the same idea, but oral dialects vary greatly. Although the so-called Mandarin (*guanhua*) dialect served (and still serves) as the lingua franca of the Chinese, officials frequently found themselves in regions with an unfamiliar vernacular.

The bureaucratic structure in China outside of the capital was several tiered. First came the provinces (*sheng*), which proliferated in number over the centuries, from ten in Tang times to fifteen in the Song to eighteen in the Manchu. A governor (*xunfu*) presided over most of the individual provinces, but the more important ones, or sometimes two lesser ones (and in one case three), were placed under a viceroy or governor-general (*zongdu*). The roster of other chief provincial officials included a treasurer, a provincial judge, a grain superintendent to supervise the collection of grain taxes, and a comptroller of salt, which was a government monopoly in mining and sales. Official salaries were traditionally small; governor-generals received the equivalent of a few hundred American dollars a year, but, by exacting bribes from local sources, they managed to inflate their incomes a hundredfold. By the ninth century, there were interprovincial circuits (*dao*) with traveling officials from the central administration, to oversee regional problems.

Each province was traditionally divided in turn into prefectures (*fu*) and then into districts (*xian*), all of whose heads were also appointed by the central government. District magistrates were key figures in local administration, yet, important as they were, they were spread thin over the 1,500-odd districts in number, each of which covered an average of 300 square miles with a quarter of a million inhabitants. Bureaucratic problems were legion. Lower rank officials, like those in upper echelons, received only minimal formal salaries, and they were tempted by ever-present opportunities for graft and corruption (accepted as normal practice unless it got out of hand), performed a stifling amount of paperwork, could hold plural offices, and in the last dynasty, shared many of their responsibilities with Manchu bureaucrats. Traditionalists predominated in the civil service, through which they had worked their way up via the examination system, but there was a minority of practical reformers, who, although coming up through the same process, tried to shake up the bureaucratic structure from time to time with modernizing, pragmatic proposals.

Lowest level political units, such as villages, families, and guilds, operating outside of the formal bureaucracy, were largely self-governing. In the villages, councils of nonelected elders and headmen who were scholars or who came from the more important families presided over official functions. Not appointed from the capital, these local officials were confirmed in their posts by district magistrates. Towns and cities were divided into wards, each also with councils and headmen. Group responsibility and autonomy were the keynotes of operation, and the government intervened only when necessary. Into modern times, a political and administrative gap existed between the district magistrate, who was appointed by the emperor and represented the central government apparatus, and the village headman, who served the mass of Chinese, who were often unfamiliar with higher echelons of bureaucracy. Even with this break in authority, over the centuries, the centralized system of government operated with a remarkably small proportion of officials to the total population, who were kept mainly in bounds by local leaders and customary behavior.

Policy Implementation

The regular bureaucracy was recruited primarily through examinations, which had their genesis in the Earlier Han, but were not systematized until the Tang, a thousand years later. The philosophy of the examination system adhered to the Confucian dictum of education for rule, not necessarily for the advancement of knowledge. Eventually, the formal testing structure crystallized into three levels, roughly comparable to the Western bachelor's, master's, and doctoral degrees.

The first round, for the "budding genius" (*xiucai*), was usually given in the districts or prefectures. Locked up in cells for several days and nights, the aspirants composed essays and poems according to prescribed rules and regulations. In the Qing dynasty, an average of about 2,000 candidates took the tests in every prefecture, but generally only one to ten percent passed. Even some of those who passed did not get appointments because there were not always enough posts to go around.

The second-rank examinations of "promoted man" (*juren*) were given in provincial capitals, usually every three years. Beijing officials administered the tests in permanently erected stalls in three-day sessions. Out of 3,000 to 17,000 examinees, usually only one out of every fifteen passed. Tests for the third and top run, for "achieved scholar" (*jinshi*), were given at the capital, also every third year, again in three-day sessions. On the average, about two hundred examinees a year passed these. In the lifelong process of upward mobility, candidates for higher positions were also sponsored by superiors, who accordingly received praise or blame for the good or poor conduct and performance of their protégés. One interruption in the rise to power was the custom of three years' mourning after the death of the official's father (usually in the son's middle age), during which time the offspring involuntarily went into a temporary period of quietude and meditation.

Although some tests related to pragmatic, practical subjects, the content of most examinations was drawn mainly from Confucian doctrine, and the forms of answering questions were strictly prescribed. By the Ming era, the eight-legged essay (*baigu wenzhang*) was a favored composition that not only stressed content but placed a premium on balanced style. Tests were administered, as noted, in practical subjects as well, but those on the orthodox Confucian canon led more readily to higher advancement. Although the examinations stressed rote, memorization, and arbitrary literary style, they brought into the government qualified and educated men who were able to give China a cultural and ideological unity through a common merit system. Outside the ranks of the bureaucrats who passed up the examination ladder were recruits to office whose numbers included imperial favorites or those who won merit on their own proven ability in civilian or military achievement and might not have passed any written examinations. Those who held position by the usual testing tended to look with disfavor upon the more nontraditionally appointed officials; cliques arose along the lines of recruitment.

The formal bureaucratic structure of government was augmented at the various levels of officialdom by informal participants such as groups or leaders who temporarily gained power in factional struggles. They included, in the lower echelons, the clerks and office runners (*yamen chayi*), who performed the routine daily chores of work. Only some of these were educated, but they were all versed and experienced in the conduct of their office. They provided local political continuity, since the imperial appointees came and went every three to six years. The clerks, although outside the traditional examination system, wielded great power. They were responsible for screening petitioners who desired to see the magistrate, and they decided what kinds of cases could be heard. Because of minimal emoluments, they also lived off bribes.

Other informal participants at the central government level included empresses and imperial consorts, who could be quite willful if they saw fit. Imperial eunuchs, who obtained favor, acquired great wealth, power, and status. Relatives of the ruling house continually tried to build up tax-free estates, and they meddled endlessly in affairs of state. Military leaders were also a continual threat to the throne, which had to gain their loyalty in times of crises.

In the governance of outlying dependencies, especially the Manchu rulers, insofar as it was possible, exerted direct rule. This was particularly true in their homeland of Manchuria, divided into three provinces, which was preserved as the ancestral place, a private domain. In Mongolia and Xinjiang, local government organs, under Manchu supervision, were kept. In Tibet, an imperial resident was stationed at the capital of Lhasa; none of the local ecclesiastical or political hierarchy could be confirmed without Manchu consent. Post roads linked these dependencies with Beijing and a relatively efficient system of communications prevailed.

Law (*fa*) as utilized by Chinese bureaucracy and in traditional political life differed considerably from those legal concepts practiced by Western countries. Legal matters related chiefly to custom, tradition, and precedent. Behavioral patterns were regulated by universally accepted precepts, embodied in *li*, a type of natural law conforming to the will of heaven. Rulers theoretically influenced and guided the populace through exemplary conduct, not by codes of law. In China joint, rather than individual, responsibility was assumed. Villages, guilds, and families were held responsible for the action of their members. Whole groups were considered accountable, and punishable, for the misconduct of an individual. Precedent, tradition, custom, proper behavior, and ethics played vital roles in Chinese law. Torture was allowed for extorting confessions; in escalating degrees, the punishment matched the crime. Professional lawyers and counsels were nonexistent; the magistrate acted as judge and jury.

Statutory law codes, heavy on injunctions and prohibitions, abounded; they dealt mainly with criminal and administrative matters. Civil affairs were largely matters of customary law and the usual procedure for litigants was to settle affairs out of court otherwise, loss of face and unnecessary complications could arise. China was ruled by a government that preached morality endlessly, legislated it continually, and practiced it imperfectly. Government meant ethics, and officials claimed the right to regulate the behavior of the populace. Government interference in, and regulation of, individual life was taken for granted in Chinese political thought into contemporary times. Moreover, the separation of church and state, taken for granted in modern societies, would have been declared unconstitutional in traditional China.

The military hierarchy was also a part of the political structure of government. Emperors maintained a standing army of mercenary troops, but they usually had to draft peasant conscripts in times of emergency and crisis. A regular military bureaucracy paralleled the civilian structure with examinations prescribed for entering the ranks and ascending the military ladder. But the military career was subordinate to the civilian because Confucian ideologues did not admit any social standing for military accomplishments. Maritime forces were negligible since most campaigns involved China's land frontiers.

At the time of the opening of China to the West in the mid-nineteenth century, the organized military structure included "banners" of separate Manchu, Chinese, and Mongol units grouped under different colors. Additionally, the Army of the Green Standard constituted a standing Chinese force. The strength of the banners and army totaled about a million men, with about two-thirds of this number in the latter organization. Over centuries of peace, the Manchu military structure became vitiated and outmoded. After the advent of the West, China began to modernize its armed forces, both at the capital and in the provinces. In the chaos of the first half of the twentieth century, these newly developed provincial forces became the bases for regional warlords who came to plague the Chinese political scene. Military force had always been necessary for any leader in China to achieve and maintain power at home and abroad, but it was the civilian bureaucrat who provided a semblance of political continuity and who kept China cohesive and viable.

Legacy

China's political cohesiveness and achievements derived from interacting practice and policy. Civil service examinations encouraged conformity of thought and the continued emphasis on orthodoxy, with little scope for individuality. Collective conformity bestowed overall stability, but it stifled change and greater possible progress. When the emperor was strong, the centralized system worked well. When he was weak, pressures to halt the imperial drift, or to remedy the dynastic decline, built up from within at court through a variety of factions or from without through revolts and rebellions. Either way, while the cast of characters might change with a new resulting dynasty, the political scenario, remaining the same in detail, would be resurrected. While dissent, contained within recognizable features and predictable results, over the centuries did not result in any enduring political changes, neither did it cause any permanent division of the Chinese homeland. As a realized end or desired goal, the concept of the Middle Kingdom held fast. It was remarkable that the imperial institution, beset by perennial problems and preserved through persisting tradition, lasted as long as it did. But in the process, and through time, Pax Sinica became rigid and ossified.

In the modern era, when China on its own soil encountered an ever-encroaching and aggressive West, it was forced to begin a process of permanent political transformation, an awesome ongoing phenomenon that kept unfolding into contemporary times. The traditional evolutionary process of leisurely advocating "change within tradition," implying only cosmetic features applied to a fundamentally decaying system, was irrelevant in a world of sovereign nations using military force to achieve radically different political ends. In perspective, the Chinese way of life in political affairs left a legacy of both boon and bane.

3

PHYSICAL ASPECTS OF LIFE

The quite worldly Chinese emphasized the physical aspects of life. Largely because of this, they fashioned material bases of living that have persisted throughout their history. Oriented toward immediate concerns, they dealt with the problems of the here-and-now, and they concerned themselves with the economic organization of society. As in other areas of Chinese life, the government, as guardian of general welfare, exerted its right to intervene, whenever it deemed it necessary, in the economy. As a regulating agency, it applied various methods of controls, management, and monopolies, as well as the issuance of licenses for certain strategic items. It advanced the economic theory of state socialism, yet the practice of laissez-faire was also noticeably present in the Chinese economy; the empire was too far flung for the government to control effectively all facets of the economy.

Moreover, the Confucian doctrine allowed the principle of individual ownership of property, although excessive acquisition of material goods was not to be the primary aim of life. Religions and philosophies other than Confucianism also tolerated economic individualism. Characteristic forms of private ownership in China embraced family holdings, business partnerships, individual merchant activity, trade, and protective guilds. The primary elements of the economic sector, those of agriculture, mining, and fishing, received the highest priority. Industry and commerce were of secondary importance. Transportation developed unevenly. Riverine systems were most widely used because road conditions were often precarious. Most trade was internal, local, or regional; a self-sufficient China did not rely to any appreciable degree on international commerce. The wealthy maintained their lifestyle through holdings of private land, expensive clothing, beautiful jewelry, jade, and hoarding silver and gold currency. Most Chinese, however, lived on the "good earth" in marginal existence.

China's greatest natural resource is its agricultural land, despite the fact that the arable area approximates only one-seventh of the country's total land area. In the early nineteenth century, about 130 million acres of cultivated land supported more than 300 million people. In modern times, some 300 million acres now support more than a billion people. Nine-tenths of the food crops are grown by four-fifths of the Chinese, who must supply themselves with an adequate food base as well as feeding the other fifth living in the cities and towns. Much of the soil is naturally fertile, especially in riparian or delta regions; interior and border areas are less so. Draft animals, such as horses, donkeys, mules, and sometimes camels, are used in the north; the water buffalo is utilized in the south. Despite numerous drawbacks, China has generally been self-sufficient in food production; only one to three percent of its food is imported. With so many people tilling relatively little acreage, the natural agricultural pattern was intensive rather than extensive (where few farmers worked large tracts of land).

Farm units, averaging three to five acres, have traditionally been small in size, with joint family ownership rather than individual ownership prevailing. Because of their topography, farms were smaller in the hilly south and larger in the flat northern plains. Utilizing scattered small tracts was often the main pattern of ownership. The percentage of peasant proprietorship varied throughout the country, with the highest proportion in the north. A study of the 1930s of landownership patterns in the lower Yangtze Valley revealed that three-fifths of the peasants owned land, one-fifth were part-owners and tenants, and the remaining fifth were tenants who paid one-half to two-thirds of the crop as rent in kind to landlords. In China, however, no comparable system existed to resemble medieval European feudalism, where the peasants were legally bound to the land. But for practical purposes, there was no place for the Chinese farmer to flee and start anew if home conditions became unbearable. Where it was feasible, particularly in the south with a favored climate, peasants often followed the practice of double-cropping, a procedure involving the planting of two crops, similar or different, in succession or simultaneously. In the colder and shorter growing season in the north, the crop cycle was limited to a single annual one. Countrywide, the Chinese acquired extensive experience in managing water supplies. Irrigation was a practice ancient to China. Archaic tradition recalled prehistoric emperors regulating floods and building ditches. Their historic descendants on level grounds constructed patchworks of canals, while on hillside terraces, gravity flow of water irrigated the crops.

China produced a great variety of agricultural products. It traditionally ranked first in the world's production of rice, tea, vegetable oils, millet, soybeans, and sweet potatoes; second in silk and wheat; and third in cotton. The Chinese diet consisted chiefly of grain: rice in the southern and central regions, wheat in the north. Fruits, vegetables, and legumes were present in all three regions. Chinese ate a fairly well-balanced array of food, with proteins chiefly derived from fish and the popular, widely used soybean curd. By the ninth century, tea, originating in India, became widespread. (A byproduct of the drink was the development of the ceramic industry, with the use of cups and bowls to hold the hot liquid.)

The south grew some bamboo and some coconut, with their all-around products of many uses. Rivers and coastal regions provided an extensive variety of fish, although interior peoples less frequently ate it. Deep-sea fishing was not practiced off the mainland coast. The Chinese were less fond of meat and animal products, except for inland non-Chinese nomads. Dairy goods were not normally consumed. Grazing land in China was not predominant, and fertile agricultural land was devoted to plant culture. The settled agricultural Chinese also tended to look down on their neighboring pastoral peoples as cultural barbarians. But there were no distinct philosophic or religious proscriptions in the matter of taste or food consumption, except among Muslims, who could not eat pork, and Buddhists, who were vegetarians.

Agriculture has been important to China, but the problems presented by the agrarian life were manifold. Caloric values in diets were marginal or imbalanced. Extreme climatic conditions and natural calamities reduced production. Crop failures were perennial. Records indicate that for the past 2,000 years some part of the country experienced at least one major famine in any given year. The county had always been threatened with soil exhaustion, and every available fertilizer has been used to replenish the land that required it, including human excrement (what Westerners euphemistically called "night soil") that spread parasitic diseases. Peasant superstitions also inhibited the development of metal farm equipment. There was a great resistance to the use of iron-tipped tools, which the peasants feared might injure the soil gods residing in the earth and crops.

Grain culture, based as it was on wet paddy fields, presented great difficulties in mechanization, although the Chinese Communists attempted to develop rice growing and harvesting machines. The peasant faced long periods of seasonal unemployment, particularly if he lived in an area that produced only one grain crop a year. He was also handicapped by the problem of raising cash from the sale of either crops or handicrafts to pay for necessary commodities and taxes. Whether he was a tenant farmer or proprietor of a tract, he still had to meet onerous rent or tax obligations in grain or in cash. Interest rates on borrowed money, often a necessary recourse to meet expenses, ranged up to 100 percent. Peasant distress was real, endemic, and never-ending.

Natural resources in China were sufficient to sustain a premodern industrial base, yet reserves were not limitless. The main concentration of iron deposits is in southern Manchuria, but it has only a 50 percent metallic content. The area also contains coal holdings. Most of this mineral ore is located in Shanxi and Shaanxi provinces. The use of coal as a source of fuel dates back to at least the fifth century A.D. A limited oil reserve, equal to only one percent of that in the United States, exists in northwestern Gansu province and border areas. The Chinese Communists are exploring offshore oil reserves. Hydroelectric power is available, and as the ultimate source of fuel, atomic energy for peaceful uses is also being developed by the Chinese Communists.

Lesser mineral deposits include tungsten (of which China is the world's leading producer), antimony (of which China is second in production), tin, mercury, uranium, and copper. Salt is mined in interior Sichuan, but it is also obtained in coastal areas by means of evaporative techniques. There are scattered deposits of asbestos, bismuth, lead, marble, and zinc. In ancient times, forests were widespread, but extensive cutting and logging over the centuries deforested much of China. This ongoing practice has resulted in great soil erosion and, in the north and west, a progressive rate of desertization encroaching on bordering agrarian lands.

Despite the overwhelming presence of the agrarian sector in China's economic life, urban centers have long existed. Chinese cities that date to Shang times primarily served governmental functions, but a few commercial cities, notably Guangzhou, also arose from early periods. Some cities were famous for certain products, such as the fine porcelain produced in the central Yangtze area at Jingdezhen, where the imperial Ming and Qing kilns were located; ivory from Guangzhou; carpets from Tianjin; and silk from Suzhou; and Shantou lace. In the cities and towns lived the bureaucrats, gentry, merchants, and artisans. Trade was governmentally supervised, with market days held at officially designated intervals. A few itinerant merchants and peddlers hawked their wares on the streets, but city trade, like that in the county, was primarily local. Despite the attempted governmental regulation of trade, weights and measures were not standardized. The various units were confusing; they could vary in volume or in dimension among differing cities or even adjacent regions. In open markets, fixed prices were not the norm; bargaining, involving compromises on middle ground, was the practice. For purposes of calculations, the use of the abacus, dating from Mongol times, was widespread. Its utilization has persisted into contemporary times; many Chinese feel quite at ease in using the mathematical aid.

Where merchants and traders did not operate on an individual basis, they formed self-sufficient family groups, partnerships, and guilds. As in medieval Europe, each guild (*hang*; *hong* in the south) had a street or urban area designated for the shops of its members. The guilds embraced both employers and employees. They fixed prices and wages, and they adopted social security measures to take care of members and their dependents. Each guild had a president and a board of directors, and it received income from the sale of goods and from fees and fines.

Along with the development of cities and towns came the growth of the use of money and the rise of banking practices. Shells were the early medium of exchange, but these were replaced in the mid-Zhou era by coinage, principally of copper. The main form of traditional coinage was "cash"—copper (or copper alloy) coins, usually round, with holes in the center for stringing in multiple quantities. Early coins were also molded to resemble agricultural implements and items of common household use. Paper money came into circulation with the Tang.

Gold was too important to use for common coinage, but silver, mined from native sources, was circulated in dust or ingot form. In the Ming, Mexican silver and coins entered China via the Philippines and were used in the original form or melted down for other uses. Many forms of metallic currency were soon in circulation, prompting the government to attempt further standardization measures through the exercise, without great success, of monopolies, controls, and licenses. During the seventeenth century, guilds of bankers grew, particularly in North China in Shanxi province; pawnshops and banks flourished. In times of financial stress, the government attempted to manipulate the economy by experimenting with debased coinage. This inflationary measure helped mark a dynastic decline.

The Chinese economy was based mainly on internal trade. The pattern of economic activity, both private and governmental, was essentially one of decentralization of operations. Each village tended to be self-sufficient in production, with periodic barter trade involving the exchange of locally produced goods at weekly markets. When the Chinese embarked on foreign trade, the goods flowing in both directions were chiefly luxury items. However, because China was economically self-contained, the Chinese were not particularly interested in foreign trade; it was usually the other countries that desired Chinese commercial items, notably silk and tea.

Transportation within China has depended, for the most part, on the major rivers with their tributary systems. To improve efficiency, since most rivers in China flow west-east, in the sixth century the north-south Grand Canal network was built and maintained over the centuries to bring the grain collected as tax from the central grain-growing centers to the northern political capitals. Coastal shipping was developed, particularly south of the Yangtze, where inlets provided favorable locations for ports. North of the Yangtze, the unindented coastline did not favor growth of seaports. Although the roads, mostly of dirt, sometimes of stone pavement, that crisscrossed the country were generally poor, they were well traveled. On main routes journeyed streams of pedestrians, carts, wheelbarrows, donkeys, sedan chairs, and in North China, horses and camels. Strong dynasties utilized the post road system, and inns studded the routes. In the late nineteenth and early twentieth centuries, China opened itself to railway travel by utilizing foreign loans. In 1929, the China National Aviation Company, the first airline company in China, was formed. The Nationalists further developed civil aviation, and the Chinese Communists have maintained an effective internal network as well as an international one, with the chief hubs at Beijing, Shanghai, and Guangzhou.

In its doctrine of state fiscal controls, the Chinese government taxed the populace in a number of ways. The main base was the land tax, which in practice amounted to as much as the official collector could extract from the owners, occupiers, or cultivators of the land. This type of tax was leveled principally on agricultural commodities, notably grain. Nonagricultural items, such as silk, copper, and finished goods, were also taxed. Customs duties on foreign items that were collected at ports of entry enhanced government income. Further revenues came from the state monopolies in mining, either through direct disposal of minerals or through the grant of licenses to private parties for the extraction of natural resources. The state acquired some income from the sale of offices, from royalties, and from property transfer fees. No large public debt existed in traditional China; no central budgets were formulated; government financing was for immediate and pragmatic ends.

China's top priority relates to the agrarian sector. Its agricultural land is of greatest importance to the economy. Yet it is sorely strained. The vast population, more than four times that of the United States, must derive its food from an arable area that is quite limited in size and can hardly be extended. The feeding of a populace of those who not only produce but also those who additionally consume in urban areas is of crucial importance to the well-being of the country. Any state reforms or blueprints for development must commence with, and assign the greatest importance to, agricultural considerations. Such a mass of people living so close to the land on such a marginal standard of living has been a source of perennial problems. Economics and political life intertwine; the bottom line of state stability must be an acceptable state of adequate livelihood. Indices of popular content or discontent are most readily evidenced in economic life, especially in agriculture and the welfare of the farmer. Decisions affecting the agrarian sector might be made by officials in far-off capitals or by bureaucrats in distant cities, but the ongoing physical health of the country is registered by real conditions in the affected countryside.

4

SOCIETY

China's most striking phenomenon is its people. Although great in number, its population is distributed unevenly throughout China proper. There, the majority resides chiefly in relatively flat and fertile areas, such as the North China plain, the Red Basin of Sichuan, the central and lower Yangtze valley, and the Guangzhou delta. The geographically harsher inland border regions sustained a lesser number. But for most Chinese, wherever they resided, life was hard and short. In premodern China, the normal life expectancy of an adult, if one survived the high infant mortality rate, was probably less than 30 years. The cycle of life had to be telescoped into a few decades.

People

Despite hardships, over the millennia, China's people have grown appreciably in numbers as revealed in official census figures taken primarily for tax purposes. At the dawn of the Christian era in the West, the Chinese population, according to a tabulation of the period, was around 60 million. By the beginning of the third century, because of extensive civil strife, the breakdown of government efficiency, and the restricted areas canvassed, the population dwindled to less than half, around 25 million. But by A.D. 600, it had dramatically doubled under the prosperous, stable, and relatively peaceful Tang dynasty. In the thirteenth century, Mongol figures revealed a slightly higher aggregate of souls, some 55 to 60 million. By the Qing era in the early nineteenth century, there were some 150 million Chinese. In the early nineteenth century, the population had doubled to 300 million, and by the mid-twentieth century, it had more than doubled again. The geometrical increases continue, and the population is now more than a billion.

Because of peace, prosperity, and the fact that ever-increasing food yields kept up with the growing population, along with the extension of arable acreage, China was able to absorb internally the demographic expansion. Population growth was essentially due to domestic factors. There were few immigrants into the country; not many of the Chinese left their homeland. Those who did, relocated mainly in border regions, especially Southeast Asia. There, in urban areas such as Yangon (formerly Rangoon), Bangkok, Jakarta, Manila, and Ho Chi Minh City, the newcomers went into retail trade and commerce. Their presence in Malaysia was particularly striking; Singapore, after Sir Stamford Raffles established a firm British colonial government there in the early nineteenth century, became almost 80 percent Chinese in population.

All that is known about the origins of the Chinese is that they derive from racially mixed sources. Over the centuries long ago, intermingling of varied strains resulted from repeated invasions emanating from northern, northwestern, and western quarters. However, by the advent of recorded history, around 1750 B.C., the Chinese had become quite homogenous in character and racially unique. Because of their numerical strength, through an ongoing racial absorption process, they assimilated minority groups. Filling up North China, they then pressed southward. To the east, the seas blocked expansion; to the north and west, deserts and hostile peoples confined movement. So it was to the south, with less forbidding topography and where fewer, weaker enemy tribes resided, that was the historic direction of internal migration. Below the Yangtze, the Chinese continued to absorb the earlier inhabitants or forced them to move even farther south through the mountain passes and river channels into neighboring mainland southeast Asia lands. The resulting overall racial uniformity in China of the ethnically purer Chinese resulted from such factors as the absence of geographical barriers, the lack of any caste system that permitted social mobility, migrations within the empire, and a tendency to promote common political and cultural goals.

Regional physical and cultural variations naturally developed among them because of the continental size of the country. Generalizations have been advanced to distinguish particularly the northern Chinese from their southern counterparts (with the Yangtze as the dividing line). Northerners, on the whole, are likely to be slightly taller, by perhaps one or two inches, a bit heavier, more strongly built, and fairer of complexion, with flatter noses and higher cheekbones, than their southern compatriots. In temperament and character, northerners tend to be more conservative, less emotional, and more relaxed. But even within the south, there is additional area diversity, since the cross-hatched mountain ranges and irregular river patterns help to semi-isolate inhabitants within their own enclaves and distinctive subcultures.

There are also differentiations between the Chinese and the various minorities who live within the political boundaries of the country. Totaling some 10 percent (more than 100 million) of the overall population, the non-Chinese reside principally in border areas. The People's Republic of China has officially enumerated fifty-five of them in number, based on differing linguistic, racial, or religious grounds.

As noted earlier, five provinces have been designated as autonomous—which implies the existence in each of a minority peoples as the most populous: Inner Mongolia, Ningxia, Xinjiang, Tibet, and Guangxi. Autonomy implies cultural and linguistic privileges, but never political ones. Even within these provincial-level administrative entities, however, are prefectural and country units designated as autonomous wherever small groups of other non-Chinese peoples are clearly the local majority. (These subprovincial autonomous units are also present in the regular provinces.) Through expressions of dance forms, dress, language, and historical background, minority peoples add much color to the national scene.

Social Classes

In the earliest dynasties, traditional Chinese society was divided into a few rulers and the many who were ruled, with a wide gap separating them. In later centuries, this gap narrowed somewhat with the addition of other intermediary social groups.

In early times, these governing classes were the aristocratic enclaves at the courts of kings and emperors, but by the eleventh century, the scholar-gentry or educated bureaucracy had emerged on top. Collectively, from benefits of officeholding, and sometimes as landlords, they constituted the government officials, ex-officials, candidates for office, and unofficial scholars. In the early nineteenth century, the scholar-gentry and their families probably constituted two percent of China's population. The class received a disproportionate one-fifth of the national income, of which one-half generally derived from official services rendered, one-third from land, and the remainder from commercial activities. In or out of office, they ruled the country, both in theory and in fact. Observing Confucian propriety and ethics, they directed the affairs of state, and they passed praise and censure on people and monarch alike.

As primary producers, the peasants theoretically ranked second in the Confucian social ladder. But they were much exploited, and they existed simply as statistics for the government. The four-fifths of the Chinese people who made up this class lived as family units in villages

Ideologies

The overall Western term for the Chinese way of life is sinicism, derived from the Greek *sinai*, an oriental people. The earliest philosophic and religious beliefs of the Chinese are not precisely known, not even whether they were monotheistic or polytheistic. But by 1000 B.C., Chinese ideology seems to have incorporated such basic outlooks as reverence for, rather than awe of, nature, animism (the belief in natural spirits), and a form of ancestor worship. The main god was an impersonal entity designating heaven (*tian*), or sometimes as a deity with more personal attributes as master above (*shangdi*). Other gods seem to have been worshiped more as supermen than as divine entities. Ancestor worship, or reverence as it might more properly be called, cementing family lines, was an important part of early Chinese thought. The state of the departed spirit was considered to be materially dependent on rituals performed by the living, who in turn could receive benefits from the deceased. Revering mutual progenitors, the living family members were bound into close-knit, regulated relationships and hierarchical patterns that extended countrywide up to the emperor, and through him to the highest heavenly deities.

Sinicism included a host of lesser gods and spirits, both god and evil. Permeating the land and water, they existed everywhere. All nature incorporated the five universal elements (*wuxing*): water (*shui*), fire (*huo*), wood (*mu*), metal (*jin*), and earth (*di*). Identified with the elements were the ten celestial (heavenly) stems (*tiangan*): water (fresh and salt), fire (lightning and burning incense), wood (trees and hewn timber), metal (metallic ore and kettles), earth (hills and earthenware). A secondary cycle was the twelve terrestrial (earthly) branches (*dizhi*), represented by symbolic animals: rat, ox, tiger, hare, dragon, serpent, horse, goat, monkey, cock, dog, and boar (each also equated with a year). Popular belief embraced the concept of *yang and yin*. The *yang* connoted a wide-ranging set of concepts, such as light, heaven, life, and the male, while the *yin* embraced opposite notions such as darkness, earth, death, and the female. *Yang* and *yin* were complementary, not antagonistic; they were to be sought in balance and equilibrium; each needed the other to be defined and defined in context. Another basic Chinese concept was that of "wind-water" (*fengshui*), a principle that governed the location of buildings and temples. By this form of geomancy, much of which was practical, architectural projects were to accord with natural phenomena; hills had to block out evil influences from the north, streams had to run in certain directions, edifices were to face the south.

Superimposed on the vast though sometimes nebulous array of simple beliefs and folk thought were the organized philosophic schools. The schools generally agreed that man was basically good and that he should accommodate himself to, rather than control, his environment. The philosophies were concerned with the creation of the ideal society by surmounting the problems of man who was always placed in a social, and relative, context. These elaborated postulations were eventually incorporated by the Confucianists. The Confucian school, as the most important, flourished in the mainstream of Chinese ideology and philosophy because of its worldliness, practicality, and eclectic borrowing from other schools. It stressed humanism, optimism, moderation, agnosticism, and skepticism, and was concerned more with ethics and ritual than with theological concepts. Yet, however sophisticated the Confucian Chinese could be, they combined superstition with rationalism and readily reconciled primitive notions to intellectual concepts. On the whole, Confucianism was tolerant, but it was a toleration, through strength, for the doctrine, once officially accepted, withstood lesser challenges from competing native and foreign dogmas and permitted them to exist in less formidable forms.

Confucianism is a latinized word derived from its founder, whom the Chinese called Kongfuzi (Master Kong), 551-479 B.C. His doctrine is known to the Chinese as "the teaching of the learned" (*rujia*). It stressed the golden mean, reverence for the past, patience, pacifism, obedience, status, and social hierarchy. Agnostic as to any future life, Confucius concerned himself mainly with problems of the here-and-now. The superior educated man was to cultivate and practice five inner virtues (integrity, righteousness, loyalty, reciprocity, human-heartedness), which would reflect themselves externally. He was to govern the state through a combination of ethics, virtue, and knowledge acquired by education and elaborate ritual. Confucius lived during the politically troubled and divided Eastern Zhou dynasty, and his doctrine for the warring nobles, advanced not as unique or new, but simply as a reaffirmation of earlier thought, drew on China's golden antiquity for model rulers and advisers.

Confucianism won out over its many rival schools within a few centuries because of its practicality, middle-ground position, intellectual appeal, and emphasis on ritual. It enhanced the position of the bureaucrat and of the educated man, who gained and regulated political power. Its most important disciple was Mencius or Mengzi (Master Meng), 372-289 B.C., who affirmed the doctrine of the right to revolt. In the Han dynasty, Confucian scholars defined the classics, adopted the concept of examination for office, and wove into official doctrine such popular beliefs as *yang* and *yin* and the five elements.

Confucianism suffered a temporary setback during the unsettled Six

Dynasties, when Buddhism made its greatest impact in China. In a more stable form, it regained its stature as a state philosophy during the Sui and Tang dynasties. In the Song dynasty, particularly under the philosopher Zhu Xi (Chu Hsi), 1130-1200, neo-Confucianism borrowed and synthesized strains from the two other main schools of thought: Daoism and Buddhism. This invigorated form idealistically interpreted the universe as a duality wherein good and undesirable traits coexisted. During the Ming, a later philosopher, Wang Yangming, 1472?-1528, stressed intuition in the search for knowledge. In the Manchu period, the main Confucian activity was devoted to a critical and pragmatic study of Han classical texts. The Confucian fate in modern China has varied. Nationalist Chinese leaders observe Confucian rituals and principles, but the Communists have variously exorcised the philosophy as undemocratic and feudal on the one hand, and on the other as an exemplary code of regulated behavior requiring obedience toward superiors.

A second school of philosophy was Daoism (Taoism), essentially advanced as a contrast against a ritualistic and precise Confucianism. *Dao* literally means "way" or "road"; symbolically it can designate any religion or philosophy, including Christianity. Daoism arose in Zhou times apparently in semibarbaric areas peripheral to China proper. In its popular form, it was naturalistic and animistic, and it incorporated beliefs in traditional superstitions. It advocated placating spirits and exercises for breathing and muscular control.

In the third century B.C., amorphous Daoist thought began to crystallize around two early leaders and books ascribed to them; Laozi (Lao Tzu, Old Master), whose historicity is questioned, and Zhuangzi (Chuang Tzu), who lived in the second half of the fourth century B.C. They advocated the merging of oneself with the Dao, which was nameless, a nonbeing state. Like the Confucians, they celebrated primitivity, not because they considered it as an ideal model of former excellence, but simply because early times, they claimed, were uncomplicated. A later popular form inverted the intellectual concepts and prescribed magical elixirs and alchemies to prolong life. Alongside the many flourishing disparate sects in the fourth century A.D. a Daoist papacy in southwestern China was organized that lasted until the mid-1920s, when the Communists eradicated it. Daoism influenced Chinese philosophic and esthetic tradition in basic but intangible ways; it provided stimulus to paint impressionistic landscapes and to compose abstract literary works.

Buddhism (*Fajiao*), the third of the three main schools of thought or "three religions" (*sanjiao*) in China, was imported from India. In its Chinese dress, it taught salvation by faith in a range of heavenly beings and constructed a hierarchy of heavens and hells in the afterlife for the faithful or the backslider. Buddhist doctrines trickling into China in Han times became a major religious and political force during the fourth through the ninth centuries A.D., particularly in the north, where they were espoused by alien rulers. The early Tang favored it, but by A.D. 1000, Buddhism had begun to decline. Although the Chinese greatly modified it, Buddhism remained a foreign import, as Chinese nativists, including Confucianists, were always quick to point out. As a body, bureaucrats never subscribed to it because its concepts basically opposed Confucianism with its alien notions such as otherworldliness, lack of any appreciable sense of historicity, and advocacy of celibacy. Once politically prominent, the religion was proscribed by Chinese rulers on grounds of security rather than theology. Today, Communist China tolerates the faith, but, in the usual fashion, the religion has been subordinated to the state.

Other foreign faiths such as Islam, Judaism, and both medieval and modern Christianity made little impact on traditional Chinese thought. But many indigenous schools of philosophy, especially in the earlier dynasties, were appropriated into the mainstream of Chinese thought, while others died a natural death. Over the centuries, as Confucius was said to describe them, the "hundred flowers bloomed" in the cultural garden and the "hundred schools contended" for political acceptance. Scholars and bureaucrats were always deeply interested in philosophy, which assumes an important role in any interpretation of Chinese history.

Language

Chinese ideology has been most fundamentally preserved in the written language, which dates in recognizable form from around 1750 B.C. Chinese script, unique to the country and of unknown origin, uses up to 50,000 monosyllabic characters, or variations of them, each ranging from one to twenty-eight strokes. A literate person is presumed to know some 3,000 of the characters, although newspaper readers require a minimum of 7,000. But because of their conciseness, one character, especially in a classical context, may represent the equivalent of several English words in translation. Mastery of writing the characters entails complex memorization. For each character, the executor must know not only the number but also the sequence and direction of strokes; any modification could change the meaning of the word.

There are several types of Chinese characters. One might be a conventionalized picture of objects; for example, a small square symbol represented a mouth. Or the character might be an abstract idea in pictorial form; for example, one, two, or three straight lines would stand for these cardinal numbers respectively, while the composite character, say, for "good" combined two others representing a woman and child, a familial concept so dear to the Chinese. Or the character might be simply phonetic in nature with no explicit or implicit indication of meaning. But whatever the type of character, each contained in whole or abbreviated form one of the so-called 214 radicals, by which they were classified in dictionaries. The radicals themselves ranged in strokes from one to seventeen in number. In looking up an unknown character in a Chinese-English dictionary, the user must first identify the number of the radical within the character itself and then the number of additional strokes, if any, to the radical that completes the whole character. The present lexicography of 214 radicals was systematized from earlier schemata in Ming times; an earlier Han arrangement contained 540 radicals.

Written Chinese language has two main forms, in a relationship somewhat like that of Latin to Italian: the classical *wenyan* and the vernacular *baihua*. The characters used in both systems are the same but retain a different meaning and context. A classical passage read aloud would make no sense to a Chinese who was not acquainted with the text or to the allusions made. Classical Chinese, used in the traditional examinations, took years to learn. Moreover, since the texts were almost totally lacking in punctuation (or indexes), they resembled unending streams of characters. Books, classical or otherwise, were traditionally read in reverse Western form, from back to front, with pages read from right to left in vertical columns. The reason for this arrangement is not clear, but it may have originated before the introduction of paper (around A.D. 100) when the Chinese wrote on narrow bamboo or wooden slips. Today Chinese read and write in either traditional or Western fashion.

In the vernacular, written characters are pronounced as the spoken words they represent. In ordinary practice, as in letters, informal communications, and sometimes on paintings, abbreviated forms of characters are executed in a graceful calligraphic "running" hand. At the time of World War I, Chinese scholars and educationalists such as Hu Shih and James Yen promoted the use of the written vernacular. Lists of a thousand basic characters were published to encourage literacy and writing among the Chinese peasants. Nationalists and Communists have continued this program of adult education.

Although characters complicated the process of printing, the Chinese invented the wood-block printing method of etching texts onto wood or stone tablets, some with illustrations, usually derived from

Confucian or Buddhist classics. The British Museum has a Chinese Buddhist scroll dated the equivalent of A.D. 868, the oldest Chinese printed book in the world produced by the wood-block method (although earlier examples are present in Korea and Japan, who derived the technique from China). The Chinese invented movable type centuries before it was developed in Europe, but they discarded it because of its impracticality. Adapting Chinese writing to modern methods posed problems. Chinese typewriters are unwieldy, and telegrams require coded numbers to represent characters. After experimenting with various foreign alphabets, both Nationalists and Communists decided to retain the native characters. Some have been simplified, but essentially they remain the same. The advantages in retaining written Chinese are several, for the characters are rich and vivid in ideas, and calligraphy is a notable art. Moreover, with little variation over almost four millennia, the character script has afforded cultural continuity in East Asia, and users of the Chinese language, although geographically restricted, remain the most numerous in the world.

The written language is uniform throughout China, but pronunciation of the characters varies in the local dialects. Southern and northern Chinese in their oral versions are markedly different. A conversation among Chinese from different parts of the country is impossible unless all are acquainted with one spoken form. The most widespread spoken form is the northern "national" or "common" language (*putonghua*), which Westerns have called Mandarin and which both Nationalists and Communists have promoted. All dialects are based on tones, which have changed through time. Old sounds have been reconstructed from rhyming dictionaries compiled between the sixth and eleventh centuries A.D.

Mandarin has four tones for each character (or vocable as it is known in the spoken form); southern dialects range up to nine. As now constituted, Mandarin possesses only some 430 vocables. The presence of tens of thousands of written characters that may be pronounced in only several hundreds of vocables necessitates the reuse of similar vocables, where tones provide some versatility in meaning. Yet the nonalphabetized and monosyllabic oral language is, in some ways, less complicated and easier to learn than Western languages. It has no declensions, no conjugations, and no genders. Plural numbers and tenses are indicated by sentence context or additional particles. Compound words are formed by repeating the same character or by combining two or more of them with related meanings.

Modern life and Western impact have raised problems of oral and written communication between Chinese and foreigners. One problem was that of romanizing Chinese vocables for Western use. A basic dictionary was compiled by two nineteenth-century British sinologists, the first by Thomas Wade and elaborated on by Herbert Giles (the Wade-Giles system), who arranged the Mandarin sounds by alphabetized syllables. However, some of the romanized vocables did not resemble the true pronunciation; for instance the verb "to be" (*shih*) was pronounced as "*shr.*" Other systems of romanization more nearly reconciling phonetics and spelling have been advanced by other Western academics. In the mid-1950s the Chinese Communists developed the *pinyin* (Chinese spelling) system of romanization (that had its roots some two decades earlier), based on the national dialect, but which, like the Wade-Giles system, does not exactly replicate all Western sounds exactly. In 1979, Beijing applied the romanization to international uses, and most foreign governments and scholars shortly followed suit in changing over to the new system.

Incorporating foreign words and ideas into inflexible written Chinese has also been a perennial problem, and none of the three basic ways has been completely satisfactory. The first method is translation, or using a Chinese character with hopefully an equivalent Western meaning. For example, Catholic missionaries in eighteenth-century China translated "God," a theological concept lacking in China, as *Tian* or *Shangdi*, both rather imprecise connotations of heaven in Chinese. A second method of possible accommodation is transliteration, using characters not for meaning but for Chinese vocables similar in sound to English words; i.e., characters as *Yehehua* for Jehovah and *Yesu* for Jesus. But since the same character can be pronounced differently in spoken dialects, transliteration can create confusion in the Chinese vernacular mind. Moreover, the Chinese reader may be perplexed by two or three strange characters inserted into a passage solely for phonetic reasons rather than for meaning. The Chinese Communists have standardized transliterations of foreign words and phrases, particularly in the scientific field. The third course of action in attempting to bridge the linguistic gap is to use cultural parallels in the Chinese and Western languages. This is difficult because Chinese cultural values often do not equate with the supposedly similar values in Western thought. Again in theology, for example, there is no concept of original sin in the man-oriented Chinese society. The parable of the biblical lost sheep misfired on the Chinese, who, disdaining pastoral life, would not have sought it out.

5

CULTURE

Roots of Chinese culture, with its basic characteristics, date back to prehistoric times. From early days, the Chinese attuned their scheduled activities to both the lunar and solar calendars. Public festivals abounded; half a dozen of these were especially observed. The life cycle itself of birth, marriage, raising a family, and death was marked by decreed custom and regulated behavior. Symbols were plentiful; the most venerated related to suggestions of prosperity and longevity. Confucianism had its own folk gods; the Daoist Eight Immortals were popular; Buddhism enjoyed its own cornucopia of motifs, designs, and deities. Colors, in themselves, held significance. In the natural world, certain animals, both mythical and real, flowers, and trees connoted special symbolic attributes. Mountains and awe-inspiring peaks were venerated and identified as special by Daoists and Buddhists. A miscellany of other widely used suggestive symbols related to cosmic forces.

Cycles

The Chinese regulated their activities according to the calendar, reputedly invented in 2637 B.C. by the cultural prototype, the mythical Emperor Huang Di. His calculations took into account days, months, years, and extended time cycles. Days, commencing at 11 P.M., were divided into twelve parts of two-hour segments, each of which received a special designation and horological importance. The lunar ritual year was 354 or 355 days, divided into twelve uneven months of twenty-nine to thirty days each. The new year commenced on the second new moon after the winter solstice, which, in Western reckoning, could vary any day between January 21 and February 20. The months were simply numbered in sequence from one to twelve; they received no special descriptive designations. But the agricultural year had to be regulated according to the solar calendar, otherwise the calendrical seasons would not conform to astronomical reality. To reconcile the two systems of time, seven short months of several weeks each were intercalated onto the lunar calendar on an average of every nineteen years. These extra intercalary months received additional numerical terms, such as the second third month, or whenever it occurred, but it was never in the first, eleventh, or twelfth lunar months. Official calendars, formulated by imperial scholars, were taken seriously; human and political affairs had to be reconciled with the mechanics of the natural world. Terrestrial and celestial events proceeded in tandem.

Solar reckoning was in use from Shang times. Sundials devised in the Zhou dynasty defined a solar computation of twenty-four periods of fourteen to sixteen days each. These "months," the first commencing between the fifth and eighth days, and the second between the nineteenth and twenty-third days, were designated at least in the one-crop Yellow River basin in North China that was the early heartland of China, according to the formula: "spring begins, spring showers, insects waken, vernal equinox (second month), clear and bright, grain rain, summer begins, grain forms, grain in ear, summer solstice (fifth month), moderate heat, great heat, autumn begins, heat recedes, white dew, autumnal equinox (eighth month), cold dew, frost descends, winter begins, light snow, heavy snow, winter solstice (twelfth month), moderate cold, severe cold."

Larger cycles, possibly borrowing from a concept of the tree of life, were devised some five thousand years ago. They included the ten celestial stems, noted earlier, and the twelve terrestrial branches. The lunar years (and the two-hour periods of the day), unlike the numbered months, were named after ideally androgynous animals. Legend had it that an ancient emperor invited all the animals to a feast but only a dozen materialized; upon these guests the monarch bestowed the calendrical honors. (Buddhism later adopted the same cycle of animals, but changed the legend to the same twelve animals that appeared to bid the Buddha farewell on his deathbed.) The ten stems six times over, combined with the twelve branches five times over, in its first combination was the basic sixty-year cycle, so important in personal life, long-range chronology, and historical writing. In the 1920s, the Nationalists officially adopted the modern calendar; the Chinese Communists also use the Christian reckoning.

As based on the lunar year, the Chinese enjoyed many festivals, local and countrywide. Of the latter, half a dozen were the more universally enjoyed and favored. First in time came the New Year (*Guonian*). Shortly before this auspicious event, the family burned the image of the kitchen god, with his lips smeared with molasses to sweeten the story that the deity would report to the gods on the family's behavior over the preceding year. On the day before the New Year, he was welcomed back with a fresh portrait of him placed in the kitchen. All debts were to be settled by that date; one started out the year with a clean financial slate. The day itself was private; the family enjoyed the company of its members; ancestors were honored. Festivals subsequently went public and they continued for two weeks. On the fifteenth day of the first month, it officially ended with the Feast of Lanterns (*Dengjie*), when the lion dance was performed. Although the People's Republic of China decried the observances of traditional customs, it extended the festivities of the New Year into a three- to five-day holiday. At this time, China, always teeming with life, became especially festive.

The second, *Qingming* (clear and bright), was the only festival fixed in solar reckoning; it occurred on the fifth day of the fourth month (April 5). In a type of memorial day, family members went to cemeteries to honor ancestors, clean graves, and offer food to placate spirits, after which the offerings were eaten.

Next in time came the Dragon Boat festival (*Duanwu* or *Duanyang*), on the fifth day of the fifth month that harmonized *yang* and *yin*. The latter had been prevalent in winter and now the former was commencing with the oncoming summer months. Possibly having its origins in South China, the festival also propitiated water spirits. Boats, decorated with dragon motifs, engaged in races on rivers and lakes. The event also specially honored a third-century B.C. poet and official who drowned himself as a protest against a corrupt monarch; the races set out to find the body. Delicacies served at this time were cakes of rice and sweets filled with chopped meat, steamed in lotus leaves, and tied with colored strings.

The next holiday was one dedicated principally to women, on the seventh day of the seventh month. This recalled the legend of a weaver maid and herdsman who, after marriage, neglected their respective duties. The angry gods separated them, but on this special night, if it did not rain, magpies with their extended wings built a bridge across the Milky Way over which the maid passed to spend time with her spouse.

Last in the year was the Full Moon festival (*Zhongqiu*), on the fifteenth day of the eighth month as a type of thanksgiving celebrated the end of the harvest season; it inaugurated the advent of autumn. Devoted to children's activities, it inspired the consumption of delicious moon cakes.

The idealized family in China was one of five generations living under one roof, from one's grandparents to one's grandchildren, all of whom were addressed on the basis more of relationship status than of personal names (i.e., elder brother, younger sister). Through the practice of ancestor reverence, the family extended back in time to one's forebears, who may have lived in another region of the country.

Surnames came first in order of listing; usually two personal ones followed, the first of which could reveal clan or generational ties. Most Chinese family names were monosyllabic and were limited in number. Sometimes designated as the hundred names, the Chinese enjoyed some four hundred surnames, although four of them—Zhang, Zhen, Li, and Wang—were the most common. Modern Chinese of both sexes follow a practice of adopting a self-designated Western name in addition to their personal indigenous ones, which are then abbreviated to initials if both forms are simultaneously used (e.g., V. K. Wellington Koo).

Parents preferred the firstborn to be a male in order to continue the surname, to observe family rites, and to be more economically productive than a female. In hard-pressed agricultural families with several mixed offsprings, young girls suffered the practice of infanticide, or being sold into bondage, or they became concubines. Even today, in the People's Republic, with the general policy of a one-child family for the ethnically pure Chinese, old customs die hard; parents hope that the firstborn would be a boy. Additional children could result in social and economic sanctions taken against the parents. (Minority groups are exempt from the policy.) Astrology played an important role in the time of birth of the newborn: the two-hour segment of day, the day itself, the month, and year—all were calculated in a prognosis of future well-being or calamity. As recently as 1967, considered a disastrous year in which the combative fire element and horse symbols coalesced, the birthrate plummeted in China and abroad among Chinese who seriously followed such omens.

In villages, the child was traditionally put to work as soon as possible in the fields. No schooling was available, although a gifted male might be sponsored by a local scholar for studies in the classics that might lead through the examination system to an official job. Such an end was highly desirable because any successful candidate, through the custom of nepotism, could enfold the whole family into a more auspicious environment.

Peasant homes were simple throughout China; brick was a common and easily available material with which to build. In the friable loess lands of the northwest, homes were dug into cliff sides that provided for some warmth in winter and cool relief from hot summers. Common folk dressed in materials from fiber, mainly hemp or ramie. Cotton, originating in India, was not widely used for clothing until it was officially promoted by the Ming. Charms and amulets were popularly worn; these were meant to protect the bearer from sundry disasters and demonic spirits. Home furniture was nil; people lived at the floor level, slept on mats, and squatted for meals that were cooked in simple hearths with wood as fuel.

For most, eating was a necessity, and the diet was simple. Tea, from Tang times onward, was widely drunk and great quantities of rice liquor were consumed. Initially using fingers with which to eat, Chinese adopted the use of chopsticks—extensions of fingers—from as early as Zhou times. A unique Chinese invention, these were widely utilized throughout East Asia wherever the sinic cultural world was imprinted. A wide variety of dishes and regional cooking variations abounded. Several basic food regions were delineated, identified with gourmet cooking: Shandong, Henan, Sichuan, Shanghai, and Guangzhou. On the whole, wheat prevailed as the staple grain in the north, rice in central regions and the south. Northerners ate hotter, spicier dishes, while heavier, blander dishes prevailed in the south. Vegetables were universally consumed, less so were fruits, poultry, and fowl, with a minimal consumption of more expensive meat. Some food products also enjoyed symbolic values; mushrooms and noodles were equated with longevity. Meat-filled dumplings, possibly from ancient sacrificial rites, floating in soup, connoted a life surrounded by water. The ginseng root was in great demand as a restorative tonic for many ailments. The wide-ranging Chinese cuisine today might have been the result in part of the ceaseless Chinese search, especially in the Daoist persuasion, for the elixir of life that promoted longevity.

As for popular sports and activities, mandarins looked down on physical activity, and peasants after a taxing day in the fields were hardly in the mood for it, but the Chinese enjoyed many pastimes. They were inveterate gamblers; they used cards and dice, played *majong* that involved an exuberant clatter of collecting similar designs or numbers incised on dominolike tiles, and *fantan*, which involved a heap of many coins from which four at a time were withdrawn, and wagers laid on the number, if any, that were left. They flew kites, witnessed acrobatic acts and jugglers, and kept crickets in cages for fights. Aristocrats of both sexes went in for polo, imported from Persia by the Tang times, while the more military-minded practiced archery, falconry, and hunting. Dedicated followers subscribed to the martial arts that combined grace of movement with intensity of spirit. Eleventh-century annals mention the art of *Taiji*, with Confucian philosophic concepts. Embodying the ruling principle of the universe, it involved *yang-yin* and the five elements. Out of it came a form of boxing, practiced since the sixteenth century; one branch, the Shaolin, viewed itself as members of an esoteric group.

Premodern marriages were arranged affairs, concluded by future in-laws and others through a matchmaker. Customary law was followed, and official and ecclesiastical authorities were not involved. Marriage was not for love; that came later, if at all. Omens of the betrothed were carefully scrutinized for compatible or adverse eight signs. On the wedding day, the bride was escorted to the home of the groom, who may have never seen her before, where, after a simple ceremony involving food and drink rituals, the couple would reside. The bride kept her family name, and she was definitely an outsider, as the in-laws harassed her, until she, through her own progeny and advancing age, could in turn become an in-law and attain respect. Filial piety toward parents was scrupulously observed; the eldest male in the household held the greatest authority. Property remained in common; the eldest son administered title. If conditions or necessity warranted it, younger siblings departed elsewhere to seek their fortunes. Through regulated kinship patterns, meticulous social behavior was maintained; each family member was expected to play his or her designated familial role. If an individual brought untoward shame through misbehavior, consciously or otherwise, to the collective unit, all members would be held accountable.

Upon death, the departed would join the host of those who had gone on ahead, to be revered with the name inscribed on the ancestral tablet in the home. The Chinese practiced inhumation, or body burial. Unless devout Buddhists, they did not favor cremation with its instant destruction of the corporeal being. The departed was considered to have three souls: one resided in the grave, one in the tablet, and one in the afterlife. Until the advent of Buddhism, there was no definite belief in retribution or reward after death. When possible, because of *fengshui* considerations, the family grave (a keyhole shape was common) was carved into a hillside facing south. At the *Qingming* festival, as noted, the living came especially to honor the dead. Grave plots also abounded on flat land, where they competed with space in much needed arable land. In the countryside, the Chinese Communists have now given priority to agricultural needs over funerary; in the cities, cremation is mandatory.

Symbols

Chinese culture was rich in symbolism, especially those relating to a state of well-being. Two of the most favored characters that frequently appeared as motifs were those signifying prosperity (*fu*) and longevity (*shou*). Popular thought, incorporated into Confucianism, included a host of mythical gods who promoted individual welfare, such as deities of longevity, wealth, fire, the kitchen, and the door. Daoism, also accommodating, embraced additional ones, as well as the popular hedonistic Eight Immortals (*Baxian*), who emerged around A.D. 1000 during the Song dynasty. Identifiable by attributes, they listed the fat Quan Zhongli, the chief of them, fanning himself; Zhang Guolao, holding a musical instrument the shape of a tube or drum with two rods to strike it; Lu Dongbin, the patron of barbers and the sick, with his fly whisk and sword; the well-accoutered official Cao Guojiu, saint of the theater, clasping a pair of castanets; holding his staff, Li Tiegua, a Buddhist priest in saffron garb (tradition held that after the Buddha became enlightened, his skin turned golden); Han Xiangzi, whom musicians particularly revere, with a magic flute; and two women, Lan Caihe, carrying a flower basket, worshiped by florists, and He Xiangu, clasping a lotus, who helps in household affairs.

Buddhism also enjoyed a host of symbols and motifs. Many of these, adopted by the Chinese from the third century A.D. onward, originated in India and were rooted there in Hinduism. At the apex of those revered were the buddha (*fo*) figures (there were other nonhistorical buddhas in addition to the originator of the faith), all of whom had attributes that denoted enlightenment. Next came the bodhisattvas (*pusa*), again all fictional, who, on the threshold of enlightenment, postponed the act and unselfishly remained in the unenlightened world in order to save others. They were bestowed with their own iconography. Then followed the holy men or monks (*lohan*) of whom eighteen, the Buddha's disciples, were especially venerated in their fixed expressions and distinctive symbols. Popular were the auspicious Eight Buddhist Symbols associated with the faith: the wheel of the law, conch shell, umbrella, flag, lotus, jar, fish, and mystic knot. To these emblems were added many others. The religious numerology rapidly escalated to the 32 signs associated with supernatural beings, then 80 auxiliary qualities, and finally to the 108 evils or shortcomings attributed to mankind. (The Buddist rosary beads count this number.)

Colors, in themselves, had significance; they were associated with directions and other phenomena. In descending order of importance were five: the life-giving red (*hong*), a symbol of joy; the imperial yellow (*huang*), denoting earth, fame, and advancement; blue (*lan*) affiliated with green (*lü*), connoting high office with attendant happiness but also cumbersome responsibility; white (*bai*), the color of old age, death, and mourning; and finally the evil black (*hei*). In directions, blue was associated with the east, white with the west, black with the north, and red with the south. The Four Great Heavenly Kings (*Si Da Tien Wang*), again Indian-derived from four godly Hindu brothers, were protectors of the four directions: Chi Guo, the blue god of the east, holds a guitar; white Guang Mu of the west, holds a sword; the red southern god, Zeng Zhang, carries an umbrella; a snake envelopes the black northern deity, Do Wen, who also wears a pearl.

Animals, including birds, mythical and real, abounded as symbols. The Chinese divided the category into five subclasses. The phoenix (*fenghuang*) represented the feathered flock; the unicorn (*qilin*) the furry creatures; man (*nan*) the naked ones; dragon (*long*) the scaly animals; and the tortoise (*gui*) the shelled. All except man were designated as supernatural creatures. The phoenix appeared in times of peace and prosperity; it presided over the south, symbolizing sun and warmth. As a decorative motif in ceremonial dress, the bird was popular in costumes of empresses. The unicorn was an omen of fecundity, longevity, felicity, and gentleness. Like its Western counterpart, the male bore a single horn jutting out from the forehead; the female lacked this implement of defense. Man was never the center of the universe; he was placed in the context of, and in harmony with, nature. The popular dragon, ancient in time and dating in concept to the Shang, was a complex animal, with nine species that related to the sky, seas, or mountains, Unlike the firebreathing destructive counterpart in the Western world, the benign animal was highly revered in China as a symbol of water and life. One special variety, with the unique five claws, was reserved for imperial use. The enigmatic tortoise replicated the cosmos, with its shell equated to the vaulted heaven and the flat underside to the earth's disc. Hero of legends, the tortoise was always at the beck and call of emperors who tried to tame natural catastrophes.

The zodiac animals were also used. Tigers, now few in number, appeared as indications of strength and of vigor. They also represented the west, to counterbalance the dragon in the east. Horses stood for the military arts and speed. Fish generically meant abundance, domestic harmony, and wealth. Goldfish and carp, with their vivid colors, were valued. Birds, of free spirit, were admired. Pairs of them connoted a happily married life. The long-necked crane represented longevity; the monogamous geese, fidelity.

Among themes drawn from plant life, in the north the long-lived pine (*song*) stood for the popular concept of long life; in the south, the tropical supple bamboo (*zhu*), bending with the winds, denoted youth and strength. Several common fruits were widely cherished. The plum (*mei* or *li*), the first tree to bloom in spring and still cling to branches laden with snow, signified good luck; the peach (*tao*), immortality; the pear (*li*), longevity; persimmons (*shi*), often found in temple gardens, for affairs and undertakings in general; and the pomegranate (*shiliu*), with its myriad seeds, fertility. Willows (*liu*), with their wistful shape providing shade, were a symbol of spring. Three seasons were also connoted by common by flowers: spring by iris (*sun*) or magnolia (*hande*); summer by the peony (*mudan*); autumn by the chrysanthemum (*ju*). Two above-mentioned trees, the plum and bamboo, connoted winter. Buddhist art made much of the lotus (*lian* or *he*), symbol of purity, a beautiful unsullied flower that blossomed out of the surrounding mire. Every month had a flower symbol.

Mountains abound in China. Their anthropomorphic spirits were early respected as the source of life-giving clouds, rain, and rivers. An ancient appellation for China, and the title of its oldest book on geography, was that of a "mountains and seas" (*shanhai*) country. Mountains, in the natural world, bestowed order, permanence, and balance, as did the emperor in human life. Of the several prominent mountain ranges, that of the Kunlun, demarcating the northern limit of the Tibetan plateau and the southern edge of the Taklamakhan desert, was fabled. Here resided the Queen Mother of the West (*Xiwangmu*) with her sumptuous palaces and beautiful gardens.

Some other individual peaks, because of their special beauty, historical association, or particular location, were elevated into status as sacred. Five special mountains (*wuyue*), revered by Daoists, were equated with the center of the country and its four cardinal directions. In the middle of Henan was Songshan. To the west in Shaanxi lay Huashan. In the south, in Hunan towered Hengshan; to the north in Shanxi was another Hengshan (with a different character). Most revered, to the east in Shandong, was Taishan. Identified with the rising sun and controlling the origins of life, it was regarded as an intermediary to heaven. Here emperors offered special sacrifices. Buddhists identified four additional renowned peaks: Omeishan in Sichuan; Jiuhuashan in Anhui; Putoshan in Zhejiang; and notably Wutaishan in Shanxi, in which compound are some of the oldest wooden structures in China.

A miscellany of other widely used symbols existed. The *yang* and *yin* duality was pictorially represented (facing the viewer) by a circle with two tadpole-shaped halves denoting an egg: the yolk, the dark element, on the left or top half, and the white, or light part, on the right or lower half. Embodying the *yang-yin* concept were the Eight Trigrams (*Bagua*), dating back to divination stalks used by Zhou horologists. These were used singly or in aggregates in circles bordering the central figure. From India came the swastika, with the crampons directed toward the right. Widely used as a Buddhist symbol, it denoted good luck and fortune. Possibly related to it was the "thunder pattern," a continuous chain of interlocking curlicues, representing clouds. Similarly, ongoing wave patterns decorated blank spaces on objects. Finally, down to earth, more immediate, and readily understood were the numerous shop signboards that colorfully dotted entranceways to various commercial establishments. Images or the pictures of the articles sold, or of the trade involved, were positioned variously on the ground, suspended from eaves, printed on walls and doorways, or hung on protruding poles over the passageway.

6

LITERATURE AND SCIENCE

In these two fields, sophisticated scholarship complemented popular culture. In literary life, the Confucian classics as well as associated philosophical works were revered. Prose encompassed works of learning including dictionaries and compendia, although those forms relating to nonclassical subjects, such as novels and fictional expression, were less esteemed. Poetry, however, was valued; it was a distinguishing mark of the scholar-gentry, who were expected to compose in the medium. Printing was a major Chinese invention. All the ingredients—paper, brush, ink, woodblocks, and rubbings—were available. In the world of scientific scholarship and ingenuity, the Chinese record was uneven. Accomplishments were less evident in theoretical science, but they remained quite rich and imaginative in practical inventions, especially in agriculture, the sciences of the heavens and earth, seismography, cartography, and medicine.

Literature

Chinese literature, of both the classical and popular expression, was rich and extensive in nature. Classical literature, grounded in Confucian values, dated back in origin to the Zhou, but the scattered works were reworked and categorized in the earlier Han. All were attributed to Confucius, although their authenticity as to authorship was and is clouded. As it developed, this official canon was crystallized into and specifically defined as the *Five Classics* (*Wujing*). Two of the five relating to history have been previously mentioned: the general *Classic of History* (*Shujing*) and one relating to a particular subperiod of the Zhou, the *Spring and Autumn Annals* (*Chunqiu*). The other three classics included a book of divination known as the *Classic of Changes* (*Yijing*); the *Classic of Poetry* (*Shijing*), and the *Classic of Rites* (*Liji*), a handbook for bureaucrats.

By A.D. 1000, the neo-Confucian school of the Song, reflecting their values, added the *Four Books (Sishu)*. Two were chapters lifted out of the *Classic of Rites*: *The Great Learning (Daxue)*, and the *Doctrine of the Mean (Zhongyong)*. The others consisted of the *Analects (Lunyü)*, or sayings of Confucius, and the *Book of Mencius (Mengzi)*. Several noncanonical works from earlier dynasties, however, continued to be cited: the *Rites of Zhou (Zhouli)*; another book of rites, the *Yili*; and the *Classic of Filial Piety (Xiaojing)*, reputedly a conversation between Confucius and one of his disciples. The examination system, earlier described, demanded the candidate's familiarity with this body of classical literature. An aspiring youth with official ambitions had already been grounded in the *Three-Character Classic (Sanzijing)*, a short summary of Chinese philosophy and history composed in rhymed lines of three characters each; the *Thousand-Character Classic (Qianzi wen)*, in which none of the characters are repeated; and the *Hundred Family Names (Baijiaxing)*.

Other officially inspired works included the compilations of encyclopedias *(leishu)*. Some were limited in scope; others were of grandiose scale. In the early fifteenth century, the most extensive one that tried to incorporate all knowledge then existing in the world of China, the *Yongle dadian* was sponsored by the third Ming emperor. Running about 12,000 volumes, it was never printed; only three manuscript copies were produced, of which now a few scattered parts exist. Anthologies or collecteana *(congshu)* were compiled on various subjects. Interested in philology, scholars wrote on the pronunciation and scripts of early characters.

Dictionaries *(zidian)* were compiled; the *Erya* was one of the earliest. Various systems of classification of characters existed: by radicals, subjects, initial or final sounds. Daoists and Buddhists also contributed much scholarship. Buddhist pilgrims to India brought back works to translate; one inspired monk of the eighth century returned to transcribe texts that totaled twenty-five times the length of the Bible. Public and private libraries existed; those of the imperial ones were the most extensive but they were often subjected to destruction by invading forces or by civil strife. Most of the classical works have survived in copies or in compilations, although scattered original literary fragments date from Han times. After the advent of printing by the woodblock method, whole editions remain extant from the Song dynasty.

In other works of literature, nonclassical works of prose such as short stories and novels *(xiaoshou* or small talk), developed. Legends of ancient storytellers contributed the substance of these stories, which imparted insight into popular folklore and mores. Few outstanding individual Chinese novelists left their imprints in the sands of time; the occupation was frowned on by Confucian bureaucrats who considered works of fiction as frivolous. Short stories were composed in the Tang, but the novel did not make its belated appearance until the Yuan and the Ming, when circumstances favored its authorship. These prose forms arose then because of the loosening of Confucianism and the abolishment of the examinations in the former dynasty. Educated but unemployed intellectuals turned from the classics to authoring popular works; a literate nonofficial public now existed in the growing commercial cities who perused lighter reading; printing made multiple copies of the same text convenient. Although the names of some novelists are known, many remained anonymous. Novels used the popular rather than the literary style, and non-Confucian heroes were quite human and lifelike. The protagonists of half a dozen novels, mostly from the Ming, became famous in Chinese folklore. These have proved invaluable documentations of everyday life, since the official and scholarly works did not concern themselves with popular subjects and tastes.

Five works of fiction were particularly prominent; their substance has been shaped over previous centuries of storytelling. The *Romance of the Three Kingdoms (Sanguozhi yanyi)*, a long historical novel attributed to Lo Guanzhong, a writer of the late fourteenth century, was set in the time of political division and civil war among the three kingdoms of the third century A.D. The second, translated variously as *All Men Are Brothers*, or *The Water Margin (Shuihuzhuan)*, originated in legends about a minor bandit named Song Jiang, who lived around 1120, in the time of the Song dynasty. With three dozen cohorts, he maintained a lair in the great marshes of western Shandong province near the junction of the Yellow River and the Grand Canal. As Yuan playwrights developed the theme, the bandits became Robin Hood-like characters; their number grew to 108. Formalized in the Ming, the novel became popular fare.

In the same dynasty, a third work, the *Golden Lotus (Jin Ping Mei)*, China's first great realistic novel, borrowed its central character, Ximen Qing, from a chapter of *All Men Are Brothers*. This strictly non-Confucian novel described the pursuit of pleasure in everyday urban life and convincingly treated women characters as distinct individuals. *Monkey*, or the *Record of a Journey to the West (Xiyouji)*, the work of a single author, Wu Chengen, 1500?-1580, was the absorbing story of an omnicompetent monkey who overcame great obstacles while escorting the famous Buddhist pilgrim Xuanzang on his travels to and from Central Asia and India in the mid-Tang period. The last great novel of traditional China was in the Qing, the *Dream of the Red Chamber (Hongloumeng)*, an autobiographical account in a riches-to-rags theme of a merchant family dealing in silk.

Poetry (*shi*) is an old revered form of literature in China. The bureaucrat, or scholar-gentry, was assumed to be well versed in the knowledge and composition of the medium. The *Classic of Poetry*, as noted, contained some three hundred anonymous poems relating to miscellaneous themes. Prominent individual poets later arose. In South China, in the third century B.C., Qu Yuan (Chu Yuan), one of the earliest known poets, wrote elegies. According to tradition, he drowned himself in despair over personal and political problems (boats in the Dragon Boat festival are looking for his body). By Han times, both free verse and rigid poetic forms were utilized. Some poems were intended to be sung, others to be merely recited. By the sixth century A.D., systematized tone values played an important part in composing and reading poetry.

During the Tang dynasty, around 3,000 poets flourished, of whom the most notable in Chinese annals were Li Bai (Li Po), Du Fu (Tu Fu), and Bai Juyi (Po Chü-I). Friendship between men was a popular theme; romantic love was not, since marriages were arranged and women played a distinctly secondary social role. Daoist attitudes formed a vital poetic strain of suggestiveness and escapism. But as in other types of art, canons of styles, of rhythm, length, tone, and forms arose and tended to stifle or freeze poetry into rigid expressions. Liu Xie (Liu Hsieh), A.D. 465-522, was an early literary critic.

Books (*shu*), a scholarly symbol, were associated with the bureaucrats. On a son's first birthday, parents presented the boy with some half dozen objects including a book; if he selected the volume, the choice augured a lifetime of study. Works, particularly the classics, in the library or under the pillow of the sleeper, supposedly warded off ignorant evil spirits during slumber. Before the invention of printing in the Earlier Han, books were incised by stylus or brushes on long slips of wood or bamboo, threaded by thongs through holes at the tops and bottoms of the slats. Bulky in structure and easily subject to weathering and destruction, early specimens are few in number today, and then only in individual slabs. After the advent of paper around A.D. 100, and the use of silk, horizontal literary scrolls of varying lengths were composed; these were stored in individual oblong containers. Woodblock and stone rubbings can be traced back to around A.D. 600. This medium led to a great expansion of the number of books as well as multiple copies of many single works. Movable type, experimented with in the Song dynasty, was discarded early as impractical for a craft that utilized thousands of characters.

To carve the woodblock, soft woods, such as pear and apple, were used. To print the text, sometimes with illustrations, the characters, directly or from a pasted sheet of paper on the wood, would be chiseled by a steel graver into the wood to leave an indented text. Alternatively, the wood would be chipped away to leave a raised one. Either way, the depressed or raised text would be smeared or rolled with ink. On the blackened surface would be laid a sheet of fairly fragile paper, a generic specimen made from a coagulated and dried composite of rice straw, crushed mulberry leaves, or another shredded fibrous substance known as rice paper. Peeled away, the mirror-effect image on the reverse side of the paper resulted in a white-on-black (with a depressed text) effect, or a black-on-white effect (with an elevated text). Multiple copies could be made in this fashion. The reverse process, of first laying the paper over the elevated or depressed text, and then smudging the paper resulted in similar effects but could yield only one copy per rubbing. From these rubbings, one block each per page of text, the finished product would result. Sheets of paper for printed books were pasted back to back; the texts from the blocks would be imprinted only on one side because of the fragility of the paper. Religious texts, especially those of Buddhism, were multiplied by the use of woodcuts.

Finished sheets were sometimes given an accordion fold with paper covers; these early books were read in reverse to Western use, from back to front. A later development resulted in the now-familiar stitched books of folded sheets still printed on only one side and read yet back to front. While block printing provided a multiplicity of printed works, it was a result of a craftsman's labor, not that of a classically inclined refined scholar. Woodcuts were not well geared to the Chinese aesthetic ideal that valued spontaneity; they could never aspire to the high rank held by the arts of brush as developed in Chinese paintings and calligraphy. Low-brow labor printed the scholarly works used by high-brow officials.

Science

Outstanding in classical scholarship, Chinese genius manifested itself only secondarily in the works of scientific inquiry and theory. There were several reasons for this imbalance. Chinese philosophies stressed the adjustment of man to nature, the control of man and his mind rather than of his mastery over matter and environment. Not only were handwork and brainwork separated in traditional life, but most trained minds concentrated on mastering and conforming to the knowledge of the classics rather than to questioning them. Laboratories for experimentation were lacking. The ready availability of manpower tended to deter invention, and precluded the necessity of labor-saving devices. State economic monopolies stifled private initiative and curiosity. Even the relatively fixed Chinese written characters hindered adoption of scientific ideas. Where the Chinese lacked any appreciable degree of theoretical science, on the other hard, they advanced the boundaries of practical science. They wrought great inventions: paper and printing, gunpowder, the magnetic compass, bronze castings, and porcelain. In the first thirteen centuries A.D., China gave to Europe, among other inventions, the wheelbarrow, the crossbow, the kite, cast iron, the iron-chain suspension bridge, canal locks, and the watertight compartment for ships. From this treasure house, only an eclectic array of significant works can be outlined here.

In a land where farm life was basic and essential to the country's economic welfare, agricultural engineering was developed. Calendars, dating to the Zhou, regulated agrarian life and charted phonological phenomena that related climate to periodical biological events (as the flowering of plants in summer, the migration of birds in autumn). From early on, the Chinese farmers practiced double-cropping, raised a variety of grains, vegetables, and fruits, and promoted grafting to improve yields. Row cultivation, intensive hoeing, iron plows, and animal harnesses were in evidence.

Irrigation was practiced from ancient times. Canal systems were dug and devices invented to move water from one level to another. From the Later Han came the chain pump, first motivated by foot power and then by animals, that turned a wheel axle, scooping up water from its source into a trough of square pallet boards to pour it into ditches at a higher level. The state pursued water conservancy projects to irrigate large areas of potentially arable land. One of the oldest, from 250 B.C., and still extant, is Dujiangyan that utilized the Minjiang River on the Chengdu plain. Sea walls to control tides were constructed as well as canals to connect river systems in order to transport grain and produce for use as food or taxes. By A.D. 600, a Sui emperor had put together the Grand Canal, some 1,100 miles long (a distance comparable to the distance between New York City and Orlando, Florida, or from Paris to Belgrade). With the lack of any major north-south river systems in China, the canal in several segments, from Hangzhou to Beijing, connected five east-west rivers to provide for this need.

In their ingenuity, the Chinese have been credited with several mathematical discoveries, including the use of counting rods, cube roots, algebra for equations, geometry to describe shapes, an accurate value for *pi*, the use of a blank space for zero, and the decimal system, including decimal fractions. In an early example, a thirteenth-century B.C. Shang notation defined 547 days in terms of 5 one hundreds, 4 tens, and the leftover 7. The cumulative distillation of mathematical knowledge of the Han through the Shang dynasties was published in the *Ten Mathematical Manuals* (*Suan Jing Shi Shu*). Later dynasties added supplements.

In astronomy, literature provided for star catalogs, maps, and calendars. In 613 B.C. came the world's first recorded mention of Halley's comet. Meteorite showers were noted. By the third century B.C., solar and lunar eclipses were followed. In the second century B.C., the author of a book described sunspots. Also in that century, in the field of optics, the first periscope applied the principle of reflection in plane mirrors. Stars provided guides for celestial navigation in which "star-viewing" placed them in configurations. Abetting navigation was an ancient south-pointing floating needle. By A.D. 1100, the magnetic compass was in use, a valuable aid to mariners when adverse night weather precluded the use of heavenly navigational aids. These utilized a floating needle also, rather than an earlier-used lodestone.

The Chinese utilized certain fundamentals of physical sciences, such as the center of gravity, the law of motion, spontaneous combustion, and the concept of acoustical waves and vibrations (as applied to musical instruments). In chemistry, they practiced alchemy, not so much in the aim of Europeans who sought it to transmute base metals into gold, but in order to prolong life through the preparation of magical elixirs (*shendan*). To this end, they experimented with various minerals, including cinnabar, a bright red mercuric sulfide. In metallurgy, they had a range of at least twenty-one minerals and thirty types of rocks with which to experiment, including copper, tin, and lead. In the mid-Zhou, iron smelting, resulting in a malleable cast product, was used. By the Han, extensive coal deposits in the north were used to refine the iron ore.

The science of seismography was accentuated. China, a land of earthquakes formed by clashing tectonic plates of the southern Himalayas and the western Pacific rim, since ancient times had been ravished by devastating shakes, often ranging up to an equivalent of a six and higher on the Richter scale. By 1700 B.C., quakes were recorded. From the Han dynasty onward, detailed annals chronicled the disastrous earthquakes and noted relevant data. Observers were always on the lookout for any special warnings through foresigns, such as underground sounds, unusual weather patterns that included lightning flashes in the sky, advance shock waves, changes in underground water levels, and strange animal behavior. In A.D. 132, during the Later Han period, China produced the world's first seismograph.

According to the *History of the Earlier Han* (*Hou Han Shu*), Zhang Heng, the imperial historian at the royal court at Luoyang, the capital, invented an ingenious machine. A bronze jar, some six feet in diameter with a domed lid, had around its perimeter eight evenly spaced dragon heads, each with a ball in its mouth; directly below each head was an open-mouthed toad. Inside, in the center of the vessel, was a suspended pendulum that, when jarred, struck one of the eight levers, each connected with a dragon mouth, which would then open and drop the ball into the waiting mouth of the toad below. The resounding clang (a type of early alarm clock as well) indicated the occurrence and direction of the quake.

Although the mainstream of classical literature emphasized civilian values, such as harmony, balance, and peaceful scholarly pursuits, the Chinese experimented with implements of war. By the fourth century B.C., the crossbow was in use, a thousand years before the Europeans took it up. Around the same time, in the course of the bloody Zhou subperiod known as the Warring States, they had developed an early form of poison gas from toxic vegetable matter, such as dried mustard, pumped by bellows into tunnels dug by engineers under a city's battlements. Gunpowder, known as fire drug (*houyau*), was initially, as the name implied, from Han times used for medicinal purposes as a type of disinfectant to cure skin diseases. Later, the powder, a mixture of saltpeter (potassium nitrate), sulfur, and charcoal, came to be used widely in pyrotechnics; the Chinese enjoyed the loud, continued bursts and strings of exploding firecrackers at festivals. Not until around A.D. 1000, during the Song dynasty, was the compound channeled into use as explosives for war: fire lances, flame throwers, bombs, and rockets.

On land, the single-wheeled carts (wheelbarrows) were extensively used from the Later Han dynasty. Especially adapted for economy and maneuverability, they were widely used in the narrow hilly byways of South China. On more level land, early emperors constructed roadways, some of stone near the capitals, on which traversed two-wheeled carriages drawn by two horses. Over the centuries, the vehicles grew in size, to be drawn by up to eight horses. In more inaccessible areas, sedan chairs conveyed the well-to-do. On water, several hundred types of wooden junks, of differing sizes and displaying a wide variety of sails, each suited for a particular purpose, plied the coastal seas. Oceangoing vessels were larger. Of these, two types were the more prominent: a flat-bottomed "sand ship" (*shazhuan*) navigated the more shallow waters, while the four-decked round-bottomed so-called Fujian ships took adventurous Chinese to foreign shores as far away as the east coast of Africa.

Maps were essential for these travelers, and cartography had ancient origins in China. Legends mentioned primitive maps from around 2000 B.C., when a culture hero, the mythical model ruler Yu, divided China into nine regions. Maps, including those of military intent, were made in early dynasties, but, because of security considerations, they tended to remain secret. A mapmaker of the third century A.D. collated eighteen maps from various earlier periods. He advanced six criteria for comprehensive mapmaking: exact scale, directions, distances, elevations, contours of hills and mountains, river courses, and mountain ranges. A Tang cartographer drew a map of China and "foreign countries within the seas." Possibly based on this source, the two oldest existing Chinese maps were carved in the twelfth century on stone tablets in northwestern China. On these, mountains, rivers, lakes, and administrative regions were well defined. The coastline and the major rivers such as the Yellow and the Yangtze did not differ materially from modern maps. In the seventeenth century, longitudinal and latitudinal lines were adopted.

Medical treatises dated back to the Earlier Han, when the *Nei Jing*, the first classic on the subject was composed, around 200 B.C. Superstitions were combined with folklore to create prescriptions. In Daoist fashion, patients were advised to "get it right with nature"; the *yang* and *yin* duality undergirded much of what they practiced. Elixirs were compounded to this end for their curative, and possibly aphrodisiac, powers. Medical education through colleges can be traced to the Song dynasty, but usually the profession was left to local practitioners, who, in a proprietary fashion, handed down knowledge in a master-disciple relationship.

Pharmacopoeia emphasized herbology and the ginseng root (*renshen*). Medical practices included the study of the circulation of the blood (at least twenty-eight pulse diagnoses were noted) massages; moxibustion, the burning of mugwort on the skin to raise blisters for cauterization; and acupuncture (*zhenjiu*). By the fifth century B.C., acupuncture was already widely followed. To cure or to alleviate various maladies, especially aches and pains, sharp needles were inserted into any one or more of some 350 to 450 points of the body, although the needles, because of the dozen or so interconnected body meridians, were not all necessarily punctured into the direct area of pain. Malfunctioning of internal organs was more difficult to diagnose. Men could not examine directly women, who pointed out on carved figures the area of discomfort. Operations (except minor ones), autopsies, and dissections were frowned on because Confucianists considered the body as a gift bestowed on the individual by his parents and ancestors.

7

ARTS

The Chinese produced a rich array of arts. Among the decorative arts, used here as a loosely defined category to encompass variously related crafts, textiles were predominant. Chinese silk was world renowned; cotton, a later import, came to provide the basic clothing needs of common folk. Jade was synonymous with China; cloisonné was popularized by the Ming. Gold and silver, because of their value and scarcity, were not highly utilized. Lacquer was a popular medium with which to decorate household items. In furniture, the simple folk had only the basics, but the well-to-do, by the Ming, fashioned exquisite classic specimens, notably of wood. Folk art provided objects for practical as well as symbolic uses.

In the performing arts, drama was often combined with music to provide a type of opera; that of the Beijing area was the most noted example. Among the plastic arts, works of bronze dated back to the Shang, but by the Han, the metal came to be replaced by ceramics that developed into exquisitely fashioned porcelain, equated by Westerners with the country of origin as china. Sculpture in the round, except for Buddhistic examples, was not developed to any appreciable degree; there were small examples of funerary representations. On the other hand, in the arts of the brush, those of painting and calligraphy flourished, promoted by the scholar-gentry as intellectual pursuits, as did their aesthetically conceived landscape arts of gardens and airy pavilions.

Decorative Arts

In the field of textiles, silk (*si*) is synonymous with China, known to ancient Westerners from its derivatives as Serica, Seres, or Sinem. Silk's pictograph comes from a figure, repeated, of a silkworm coiled in its cocoon with three twisted filaments issuing from it. Sericulture was

83

supposedly invented by Lei Zu, the consort of the mythical cultural hero Huang Di; she is venerated as the goddess of silk. Archaeological evidence supports the presence of silk in Neolithic times, as well as during the Shang. Zhou texts mention the fabric; fossilized cloth from silk, oxidized on wrappings around funerary bronze vessels, can be discerned. Remnants are extant from the Han period, when silk bolts of standard length were used as money in kind, a practice that persisted into the Tang. Paintings on silk, as on paper, also date back to this time.

Romans marveled at the pristine qualities of the cloth. Their extensive purchase of the commodity through intermediaries caused such a gold drain in the empire that Emperor Tiberius (ruled A.D. 14-37) forbade its importation. The source of silk remained a secret until the sixth century when silkworms, always guarded jealously by the Chinese, were smuggled out to the West. The main commercial land routes to Europe, which came to be called collectively the Silk Road by the end of the nineteenth century, traversed deserts and mountain passes. An alternate sea route from South China led to the port of Haiphong in northern Vietnam, where silk was transshipped to the Red Sea and to Mediterranean ports.

Considered to be a woman's occupation, sericulture was widely practiced in China; an ancient rule supposedly mandated that all girls above fifteen years of age should rear silkworms. Leaves of mulberry trees provided the basic staple for larva. Consisting of two varieties of growth, the wild and the domesticated, cuttings from the latter were grafted onto the former. Trees matured after five years, up to six feet in height, after which leaves were plucked and fed to the worms. Mulberries were usually planted in plots surrounding the homes or along the borders of nearby fields. Each fully grown tree could produce some eighty pounds of leaves a season. The voracious worms consumed four hundred pounds of leaves, the quota of five trees, to produce a pound of reeled silk.

All the stages in silk production were closely monitored. The process commenced when the silk moth laid its eggs, which were collected and kept in cold storage until mid-April. They were then incubated at room temperature. After ten days, they hatched. The small, thin bodies were brushed into bamboo trays and fed with fresh, finely chopped mulberry leaves, their sole diet. After one month of feeding, worms went through four moltings until they were two inches long, by which time they had consumed twenty times their body weight. Suddenly feeding stopped; the larva were ready to spin. In five days, they had industriously encased themselves into cocoons, from two strands of silk extruded from glands, the length of the body in figures of eight sealed with ericin, a gum, that bound the dual strands into a single filament. Cocoons, highly temperamental, throughout the whole evolutionary process, were sensitive to noise and vibration effects. The whitest and hardest cocoons were then set aside for breeding purposes, where, after ten days, moths emerged and paired, with the female laying eggs and dying the same day; these provided the genesis for the next crop. Half of the remainder became the reeled silk; the other half, rough silk (the first few yards of the reeled silk).

Those cocoons selected for reeling were dipped into boiling water, long enough to kill the chrysalis inside but not long enough to damage the filaments. While immersed, the cocoons were unraveled by the teeth of bamboo combs that caught and extracted the filaments, which were combined, with six to seven forming the finest strands. These were fed to reeling machines and agglutinated into threads. As each thread became exhausted, a new filament was grafted onto the old to form skeins of the finished fiber product. In some areas, through intensive labor, it was possible to produce up to four or five silk crops a year. The coastal provinces of Zhejiang and Jiangsu came first in volume of silk production. A type of coarser-brownish, off-white raw silk, derived from larva fed on oak, was produced in Manchuria, Shandong, and Hepei. The lovely, purer, gossamer material, cleaned by washing, was worn at home by the well-to-do of both sexes; surplus material was exported. Over time, silk garments became progressively more elaborate in design and finer in texture. The cut silk (*kosi*), more delicate in nature than any Western counterpart, was used not only for dress but for decorative purposes and as painting surfaces.

China's ruling classes dressed in courtly elegance in gowns made especially from silk. An official's rank could be identified from the garments that he wore; each of the nine bureaucratic ranks, in addition to the royal family, had its own unique insignia and theme. The Qing imperial dragon robes were sumptuously decorated with rich, and appropriate, designs, all mandated by court law. Other silk-derived textiles were used: satin, damask, and taffeta of smooth lustrous appearance; brocade, with raised patterns or designs in gold or silver thread; embroidery with its hand-stitched designs; and tapestry, introduced around A.D. 800 from the Near East, with lush landscape panels, usually woven by imperial craftsmen at factories centered in the lower Yangtze region.

The more plebeian cotton (*mian*) came into China introduced from India via Central Asia and southern sea routes; it was first recorded as clothing used by Buddhist monks at the end of the Han dynasty. By around A.D. 1000, it was grown indigenously in the drier areas of North China, the wetter coastal areas of the south, and by non-Chinese in hilly Yunnan province. A cash crop, it competed with grain and food crops for valuable agrarian land in the more fertile areas of the country. Cotton fabrics replaced the vegetable fibers, such as ramie and hemp, used by most from ancient times. In the early twentieth century, with the end of imperial rule and sumptuary ostentation, cotton became the common staple cloth, even for leading political figures. Wool from camel, sheep, or goat fleece was produced mainly in the northwest. That of the camel, the finest, was spun into twisted ropes up to a half-foot in diameter and wound into bales. Of fine fiber, the wool was manufactured into cloth, sometimes mixed with silk, as yardage material. Wool was also used in floor coverings, especially as the well-known Tianjin and Beijing carpets, with their local designs. The modern cashmere came from the soft fine underwool of a type of goat by that name. Minorities in border provinces wove coarser ones with their own colorful and unique ethnic patterns.

As with silk, jade (*yu*) is also equated with China, where it was considered as a most precious material, more valued than even gold. Of varying textures and colors, of which the imperial green was highly prized, jade is derived from either nephrite ore (a calcium and manganese compound) or jadeite (of aluminum and sodium). A hard stone, it was shaded and polished by skilled artisans using even harder abrasives. Scattered native deposits in the northern, central, and southern regions were exhausted by the eleventh century A.D., except for the so-called "mutton fat" white jade from the Kunlun mountains near Hotan in Xinjiang province. Most supplies now come from Central Asia or Burma. Valued for its beauty and rarity, the stone is a form of wealth that also possesses an aesthetic appeal. The skin of a beautiful woman was likened to that of the color and smoothness of jade. The mythical Jade Emperor, Great Ruler of Heaven, was a popular god.

Jade objects dated to the Shang, who used the material variously for weapons, mythological symbols, and ritual implements. Heaven was represented by a perforated jade disk (*bi*); earth, a perforated tube (*zong*). Into the Song dynasty, jade objects were buried with the wealthy to confer immortality and happiness in the afterlife. A piece of jade in the mouth of the deceased was believed to prevent decomposition of the body. In later periods, the stone came to be valued more for the living in personal uses or as a decorative art than as funerary items. A representation of virtue, its amulets bestowed on the user protection from evil forces. A jade emblem in the shape of a short curved sword (*ruyi*) was extended as a gift signifying good wishes and prosperity to the receiver. Uses included a wide variety of other objects, including royal insignias. Court edicts were sometimes inscribed on jade tablets.

With an interest in antiquity, Qing emperors had fashioned jade objects into the likenesses of archaic Shang vessels.

The art of jade carving was also utilized to make small vessels, such as the ancient medicine bottles (*yaoping*) and snuff bottles (*yenhu*). Probably first used during the Han dynasty, medicine bottles, in various animal shapes, held aromatic powders, rare drugs, or herbs. Snuff bottles dated no earlier than the sixteenth century, when tobacco, indigenous to the Western Hemisphere, was introduced into Asia by Portuguese and Spanish mariners. Without success, the late Ming and early Qing emperors interdicted the use of the weed. Its use spread, and with the permanent advent of Westerners in China, the Chinese also adopted the foreign use of snuff as a pulverized tobacco. Because of their variety and compact size, snuff bottles have for long periods been avidly collected by Westerners. Those carved in rare jade colors are the most valued.

The Chinese executed cloisonné (*fa*) from the French word for partitioned, which is a decoration on metal of enamel (a ground glass paste that hardens again when fired), outlined into patterns stenciled by thin pliable metal strips to keep the various colored segments in place. The enamel process, imported from the Middle East in the fourteenth century, was avidly adopted by the Chinese. But the solder sometimes melted in the high-degree firing until Ming artisans, through trial and error, developed the use of tempering adhesives that themselves burned away to leave only the enamels as the binding agents. Yuan examples were highly decorative. Those from later dynasties refined colors of great purity, especially blues, purple, and pink. The Chinese were less fond of champlevé (lifted) and repoussé (pushed back). In the former process, the enamel cells themselves were placed into incised patterns on the surface. In the latter, depressions were filled with enamel and hammered onto sheet copper. Glass (*liao*), less highly developed, was imported into China from the Mediterranean area around A.D. 110. Many glass objects, usually of small scale, were produced, but these were not outstanding.

Gold (*jin*) and silver (*yin*) were not so highly used by Chinese. Deposits of gold were limited, although silver was more abundant. In early dynasties, gold specimens were made chiefly of cast metal. In the Tang, beaten gold was introduced from Persia. This lighter and more delicate variation lent itself to the use of finely tuned personal adornments or jewelry. Silver techniques were similarly adopted from the neighboring country, as well as Middle East motifs and designs. Pewter, an alloy of tin, lead, with some copper and antimony, was fashioned into plain utensils or adorned with handmade engraved designs. Ming examples were the best. Imitating gold and silver, the alloy served as a substitute for these more expensive metals.

In the art of preparing and applying lacquer (*qi*), the world's first plastic, the Chinese were skilled. The medium is the sap from the lac tree, cultivated in central and southern China, where it grows to a height of some 20 feet. After several years of cultivation, the tree furnishes the sap, which is collected in summer mornings from cuts made the previous night in the trunk near the base. Upon oxidation, the resinous gum, a poisonous substance, turns black. Artisans, often overcome by its noxious effect, mix it with other ingredients such as wood oils that form the blended result. By brush or spatula, the lacquer, sometimes colored, is applied, thinly on wood surfaces, in many individual layers, hardened each time through a low firing process, for visual beauty or as a practical preservative. The lacquered surface is then often incised or painted with conventional, symbolic designs or configurations, sometimes with a background of dusted silver or gold. Funerary lacquer ware dated to the Han dynasty, when coffins of the wealthy were rubbed with the finish, as well as accompanying utensils and cosmetic boxes. Highly resistant to decomposition, the lacquer was applied as well to accouterments of the living, and their furniture and kitchen utensils.

While homes in poorer classes stayed bereft of furniture, those of the well-to-do accumulated refined home furnishings. An early type of bed, used also as a bench or stage, was a hollow brick sleeping platform (*kang*) heated in cold weather by internal flues. Then came raised beds (*chuang*), which doubled up as chairs upon which one sat crosslegged. Some beds were four-posters with elaborate canopies of wood or fabrics. Hard ceramic pillows, shaped with a slight concave, fitted the hollow of the neck. Chairs themselves materialized around A.D. 1000; with them came wooden stools and tables of proportionate height. All were superbly crafted from firm-grained aromatic woods (such as ebony and rosewood), without any use of nails, through the fitting of finely beveled parts. Small accessory tables of varying shapes and heights were utilized to display books, curious, and objets d'art. The Ming dynasty was especially noted for producing fine furniture.

While the rich enjoyed the luxuries of more refined decorative art forms, the common folk shaped their own artistic objects (*renmeishu*), especially ones related to utilitarian purposes. In the south, bamboo (*zhu*) and rattan (*teng*) were widely used for simple products. These supple commodities easily fashioned home furniture such as chairs, cabinets, and head rests. Mat weaving, and its derivative of basketry, dated to ancient times. Again made chiefly from bamboo, these matted utensils and containers were used to store food, to provide cages for chirping crickets and birds, and for floor coverings. The reeds as well were woven into articles of footwear, such as sandals and shoes. Cotton, besides its use as clothing in simple forms with dye-resist patterns, was utilized for wall hangings, bedcovers, stenciled sheets, baby items, and appliquéed works. Utensils of wood included carpenter tools, spindles, containers, and cases. Gourds, in their natural forms, provided a variety of kitchen ware.

In addition to practical uses, other folk art was symbolic. In homes, carved wood statuary represented ancestors, folk heroes, or gods. Paper products were widespread and familiar. In addition to its use on flat surfaces for calligraphy, painting, and printing, the material was cut out into two- and three-dimensional objects for toys, stenciled animals, and floral designs. Kites were a special work of art with their colorful symbols and long-stringing tails. Funerary paperworks imitated real-life objects. Plain or colored paper fashioned rosettes, charms, and substitutes for the real, expensive items. Burnt at burial ceremonies, these supposedly transformed themselves into reality in the next world.

Performing Arts

On a more structured, elaborate, and organized level than popular amusements were the performing arts. Drama (*qu*) evolved through several forms. Ancient pantomimes with music created the characters of lives of ancestors as well as popular heroes. There were exorcist dances by shamans in the Zhou dynasty. Later, professional storytellers, acting out recitations, performed before the illiterate inhabitants of the towns and villages plays with themes much like those of the morality plays in medieval Europe. In the Tang court, theatricals were developed; an emperor of the dynasty founded the Pear Garden School, a type of college of dramatic arts. During the Song dynasty, performances broadened in popularity with city folk. During the Yuan period, in peaceful and prosperous times, with the suspension of the examination system and Confucian scholars out of jobs, some turned to producing dramas, at which time they reached a peak in numbers of production. The first extant dramatic texts date from this dynasty. Histories list about a hundred dramatists, all native Chinese but one, who composed an aggregate total of more than five hundred fifty plays. Drama in its present form crystallized in the Ming and Qing eras.

Of the many theatrical forms, which varied from province to province, Beijing opera was the most important. The plays with music and dance, enjoyed by both the literate and the illiterate, were another means of popular education. They emphasized a story line rather than any psychological or character portrayal. Themes drew from both comic and tragic situations, from both historical and fictional sources. Beijing opera composers displayed an inferior craft as was revealed by the leveling content of their plays; China never produced towering counterparts to Shakespeare, Ibsen, Chekov, or Shaw. Itinerant troops, large and small, staged the plays, which were performed in the open air, in temples, at market fairs, and in formal theaters. These structures were usually of simple design, with a raised platform at one end, benches in the orchestra, and galleries on the three sides. Stage props were minimal; there was little scenery. But costuming and makeup were brilliant and largely symbolic; a red mask denoted an upright man; a black one, a cruel man.

The typical play consisted of several acts with featured main stock characters. Chief roles included those protagonists portraying a male, female, or a comic. Orchestras of eight to ten instruments played in a corner of the stage. Audiences, who knew the stories well, were rude and loud-mouthed in behavior and response; plays were accompanied by a cacophony of noise and confusion among those attending. As in Shakespearean theater, women's roles were acted by men, since Confucian moralists disapproved of the mingling of the sexes in the theater. Despite their hard training, actors were accorded with very low social status. Descendants of actors for three generations were forbidden to compete in the bureaucratic examinations. Puppetry, juggling, and acrobatic acts were spaced along with formal productions.

The musical tradition that embraced opera is ancient to China. A classical text on music mentioned by Zhou scholars has long since been lost. Confucius considered appreciation of music (*jinshi*) a necessary element of a man's total character because music reflects the natural order. Rows of bells of varying sizes with differing pitches were strung up and struck by rods of wood or metal; Chinese bells have no clappers. From early times, a twelve-tone scale had been used, although a pentatonic scale eventually became more common. Music achieved heights in the aristocratic grandeur of the Tang courts, whose orchestras used eighty-four scales based on each of seven intervals. The Japanese imperial line adopted Tang music and dance, which died out in China; it is preserved in Tokyo to this day as the oldest continuous authenticated dance tradition in the world. Chinese music was written in vertical rows of characters. Musical instruments, fashioned of stone, gourds, skins, bamboo, and strings, included harps, cymbals, gongs, drums, clarinets, reed mouth organs, and musical stones. Some stringed instruments were plucked; others were played with bows.

Plastic Arts

Bronze (*tong*) was early fashioned in China, where it enjoyed connotations not only of utility but of an inspired magical nature. The character is a written composite of two subparts, one half representing the idea of a valuable metal or gold and the other referring as something similar to it. Chinese histories claim that in the as-yet legendary Xia dynasty, the nine provinces sent as tribute to the sovereign nine bronze tripods, each inscribed with its own particular map. In the 1920s, in the Anyang area of Henan province, where the ancient Shang kingdom had been centered, royal gravesites yielded quantities of beautifully executed bronzes with the earliest examples of Chinese writing (a valuable source of history). They also had incised intricate geometric or zoomorphic designs, notably that of a stylized head-on animal mask (*taotie*), one that perhaps endowed protective status on the user. The ceremonial or utilitarian vessels, some with three legs, some with four, others with none at all, came in conventional circular or square shapes; other forms represented birds or animals. Bronze weapons and chariot fittings connoted the presence of a military aristocracy. The components of the metal, an alloy of copper, tin, and lead, were all at that time found in the hills near the capital. Long buried in royal tombs, the artifacts usually had an appealing green patina on them, a color resulting from chemical action on the metal in the ground over the millennia.

Some Shang bronze forms seemed inspired by similarly potted shapes of an earlier Neolithic period, but with an ensuing archaeological gap of several centuries between the two periods, there was no clear record of any conscious evolution of a bronze craftsmanship developing from primitive pottery to sophisticated Shang ware. These beautiful specimens, as adduced from the many broken clay shards in the area, were cast in one of two ways from sectional pottery molds or through the cire perdue (lost wax) process. In the latter method, some half dozen steps were consecutively involved. First, an exact wax model of the artifact was molded, with its sharply incised surface patterns or inscriptions. The model was then coated on both sides with fine clay that filled in the intricate designs; these were built up into a thick overall mold with drain holes punched into the bottom of the model. The clay was then fired; the melted wax oozed out through the bottom holes, to leave a hollow space between two rigidly based shells. Molten bronze was poured into the space. After the metal hardened, the clay shells were broken away; if necessary, incised surfaces were retouched.

The Zhou and the Han dynasties continued the art of casting bronze, but results became bulky and stereotyped. In the ensuing periods the craft became subordinate to that of ceramic making. The first extensive treatises on the ancient art of bronze casting appears in the Song dynasty, an era noted for its special interest in antiquity. Later eras revived the art, but specimens remained inferior in quality to the Shang prototypes. The circular bronze mirrors (*jien*), however, always remained popular. While the polished side served as the reflector, on the reverse side were carved beautiful stylized designs, astrological symbols, and other representations that might bestow good fortune on the owner.

In China, the art of ceramics (*ci*), or sculpting forms from a clay base, has survived in artifacts through continuous evolution from simple prehistoric hand-fashioned items to delicate translucent porcelain in later imperial dynasties. In this field, although fame came late, as early as A.D. 1000 China enjoyed no peers; the name of the country itself was later equated with fine pottery. Most indigenous activity with regard to its subsequent manufacture centered in the Yangtze River valley with its abundance of clay, the ease of riverine transport of raw materials to kilns, and then that of the finished product to imperial centers or the populated delta and coastal communities. Although porcelain masters came to be highly sophisticated, the occupation was considered more as a craft than as an art. Individual pieces have no signatures or seals. Those producing the beautiful ware were lost in anonymity.

In their usual fashion, Chinese sanctioned in antiquity the origins of the craft. Around 2700 B.C., the mythical emperor Shen Nong was credited with the invention of pottery. Early on, to give it the imprint of imperial favor, a successor, Huang Di, the legendary Yellow Emperor, appointed a superintendent of pottery to supervise imperial kilns. As documented by archaeological evidence, by 3000 B.C. in the valley of the Yellow River, Neolithic peoples were fashioning handmade utilitarian vessels of white, gray, and painted clay, with geometric designs added to the upper half of the utensils. By the advent of the Shang in the mid-eighteenth century B.C., the Chinese claimed the discovery of the potter's wheel, one that could more easily produce the symmetrical round shapes. The Shang themselves made a type of white stoneware, and they were credited with additional ceramic discoveries. One was the use of kaolin, a fine white clay of decomposed granite containing feldspar (a fusible element). Another was the art of glazing, which when combined with feldspar, silica, and kiln ash, produced a glassy surface impervious to liquids.

The next nine-centuries-long Zhou dynasty did little to advance the art, although it utilized a low-fired copper green glaze, a type of proto-porcelain that produced a ringing sound when struck. By now, the process of producing ceramics was growing in complexity; a division of labor at kilns included the potter, the decorator (if the object were to be inscribed with designs), the glazer, and the kiln supervisor. To maintain imperial control of both royal and private kilns, the contemporaneous literature commented on the sites, possibly idealized, of a royally appointed bureaucrat, the secretary of pottery. In the Han period, glazed items—blue was a favored color—were commonplace, both in domestic utensils used by the living and in funerary ware, where objects familiarly used in life were interred with the deceased. Recovered small-scale models of houses, gazebos, granaries, animals, carts, toys, and utensils help to shed light on the life and times of the Han era, an empire that territorially dipped south into Vietnam and northeast into Korea, where tomb figures from the time have also been unearthed.

After a hiatus of about four centuries, with the advent of the Tang dynasty in A.D. 618, a great outburst of activity took place. Dynastic annals mention sixteen kilns. Domestic wares took on harder glazes that utilized lead and were formed by higher firing temperatures. Household items were mass-produced; more colors were utilized. The three-colored (*sancai*) finish of green, yellowish brown, and white glaze was popular. An international trade from China through southern sea lanes and by land across western routes saw the export of Tang ware abroad. New Islamic art forms and designs were imported, especially from the Middle East, some of which were incorporated into Tang products. In the following Song dynasty, Chinese porcelain reached its height of refinement. Where the Tang had sought quantity, the Song found quality in fashioning a variety of translucent glazed vessels, crackle ware, and the green-glazed celadon. Kilns each turned out their own distinctive products. Five operated at Kaifeng, the Northern Song capital (960-1127), and two at Hangzhou, the later Southern Song political center (1127-1278). As in their studies of ancient bronzes, the Song, with an antiquarian taste, took pleasure in executing ceramic copies of Shang and Zhou artifacts.

The alien dynasties of conquest, with their Central Asian ties, that drove the Song southward and later resulted in the establishment of the Mongol or Yuan dynasty over all of China, reinforced Islamic representations, such as ewers and flasks. The ensuing nationalist Ming was noted for painted porcelain and colored glazes, especially the white and cobalt blue. By this time, the kilns at Jingdezhen in Jiangxi province had become prominent. The extensive area deposits of raw kaolin were mixed and refined, pulverized, and moistened, then shaped into bricks and dispatched to the manufacturing center, where, in the reverse process, the bricks were broken down, mixed again with liquids and made more malleable. Along with sand and petuntse (a fusible, weathered, crystalline rock containing feldspar), mica, and quartz, the resulting compound was fired under high temperatures to produce beautiful polychromatic wares.

By this time, with the arrival of Europeans in China and their ambitions of trade, if not of conquest, the Portuguese-derived word porcelain (from the polished cowrie shells, whose shape resembled the rounded back of a piglet or *porcella*) was applied collectively by Westerners to the beautiful ceramic ware. As the final imperial dynasty, the Qing continued to center operations at Jingdezhen, where some 3,000 kilns turned out monochromatic wares (such as yellow and ox-blood) and polychromatic ones (including the famille rosé and famille verte). Especially renowned for the production of ceramics were the long reigns of Kang Xi (K'ang-Hsi), 1662-1722, and his grandson Qian Long (Ch'ien-Lung), 1736-1769. Export ware, some commissioned by the European and American merchant firms then resident at Macao and Guangzhou, displayed Western heraldic symbols, genealogical representations, patriotic themes, or historic emblems. Armorial china collections graced the halls of New England mansions as well as castles in Europe, where commercial production of China-inspired porcelain, as in Delft and Meissen ware, commenced.

Sculpture (*diaoke*) was not so highly developed or regarded as bronze and ceramics. No counterparts to Michelangelo or Rodin appeared. As in ceramic making, only a mass of nameless, faceless artisans left behind their results. Late in appearing, pre-Buddhist secular sculpture dated only to the Han dynasty, where it resulted in two forms. One was of the flat horizontal bas-reliefs, usually lining tombs of famous civilian or military persons and depicting historical or fictional scenes. The other was freestanding, also associated with grave sites, either in monumental figures lining the "spirit path" south from the funerary mounds, or small ones placed inside to represent those figures associated with the deceased in his lifetime. Both the flat bas-reliefs resembling stone scrolls and tomb figurines of terracotta (fire clay, either glazed or unglazed), usually about a foot high, depicting household members or servants, animals, or architectural forms, are excellent sources of history. Only three examples of freestanding monumental sculptures from the Han period exist. Dated 117 B.C., near Xi'an in the Wei River valley (the political center of the Former or Western Han empire), at the burial mound of a Han general, is a representation of a horse trampling a nomad. From the Later or Eastern Han era, two stone lions (A.D. 147) guard a family tomb in Shandong. In Sichuan, a winged tiger (A.D. 209) performs a similar task.

Some later Confucian and Daoist deities (especially the Eight Immortals) were sculpted, mainly of wood; these fragile items have long since disappeared. But the golden age of sculpture in China was equated with the introduction around A.D. 300 of Buddhism from India and its spread over the next five centuries. Imitating styles and conventions imported from the neighboring country, the Chinese fashioned myriads of buddhas, bodhisattvas, and other divinities associated with the faith. Most, in this archaic form, were flat and viewed frontally. Some were carved out with texts on stelae, upright stone slabs sometimes resting on animal representations, especially the tortoise, the legendary supporter of the earth. Other figures were related to cave art; these were hacked out of cliff sides (as in India) to create artificial caves or grottoes. Non-Chinese rulers of the northern Wei dynasty (386-523) coming from the steppes and deserts to conquer northern China, carved out a Buddhist cave complex at Yungang, their capital in the fourth century A.D., and then, after relocating farther south, again at Longmen. In the west at Dunhuang, where the trade route heading west split to continue north and south of the vast and forbidding Taklamakhan desert, they, as well as subsequent dynasties, fashioned an astounding aggregate of caves that unfold sculpturally and pictorially a thousand years of Chinese Buddhist and related secular art (ca. A.D. 350 to 1350).

Buddhist sculpture reached its height in the early Tang (seventh and eighth centuries A.D.). Emperors added to the already existing grottoes more Buddhist figures, full-bodied and plump, a physical state that reflected the self-satisfaction with the peace, prosperity, and plenty of the period. The sovereigns also executed monumental animal figures in the open to line paths to tombs, and inside them etched out bas-reliefs, notably those depicting horses, now a familiar animal in the Chinese annals of conquest. With the subsequent ebb of Buddhism and military might, inspiration for sculpture in later dynasties was channeled into conventional forms. The Song, in wood, concentrated on the compassionate and merciful bodhisattva Guanyin, a rare female Buddhist deity. (The Indian prototype, Avalokitesvara, had been male.) Ming and Qing artisans continued religious imagery with stereotyped representations. For all their emphasis on a man-oriented society, the Chinese failed to create any exemplary statues of the human figure, draped or nude, to compare with those of the Greek, Roman, and later European Renaissance sculptors.

Arts of the Brush

Throughout their long history, the Chinese have particularly excelled in the three uses of the brush to produce painting (*shanshui*—mountains and water), calligraphy (*shufa*), and poetry (*shi*). In painting, the Chinese early emphasized a man-centered approach as subject matter. Not until later dynasties, into the Song, did they display any genuine talent for landscapes, a subject matter now most familiar in Chinese paintings. Usually impressionistic in portrayal, these nature scenes were meant to reflect the Dao, the harmony of man with his surroundings. The essential spirit of the composition was to be absorbed and conceived before the painting was executed in swift, bold brush strokes. Subjective, suggestive, and evocative, the landscapes in monochrome (black and white), or in color, emphasized flora and fauna, mountains and water. Man, as part of the painting, was subordinated to blend insignificantly with the natural world, a philosophical outlook held in common with all three major schools of Chinese thought: Confucianism, Daoism, and Buddhism. Brush strokes were characteristically masterful, disciplined, and flowing; once executed, they could not be retouched. Perspective was created not by converging lines of depth but by presenting the scene as from above or from different eye-level viewpoints. Flatness was avoided by sketching in mists, fog, and clouds.

The earliest Chinese pictorial representations were cave paintings and decorations on Neolithic painted pottery. Annals relating to Zhou times recorded the art of painting, but few specimens from the time exist. Dating from the fourth or third century B.C., etchings on silk fragments have been recovered from tombs near Changsha in Hunan province. About the same time, tomb murals reflected the cosmology of the mythical afterlife to where the departed was going. Subsequent Han tomb art in North China and Korea reveals that man and animals were predominant subjects, populating the imagined celestial and terrestrial spheres as well as the underworld. For several centuries following the Han dynasty, painting related mainly to some frescoes, tomb tiles, decorated lacquer work, and Buddhistic-inspired paintings that depicted a mythical paradise. One of the earliest notable individual painters was Gu Kaizhi (Ku K'ai-zhih), who flourished in the early fifth century A.D. To him is attributed the colored silk scroll entitled "Admonitions of the Instructress at the Palace," (now in the British Museum). The sixth-century master Xie He (Hsieh Ho) developed six canons of painting that became gospel for professional artists: rhythm, structure, naturalness, suitability of colors, line composition, and finish.

During the expansive Tang times, artists portrayed court figures and tribute bearers with their gifts. As classified by their painting styles, northern and southern schools emerged. Not necessarily related to the geographic origin of the artist, the former stressed realism and the latter refinement. Whatever the style, toward the later decades of the dynasty, the paintings by subject matter were categorized into three main branches: figure painting, landscapes, and birds and flowers. Buddhist paintings, in caves or on scrolls, continued to be executed. From the late Tang into the Song period, landscapes came to predominate, in part because the Chinese mind turned inward because of disillusionment with the weak military and political condition. Reaching full flower in the Song era, in both its northern and southern political subperiods, there appeared many of the greatest landscape artists. After the golden age of the Song, themes and styles of painting became stereotyped. One later, seventeenth-century, canon for painters, the *Mustard Seed Garden Manual,* by Wang Kai, once again summed up the rules and regulations of how best to present the art.

Chinese paintings were usually executed on silk or paper. Popular forms were vertical or horizontal scrolls (*lien*). The latter, usually about a foot in width but with no fixed length, were appreciated in segments as they slowly unwound in panels from right to left. Subjects were also painted on folding and square fans, removed from their ribs and mounted in albums. Other media included screen panels, tiles, and frescoes that were widely executed in the earlier Tang dynasty. Depending on the desired fineness of stroke, brushes were made of a variety of bristles, using the hair from such animals as the fox, pig, camel, and rabbit. These were pressed into a compact bundle with a pointed tip.

To make black ink, sticks of compressed soot from wood or coal products were scraped; the filings were softened with water on the ink stones (a favored object for collectors). Colors were made by grinding appropriately colored vegetable or mineral matter and similarly moistened. The artist placed his chop (*yin*) or seal on the painting usually in the archaic script of characters dating to the Shang. Some owners did similarly; many old Chinese paintings came to be cluttered with conspicuous family, or royal, seals of the several successive owners. Unlike the creators of the plastic arts, these artists, who imprinted their works with seals of their authorship, enjoyed high status by the advent of the Song dynasty. As part of the literati, they, as well as scholars who collected the paintings, formed an elitist group in the Chinese art world.

Closely related to painting in the arts of the brush was calligraphy, the Chinese equivalent of fine penmanship. Not only did specimens of writing grace the painted scrolls, but calligraphy in and of itself was often the sole subject. Vertical hangings, usually in pairs, were purchased or highly valued as gifts from friends. Calligraphic examples on paper or silk were numerous and varied; they ranged from copybook exercises to classical quotations. Works of master calligraphers, with their seals, were easily identifiable to knowledgeable Chinese.

The execution on paper or silk, as in brush painting, was the result of prior conceptualization translated into subsequent reality through sure, bold strokes. A dozen recognized styles existed, from the formal pattern style (*kai*) in office use through the running hand (*xing*) to the grass hand (*cao*), an extremely abbreviated form. Characters were also often inscribed in stone on city gates (*chengmen*), memorial arches (*pailou*), and funerary sites.

Early specimens of calligraphy exist from Qin and Han times, but the first calligrapher to achieve fame was Wang Xizhi (Wang Hsi-chih), A.D. 321-379, whose works were copied, and the copies recopied, over generations by individuals through rubbings and block printing. For fifteen years, it was related, the master concentrated efforts to replicate the character for eternity (*yong*), one that contained all eight basic strokes of the Chinese script. A later Buddhist monk, who was a seventh-generation descendant of Wang, persevered for four decades to master the art; his transcriptions of monastic charts and quotations were highly favored. A Ming dynasty calligrapher labored at his task for most of his ninety years. For others, perseverance did not pay off. The results of a Qing dynasty calligrapher, who studiously practiced the craft for two decades, were dismissed by critical viewers as nauseous.

Landscape Arts

The earliest evidences of landscape art, as deduced from literary and pictorial representations, were the extensive hunting grounds and royal gardens (*shu*) of the early Qin and Han emperors. Ostentatious and extravagant in spirit, they flaunted imperial prestige with numerous specimens of animal and plant life. This expansive imperial spirit carried on into the Tang and Song periods, whose emperors raided their empire, as well as gardens of private citizens, to obtain unique plants and rock formations. Ming and Qing rulers continued the grandiose pattern of landscaping. The great Manchu emperor Qianlong, among other projects, in the mid-eighteenth century, constructed near Beijing the Yuan Ming Yuan (Old Summer Palace), which, after a century of use, was looted and destroyed by an Anglo-French force in the course of a punitive expedition. His successors relocated at the present Summer Palace, now a favored tourist site for both local and foreign visitors.

Another approach, more intimate, elegant, and scholarly (*ya*), was developed by the literati, who, as active or retired bureaucrats, built homes and surrounding gardens to reflect their personal tastes. Tao Qian, one of the first, in the fourth century A.D., resigned in disgust at official life and duties after only three months of service to return home and live a simple life in his walled estate in harmony with nature. Lu Hong, an eighth-century Tang scholar, was so much admired by his emperor, Xuanzong (Hsüan-tsung), that the monarch permitted his bureaucrat, the recipient of royal stipends, to retire to his beloved home and gardens. A contemporary, Wang Wei, constructed a more ostentatious rambling garden, the Wangchuan Villa, near the Tang capital of Chang-an (modern Xi'an). Later scholars continued to design their own homes and gardens and enjoyed the creative challenge to reflect their personalities in an eremetical life. The *Yuan ye*, completed by Ji Cheng in 1634, was a garden building manual that praised this secluded life in an urban area, an oasis of beauty sealed off from the "vulgar" neighborhoods.

Landscape arts were closely affiliated with landscape paintings, which had also been created by the scholar-gentry class. Both portrayed idealized settings. Gardens, as did the paintings, in a planned controlled atmosphere, consisted of several basic components, all to blend man in with nature, as in the larger world. Water (*shui*) was present, usually manifested by a central pond with floating beds of lotus or hyacinths. Running streams were crossed by gracefully carved rainbow bridges or zigzagged walkways. Piled rocks (*jiashan*) or a monolith one (*feng*), as the "bones of the earth," represented mountains or a single peak. Some rocks were miniature in size, others were large. Plants and vegetation were not predominant, although potted flowering plants spaced throughout the garden added color. Trimmed dwarf trees (the prototype for the Japanese *bonsai*) dotted the grounds. Paths of gravel or stone (*qulang*) wound around the courtyard, connecting paved areas or the variously scattered buildings.

Since people were to live among and enjoy the gardens adjacent to the residence, domestic architectural features were prominent. Besides the chief domicile, which had viewing windows or doors of various types (the moon-shaped entrance was popular), were scattered freestanding structures, some with inscriptions identifying them: open pavilions (*ting*), extended large halls (*tang*), or more intimate ones (*xuan*). A central concept of overall planning was that of *yang* and *yin*, the complementary and necessary opposites. Dark areas balanced the light; low and high spaces coexisted. Gardens, and their living quarters, were often bestowed with names bearing historical and literary allusions. In viewing the particular site, as in viewing paintings, the educated observer could relate the scene to its appropriate literary reference or allusion.

The Jiangnan area (south of the Yangtze River) abounded with beautiful gardens. With its abundance of water and easy riverine routes, in a rich delta region with agricultural and commercial wealth, the cities of Yangzhou, Hangzhou (the Southern Song capital, then known as Li Nan), and Suzhou were rich in gardens. Suzhou was particularly famous for them. Near Lake Tai (*Tai Hu*), its artisans collected the famous wildly shaped and pockmarked stones for use as landscape ingredients. Two prototype gardens there are cited as outstanding. One, the Garden of the Unsuccessful Politician (*Zhou Zhengyuan*), dated from the Ming original, with later Qing era additions. On an east-west axis, it consisted of the original house (now gone), and three adjoining gardens. Its area encompasses thirty-one named sites. The other, now known as the Garden of the Master of the Fishing Nets (*Wang Shiyuan*), dated to the twelfth century, when an official desired to emulate what he perceived as the uncomplicated life of a fisherman, and called it the Fisherman's Retreat. After his demise, the garden slipped into oblivion until the eighteenth century, when it was rebuilt and renamed, in a play of words, by an official of the emperor Qianlong. Various successors continued to modify the gardens. One paved courtyard and the adjoining structures have been replicated in the Chinese Garden Court at the New York Metropolitan Museum of Art. In Japan, where so much has been borrowed from the mainland, many private gardens and old Buddhist temple grounds preserve the tranquillity and beauty of the original Chinese models.

8

ARCHITECTURE

A survey of traditional Chinese architecture (*jianzao*), in which order, form, and balance were fundamental indigenous elements, reveals several distinct characteristics. First is the continuity of style that has persisted from prehistory into the modern era. The classical buildings of China did not evolve through the distinct phases as did those of Europe, where the latter proceeded through the Byzantine, Romanesque, Gothic, Renaissance, and Baroque periods. The organization of shape and material also remained constant throughout the millennia. Modest homesteads, private compounds of the well-to-do, and imperial residences all were undergirded by similar basic principles of planning and construction. For surface spaces, the rectangular bay room (*jian*) provided the standard measurement; this unit was expanded into groups of them that formed halls (*ting*), buildings in compounds (*yuan*), palaces (*gong*) and into city planning (*cheng*). Wood, more available in these earlier years, was the chief medium of structures. Location of sites (*fengshui*) was critical. Hills in the north saved the edifice from cold winds; a southern exposure gave life and warmth. Accordingly, in keeping with the north-south orientation, buildings were laid out on a longitudinal axis; the whole compound, including courtyards, was surrounded by walls.

The building itself, usually of rectangular shape, was composed of three basic elements: a platform; on this rested the wooden framework where, in trabeate fashion, horizontal trusses were tetoned into upright bracketed pillars; and a tiled roof that swept gracefully down in concave fashion from the ridge beam. In part, because of climatic reasons, to alleviate the effects of great precipitation the built-up platform, ascended by central steps, was erected to about a three-foot height. The simplest elevations were of rammed earth; later forms encased this with brick or stone facing. Directly placed on the platform, or on inverted upright bases, were the vertical wood pillars; this prevented rot by not being implanted directly into or on the ground. During the

Qing, to correct optical illusions, the facade pillars swelled slightly out below the middle section, while the corner ones were inclined slightly inward. No capitals adorned the top of the upright pillars, although pyramiding brackets (*dougong*) helped to distribute the weight of the transverse beams. Over time, the bracketing system (which was one way—through style—to date buildings) became more complex; extended brackets supported others until a multitiered effect was realized. The standard timber used for a bracket arm (*cai*) became a fixed measurement as well as the *zu cai*, which was the *cai* plus the space between another superimposed bracket arm.

Ceilings were flat or vaulted; some were decorated with small squares and a central roundel. The roofs were sharply inclined outward into overhanging eaves, again for climatic reasons to drain off precipitation and keep the interior cool in summer. Inside, a series of ever-shortening transverse ceiling beams, in pyramidal fashion, supported the ridge and roof beams. Roofs were gabled (full roofs front and back but flat vertical sides), hipped (four full roofs), or a combination of both. On the roof, rows of half-circled tiles were laid one row with rounded half holding the next row with rounded tops, some rows ending in embellished finials. Often, for ornamental purposes, at both ends of the ridge beam were placed sculpted figures as well as on the up-turned saves. Receded second or third roofs were sometimes added to the primary one. Since the pillars supported the heavy roofs, this function of the walls was secondary. Full walls partitioned off private rooms, but often partial walls of decorative latticework were utilized to divide spaces.

Different colors were often applied to the various components of the building. A white platform supported the brilliant red pillars and facade; blue or green glazed tiles adorned the eaves; the roof sparkled with yellow hues. The overall use of wood also had practical purposes. In compounds, clusters of buildings were set far apart enough to obviate the spread of fire from one area to another. Wooden structures were better able to survive earthquakes, with their lateral tremors, than those made with stone or masonry. The disastrous earthquake of 1976 that collapsed many buildings in the Tianjin area left unaffected there the thousand-year-old wooden Pavilion of the Goddess of Mercy (*Guanyin*).

Historical Evolution

Because of perishable material and destruction caused by wars, invasions, and natural catastrophes over the centuries, few pre-Ming freestanding structures exist. As adduced from archaeological evidence, the earliest Chinese, such as Peking man from around 500,000 B.C., lived in caves. In South China, perhaps they resided in trees. In Yunnan, the domiciles of the minority Dai people are built on stilts with large thatched roofs that resemble birds' nests, from which their design may have been derived. Although many Chinese in the north still dwell by choice in comfortable loess caves, by 6000 B.C. most, as agricultural people, had now settled down into fixed homes.

At Banpo, a Neolithic site near Xi'an, excavations revealed floor plans of partially subterranean dwellings in several shapes: circular, oblong, or square. A moat separated the residential area from an adjacent cemetery; both sections were enclosed by one overall encompassing wall. Saplings framed the walls of huts and were filled in with loess; the open entrance led into a single room with a plastered floor and central hearth. By 2000 B.C., a pillar-and-beam construction pattern was evidenced in the middle Yellow River plain. In the cold north, in the Amur River reaches, subterranean dwellings continued, while to the warmer south, homes remained on stilts. The kings of the later Shang dynasty (ca. fourteenth to eleventh centuries B.C.) at their royal capitals in the Anyang vicinity of Shanxi province initiated the style of traditional palace architecture: a platform of rammed earth several feet high that supported a framework of wooden columns, beams, and rafters, and a thatched roof. Pit burial grounds were placed in a separate area.

Several of the subsequent major dynasties relocated west of the last great bend of the Yellow River in the Xi'an region on the Wei River. From Hao, the earlier or Western Zhou (ca. eleventh century to 771 B.C.) capital on the Feng tributary, nothing remains. However, as composed during this period, the *Zhouli* contained sections relating to architecture and early ideas in city planning that emphasized an idealized agrarian pattern as a basis: that of the well-field system (*jingtian*) with nine squares, three across and three down, for eight families to cultivate individually the eight peripheral plots with the central one reserved for communal purposes. Nothing also remains of the Later or Eastern Zhou (771 to 221 B.C.) sites. However, Shi Huangdi, founder of the Qin dynasty and the first emperor of China (ruling from 221 to 206 B.C.) left a grandiose imprint. In the course of his short rule, at his capital of Xianyang, northwest of present-day Xi'an, he erected a vast array of palaces of which the Epang was the greatest. The complex was erected on a platform ranging some 700,000 square yards in area, with a floorspace itself for buildings one-seventh the total size. To the city, from which today only mounds remain, he relocated 120,000 families.

Obsessed with the afterlife, he drafted 700,000 men to work on his three-tiered tumulus at Qin Ling, which still rises today some 150 feet about the surrounding flat plain, several miles east of Xi'an. The site is surrounded by a double wall: an outer one of almost four miles in circumference, and an inner of one and a half miles. With him were buried manifold treasures, all of which were looted shortly after the emperor's death by a general in the course of a civil uprising. As accidentally discovered in 1974, the emperor also had laid out underground chambers in the four cardinal directions from the central mound. A mile distant from the tomb, the excavated eastern flank, three times the size of a football field, unearthed almost six thousand six-foot tall terracotta warriors, with some horses and chariots, ostensibly to protect him from any pursuing enemies in the future existence of whom he had made many in the course of the empire's consolidation to the east.

Shi Huangdi was also noted for consolidating the Great Wall, known in China as the *Wan Li Chang Cheng* (Ten Thousand Li Long Wall) which meandered along hill crests, gorges, and rivers. It stretched from the China Sea town of Shanhaiguan over 3,000 miles westward into Gansu province (a distance comparable to that between Los Angeles and Boston, or London and beyond the Urals). From earlier times, stretches of wall had existed in North China to contain the non-Chinese forces invading from the north and northwest (the traditional enemy territory). The emperor's contribution was the fashioning of one overall line of defense. In some strategic areas, two or three overlapping segments existed. North of Beijing, tourists visit the Badaling stretch (restored by the Ming), where the walls appear massive. Indeed they are. At its most extensive measurements, the Great Wall had a 15- to 50-foot base, rose some 15 to 30 feet to a top of 12-foot or more ramparts, with guard towers at intervals. Great granite blocks, up to 14 feet long and 3 to 4 feet thick, face the wall, filled with rammed earth.

In its western stretches, it is less impressive and has disappeared altogether, but the Ming (and the Chinese Communists) have restored the traditional western terminal gate at Jiayuguan. Earlier dynasties, such as the Han and Tang, carried the wall, mainly of earthen ramps and towers, farther west into the edges of the Taklamakhan desert. An awesome engineering feat, built at great cost of human life, the Great Wall is one of China's great architectural accomplishments. (One astronaut allegedly claimed that it was the one man-made structure visible from outer space.) Ironically, the Great Wall never effectively performed its task of military deterrence. Any enemy of sizable force could, and did, penetrate its defenses. It came to be seen not as a military phenomenon but as a psychological barrier: "we" are Chinese south of the Wall; "you" are cultural barbarians north of it.

As successors, the Western Han, as did the Qin and Western Zhou predecessors, continued imperial presence in the Xi'an area, a distance northwest of the present city at Chang'an. In an early instance of a totally planned city, following strictures laid out in the earlier *Zhouli*, the first dynastic ruler laid out in grid fashion to house 300,000 a rectangular walled city, some five miles running north and south, and six miles running east and west, with broad parallel streets marking off districts. Twelve gateways pierced the walls. (In China, walls and cities are synonymous; both retain the same character, *cheng*.) The main gateways faced south, the life-giving direction, as did tile Changle palace in the center of town, which took two years to build. Extensive platforms supported the post-and-lintel framework of the palace, but the Han took to elaborating the half-circle tiled roofs and ridges ornamented with animals. Little is left of either palace or city. Outside the urban center, to the south lay temples where emperors conducted rituals. When, because of enemy pressures, the Later or Eastern Han relocated at present-day Luoyang (as had the earlier Zhou), A.D. 25-220, they replicated there many of their earlier architectural and city features.

Some Han tumuli exist in the Xi'an district, under which, in stone vaulted chambers (an early Chinese use of the arch), members of the imperial family or prominent generals were buried along with personal possessions and valued items. At Leshan in Sichuan are some Han rock-hewn tombs. In Turfan, on the edge of the Taklamakhan desert, the tomb of a Han general has been excavated; inside the single stone-lined chamber on the walls are depictions of birds and animals, some mythical. From another Han general's tomb was recovered the famous bronze heavenly horse, now in the Gansu provincial museum at Lanzhou. Small in size but perfectly executed and in exquisite balance, the galloping animal's rear right hoof rests on a swallow.

In the almost four centuries of political division that followed the Han demise, little of architectural note was recorded in the secular sphere. Buddhism entered with some distinctive structural features (discussed below), but the alien rulers over northern Chinese territories absorbed Chinese building patterns. With the reunification of China by the short-lived Sui in the late sixth century A.D., followed by the long-lasting Tang of three centuries, grandiose palace architecture and city planning were revived. The capital was located again, for the fourth time, in the Xi'an area, and similarly renamed Chang'an. (An additional association for China was as a "country of peace," or *an*. The Tang marked their four protectorates in the border areas according to the cardinal directions. That one to the south was An-nam, a term today still applied to central Vietnam.)

Like the Han, the Tang embarked once again on ambitious city and palace designs. Chang'an, with possibly some two million people, became another large walled rectangular urban configuration embracing eastern and western halves, each with a central market and each divided further into districts (*fang*) composed of city blocks. It covered an area larger than present-day Xi'an and served as a model for the Japanese, then embarking on national life, for their first fixed capitals: first at Nara (710-794), and afterward at Kyoto, then called Heian (City of Peace and Tranquillity). Broad parallel streets in Chang'an ran longitudinally. The palace grounds, a second walled complex, lay to the north, facing south, toward the main gate. In their lateral grandeur, Chinese cities were quite flat in overall appearance; no towering structures pierced the skyline. From a distance, only the high city walls and gate houses, hiding the enclosed city structures, were visible.

The eighth-century Da Ming palace of the Tang emperors, details of which have been derived from excavations and contemporaneous paintings, was, in the usual fashion, surrounded by walls with pillared galleries inside, punctuated by the four gate pavilions and corner towers. The palace was symmetrical along the north-south axis, as was the city, except for a detached tower to the immediate east of the central hall. Early dynastic monarchs at nearby Huaqing hot springs erected a complex of graceful pavilions, gardens, and pools. Some Tang tombs exist; these are some distance north of Xi'an at Qianling. Those of Gaozong (Kao Tsung), the third emperor, and his empress, lay beneath a large mound. The overall setting enjoys a natural landscape. According to *fengshui*, the high peak to the north entombed the monarchs while two smaller ones guard the southern flank as well as the monumental sculptures lining the "spirit path" to the central graves.

Although the Song was noted for beautiful porcelain, painting, and gardens, little exists from architectural specimens. However, in A.D. 1103, Li Jie composed the *Ying Zo Fa Shi*, a technical guide for building techniques. During the ensuing Yuan empire, the Mongol rulers opted for Chinese architecture. (Nomadic desert tents and yurts were impractical for use by the foreign ruling class in settled China.)

The center of political gravity now shifted from the northwest and Yangtze regions to the North China plain in the vicinity of Beijing, which had enjoyed no particular auspicious natural or geographical setting. The city, however, had earlier been a regional political center. During the Zhou dynasty, Yen, the capital of the state of Chi, was located there. (Yenjing remains a romanticized name for Beijing.) The two predecessor non-Chinese states to the Yuan also had also been centered there. In A.D. 936, the Liao made its southern capital there (called Nanjing) as did the Jin, in 1122 (renamed Chung Du). In 1267, Kublai

Khan established Dadu (Xanadu to later English poets). A so-called Tartar town was established in the present-day northern sector of Beijing, but nothing remains of this grid city that Kublai had laid out.

The nativistic Ming, overcoming the Yuan, embarked on a crash program of fortifying cities and rebuilding walls to provide security, if only on a psychological note. Much of what is architecturally pointed out today to tourists in China dates back only to the Ming, including the impressive city walls of Xi'an (Western Peace), so-renamed at the time from Chang'an (Eternal Peace). After initially presiding at Nanjing (this one on the lower Yangtze banks), they relocated to Beijing. Just south of the Tartar City, in 1402, Yongle, the third Ming emperor, commenced the fabled Imperial and Forbidden City, now collectively called the Palace (*Gugong*) Museum, on which his Qing successors elaborated. Along the familiar north-south axis, a progression of gates and courtyards and buildings led from public to private quarters. Its south wall demarcates the northern limits of the adjacent Tian'anmen (Heavenly Gate) Square, the largest in the world.

Facing the square in the north is Tiananmen (gate) with five openings and five bridges across the River of Golden Water (*Jinshuihe*). Entering, one immediately confronts a second, even more forbidding, awe-inspiring gate and walled courtyard, that of the Meridian Gate (*Wumen*). Through it one proceeds into the Imperial City proper, with another immense Outer Court (*Waichao*) and its winding River of Golden Sand (*Jinsha*), also with five white marble bridges. Directly ahead is the wall and Gate of Great Peace (*Taihemen*), with its lateral and corner pavilions. Entering that, one comes into the vast central courtyard with three buildings on an axis, all raised on one common three-tiered marble platform. Here, official ceremonies were centered. The first and largest of the three is the Hall of Supreme Harmony (*Taihedian*), the reception hall; next is the more intimate Hall of Middle Harmony (*Zhonghedian*), where the emperor robed; and finally comes the mid-sized Hall of Protecting Harmony (*Baohedian*), where top scholars were received.

Beyond more walls lies the Forbidden City or the Inner Court (*Neizao*), with its many intimate courtyards and buildings that constituted the living quarters. The total grounds encompass some 10,000 structures, a multitude of large and small courts, Prospect Hill, and three lakes. Outside the city, to the south, as in Han times, lies the ritual temples centered on the open-aired three-tiered marble terraced Altar of Heaven (*Tiantan*) in a circular arrangement; the single story round Imperial Vault of Heaven (*Huangqiongyu*) with the surrounding Echo Wall; and the triple-eaved, also rounded Hall of Prayer for Good Harvests (*Qiniandian*). Previously mentioned were the two summer palaces, the old (*Yuan Ming Yuan*) and the new. Another royal complex was located at Chengde, some 150 miles northeast of Beijing, in Qin home territory. The evolution of imperial architectural grandeur of city and palace that began with the Shang in Anyang climaxed with that of the Qing in Beijing.

The Ming and the Qing also had their tomb complexes. That of the former was at Changling, thirty-five miles northwest of Beijing; it is usually included in a tourist itinerary that takes in the Great Wall at Badaling the same day. In an appropriate natural *fengshui* site, bounded to the north, east, and west by ranges, the thirteen tombs of the Ming who ruled at Beijing are spread out over a twenty-five-square-mile area. One enters the overall site through a memorial arch and proceeds down the spirit path lined by eighteen pairs of statuary, figures of men or animals, to a tomb of one of the emperors. The walled-off tomb, typical of the others, is surrounded by gardens and a stele that recorded imperial accomplishments of that particular monarch. Proceeding down the steep bank of steps inside, the visitor enters the main stone vaulted chambers, with separate central platforms that held the coffins of the emperor and empress, and a couple of side rooms. Nothing is left of the contents; everything, human remains and artifacts, has long since disappeared. Some of the Later Qing imperial line are buried near Shenyang (Mukden).

Other Structures

Chinese ingenuity manifested itself also in other structures. Though the use of the arch (*gung*) was not pronounced in China in domestic architecture, the commemorative arch was a familiar sight. These could be erected in memory of prominent officials, famous women, generals, or royal figures. During Qing times, they could be erected only on imperial sanction. Mostly constructed of stone, they contained one, three, or five openings. The arch was also utilized in bridges (*qiao*). The oldest one in continuous use is the Zao Zhou (An Ji), built A.D. 605-617, over the Xiao He in Hebei province. Spanning a hundred feet, this single-arched bridge at both ends has a spandrel, each of which again has two small arches to help distribute the weight. Two other types of bridges were the beam, with piers to support the usually flat traverse way, and the suspension, widely used across river gorges of south and southwest China.

Among religious edifices, Daoism lacked any appreciable structures, since most of its activities transpired in the open country in contemplative stance. Confucian temples, however, dotted the countryside.

The birthplace and home of Confucius at Qufu, in Shandong province, was preserved with a temple much in accord with palace architectural style. With the introduction of Buddhism, its temples (*miao*) grew in popularity; these again were modeled along traditional lines. More unique was the pagoda (*ta*) that drew on two sources: the several-tiered Han dynasty watch towers, and the tiered finial of the rounded stupa that derived from India. Pagodas rose, according to *yang-yin* principles, in a sequence of odd-numbered eaves or roofs, from one up to fifteen. An old wood pagoda in Yingxian, Shanxi province, is 221 feet high; the oldest brick one, a twelve-sided pagoda, dating to A.D. 523, is part of the Songshan temple in Henan province. The early versions had a high first story, followed by a series of recessed close-set eaves demarcating stories, each section repeating the basic pattern in diminishing proportions. Pagodas were built of varying materials (wood, brick, stone) and in several shapes (square, hexagonal, octagonal). A few domed-stupa style ones exist from the Yuan rulers, who were converted to the Tibetan version of Buddhism inspired by Indian models. Some were built with a pedestal that holds five pagodas on its base, a number dedicated to the five buddhas of Vajradhutu, the realm of total reality according to Tantric briefs that encompassed the concept of a magical circle.

The pagoda was a central element in the Buddhist monastery, one that was laid out much like a palace complex. Enclosed by walls and colonnades, one entered the temple courtyard by the great southern gate. The earliest pagodas were placed directly behind the gate. (Later they were moved to one side or eliminated altogether.) Then came the main temple with statuary; off to the sides were auxiliary buildings. Many of the early wooden structures in ancient sites have been destroyed. But Buddhist pilgrims coming to and going from China in the seventh and eighth centuries preserved these styles, now lost in the homeland, in Korea and Japan, where indeed, the oldest wooden buildings in the world, a pagoda and temple from the early 700s, exist in the Horiuji temple compound near Nara.

Islam (*jiaomen*) added its own distinctive architectural features. In the eighth century, the faith entered China via two routes: a southern sea one into Guangzhou, where a mosque (*si*) exists; and by the western deserts, where the majority of peoples are still of Islamic faith, one that supplanted an earlier Buddhism. In western China, Central Asian architectural features were pronounced in Islamic buildings with their minarets and assembly halls with semibulbous domes, lovely tile decorative work, and Arabic calligraphy. The Great Mosque at Kashi, built in 1861, is an open-air one; the nearby Aba Khoja mausoleum-mosque-cemetery is quite typically Central Asian in character. In Turfan, the

Imin mosque, dating to 1778, maintains the traditional minaret and assembly hall.

In Xi'an, the Hui people, of Chinese ethnic origin, but converted and remaining true to Islam (the only minority in China that is distinguished by religion and not by race or language), have erected Islamic structures but in Chinese style. As the largest mosque in China, it is an intriguing blend of Islamic concept and Chinese execution. The walled Great Mosque (*Hua Jiao*), reconstructed by the Ming in 1392, lies on an east-west axis (Mecca lies to the west). But in true Chinese style it keeps the axial progression from the gateway (*pei fang*) to a three-roofed octagonal minaret in pagoda style (*shengxin lou*). This is followed by the Phoenix pavilion, leading to the main praying and assembly hall on a raised platform, with the wooden pillar-and-lintel system supporting a heavy steep roof so typical of traditional Chinese imperial and religious structures. In architecture, as in other ways of life with ideas from abroad, the Chinese adapted them according to their own needs. As usual, they had the final word on interpretation.

Chronology: Highlights of the Chinese Genius

B.C.

by mid-18th century	Writing appears; political state organized; calendar formulated; bronze technology adopted; agricultural economy appears; basic ideology (sinicism) formed; maps used; silk spun; jade fashioned; potters wheel utilized; palace architectural pattern set; earthquakes recorded
ca. 750	Coinage used, iron smelted
613	First mention of Halley's comet
ca. 500	"Hundred schools" of philosophy, out of which Confucianism develops as major one; coal used
300	Solar and lunar eclipses noted; crossbow in use; acupuncture; painting on silk fragments
250	Earliest irrigation project
210	Segments of Great Wall united by first emperor; first medical treatise
117	One of first animal sculptural representations
ca. 100	Inception of examination system; five classics defined; first individually authored history; sunspots discovered; first periscope; ceramics developed; planned imperial city outlined

A.D.

100	Paper appears
132	First seismograph
200	What later developed into gunpowder was used for skin diseases; a sophisticated collated map compiled; cotton utilized; glazed ceramics commonplace; early calligraphic specimens
300	Buddhism introduced into China from India via Central Asia
523	Oldest brick pagoda
600	Grand Canal built
605–617	Oldest bridge
868	Oldest printed book (by wood-block method)
by 900	Paper money; theatricals developed; musicology sophisticated
1000	Neo-Confucianism stamped as official state philosophy; explosives used; complete printed books extant; height of porcelain and painting arts
1100	Magnetic compass in use; two old maps compiled
by 1300	Wheelbarrows; kites; cast-iron chain suspension bridge; canal locks; water-tight ship compartments; drama at height
by 1400	Novel appears; freestanding walls and buildings exist, such as the first structures of the Forbidden City complex in Beijing

Part Two

ANCIENT CHINA

Prehistory to 221 B. C.

Pre-imperial China is lost in antiquity. Earliest recorded traces of hominids as revealed by archaeology date back almost two million years. The Chinese themselves have spun creation myths to outline their origins. Paleolithic (Old Stone) Age artifacts of the so-called Peking man, some 500,000 years ago, reveal life in the North China plain, while evidence of existence from the Neolithic (New Stone) Age become more widespread. Alleged to have existed during this latter period, the first traditional Chinese dynasty, the Xia (Hsia), ruled by kings, is as yet unsupported by fact.

That of the ensuing dynasty, the Shang, on the other hand, is quite well documented in its life between the eighteenth and twelfth centuries B.C. A remarkable state, its legacies have been handed down to present generations: an organized political entity based on a settled agrarian economy; a written language in characters recognizable today; and beautifully worked arts, including bronzes. The next dynasty, that of the Zhou (Chou), longest in Chinese history, lasting between the eleventh and third centuries B.C., was overall a militarily muddled period but a culturally brilliant one. Among other bequests, it produced China's most famous philosophers and classics of literature. These predynastic eras and first ruling houses are those covered in this part which ends in 221 B.C., when the monarch initiating the next dynasty escalated his title and structure to those of emperor and empire.

9

FROM LEGEND TO HISTORY

(Prehistory to 1122 B.C.)

A variety of archaeological sources indicate antecedents of the Chinese that date back over many thousands of years. Physical and cultural anthropologists have recently discovered Stone Age existence located principally in the North China plain. Since the 1920s, and into the People's Republic of China, Chinese and Western archaeological expeditions have excavated northern and northwestern sites of early civilizations, and much has been uncovered. The various artifacts and the animal and human skeletal remains that have been discovered there lend some credence to the myths, literature, and historical works that later described Chinese beginnings and evolution.

Chinese origins can only be surmised, but several hypotheses have been advanced. According to a diffusion theory, the Chinese originated somewhere in Africa, the Middle East, or Central Asia, and subsequently migrated into China. The civilization of ancient China was similar in some basic outlines to those of the latter two cultures: the presence of domesticated animals, grain crops, the use of the wheel and chariot, and bronze and iron tools. Yet China, unlike other early cultural centers, was unique in using the stone chopper rather than the stone ax, and in developing the long-bladed hoe rather than the plow. China also discovered the cultivation of silk. A second hypothesis posits Chinese origins in southwestern China or India, for the earliest extant Chinese racial strain is the Tibeto-Burmese family in Yunnan province. Rice and the water buffalo, the predominant beast of burden in South China, originated in the land to the south, across the Himalayas. A third theory holds that the early Chinese evolved independently in North China. In any event, historic Chinese civilization arose in the north, in the Yellow River plain. Why it commenced there is conjectural, but undoubtedly the loess soil was fertile, and the land, although it tends today toward climatic extremes, may have been a more habitable place in which to live.

Prehistory

Traditional Chinese accounts supported the historic fact that the North China plain was the homeland. Centering on this region, the native myths, oral histories, and written classics described superhuman progenitors or deities who "invented" clothing, food, the institution of marriage, and other basic features of life. These stories, with their man-centered cultural values, beliefs, and ethical principles, emphasized the importance of the family, the dominance of agriculture, and rule by priest-kings. The creation chronicles varied in details, but the general outline can be sketched.

These told of Ban Gu (Pan Ku), the creator, who helped to shape the universe in the vast interaction of the forces of *yang* and *yin*, over a period of 18,000 years, a major multiple of the sixty-year cycle. There followed a dozen celestial emperors (Heaven Kings), all brothers with serpent bodies, each of whom also reigned for 18,000 years. Next in line were eleven terrestrial emperors (Earth Kings), also all brothers and also with gross shapes, with each again ruling for 18,000 years. Finally, nine human emperors (Human Kings), also all brothers, ruled for a total of 45,600 years, each over his own ninth portion of the world. The stories sketched a subsequent obscure period of sixteen sovereigns, of whom little was known but their names.

They were followed by three outstanding legendary monarchs (*huang*) credited with the invention of many arts and crafts. Fu Xi (Fu Hsi), 2852-2734 B.C., who ruled over 120 years, domesticated animals and invented fishing, the eight trigrams, music, writing, and the worship of *shangdi* as the supreme being. He shared his rule with Nu Wa, his sister consort and wife (the couple is credited with inventing the institution of marriage), and first created flood control and water management, so crucial to the well-being of the Chinese state. The couple is often portrayed intertwined with human bodies and dragon tails. The successor, Shen Nong (Shen Nung), 2734-2697 B.C., with a shorter reign of almost four decades, took up agriculture and fathered medicine. The third, last, and most famous, the father of the Chinese people, Huang Di, the Yellow Emperor (2697-2595 B.C.), ruled for over a century, fought barbarians, and invented bricks, the cart, the sixty-year cycles, and the writing of history. He supposedly reigned at the same time that the Egyptian pharaohs were building their first pyramids. His wife, Lei Zu, the first to be designated as empress, was credited with the establishment of the silk industry. Huang Di's legendary tomb is said to be at Qiaoshan, some 120 miles north of Xi'an on the road to Yan'an. (Tombs in Gansu and Henan provinces are also claimed to be his.)

Five other monarchs followed in succession, not by eldest son, but by ablest man. The last two of these five, Yao, grandson of Huang Di, and Shun, who invented weights and measures, and their successor, Yu, were called the Model Emperors. All three continued efforts to control floods and to bring prosperity to their subjects. The two-part character for law (*fa*) is derived from this idea of water control; the right half stands for the verb go and the left is the radical for water. A hard worker, Yu supervised with efficient authority and superhuman efforts the affairs of state, and he began the custom of hereditary succession (not necessarily by primogeniture, but by ablest son). He is also credited with the founding of the Xia, the first traditional dynasty in Chinese history.

Archaeology supports the traditional thesis that Chinese civilization developed in the northern plain. The Chinese created primitive riverine cultures, much like those in the Middle East, during the Paleolithic or Old Stone Age, which in China lasted to around 20,000 B.C. Twentieth-century archaeological finds confirm the ethnocentricity of ancient China. In 1965, several tooth specimens, dating back 1.7 million years, were found at Yuanmou, 65 miles northwest of Kunming in Yunnan province. The discoveries were classified as an early form of *Homo erectus*. Earlier excavations, in 1963 at Lantian near Xi'an, revealed evidence of later human existence, to around 600,000 years ago. In 1927, at Zhoukoudian (Chou-k'ou-tien), 30 miles southwest of Beijing, an archaeological group financed by the Rockefeller Foundation discovered remains of the so-called Peking man, who flourished around half a million years ago. He was a hominid, a proto-human being, who walked upright on his feet and possessed a brain capacity larger than that of a gorilla, but less than that of a modern man. Partial physical remains, such as skulls and teeth, reveal several characteristics common to both early Peking man and modern man in Eastern Asia, including shovel-shaped upper incisors and bony outgrowths on the inner side of the lower jaw.

The Chinese Communists continued to excavate in the Beijing area and in the northwestern provinces of Shanxi and Shaanxi. In Shanxi, at Kehe, just inside the elbow of the Yellow River as it takes its last great turn from south to east, they uncovered eleven sites that contained animal fossils and at least five types of Paleolithic stone tools, but no human skeletal remains. Animal, stone, and human finds in North China indicate that Paleolithic man used fire. In the warmer climate of that time, he hunted the rhinoceros, ostrich, gazelle, antelope, hyena, and bison. He did not employ a wide variety of implements, but used a few, such as fish bones or bone needles, for many purposes. He wore beads and painted his teeth red. In the latter part of the Paleolithic Age, living conditions changed greatly when glaciers descended into China and an ice cap moved into Central Asia from the Urals. Turbulent winds stirred up by climate changes brought dust and soil, which settled as fertile loess in the Ordos region, enclosed by the big bends of the Yellow River in Shaanxi and Shanxi provinces. The winds may also have blown some of the early inhabitants across the narrow Bering Strait into North America to become the ancestors of the Eskimos and Indians.

There appeared to be no extensive life in China in the Mesolithic or Middle Stone Age, but by the Neolithic or New Stone Age, which began at an unknown time but ended around 2000 B.C., the Chinese had settled down to agricultural pursuits. Now they used stone-bladed hoes to cultivate vegetables, millet, and possibly other types of grain. They raised pigs and dogs for meat. They produced tools and weapons of polished or ground stone, including a unique stone knife shaped like a half-moon. They hunted with bows and arrows, wove baskets and cloth, and sewed with bone needles. Wearing clothes of skin or hemp, they lived in sunken pit dwellings, a type of dome-shaped lodge in the ground with an outlet at the top to serve as an entrance for the occupant and as an escape for smoke.

Several cultures of the Neolithic period were revealed through the existence of major pottery types. One was called Yangshao, after a site located in northwestern Henan province, south of the Yellow River near its last bend. Part of an overall Neolithic culture in Asia that spread from Xinjiang province to Manchuria, but with Chinese variants this culture appeared first in Gansu province. It then spread eastward, but it lasted the longest in Gansu. Banpo village, an excavated Yangshao site near the Xi'an loess, has pits of varying shapes (rectangular, square, and circular) over which wattle and mud huts were erected; thatched roofs with a hole at the top-center let smoke out. A defensive moat surrounded the one huge loghouse, twenty-four domiciles, and one hundred sixty storage pits; beyond the ditch lay the cemetery. The Yangshao period, with specimens from Banpo and other sites, was noted for its red or painted pottery, especially its large bulbous red pots with painted black geometric designs, the more refined pottery being fashioned by the potter's wheel. The pottery, used variously for funerary, ceremonial, and culinary purposes, had few naturalistic patterns.

Another culture, that of fine black wheel-made pottery sometimes less than a millimeter in thickness, is called Longshan or Chengziyai, the latter a site discovered in 1930 in western Shandong province. This phase also had characteristics in common with the general Neolithic subperiod in Asia, but it anticipated the Shang dynasty. Black pottery diffused in Chinese migrations throughout the North China plain and went southward into the Yangtze valley to Hangzhou. The life of the plains and villages was relatively well advanced. The political center of Chengziyai was surrounded by a mile-long wall built of pounded earth, which still stands in some places, more than 30 feet wide at the base and ten feet high. This warlike people used the ox and the horse, but no vehicles have been discovered. They practiced agriculture, caught fish, and raised sheep and cattle. They used shells for ornaments and implements; practiced scapulimancy, a form of divination adduced from cracks produced by scorching animal bones and turtle backs; continued to live in primitive dwellings such as flat-bottomed circular pits; and followed the unusual practice of face-down burial. A third culture, Xiao Tun, was derived from artifacts recovered from ruins of that name at Anyang, where it was first discovered in a pure form. Its predominant feature was a grey-ware, shaped with the use of a pad and beater. The Neolithic Age ended with the advent of bronze during the legendary Xia dynasty.

The Xia Dynasty

Early Chinese histories date the Xia, whose family name was Si (the first of the Three Dynasties), variously meaning Great or Spacious or Summer, as ruling 2205-1766 B.C. (or alternatively 1994-1523 B.C.). All purported evidence concerning the period is yet conjectural. The dynastic name itself is ill-defined; Xia might be a culture, a region, a state with a succession of rulers, or even a tribe. No definite archaeological evidence has been uncovered to prove that such a dynasty or state ever existed. If it did, the Xia culture, like most of the earlier Paleolithic and many of the Neolithic ones, was centered near the banks of the Yellow River, in its middle reaches. The most promising sites for excavation are thought by some to be in the Luoyang plain in central Henan province and in southwestern Shanxi province. Erlitou village, two miles from Luoyang, has yielded several cultural levels, the lowest two of which might be from Xia times. Yangcheng (Sun City), the legendary dynastic capital, is sometimes placed at Wang Cheng Gang (Royal City Mound), near Dengfeng city in western Henan province, where the topography matches descriptions of it in later annals.

During the five-century dynasty, seventeen sovereigns ruled for a total of 439 years over groups of city-states strung out along the north China plain. According to Chinese histories, Yu, the last of the three Model Emperors, founded the Xia. A vigorous, virtuous ruler, he divided his kingdom into smaller units and devoted all his time and energy to a just rule. He bequeathed the kingdom to his son, but through time, the royal line weakened. The dynasty's vigor declined until Jieh, the last depraved monarch, was overthrown in a revolt led by Tang, another branch descendant of the Yellow Emperor and lord of the city-state of Shang. He began the dynasty of that name, which his successors re-named Yin because it was eventually located in the marshes of that name in Henan province.

The cycle of personal factors was now established in Chinese history whereby great, strong, virtuous men initiated dynasties; debauched ones ended them by losing the mandate of heaven, which required virtue to rule, appease the gods, and placate the subjects. The tradition of the right to revolt against despotic monarchs was thus established early in Chinese history. Rulers might have had a divine mandate to rule, but they themselves were not divine and could be removed from office by force.

Although everything about the Xia is supposition, several plausible arguments support the existence of the dynasty. The ancient Chinese chronicles, although they vary in dating the period, unanimously ac-cepted the validity of the dynasty. In the histories, the Xia rulers seemed more lifelike than the earlier legendary demigods. They reigned for realistic lengths of time. As a cultural transitional link, the Xia might reasonably have filled the historical gap of several centuries (or over-lapped) from the black pottery of Neolithic times and the beautiful, highly developed, and fully executed bronzes of the later Shang. Ex-cavations may yet support the historicity of the Xia as they did, belat-edly, that of the Shang. At any rate, by the first half of the second millennium B.C., historic China had emerged.

The Shang Dynasty

The first authenticated dynasty is that of the Shang, 1766–1122 B.C. or 1523–1027 B.C., with a family name of Zi, who developed a re-markable civilization in the North China plain. Sources documenting the period include some of the later classics, especially the *Classic of Poetry*. The traditional accounts of life, the first recorded civilization in East Asia, have been confirmed by archaeological discoveries. Excavations since the 1920s in the area of present-day Anyang in northern Henan province have brought to light remains of the later royal Shang city, sculptured marble fragments of birds and animal heads, bronzes, and bones and shells, of which one-tenth are inscribed. That so much is left is remarkable because of the antiquity of the period, the historical political vicissitudes, banditry, and the continual dese-cration by robbers of early graves.

One major archaeological source of Shang life has been artifacts of divination on oracle bones and shells. Fragments of these were first discovered in Beijing pharmacies around 1920 and were traced to sites at Anyang, some 80 miles north of the Yellow River and 300 miles from the sea. About 2,500 signs of the early writing scratched on bones and shells are recognized to this day. Remains have been plentiful; 17,800 specimens were discovered in one Anyang site alone. Incisions were made with a sharp instrument on tortoise undershells or on bones, usually in the flat scapula or leg bone of cattle, by shamans to divine responses to inquiries of varying sorts by clients, many of them royal. Hot wood or metal was then applied to form additional cracks, from which answers could somehow be fathomed. Shells or bones could be used more than once. Later, the extended questions and the more involved answers themselves were recorded on the shells or bones; some diviners signed their names (about 120 of them exist).

The average inscription generally consisted of about a dozen characters, although some had as many as sixty. The questions and answers related to such subjects as the efficacy of sacrifices, announcements to departed spirits, prognostications on hunting, fishing, war, crops, weather, sicknesses, and the feasibility of commencing journeys. In the late Shang, kings of the so-called New School appropriated the diviner's function themselves and transformed it into a royal prerogative. The Shang also wrote on strips of wood or bamboo, but remains of these have long since disappeared through the attrition of time.

A second major archaeological source documenting Shang life is the pottery and bronzes. Only highly developed forms of bronze have been uncovered, some with inscriptions and designs; excavations have not as yet revealed any in a more primitive stage. Anyang, possibly deriving the technique of bronze casting from peoples to the west of China, smelted and cast its own bronze in primitive blast furnaces, sometimes by the lost wax process (cire perdue). Other bronze vessels were cast in parts and fitted together. Some ran quite large—up to 400 pounds—a size that necessitated control over the coordinated efforts of hundreds of workers.

The bronze artifacts consisted of both weapons and elaborate ceremonial containers. The latter included a variety of shapes of cups, round and square pots mounted on three or four legs respectively, and other covered jars with grasps or movable handles. On the bronzes, the patterns were conventionalized designs or geometrical forms, often in delicate incised lines or in high relief. One stylized representation was the *taotie* (animal mask), a front view of an animal head, usually that of a ram with the design centered on a nose-eye axis with the ears spread out. (Animal forms in profile came later into Chinese art.) These highly conventionalized figures, with their balance of design, form, and order presupposed a long history. The animals, in numerous shapes and in combinations, included oxen, sheep, snakes, cicadas, dragons, and birds.

Most of what is known from the oracle bones and bronzes, or later literature about this dynasty, involved the kings, court, and aristocracy. Tang, the dynastic founder, with his able prime minister Yi Yin, emulated the Model Emperors with his dedicated work ethic to promote the common good. In its early years, the Shang, whose name derived from Tang's geographic domain in the Xia, probably occupied several capitals. With some sixteen sovereigns, early Shang settlements are identified with cities including Zhengzhou, the capital of Henan province. Around 1400 B.C., they settled in the marshes of Yin near Anyang on the banks of the Huan tributary, just before it empties into the Yellow River. Built on earlier Neolithic sites (as Xiao Tun), the royal house ruled areas in North China that expanded or contracted according to the fortunes of war. Their principal hegemony held sway from Yin into parts of the surrounding Hepei, Henan, Anhui, Shandong, and Shanxi provinces. At its widest extent, the royal domain was strung out tenuously from what is now Beijing to the Yangtze and from the coast to Gansu province. But its power seldom reached far beyond the capital city, which governed through indirect rule over the vassal city-states. At Anyang, the royal cemetery with its several tombs has now been excavated. (The tomb of one king was 43 feet deep and 65 feet square.) A dozen monarchs, at least, ruled at Anyang, with reigns ranging from two to seventy-four years. Succession was as often from brother to brother as from father to son. Kings (*wang*) had one or several wives. They performed the high rites, commanded armies, and conducted hunts. As far as they could, they ruled with absolute authority over their subjects.

The centralized bureaucracy consisted of councilors, historians, diviners, and priests. The scribes at the royal court provided some of the earliest historical accounts and records. These proto-historians facilitated governmental affairs, which depended on calendrical accuracy. They fashioned the traditional Chinese calendar, reconciling the solar year of 365 days and the lunar one of 354 or 355 days with the periodic interjection of short intercalary months. Days were grouped into ten-day weeks, and each day of the week had a royal designation with rites to be performed on that day by those associated with the symbol or name. Hereditary nobles ruled over substates of varying size, with power concentrated in local towns, and supported or fought the king, who in turn protected or fought them.

The *Classic of Poetry*, a major source of Shang life although compiled in the Later Zhou dynasty, indicated that the aristocracy was much concerned with ritual. As the high priest, the king performed numerous ceremonies. The nobility worshiped *tian* (heaven) and *shangdi* (ruler above), a sky deity possibly considered to be an ancestor who was entreated for successful crops and victory in battle. A multitude of other divinities were honored, such as a dragon woman, an eastern and western mother, and animistic gods of the winds, rivers, and earth. The condition of the spirits depended in great part on the nature and efficacy of open-air sacrifices of food, animals (cattle, sheep, pigs, dogs, and horses), and human beings, usually in multiples of ten. Sacrifices accompanied the dedication of buildings, and often animals or human beings were buried alive with their masters or kings. Shang culture could be violent; hundreds of victims of war or sacrifices were slaughtered or buried "accompanying in death."

Shang palaces and public buildings set an architectural style that is still followed. A pounded earth platform supported foundation stones, in which wooden pillars were erected to support a gabled roof over a rectangular structure. At first, the walls were of pounded earth and then of brick, but the pillars, not the walls, supported the roofs. Stone was plentiful, but the early Chinese, unlike the Greeks, did not use it (possibly for seismological reasons). Buildings were large; one measured 26 by 92 feet. According to *fengshui* principles, they faced south.

From these palaces the king and the aristocrats went out to do battle against each other, or to repulse invaders from the border regions. Besides defensive purposes, wars were waged to collect tribute or simply to loot and plunder. In an era of continuous fighting, the average army was composed of 3,000 to 5,000 conscripted men. Spike-wheeled chariots (possibly an importation from Central Asia) were drawn at first by two horses (later by four), and each carried three men: the king or noble, a charioteer, and an armed man or spearman. Leaders wore bronze helmets and leather armor reinforced by bone and wood. The main brunt of the fighting was borne by infantry equipped with spears, halberds, and bows and arrows tipped with bronze or stone. In the then more temperate climate, hunting was a popular aristocratic sport. It was organized on a large scale with chariots and yoked horses, and used for various purposes, such as for exterminating dangerous animals, capturing others for sacrifice, and accumulating ivory, hides, furs, plumes, and horns.

Life for the mass of the people was drudgery. Because of the great gap between the rich and poor, the latter continued to live in crude Neolithic pit dwellings and loess caves, at least in winter, or in simple one-roomed thatched huts. There is no proof that Shang society was based on slave labor. The main industry was farming, and the chief crop was millet. Possibly wheat and wet or irrigated rice were also cultivated. Peasants used spades, hoes, and foot plows. They raised pigs, dogs, sheep, goats, cattle, and horses, although sheep were not sheared and cows were not milked. Even in ancient times, the Chinese had eschewed milk and dairy products. A beer was made from millet. Fowl is not mentioned in literary works and rarely depicted in art; possibly it was introduced later from the Burma region.

Artisans worked with bronze and carved stones, bones, and ivory, the surfaces of which were often inlaid with turquoise or mother of pearl. Jade was carved into many shades representing men and animals, into royal ornaments such as the large jade tablet fastened to the imperial gown, and into symbolic ritual objects. Possibly used in seasonal sacrifices and in ancestor worship, these included discs with pierced centers (*bi*) to represent heaven and cylinders fitted into cubes (*cong*) to represent earth. Sculpture, up to a yard in length, included incised marble blocks representing mythological creatures, but this art disappeared in time. White and glazed pottery was manufactured, although the latter was quite unusual. The method may have been the secret property of a family or two because the technique died out and was not revived for many centuries. Silk was produced, and the cocoon figure appeared in bronze designs of the time. Clothing consisted of furs and textiles. Musical instruments included the ocarina and musical stones.

A merchant class dealt in salt, shells, and metals. Since the making of bronze involved copper, tin, lead, and antimony, some of which were not found in northern China, they probably were imported over long distances from southern supply centers. Cowrie shells were used as currency in early China as elsewhere, but although cowries were found along the southern China coast, the Shang apparently used shells like those found as far afield as the Indian Ocean.

The end of the era saw a recurrence of the signs that supposedly terminated the Xia. Zhou Xin (Chou Hsin), the last Shang ruler, like the last Xia ruler, was supposedly evil, debauched, and tyrannical. The long-suffering people rose in revolt led by a subject, Wu Wang (King Wu), and his brother Zhou Gung (the Duke of Zhou), whom Confucianists revered as a prototypal adviser. The remnants of the Shang royal family and its adherents were scattered far and wide. Korea traces its legendary beginnings to one such group. Other refugees retreated to Central China and maintained the ancient rituals and customs for several centuries. As the earliest historic Chinese, the Shang left a distinct legacy. Writing and artistic skills were highly developed. In a centralized class-stratified two-layered state of the rulers and the ruled, the kings, through centralized management, exercised the control of writing, the arts and crafts, the use of chariots, and the calendrical rituals. Through ancestor worship, the Shang perpetuated the family system, projected their origins into prehistoric antiquity, and emphasized hierarchical ties of obligation and servitude from the ruled, through the rulers, to the gods above. Chinese civilization began to radiate from the northern heartland into other regions of China proper and out into neighboring countries.

Chronology

B.C.

? to ca. 20,000	Paleolithic (Old Stone) Age
20,000 to ?	Mesolithic (Middle Stone) Age
? to 2,000	Neolithic (New Stone) Age: Yangshao (red or painted pottery), Longshan or Chengzuyai (black pottery), and Xiao Tun (grey-ware)
2205-1766	Traditional dates for the Xia dynasty
1766-1123	Shang dynasty
ca. 1400	Shang settle down at Yin

A.D.

1920s	Discoveries at Anyang of Shang/Yin existence
1927	Remains of Peking man discovered
1930	Chengdzuayi sites discovered
1960	Discoveries at Kehe of eleven Paleolithic sites
1963	Discoveries at Lantian of man dating to 600,000 B.C
1965	Discoveries at Yuanmou of man dating to 1.7 million years B.C.

Chinese Sovereigns: Legendary
(Dates of rule conjectural)

Ban Gu, creator, 18,000-year reign

Twelve Heaven Kings, 18,000 years each

Eleven Earth Kings, 18,000 years each

Nine Human Kings, total reign of 45,600 years

Sixteen sovereigns, reigns ?

Three legendary monarchs:

Fu Xi, 2852-2734 B.C., and wife, Nu Wa

Shen Nong, 2734-2697 B.C.

Huang Di, father of Chinese people, 2697-2595 B.C., and wife, Lei Zu

Three sovereigns, reigns ?

Three Model Emperors:

Yao, 2357-2257 B.C.

Shun, 2257-2205 B.C.

Yu, 2205-2198, who founded the Xia dynasty

Xia dynasty, 2205-1766 B.C., with sixteen successors:

Chi, 2197-2189

Da Kang, 2188-2160

Zhong Kang, 2159-2147

Xiang, 2146-2119

Shao Kang, 2118-2058

Zhu, 2057-2041

Huai, 2040-2019

Mang, 2018-1997

Xie, 1996-1981

Bu Jiang, 1980-1922

Qiong, 1921-1901

Jin, 1900-1880

Kung Jia, 1879-1849

Gao or Hao, 1848-1838

Fa, 1837-1819

Jieh or Lu Gui, 1818-1767

Chinese Sovereigns:
Shang and Yin Dynasties
(Dates of rule controversial)

Shang dynasty:

Cheng Tang, 1766-1754 B.C.

Tai Jia, 1753-1721

Wu Ding, 1720-1692

Tai Geng, 1691-1667

Xiao Jia, 1666-1650
Yung Ji, 1649-1638
Tai Wu, 1637-1563
Zhong Ding, 1562-1550
Wai Ren, 1549-1535
Jian Jia, 1534-1526
Zu Yi, 1525-1510
Zu Xin, 1509-1489
Qiang Jia, 1488-1466
Zu Ding, 1465-1434
Nan Geng, 1433-1409
Hu Jia, 1408-1402

Yin dynasty:
Pan Geng, 1401-1374
Xiao Xin, 1373-1353
Xiao Yi, 1352-1325
Wu Ding, 1324-1266
Zu Geng, 1265-1259
Zu Jia, 1258-1226
Lin Xin, 1225-1220
Kang Ding, 1219-1199
Wu Yi, 1198-1195
Wen Wu Ding, 1194-1155
Di Yi, 1191-1155
Zhou Xin, 1154-1123

10

THE ZHOU DYNASTY

(1122 to 221 B. C.)

The Zhou dynasty (1122 or 1027–221 B.C.) derived its name from the character meaning "complete" that it bestowed on its territory. The family name was Ji. It was the longest dynasty in Chinese history, but because of extended periods of warfare and the existence of strong city-states, the central authority was often only a hollow name. The origin of the Zhou is unknown; possibly the house first rose to power in the Tibeto-Burman areas or in the plateau north of the Yellow River. By the time Chinese history gives the Zhou notice, after their wanderings, the state was centered at the city of Hao in the Wei River area near present-day Xi'an (the first of several major Chinese dynasties to be located there). According to the traditional accounts of the Zhou assumption of the mandate of heaven, Wen Wang (King Wen, a posthumous title) was entreated by the people to end the rule of the wicked Shang. As a loyal subject, he hesitated; instead, the titled vassal, also called Count of the West, was imprisoned by Zhou Xin, his overlord. The Count's sons, Wu Wang and Zhou Gong, had no such compunctions about loyalty. Leading their forces, the two invaded and destroyed Anyang.

After a few years of rule, Wu Wang died and his brother became the regent for the monarch's son and heir. The regent began the process of assimilating Shang features into the political process. To assure control of the eastern regions, he built a subsidiary capital at Luoyi (now Luoyang). It took two more decades to conquer the other fifty Shang city-states. The Zhou initially kept the capital in the Wei valley, where the state had matured. They were in a location that permitted a mixture of the border martial spirit with the more advanced settled civilization of the previous dynasty. The population of China under the Zhou is not known, but the people multiplied rapidly. By the end of the dynasty, in the third century B.C., the Chinese probably had become in any one country the largest aggregation of human beings in the world, as they are today.

For the first four and a half centuries, the Zhou kept the political center of power in the Wei valley, ruling a triangular area bounded by southern Manchuria, the Yangtze River, and Gansu province. With its thirteen kings over this time period, political indirect rule prevailed; vassals governed the outlying regions. Of this Earlier or Western Zhou period (1122 or 1027-771 B.C.), not much is recorded in Chinese literary or historical works; no archaeological remains exist. From what little is known, life and culture appeared similar to that of the antecedent Shang: the theory of absolute kings, a bureaucracy run by nobility, the veneration of ancestors, the continuation of divination. Civil strife periodically broke out; in 841 B.C. (the first authenticated date in Chinese history), a harsh king was overthrown and replaced by the crown prince. Civil strife prevailed. Finally, after the capital was sacked by barbarians in 771 B.C., the Zhou rulers moved east to Luoyi, a better protected area in western Henan province.

Fairly detailed and reliable records chronicle the Later or Eastern Zhou (771-221 B.C.), who were now relocated in the cultural heartland of China. Its twenty-two monarchs lost effective rule to the nobles. Throughout these five and a half centuries, kings reigned but did not rule. The aristocracy became more independent and in the continual wars and strife, feudalism rose. Monarchs were manipulated by a league of vassals headed by an overlord, the most powerful of them. Somewhat like medieval Europe, China became a collection of states with fluctuating boundaries. The troubled latter half of the Zhou is sometimes divided into subperiods such as the Spring and Autumn Epoch (*Chunqiu*, 722-481 B.C.), named after the classic that narrated the events of these years in Confucius's home state of Lu in Shandong peninsula, and the Period of the Warring States (*Zhanguo*, 480-221 B.C.), after a book devoted to these centuries. Yet despite political turmoil, the Zhou was an era of great creativity, cultural vitality, and literary and philosophical advancement.

The nominal head of the kingdom at the capital was the Zhou king (*wang*), the chief priest and the leader in war. His royal symbol was the ax. As a superhuman person, he converted the earlier celestial title of *Shangdi* into the terrestrial Son of Heaven. He reigned by moral virtue and by the mandate of heaven, assisted by a chief minister amd six ministries (some of which persisted into the twentieth century): agriculture, army, public works, religion, punishments, and the monarch's personal affairs. The state functioned as an elaborate bureaucracy based on wealth, title, and appointment. The land was divided into circuits called *zhou*, each administered by one man. The king received tribute and taxes directly from his royal domains and indirectly from lesser lords scattered in their feudatories. These obligations were paid for chiefly in silk and agricultural products.

Because the country was large, communication poor, and centralized rule weak, the king delegated authority to the lords or vassals, who owned land and maintained miniature courts in their own political centers. Until the eighth century B.C., the aristocrats came to the capital of Hao for ceremonies of investiture, but in the Later Zhou, the lords, as they became more powerful, disregarded central authority. An aristocratic hierarchy, growing more complex in time, arose with five ranks, usually translated into English terms: duke, marquis, earl or count, viscount, and baron. Each had his own power center, of which there were some one hundred seventy by the eighth century B.C. In these centers, the nobles maintained palaces, temples, and altars. The timber houses were protected from their traditional enemies, the northern nomads, by town walls of stone or pounded earth with gates and wooden signal towers. Vassal states in the north, bordering the source of traditional enemy forays, erected segments of extended walls, later to be incorporated into the Great Wall. There were public markets in the urban centers and schools for the sons of nobility, who studied the arts of music, archery, chariot driving, and writing.

In the Later Zhou, between the eighth and third centuries B.C., a dozen leading states emerged from out of the political turmoil in alliances that shifted with the vagaries of war and conquest. Various unstable hegemonies flourished on the periphery of the Zhou royal domains, which had, in effect, contracted to the Luoyi area. The more important states that challenged the power of the Zhou came to include, in the Beijing area, Yen; Jin, southwest of it; Shu, situated since the Neolithic era in Sichuan in the Chengdu plain; and Wu at Nanjing, whose people spoke a polysyllabic language (and bequeathed the term *wu* to the present dialect and peoples of the lower Yangtze delta, including Shanghai).

Another state, that of Chu, was centered in the agriculturally rich central Hankou region. Of Thai ethnic background, its people blackened their teeth, cut short their hair, and tattooed themselves. They were hardworking and prosperous in agricultural and commercial activities. In the sixth century B.C., the first Chinese reference to irrigation is to their state. Still other peoples, the Yue, were spread along the southern coastal areas. According to chronicles, they were lazy because of an abundance of readily available food. By the third century B.C., they had been forced, in part because of hostile neighbors, into northern Vietnam to the eighteenth parallel, a boundary that came to be the approximate limit of historic Chinese expansion in that part of mainland Southeast Asia. They brought their artifacts and way of life; with them came the introduction of a higher civilization based on iron and bronze into southern peripheral lands.

Meanwhile, two more states were consolidating power. Qi flourished in eastern China in Shandong and Hebei provinces. Annals depict its people as warlike and lacking in tradition. Its centralized bureaucratic government developed an efficient tax system. Its wise rulers, who appealed to Chinese historians, promulgated laws, regulated weights and measures, and enjoyed monopolies on salt and iron. The other centralized state of Qin evolved in the northwestern region, where previously the Zhou had risen to power. According to tradition, its model adviser, Wei Yang, gave the peasants ownership of land. In long drawn-out campaigns the Qin eventually defeated the Zhou and captured the capital of Luoyi in 256 B.C. (a date sometimes reckoned as the end of the Zhou). All other rivals were subdued by 221 B.C., when the Qin monarch established the Chinese imperial structure.

Although the centralized Zhou state was in fact weak, the results of the multistate struggles were significant. The continued contacts, albeit mainly military, brought peripheral states into the Zhou cultural context, inherited from the Shang. The civil commotion promoted a greater degree of social mobility; feudal domains were replaced by fewer territorial states, managed by career civilian and military bureaucrats. Interregional trade flourished; commercial urban centers arose in part through a more efficient agricultural system that produced surpluses to support nonfarming communities. Most importantly, schools of philosophies, with their literary texts, flourished to propound various solutions to vexing social problems.

Society

War was an integral part of Zhou life, and over the centuries, three basic military units were developed. Chariots continued in use by kings and nobles in the Earlier Zhou. As during the Shang, each vehicle carried three men; horses still were not mounted. The chariots fought singly, and each noble had his own standard. Spears were used but were not thrown. Some horses had leather armor. To augment the charioteers, infantry units numbering tens of thousands were led by officers drawn from the nobility. The conscripted foot soldiers wore sheepskin jackets and used slings and bows with bronze-tipped arrows. By 340 B.C., they had adopted the crossbow, a weapon not used by the Europeans for another six centuries. In Later Zhou times, cavalry replaced the clumsier chariots. For the first time, probably derived from

Central Asian games, horseback riding came into fashion and changed the nature of warfare in North China because of greater speed and mobility. It also changed Chinese dress, for on horseback the traditional gown was much less convenient than the adopted trousers.

Excuses for war were manifold: to punish enemies, to expand domains, to settle private squabbles, or simply to plunder. The large armies consisted of an advance guard; center, left, and right flanks; and a rear unit. Requiring vast quantities of dried meat and grain, they lived off the land. Omens were taken before battle. Drums were beaten to signal advance and gongs for retreat. Battles were usually chaotic, and there was no overall strategy other than to capture the enemy leader. Siege-craft was known, and tunnels were burrowed under town walls. In the Earlier Zhou, battles were chivalrous, but in later periods they degenerated into grim all-or-nothing campaigns.

Like that of the Shang, Zhou religion recognized a supreme god, *tian* (heaven), sometimes confused with *shangdi*, the ancestral deity. As the Son of Heaven, the king claimed the sole right to worship *tian*. As mediator between heaven and earth, and between man and nature, at ceremonies he performed the kowtow, or the three kneelings and nine prostrations. Other important gods were *ti*, the goddess of earth and consort of *tian*; the god of soil, who was worshiped at earthen mounds in each community; a millet god; a rain god; the god of agriculture, who was conceived by virgin birth; and the god of the Yellow River, who was a type of merman with the body of a fish and face of a man. These gods, as carryovers from Shang times, were portrayed as superhuman rather than as divine.

Nature and ancestor worship persisted. Sacrificial animals included cattle, sheep, swine, and horses; some human sacrifice continued, but these ended by the sixth century B.C. The use of oracle bones tended to die out, to be replaced by other methods of divination. Among sacred animals, the supernatural dragon held a paramount position. Unlike the dreaded mythical creature of medieval Europe, the grotesque Chinese dragon, probably derived from the alligator and associated with rain and water, was considered a beneficial animal.

The two main groups of society continued to be the rulers and the ruled, the privileged and all the rest of the populace. Aristocratic clans, bound more strongly by religious than by economic or blood ties, worshiped through a hereditary leader, a common ancestor, a man, or in some instances, a bird or animal. The clan, divided into family groupings, did not necessarily live together in a territorial unit. Polygamy was permitted, but wives could not come from the husband's clan. Women could not own land or aspire to political leadership. The law was imposed only on commoners, who for various infractions received such severe penalties as death, the tattooing of faces, amputation of noses or feet, and castration. The lords enjoyed unlimited power in their lands; they owned the holdings and their stewards supervised the cultivation.

Nobility wore long flowing gowns or trousers, furs, ornamental shoes, and headgear that identified the different ranks. Hunting was popular as a sport or training ground for war, and hunting parks increased in size and number, but game laws were severe. Nobles ate meat and were fond of drink. By the third century B.C., chopsticks were in common use. Furniture was minimal; chairs and tables were still unknown in common homes. The rich enjoyed music played on bells, flutes, whistles, musical stones, and mouth organs. Burial customs varied. In the northwest, cremation was sometimes practiced, but generally the custom of inhumation of the deceased in coffins was followed. Bodies were covered with a red pigment. Wealth was interred with the dead; twelve chariots and seventy-two horses have been found in a single tomb. Tombs, particularly those for kings, were marked by large mounds or pyramids erected over the vaults.

The governed class consisted mainly of peasants in a type of serfdom. They were not slaves, but for all practical purposes they were bound to land from which they could not flee or own. They were valuable assets to their lords: it was a cause for war when a lord took peasants from the land of another. They lived in Neolithic-type dwellings, ate millet, and observed fertility and animistic rites. During growing seasons the peasants lived on the land under cultivation, but during the winter they gathered in the walled villages surrounding officials' residences, where there were marketplaces and public grounds.

The other two classes remained small in number. Artisans continued to execute bronzes, which became more massive, bulky, and formal, and less inspired than Shang prototypes. Animal designs in silhouette, derived from Western and Scythian sources, were now portrayed in art forms. By the fourth century B.C., lacquer had been developed as a finish for wooden objects. Jade was carved into a variety of forms and worked with gold filigree. The merchant class increased in numbers but was ranked by the aristocracy, possibly out of jealousy or in social self-defense, at the bottom of the Chinese social scale. Outside the class structure were slaves, usually captives or criminals, who were bought and sold and who performed domestic chores.

Agriculture was the foundation of economic life. Millet, wheat, barley, and rice were the main crops. The ox-drawn plow came into use. Pigs and chickens were household animals. The most interesting agrarian feature, which may have been merely a later idealization of

Zhou peasant life, was the well-field (*jingtien*) system, so called because the land pattern resembled the form of the character for well (*jing*). Land was parceled out to eight peasant families; each family had a peripheral field for its own use, and all eight families together tilled a ninth, central field for the lord. Land was periodically reassigned as it became impoverished. Not until the third century B.C. was the peasant allowed to own land, at which time the well-field system, if it ever had existed, withered away.

Trade and commerce involved bartering goods or using cowrie shells, grains, and rolls of silk for currency. Around 500 B.C., metallic money was introduced. Minted bronze and copper coins constituted tokens for equivalencies in grain. Some coins resembled agricultural impliments such as spades and hoes. In the Later Zhou, copper cash came into fashion. These round coins with square holes in the middle were strung together into long strings. The coins had inscribed characters, which have served as a form of numismatic historical source.

In the technological field, China entered the iron age during the Zhou. About 500 B.C., iron became a substitute for bronze, in part because charcoal had come into use for smelting ore. A wide variety of iron tools and weapons were created: ox-drawn iron-tipped plows, hoes, scythes, axes, wheels, chisels, drills, knives, and needles. Swords up to three feet in length were fashioned. Astronomical knowledge was present. Earlier, in 1311 B.C. a lunar eclipse, and in 1137 B.C. a solar eclipse, were recorded in annals. By 350 B.C., the movements of Jupiter and Saturn were known in detail, and in 240 B.C. Halley's comet was described.

Other scientific and technological feats were recorded. In the third century B.C., the Pythagorean theorem was mentioned and the concept of *pi* advanced. The first treatise on trigonometry was composed. Hydraulic engineers developed efficient irrigation and flood control measures. Sections of what later became the Great Wall in the north were built. Efforts were made to standardize weights and measures by basing them on a standard tone frequency of a pitch pipe. Although the Chinese continued to use the lunar year for ritualistic purposes, by 444 B.C. the solar year was calculated at 365.25 days. Despite political confusion, the Zhou dynasty produced new achievements by the Chinese people.

Literature

The Zhou, especially in its latter centuries, was also a period of literary and intellectual activity. In the midst of the changing conditions of the politically fluid times, men reassessed or confirmed traditional values and proposed various alternatives to resolve the political chaos. Feudal lords gathered around them philosophers, advisers, and writers to examine the issues and to enhance the prestige of their courts. This wealth and patronage created a milieu favorable to literary and philosophic schools. The response of these schools to the physical challenges of the day was basically humanistic. Man was viewed as a political and social personality in a group context, rather than in an individual one. As practical men and as politicians, the philosophers and writers paid more attention to human endeavor and activity than to metaphysics or theories of divine origins.

The most notable body of literature that emerged during the Zhou dynasty was the classics. The term *classics* (*jing*) in China was not just a vague designation for early literature; it represented a specific set of five books associated with the orthodox Confucian doctrine, which in time won out over other philosophies. Defined and categorized later in the first century B.C. during the Han dynasty, the material was all present in the Zhou. The classics became the standard corpus for educated men to study, to emulate, and to use for the bureaucratic examination system. Tradition attributed them to Confucius as author or editor, but it is doubtful that he was associated with any of them. Some of the earlier sources of the classics predated Confucius. But the philosopher was cast in the role of transmitter, editor, or commentator by the history-minded Chinese out of reverence for the past as a golden age and through their respect for the written word. Much in the volumes is spurious, and the archaic phraseology and hidden meanings obscure the precise ideas of the anonymous authors. The five classics, as compilations of poetry, divination, ritual, a general history of China, and a history of Confucius's home state, revealed the Confucian sense of values.

As the first Chinese work of literature in point of time, the text known variously as the *Classic* or *Book of Songs*, of *Poetry*, or of *Odes* (*Shijing*) is an anthology of 305 songs composed probably between the tenth and seventh centuries B.C. dealing with love, politics, life, and the rites of Zhou times, although one section purportedly contained Shang ceremonial songs. Some poems are folk songs from the various feudal states of the Earlier Zhou times; other are passages that were chanted by the nobility in ceremonies and official functions. The odes adhere to exact patterns of meter, rhyme, and rhythm. Confucius was supposed to have selected the poems from a much greater body of material. Modern scholars deny this, but they accept the authenticity of most of the poems. The educated man in China was supposed not only to be familiar with this classic but also to be able to compose poetry.

The *Classic* or *Book of Divination* or *Changes* (*Yijing*) is a diviner's source book. As an alternative to scapulimancy, this form of divination involved the shuffling and drawing of even or odd number of stalks, usually of milfoil, a common herb, to form short or long lines of a trigram. The eight basic trigrams are three-lined combinations of straight or broken lines; they range from three straight unbroken lines over each other to three broken (in half) lines, with six variations in between. The long work explains the significances of the resulting eight trigrams and sixty-four hexagrams, the creation of which one tradition ascribes to Wen Wang, the father of Wu Wang and Zhou Gong. The classic is attributed to ancient authors, but Confucius is supposed to have written the appendixes (actually composed later in the Qin or Han dynasty), which elaborate on metaphysical interpretations and the symbolism involved.

This text contains both specific and vague auguries and much popular lore such as the *yang-yin* philosophy of complementary opposites. For instance, the first trigram of three unbroken lines may connote a multitude of concepts that include father, dragon, horse, heaven, south, late autumn, early night, king, deep red, head, force, roundness, expansiveness, and giver. The final one of three broken lines stands variously for mother, ox, mare, earth, north, early autumn, afternoon, people, black, abdomen, docility, squareness, form, and receiver. The sixty-four hexagrams ranging from six unbroken to six broken lines take on similar varying connotations. The *Classic* or *Book of Rituals* or *Rites* (*Liji*) is a second-century compilation of earlier rituals and etiquette, so important to Confucianists; these range from philosophical treatises to minute rules for everyday conduct. The *Liji* contains two particularly venerated passages, that of the *Great Learning* (*Daxue*), which stresses self-cultivation of socially accepted ends, and the *Doctrine of the Mean* (*Zhongyong*). which, as the title implies, advances a thesis of balance and moderation in all pursuits. These chapters were singled out a thousand years later in the Song dynasty for inclusion in the *Four Books* (*Sishu*), further doctrinal embodiment of Confucian ideas that also embrace the sayings of Confucius, the *Analects* (*Lunyu*), and the book of *Mengzi*, his chief disciple.

Another book inspired by the *Liji* was the *Classic of Filial Piety* (*Xiaojing*) of the Later Zhou period, which was a reshaping for instruction in primary grades of ideas on proper behavior found in the *Classic of Rites*. The Chinese also revered two other compilations of rituals: *Ceremonies and Rituals* (*Yili*), a portion of a larger work of undetermined origins, and the *Rituals of Zhou* (*Zhouli*), earlier known as the *Officials of Chou* (*Zhouguan*) and traditionally ascribed to Zhou Gong, although it is possibly from the Later Zhou era. The *Zhouli*, an idealistic plan for governmental administration, influenced many social and political reformers.

The fourth major *Classic* or *Book of Documents* or of *History* (*Shujing*) is a general Chinese history. In it exists much forgery, an honorable tradition in Chinese historical writing in which, by way of flattery rather than from deliberate falsehood, authors attributed their own works to favorite predecessors. By the second century B.C., two versions of the classic existed. The *Old Text*, found in the house of Confucius where it was hidden by descendants, has sixteen chapters not contained in the *Modern Text*, which was written in Han dynasty script. As the *Shujing* now stands, it has fifty-six chapters, of which probably only half are genuine. It embraces a great number of short statements, speeches, and oral reports said to have been made by various ancient ministers and model emperors through the Earlier Zhou period. The style is terse, dry, and flat. The collection was supposedly edited by Confucius, with his short prefaces to each document explaining the circumstances of its composition.

The fifth and final classic, *Spring and Autumn Annals* (*Chunqiu*) was a chronological recitation of events between 722 and 481 B.C. in Confucius's home state of Lu; the title, as noted, bestowed its name to a subperiod of the Later Zhou history. The title refers to the one-crop agricultural year in North China where grain was planted in spring and harvested in autumn. The chronicle is similar to histories of other states, and its traditional author is again Confucius. Like the *Shujing*, it is terse and factual, but it appears to be accurately dated. Three commentaries are appended to explain the background of the events referred to in the texts. The *Tso Commentary* or *Tradition of Tso* (*Zuozhuan*) of the fourth to second centuries B.C., with authorship attributed to one Zuo Shi, is an independent work chopped up to fit in with appropriate sections of the *Chunqiu*. The *Tradition of Kung-yang* (*Gongyangzhuan*) and the *Tradition of Ku-liang* (*Guliangzhuan*) are two simple commentaries that date from the final century of the Zhou.

Other works, including historical ones, though not elevated to the status of the classics, flourished in the Zhou. The *Bamboo Annals* (*Zhushuqinian*) record events in the state of Jin. Buried in a grave in 295 B.C., they were discovered in 279 A.D. They had been written on bamboo slips and were obviously ancient and anachronistic for the times, since paper was in general use by the third century A.D. The *Bamboo Annals* were subsequently lost again; only a forged text exists today. Other works of history included the *Discourses of the States*

(*Guoyu*), which complements the time and subject matter covered in the *Zuozhuan*, and the *Intrigues of the Warring States* (*Zhanguoze*), which describes a political subperiod (480-221 B.C.) of the Later Zhou. From the third century B.C. the *Erya*, a collection of commentaries on literary texts, is an early lexicographic work.

In the later decades of the Zhou, in another category of nonclassical literature, poetry assumed new forms and individual poets flourished. China's first great poet of note, Qu Yuan of the early third century B.C., composed poems and elegies, most of which constitute the anthology of the *Elegies of Ch'u* (*Chuci*), his home state in South China. An aristocrat in exile and in despair, he wrote impressionistic poems, most notably the long *Li Sao*, about his condition, his dreams, and his search for a model ruler to heed his advice on running a state. According to tradition, despondent, he eventually drowned himself in protest, and the Dragon Boat festival, according to one theory, is a search for his body. His fanciful, sophisticated, and exuberant poetry greatly influenced later generations of poets.

Philosophy

Augmenting literary activity was philosophy. The greatest intellectual achievement of the Zhou dynasty was the schools of philosophy, which borrowed largely from the earlier ethical and religious beliefs of the Chinese people. The political anarchy of the warring states encouraged diverse philosophic systems as scholars, philosophers, and tutors gathered disciples and attached themselves to the feudal lords. Others wandered with their followers throughout North and Central China to promulgate their doctrines by the nobility. They asked the usual time-honored questions on the nature of man, but their main accent was on political thought and the improvement of society in anarchic times, on political panaceas, and on utopias. Two main streams of thought eventually emerged: Confucianism, with its pragmatic, ordered, and man-centered orientation, and Daoism with its nonpersonal, intuitive, and reflective character. Other minor schools flourished at the time but what won out at the end of the Zhou was Legalism, a combination of traditions that offered authoritative answers to the perplexing social problems of the day.

Confucianism, which stressed balance and moderation, was only one of the leading schools of the day and it did not emerge as the paramount one until several centuries after the Zhou. Its founder was Confucius (Kongfuzi, Master Kong), a contemporary of Pythagoras and the Buddha. His traditional dates, as established in the much later Song dynasty, are 551 to 479 B.C. Despite much fanciful information, his life can be reconstructed in the main from various passages of the *Analects* (*Lunyu*), probably written by his disciples or later followers. The philosopher was born in the state of Lu of an aristocratic family. His elderly father died while Confucius was in his infancy, and his mother reared him. He was studious as a youth and early began to attract followers. He traveled, raised a family, and achieved the top office of his native state. According to tradition, he retired in middle age in protest against the unethical conduct of his prince. Confucius then went from state to state in search of a lord who would accept his principles of government. In old age he returned to Lu, where he died after more years of teaching and study. His tomb at his hometown of Qufu in Shandong province became a national shrine; his birthday was commemorated, and his descendants were honored. Although Confucius's political ideas were not accepted in his own time, he was revered as a philosopher in later generations.

The conservative Confucian doctrine is flat and unexciting. Its most important tenets are collected in the twenty chapters and 497 verses, many of them terse and cryptic, of the *Analects*. The book in the main comprises Confucius's replies to his disciples' questions. The philosopher was not interested in death or the afterlife but in the here and now, in the creating of an ideal society. An agnostic, he claimed that inasmuch as man did not understand life itself, he could not grasp any concept of life after death. For models and precedents of wise rulers he turned to the ancient emperors, particularly the founders of the Zhou dynasty, who were the forebears of the rulers of Lu. Confucius has been called China's first moralist; he advocated a government of ethics, the training of character, and the education of the superior man (*junzi*), a term already in use to mean the aristocrat or ruling lord.

Confucius believed that the road to good government lay in the observance of correct ritual, executed by properly educated men. Impeccable behavior and the unimpeachable character of the ruling classes, rather than force, were to hold society together. The Confucian training for the perfect man included the cultivation of the five inner virtues of integrity (*zhi*), righteousness (*yi*), loyalty (*zhong*), reciprocity (*shu*), and graded love (*ren*) in the sense of human-heartiness. The *junzi* was also to possess culture (*wen*) and ritual (*li*), a proper understanding of etiquette. The doctrine also stressed proper behavior in the five basic relationships of ruler and subject, husband and wife, father and son, elder and younger brother, and friend and friend. All had assigned roles to play in a hierarchical society, a concept later called the "rectification of names," which implied that words, including names, should mean what they had been intended to mean according to the structured Confucian scheme of social behavior and role-playing.

Toward the latter centuries of the Zhou, others grafted additional tenets onto the Confucian tradition. The St. Paul to Confucius was Mengzi (Mencius, Master Meng), 372-289 B.C., who lived some two centuries after his master and was a contemporary of Socrates. His thought is contained in his book, the *Book of Mengzi*, written like the *Analects* in dialogue style. A wealthy and idealistic aristocrat from a state near Lu, he wandered around North China as an itinerant philosopher-statesman. He proclaimed that man was by nature good. He posited that everyone had an innate moral sense that could, however, be changed by environmental factors. To avoid such change, one had to practice self-cultivation and love. Mengzi also advocated rule by good example and the right to revolt against evil kings. A good and wise monarch provided for the material and educational well-being of his subjects; if he did not, he was not worthy of the mandate of heaven and could be deposed. Such a doctrine justified and legitimized the Zhou overthrow of the Shang and the earlier Shang overthrow of the Xia. Needless to say, the right to rebellion was effective only when the rebels were successful. But Mengzi's legacy to Chinese intellectual and political thought was deep-rooted and influential, especially his interpretation of the moral worth of every individual and his idea that government was based on the tacit consent of the people.

A second major Confucian disciple was Xunzi (Hsün-tzu, Master Hsün), 300-237 B.C., who was a younger contemporary of Mengzi. Both a teacher and a practical politician. He wrote organized essays collected in a book of thirty-two chapters. he left a great mark on early Chinese intellectual history, but in the twelfth and thirteenth centuries the Chinese rejected his ideas. Living in a time of increasing political anarchy, he contradicted Mengzi and claimed that man, because of conflicting emotions and urges, was essentially unethical, although through education he could improve his nature. An authoritarian agnostic, Xunzi emphasized the role of the master, the necessity of formal education, the study of important works, and the observance of ritual. Like Mengzi and his contemporary rulers, he interpreted society on an economic basis.

These two and other contradictory thinkers were grouped together into the historic Confucian school. Although they differed in some interpretative details of human behavior, as common ideological denominators they advocated man's duty to man, the necessity of education, the ethical conduct of rulers, the improvability of human beings, and as members of the ruling class, ritual as a means to promote good behavior. Their general disbelief in spirits and personal deities reinforced the agnostic strain in Chinese religious life, and their stress on proper conduct according to social status strengthened the growing paternalism in political affairs.

Next in importance to Confucianism was Daoism, which, taking on the cause of the common man, protested against authoritarianism and the constrictions of ritual. In stressing the independence of man, it advocated the doctrine that one should accommodate oneself to nature rather than to other people in a social context. Daoism, which arose in the peripheral sinic states of the Yangtze valley, might be considered as a "barbarian" contribution to Chinese life. The philosophy incorporated pre-Confucian mysticism and such related beliefs as the placating of spirits, the merging of man into the universe, and the practice of breathing exercises. Much in intellectual Daoism, which derived essentially from two men and three books, is vague and nonhistorical.

Laozi (Lao Tzu, Old Master), an elder contemporary of Confucius, reputedly founded Daoism in the sixth century B.C., but his historicity is questioned. He might be a composite figure created by Daoists in later times, for the earliest reference to him constitutes a brief passage in a history written about four centuries after his alleged death. The book attributed to him, a brief and terse repository of various beliefs called the *Classic of the Way and Power* (*Laozi* or *Daodejin*), was probably written in the third century A.D. A second figure, the historical Zhuangzi (Chuang Tzu, Master Chuang), 369-286 B.C., was a contemporary of Mengzi. The book by his name, *Zhuangzi*, set forth Daoist ideas in vivid poems, parables, and metaphors. He wrote to free the individual from external pressures and from the narrow confines of his own mind. A third Daoist work, the *Liezi* (Lieh-tzu, Master Lieh), similar in thought and style, appears to be of later provenance.

Intellectual Daoism advocated that man merge with the Dao, the way, the nonbeing, the nameless. Merging consisted of passivity and inaction (*wuwei*). The Daoists were fond of an analogy of soft water in time wearing down hard rock. Dao was the great underlying principle in which all had their being, and knowledge of it was to be attained mystically by intuition and illumination, rather than by scholarship and rationality. Daoists advanced the idea of the unity of opposites: rules exist because of the presence of anarchy; filial piety because of impiety.

Like Confucians, but for differing reasons, Daoists espoused the ideal of political primitivity. As early anarchists, they professed to see no good or evil and no binding ritual in ancient society. Their ideal state was minuscule in size, one so small that a person could hear the cocks crow and the dogs bark in a neighboring state but would know nothing about affairs there and would care even less. Antischolastic and antiritualistic, early Daoism advocated laissez-faire to avoid friction in political affairs. Later, popular Daoism inverted some of this doctrine by stressing proto-scientific magic in search of alchemies and elixirs for prolonging life. Although Zhou Daoism did not appeal to the educated class as much as Confucianism, it was accepted as a healthy balance to the other doctrine. It promoted much creative and aesthetic vitality in artists and poets. Despite the doctrinal contradictions, an educated Chinese could properly be concerned with social problems and Confucian observation of ritual and decorum in the course of official duty and yet pursue pleasure and personal Daoist aesthetics on his own. Many Chinese did not regard religions or schools of ethics and logic as necessarily exclusive; a person could well be influenced by two or more philosophies without formal identification with any.

Other schools of thought existed in the Later Zhou, but they tended to lose significance in later dynasties. Mozi (Mo-tzu, Master Mo), 470-391 B.C., in a book bearing his name formulated a doctrine of universal love, not a Confucian regulated and hierarchical love, but a love for others as for one's self. His concept was utilitarian in that universal love was considered necessary to fulfill immediate practical and material human needs as well as any egocentric love. Mozi thought ritual useless and aesthetics unimportant. Utilitarian and authoritarian in politics, he thought it the duty of the prince to enrich the country and to increase its population. The Mohist school measured all acts by degree of utility to all people; hence its objection to war and its plea for simplicity.

A few other philosophers and schools of the time never became popular. The individualistic Yangzhu of the fourth century B.C. was pessimistic, fatalistic, and nihilistic. He accepted life as it came because he claimed that one could not control its vicissitudes. Founding no school and gathering no followers, he left little permanent imprint on Chinese thought. The Dialecticians, or School of Names (*Mingjia*), posed linguistic, semantic, and philosophic problems, such as "What does one mean by a 'white horse'?" Since the Chinese did not naturally take to abstract reasoning, the school was not popular. More important were the Naturalists, a school of cosmology, who explained nature in terms of such popular notions as the dualism of *yang* and *yin* as rhythms in life and nature; *fengshui*; the ten celestial stems and twelve terrestrial branches in the calendar; and the five powers or elements: wood, metal, fire, water, and earth. Their populist beliefs were incorporated into later Confucian thought.

The school of philosophy with the most immediate impact was the Legalists (*Fajia*), for their ideas were subscribed to by the rulers of Qin, who overthrew the Zhou and established the first unified Chinese empire. Three chief ministers were associated with the Legalist tenets. Wei Yang, also called Shang Yang or Gong-sum Yang, died in 330 B.C. The *Book of Lord Shang* (*Shang Zi*) is falsely attributed to him, but it contains his basic policies. Wei Yang helped to reorganize the state of Qin by replacing its political decentralization with a strong prince governing through a bureaucracy. He denied that the traditional Confucian values of righteousness, propriety, and humanity were effective political ideas and instead advocated force to compel obedience and loyalty. To make the state economically self-supporting, he discouraged foreign trade, and he replaced the so-called well-field system of landholding with peasant proprietorship. He promulgated severe laws and punishments and organized families in groups, the better to control them.

A second Legalist, Han Fei, who died in 233 B.C., left a collection of writings under his name. He was influenced by the view of his Confucian master Xunzi that man was unethical, but improvable. He rejected the ethical basis for politics in favor of a government of laws as interpreted by leaders of men. He was forced to commit suicide by the opposition of the third chief Legalist philosopher and statesman, Li Si (Li Ssu), who was an adviser to the first Qin emperor.

Legalism drew from other schools, but its central emphasis on political authoritarianism was its own. The prince was permitted to follow any tactics that gained and maintained power. The prince knew everything, the people knew nothing; they had merely to do as they were told. Not surprisingly, such a totalitarian rule created laws with wide-ranging rewards and stiff punishments. Authoritarianism had always been present to some degree in Chinese thought, but the Legalists carried it to this extreme.

This variety of philosophies and abundance of literature, which luxuriated in times of political disunity and flexibility, comprised the main heritage of the Zhou dynasty, in its latter half, to Chinese history. Some notable accomplishments were achieved in art, society, and economics, and despite the turmoil, Chinese culture continued to flow out into North and Central Asia. With it, spread the Middle Kingdom (*Zhongguo*) concept, the sense of Chinese uniqueness and superiority over the surrounding cultural and racial barbarians. From this time, the ancient ethnocentric attitude of "we" as against "they," given definite imprint, has persisted into the twentieth century.

Zhou Classical Literature:
A Basic Schemata

Five Classics (*Wujing*), as defined in Han dynasty:
   Classic of Songs or *Book of Poetry* (*Shijing*)
   Classic of Changes or *Book of Divination* (*Yijing*)
   Classic of Rites or *Book of Rituals* (*Liji*)
   Classic of Documents or *Book of History* (*Shujing*)
   Spring and Autumn Annals (*Chunqiu*)
Four Books (*Sishu*), as defined in Song dynasty:
   Two sections from the *Classic of Rites*:
      Great Learning (*Daxue*) and
      Doctrine of the Mean (*Zhongyong*)
   Analects (*Lunyu*)
   Mengzi
Other works:
   Bamboo Annals (*Zhushuqinian*)
   Ceremonies and Rituals (*Yili*)
   Classic of Filial Piety (*Xiaojing*)
   Discourses of the States (*Guoyu*)
   Erya
   Intrigues of the Warring States (*Zhanguoze*)
   Rituals of Zhou (*Zhouli*) earlier known as *Officials of Zhou* (*Zhouguan*)
   Tradition of Ku-liang (*Guliangzhuan*)
   Tradition of Kung-yang (*Gongyangzhuan*)
   Tradition of Tso or *Tso Commentary* (*Zhozhuan*)

Chief Zhou Schools of Philosophy:
A Basic Schemata

Confucianism:
   Kongfuzi (Confucius), 551-479 B.C.; *Analects* (*Lunyu*)
   Mengzi (Mencius), 372-289 B.C.; book by the same name
   Xunzi (Hsün-tzu), 300-237 B.C.; book by the same name
Daoism:
   Laozi (Lao Tzu), 6th century B.C.?; *Classic of Way and Power* (*Daode jing*)

Zhuangzi (Chuang Tzu), 369-286 B.C.; book by the same name

Liezi (Lieh-tzu, dates?); book by the same name

Legalists (*Fajia*)

Wei Yang (or Shang Yang or Gong-sum Yang), d. 330 B.C.; *Book of Lord Shang* (*Shang Zi*)

Han Fei (Han-fei-tzu), d. 233 B.C.

Li Si (Li Ssu), d. 208 B.C.

Other schools:

Mozi (Mo-tzu), 470-391; and Mohist school

Yangzhu (Yang chu), 4th century B.C.; individualist

Dialecticians or School of Names (*Mingjia*)

Naturalists or Yin–yang School (*Yinyangjia*)

Chronology

B. C.

1122 or 1027-221	Zhou dynasty
1122 or 1027-771	Earlier or Western Zhou
841	Earliest authenticated date in Chinese history
771	Move from Hao to Luoyi
771-221	Later or Eastern Zhou
722-481	Spring and Autumn period
6th century	Daoist founder Laozi (of questionable historicity)
551-472	Confucius (Kongfuzi)
ca. 500	Iron Age begins in China
480-221	Warring States period
470-391	Philosopher Mozi
4th century	Philosopher Yangzhu
372-289	Confucian philosopher Mengzi
369-286	Daoist philosopher Zhuangzi
330	Death of Legalist philosopher Wei Yang
300-237	Confucian philosopher Xunzi
3rd century	Poet Qu Yuan
233	Death of Legalist statesman Han Fei
208	Death of Legalist statesman Li Si

Chinese Sovereigns: The Zhou Dynasty
(Dates of rule may vary into the ninth century B.C.)

Western Zhou dynasty:
   Wu, 1122-1116 B.C.
   Cheng, 1115-1079
   Kang, 1078-1053
   Zhao, 1052-1002
   Mu, 1001-947
   Gung, 946-935
   Yi, 934-910
   Xiao, 909-895
   Yi, 894-879
   Li, 878-842
   Gung Ho, 841-828
   Xuan, 827-782
   Yu, 781-771
Eastern Zhou dynasty:
   Ping, 770-720
   Huan, 719-697
   Zhuang, 696-682
   Xi, 681-677
   Hui, 676-652
   Xiang, 651-619
   Ching, 618-613
   Kuang, 612-607
   Ding, 606-586
   Jian, 585-572
   Ling, 571-545
   Jing, 544-520
   Jing (another character), 519-476
   Yuan, 475-469
   Zheng Ding, 468-441
   Kao, 440-426
   Wei Lie, 425-402
   An, 401-376

Lie, 375-369
Xien, 368-321
Shen Jing, 320-315
Nan, 314-256
Under Qin control:
Zhao Xiang, 255-251
Xiao Wen, 250
Zhuang Xiang, 249-247
Shi Huangdi, 246-211

Part Three

IMPERIAL CHINA

First Phase—221 B.C. to A.D. 589

In 221 B.C., China's first political revolution established the Chinese empire, one that lasted more than twenty-one centuries. The first phase of the long imperial period involved a four-century rise and decline of two dynasties as well as an almost equal span of political division. Though short-lived, the first, the Qin dynasty, 221–206 B.C., founded the imperial structure. It was followed by the Han, 206 B.C.–A.D. 220, a long dynasty of two subperiods, earlier and later, separated briefly by an interregnum of non-Han rule, A.D. 8-23. The Han consolidated gains, gave lasting imprint to the imperial foundations, and expanded Chinese rule into Eastern and Central Asia. Intellectual and artistic creativity flourished. Because of the many dynastic achievements, the Chinese proudly, and justifiably, call themselves the Han race. The great empire then dissolved into an extended period of political divisiveness, during which no one ruler of the several dozen petty kingdoms had the power to reunite the country until 589. But technological achievements continued and Buddhism entered the country to contribute richness and variety to cultural life.

149

11

QIN AND HAN DYNASTIES

(221 B.C. to A.D. 220)

The Qin Dynasty (221 to 206 B.C.)

Although the brief Qin dynasty essentially consisted of rule by one man, it had lasting significance. Its founding monarch established the empire according to authoritarian ideas of the Legalist school formulated during earlier generations. Many of the Qin imperial ideas and programs had already been adopted before 221 B.C. by earlier kings and by some of the neighboring feudatories. Within the broader context of the Asian setting the Qin imperial experiment was, however, not unique. Three centuries earlier, Darius had fashioned a great empire in Persia; around 300 B.C., in North India, the Maurya had established a similarly centralized empire.

The Qin state was mentioned in Chinese annals as early as 714 B.C. Its capital, which has been excavated by the Chinese Communists, was Xianyang in Shaanxi province near the Earlier Zhou capital. In this favored location, the Qin faced both nomadic and Chinese cultures. The rulers controlled the northwestern defenses and with a mobile cavalry, repelled repeated intrusions. Its location on the Wei River, a tributary of the Yellow River, enabled its rulers to develop and manage water supplies and irrigation projects. In slow but sure expansion, the Qin conquered a coalition of northern Zhou states. In 318 B.C., it vanquished the Sichuan area and its rich Red Basin, where it inaugurated irrigation projects that have alleviated droughts and floods to this day. In 256 B.C., it defeated the Zhou regime at Luoyi. By 221 B.C. it had conquered all of China as it then existed. In the preimperial phase, strong Legalist ministers advanced effective authoritarian rule, especially Wei Yang, who advised the feudatory monarchs from 360 to 338 B.C. The entire populace, he maintained, was to be productively employed and was subject to specific rewards and punishments for actions taken. An aristocracy based on military might strengthened security measures through mutual responsibility and a network of spies.

Parallel military and civilian bureaucracies at Xianyang controlled all state territory, with prefectures at the local level. To avoid competition and any possible threat to the throne through consolidation of regional power, political fifes were not hereditary. Similar doctrines were subsequently promulgated by the later advisers, Han Fei and Li Si. The latter was minister to Zheng, the young Qin king, at the time of the final Qin conquest of China. An ambitious man, Li Si sought strong measures of state, in the course of which he imprisoned friends and cut down enemies.

In 246 B.C., the young monarch ascended the throne at the age of twelve; nine years later he came into actual rule. A strong monarch, a strong advisor, and a strong philosophy commenced an epochal political cycle. Upon assuming the throne of all China at Xianyang, he took the imperial title of Shi Huangdi: Shi meant first and Huangdi was a celestial title (though a homonym, it was a different character and meaning from the *Huang* of the Yellow Emperor). The heaven-sent emperor meant to make a clean sweep of the old kingdoms, to set precedent and achieve prestige through the creation of a new imperial structure. The monarch had a complex personality that combined intellectual with superstitious activity. He daily read quantities of official documents written on bamboo or wooden slips. He kept close tab on affairs of state and he traveled widely. Yet he held primitive beliefs, and he feared death; he ceaselessly sought the elixirs of life. Often he went to Shandong, a region associated in Chinese lore not only with Confucius but also with mystics and magicians, to consult oracles.

As in the preimperial phase, Shi Huangdi's domestic programs, like the earlier systems, emphasized unification, standardization, and centralization. He erected at the capital a huge palace, some 2,500 feet in length east-west and 500 feet in width north-south, which housed 10,000 people. He was in constant fear of assassination, with good reason. At least three attempts were made on his life, so he constructed a network of secret tunnels throughout the palace. He also built numerous nearby subsidiary palaces; within a 60-mile radius of the capital there were over 250 other imperial edifices.

Under the big bureaucracy at the capital, China was divided first into thirty-six and then into forty-one military regions or commanderies (*jun*). A triad of top officials in each of these included a military governor, a civil administrator, and a supervisory bureaucrat. These administrative units were subdivided into counties (*xian*). After 238 B.C., no new fiefs were granted, and under these measures of political centralization, the feudal system in China began to break up. As in preimperial Qin rule, peasants owned land privately, but it was subject to taxation. Stringent controls held down the nobility. Gifts and services to the emperor, rather than birth, were the criteria for entry into the nobility, whose families, some 120,000 in number, were maintained at court, in effect as hostages.

Drastic domestic measures included the shifting about of whole populations according to labor needs and military necessity. The southern provinces began to fill up with involuntary immigrants. State monopolies were imposed on salt and iron. Currency was unified; weights and measures were standardized. Irrigation networks were expanded, and canals funneled grain taxes to the capital. Artificial waterways linking two tributaries in South China completed a continuous transport system between the Yangtze and West river systems. There was also an efficient network of roads, radiating out from the capital. Axles on carts were standardized, mainly to reduce ruts on the loess roads in northwestern China.

Going to great lengths to organize life and customs, the emperor formalized written Chinese into a basic script, which has persisted to this day. He instituted, upon Li Si's initiative, a program of thought control (whose stringency is questioned by some modern scholars since the information derives, essentially, from Confucian-inspired historians who disliked the monarch). He allegedly killed off intellectuals who opposed him; in 212 B.C., he executed 460 of them. The year before, in a campaign that involved the burning of books, he sought to eradicate all political and philosophic systems other than that of Legalism. The program was relatively easy to implement because the books of the time, before the invention of paper, consisted of unwieldy bamboo or wood and were difficult to hide. The proscription exempted only utilitarian or noncontroversial volumes on such subjects as medicine, divination, and agriculture, as well as the imperial archives and the Qin house history. This destruction, again recorded by historians of the Confucian persuasion, and who had the final say in historical interpretation, earned for the emperor and his minister unflattering roles in Chinese annals.

Qin Shi Huangdi defined and expanded China's frontiers by the use of large armies filled with recruited draftees. In the north, he held the line against invaders by consolidating the Great Wall, building new sections and connecting others, until the massive engineering marvel stretched 3,000 miles from the sea into Gansu province. (Portions were added until the sixteenth century; the wall in present form dates mainly from the Ming dynasty.) The main purpose of the wall was to help border patrols contain barbarian invaders at bay until local reinforcements could arrive. The wall never kept aggressive invaders out of

China, for it was continually breached. As noted earlier, its main value was psychological; as a cultural dividing line, it defined the area to its south as Chinese and to its north as barbarian.

The emperor also contained the western branch of the Xiongnu (Huns), perennial invaders of China. He temporarily subdued them, but they later returned in strong and mobile confederations. In another direction, to the south, Chinese expansion was notable. From that source, geographic barriers were weaker and no strong indigenous tribes blocked emigration and imperial campaigns. By 214 B.C., his troops had penetrated northern and central Vietnamese valleys and coasts as far as present-day Hué to inaugurate over two millennia of vital Chinese interest in, and concern over, what transpired in the territory of that southern neighbor. For the first time, foreign conquests and expansion rounded out the map of China proper approximately to its existing borders today.

Qin Shi Huangdi believed that his empire would last for ten thousand generations. His own dynasty continued for only a few more years, but his imperial structure remained for 2,133 years more, until 1912. In 210 B.C., the emperor died while on a trip away from the capital. To avoid political turmoil and revolt, Li Si returned the body in a sealed carriage to Xianyang, where it was later buried under a great pyramidal mound in the Wei valley. (In 1974, to the east was discovered the terracotta army that was to protect the emperor from his enemies in the afterlife.) The minister, along with the connivance of Zhao Gao, a court eunuch, changed the wording of the emperor's will that had designated Fusu, the elder son, as successor, in favor of a younger and weaker son, Hu Hai. Upon returning from a western campaign and learning of the change in succession, which he believed to be his father's wishes, the original heir committed suicide. After three years of rule, the second monarch (called Er Shi) was killed by his sponsor Li Si, who, in the ensuing fight among contenders for the throne, was also put to death. Zhao Gao met a similar fate.

The Qin came to a sudden end. In its dependence mainly on the founder's policies and autocratic person for success, the dynasty lacked any ongoing political basis and personalities to sustain power through immediate successors. Shi Huangdi had introduced into China too many ideas too suddenly on too grand a scale. His many severe measures alienated the nobles and people alike. On the other hand, by capitalizing on the developing ethocentricity of the Chinese, Shi Huangdi pinpointed Zhongguo as China territorially south of the Great Wall. Despite drastic measures, this put into effective practice the notion of Chinese cultural unity under a hierarchical, bureaucratic, centralized, government responsible for law and order. He initiated the longest lasting political institution known to history. In terms of duration, the short-range dynasty failed; in terms of significance, the legacy persisted. It is no accident that the western name for China derives from Qin.

The Western Han Dynasty (206 B.C. to 8 A.D.)

In the course of the political confusion that arose at the end of the Qin, several factions contended for successorship. These included the remaining troops of the Qin and the army of the state of Chu in the Yangtze River valley under Xiang Yu, a professional general. His colleague, Liu Bang, was a peasant who came up through the ranks and established himself as ruler of the Han River area in 206 B.C. Subduing his rivals and his former associate, Liu Bang, after another four years of fighting, received the mandate of heaven and established the Han dynasty in 202 B.C. With only a brief interregnum, the Han, contemporaneous with the rise and spread of the Roman Empire, held China together for most of four centuries, an unusual duration for a dynasty. The period was divided, as the Zhou had been, into the Earlier or Western Han, 206 B.C.-A.D. 9, and a Later or Eastern Han, A.D. 25-220. The interregnum between these two periods was the Xin (New) dynasty of Wang Mang, considered a usurper by traditional Chinese historians since he was not a member of the imperial family.

Han emperors were pragmatic and shrewd. Although they decreed Confucianism as the state doctrine, they tolerated a diversity of philosophic opinions. The people gave their support to the rulers. Institutions that commenced under the Zhou and the Qin reached their fruition during the Han to establish the political and cultural bases of China: a modified form of Confucianism, an emperor ruling by virtuous example, and the beginning of the principle of a merit bureaucracy recruited through examinations. The sources of information on the Han include voluminous works of history and literature that have been handed down in copied form, as well as of archaeological finds in tombs, located not only in China proper, but in border areas, where the dry desert air preserved artifacts in pristine form.

The founder of the Han dynasty was of humble origins. A former village official from eastern China, Liu Bang turned bandit before joining the forces of Chu. In a rags-to-riches story, he first proclaimed himself the king of Han in 206 B.C., an area between the Yangtze and Yellow rivers. After four more years of civil strife, he then defeated Xiang Yu, his former colleague and later principal rival, vanquished other contenders from other states, and then, acclaimed by his troops, set himself up as emperor of China in 202 B.C. (an alternative date to commence the Earlier Han period). He located his capital at Chang'an (Eternal Peace), near modern Xi'an, by now a traditional site for Chinese political centers. The dynasty took its name after the upper valley of the Han River, which had been Liu Bang's home territory during his tour of duty in the Chu military forces. He adopted the Qin system of centralized imperial government, but unlike the Zhou kings or Qin emperors with their aristocrats and nobles, he surrounded himself with rough and ready men. In his search for capable men, he slowly replaced Legalists with Confucianists to act as bureaucrats and tutors to the heir. Historians bestowed on him the posthumous or temple name of Gaodi or Gaozu (High Progenitor), a practice that began at this time and continued into the Mongol dynasty.

In what appeared to be a strategic retreat, the Gaozu emperor temporarily reinstituted the system of vassalage, a step necessitated in part to reward his supporters by investing them with vast tracts of land. He conferred authority in the local lords to accept taxes and to protect estates. But as the emperor, in time, grew stronger and consolidated his position, he abolished some of the lesser feudatories. His successors continued to whittle away at the power of the remaining nobles, until by 154 B.C., the several hundred estates had been reduced to some 20 small ones. Territory was taken away if the lord offended the emperor in any way, and fiefs were further weakened by the practice of the eldest son sharing the father's estate with all the younger brothers.

The emperor also faced the continued menace of the Xiongnu in the north and west. The nomadic Huns had originated in Mongolia during the Zhou, whose annals mentioned them as early as the fifth century B.C. The periodical failures of limited food supplies in their homeland made them restless and aggressive. The magnetic attraction of a rich and fertile agricultural China, combined with temporary but strong Hun federations and leadership, helped to make for unsettling political conditions along the nothern Chinese border. When Liu Bang ascended the throne, the state of affairs favored the Xiongnu. In one campaign, they captured the Son of Heaven himself, who had to buy his way free through the marriage of a princess of the imperial family to a Hun chieftain. After this humiliation of the Chinese, the Huns remained in and around the capital for many years. Other tribes in Manchuria and western China, such as the Yuezhi (Yüeh-chih), whose language was derived from the Indo-European linguistic group, also became aggressive. The political interaction and military confrontations along the northern and northwestern borders between Chinese and barbarian lands, with one or the other party the more forceful, recurred again and again through Chinese history.

In 195 B.C., Liu Bang died, and the family of his consort, the Empress Lu, took charge. Chinese emperors, although having only one legal wife, as empress in title, were polygamous, and when a son was designated heir apparent, his mother, if not already on the throne, was recognized as de facto empress. (All children of imperial wives were considered legitimate.) Upon accession of the son to power, the mother, in the role of empress dowager, became dominant in court affairs. After Liu Bang's death, and with the succession of two children to the throne, the Empress Lu became, in effect, China's ruler for seven years. She presided with a firm hand and appointed family members and favorites to top positions in an effort to create a new dynasty. After her death, her relatives were massacred by those loyal to the Han founding family of Liu. Yet despite succession struggles at the capital during the early Han period, peace and prosperity reigned in the empire. The Han reduced forced labor and taxes, eased punishments, and in general, lessened the severity of Qin Legalistic measures.

Half a century after Empress Lu's death, the Western Han reached its apogee of political power in the reign of Han Wudi (the posthumous title meaning Martial Emperor), 141-87 B.C. The outburst of energy during his rule of fifty-four years, the longest of a native Chinese emperor, stimulated in China one of the country's several historic peaks of political and cultural grandeur. This delayed dynastic climax, a century after its founding, was one variant of the dynastic cycle: an able founder was followed by a generation or two of relatively mediocre rule, until a greater monarch gave the line a later revival of power. Han Wudi believed in firm and highly centralized government. As the embodiment of the virtues of a strong emperor, he reinvigorated and performed the imperial rituals of the sacrifice to heaven (*feng*) and prayers to earth (*di*). He also worshiped the gods of the four cardinal directions and the central one, the omniscient deity *Tai Yi*. The imperial identification with the spiritual structure of the universe as well as with the political system on earth reinforced the all-encompassing importance of the throne. It was in his reign that the practice commenced of using several reign titles in lifetime periods to indicate calendrical time or descriptive designation in a lifetime (in his case, eleven of them).

The eighteen grades of the bureaucracy, concentrated at the capital of Chang'an, serviced the emperor. The examination system was inaugurated for appointing some officials from the ranks of the wealthy and the educated. China was redivided into more than a hundred provinces, in turn subdivided into counties. The traditional distinction was maintained between the rulers and the ruled, but the governing class consisted now of appointed officials rather than hereditary aristocrats.

By 100 B.C., the bureaucracy numbered some 130,285 persons, controlling a population of about 60 million people. Such a low ratio of officials to people, in this instance of 1 to 400 or 500, was typical also of later empires. What kept society in bounds was not so much a heavy layer of officialdom but the webs of accepted, unstated social obligations and relationships. Having little direct contact with the people, the bureaucrats were interested in the masses only as taxpayers. At the top, around the emperor, swirled the court; at the bottom rung of society, perhaps one percent of the population, were serfs, criminals, and slaves.

Strong economic measures, directed more toward filling state coffers than toward ameliorating public welfare, supported Han Wudi's ambitious domestic programs and foreign campaigns. Because the Legalist practice had lapsed during the early prosperous days of the Han, the emperor reinstituted state monopolies or licensing systems for the sale and production of commodities, such as the minting of copper coins or cash. In 119 B.C., the emperor reintroduced monopolies on salt, iron, and liquor. In 110 B.C., he established the leveling system, which provided for granaries to store surplus produce bought in times and in regions of plenty in order to sell it in times and in areas of food deficiency. Price stabilization was a motive, but the main purpose was to ensure guaranteed profits for the treasury. As in later times, the stabilizing granaries proved to be controversial, and bureaucratic debates raged over their utility. The government imposed taxes on commerce, ships, carts, artisans, and merchants. Fines replaced punishments, and the sale of ranks, which contradicted the merit system, was countenanced. The currency was debased, and worthless script, such as deerskin certificates, were issued to nobles, who were forced to buy them for as much as 400,000 coins apiece. The measure contributed to the subordination of the nobility.

Han Wudi embarked on a series of campaigns of defense against the Xiongnu and of territorial expansion. It was expensive, but the prestige he won was high. The emperor continued the Qin probings to the south by waging military campaigns in South China and northern Vietnam. As a result of his conquest in 111 B.C., northern Vietnam was incorporated into Chinese territory for over a thousand years. To outflank the Huns from the east, the emperor dispatched troops simultaneously into southern Manchuria and northern Korea. In 108 B.C., these areas were likewise assimilated into the Chinese empire as Chaoxian and divided into four provinces. Han power there centered at Lolang (now Pyongyang), which had a population of over 300,000 and which remained a Chinese outpost until A.D. 313. Transformed into an early center for sinic culture, Korea in turn exported Chinese ideas to Japan from the turn of the fifth century A.D.

To stop the rising Xiongnu in the north and west, Han Wudi also extended the Great Wall westward into the desert to Yumen in the Gansu corridor and transplanted about 700,000 colonists into that corridor. With troops, cavalry, infantry, and supply forces numbering between 50,000 and 100,000, the emperor fought the Huns in immense campaigns. By 127 B.C., after a great loss of life, the Chinese drove the Huns out of the Ordos back across the Gobi. A period of uneasy coexistence resulted between the opposing forces. Opportunistic officers of mixed origins in the Chinese border armies took first one side and then the other. By the mid-first century A.D., the Xiongnu had declined in power, but other barbarian groups rose to plague the Chinese.

The emperor also employed diplomatic strategy against border tribes. In 119 B.C., he dispatched Zhang Qian (Chang Ch'ien) a remarkable soldier-statesman, to Central Asia to make an alliance with the Yuezhi, whom the Xiongnu had pushed out of Gansu into Central Asia. By this time, however, the Yuezhi were relocated in what is now Russian Central Asia and safe from their traditional enemy; they were not interested in fighting the Xiongnu. Unsuccessful in attaining his objective, Zhang Qian was nonetheless gone for twelve years, ten of them spent in captivity with the Huns, one of whose women he married. Upon his release, he returned to report a wealth of information on conditions in Central Asia. His second mission in 115 B.C. to the Ili valley also proved diplomatically unsuccessful, but it broadened Chinese interest in the area, including the "heavenly" horses so remarkable in warfare and mobility. Under Han Wudi, Chinese probings into Turkestan reached their farthest limits between 104 and 102 B.C. Subsequently, in 42 B.C., the Chinese pressed on into Central Asia, where they fought the Xiongnu and possibly met the Romans. By that time, at the end of the first burst of Chinese imperial expansion, the men of Han had advanced some 2,000 miles from their capital city, much farther than the Romans had ever ventured from theirs.

In their relations with surrounding tribes, the early Han emperors proved to be pragmatic. They allied with one barbarian group to defeat another. Where feasible, they practiced divide-and-rule tactics. They fought the enemy, married into their ranks, or bought them off. They did not rely solely on their walls, and the founder of the dynasty, as noted above, was once himself captured by the enemy. The Chinese successfully contained the foreign threats, but after Han Wudi there were no emperors of note. Chinese fortunes contracted, and within a century a usurper replaced briefly the line.

Interregnum:
The Xin Dynasty (A.D. 9 to 23)

After serving as regent for two young emperors, Wang Mang, not of the Liu family, took over the throne from A.D. 9 to 23 and established the one-man dynasty, the Xin (new). The traditional Chinese interpretation of this act was that as a member of a new family he had unlawfully occupied the throne and so earned the condemnation of later historians. His foreign policies were not outstanding, and his internal ones were recorded unfavorably. He came to power with a program of reviving Confucian doctrines and sought support from the Confucian bureaucrats, but he merely donned a Confucian cloak. Once in power, he revived the Legalist tradition of strong authoritarian rule. He strengthened the bureaucracy, created more monopolies, reinstituted the ever-normal granaries, and extended agricultural loans to peasants. He debased currency by introducing coins of different denominations and stipulated that gold be exchanged for bronze and copper coins. Termed China's first socialist, Wang Mang nationalized the land. In A.D. 9, he decreed the end of the great private tax-free estates that had grown up over the previous century, and he parceled out land among tax-paying peasants and abolished slavery. But because both land and antislavery policies were too drastic and could not be enforced, they were retracted within a few years.

The vigorous imperial reforms cost Wang Mang the support of the bureaucracy and the rich families. Toward the end of the one-man dynasty, indications of decline became obvious. Bad harvests plagued the countryside and omens foreshadowed a dire future. The Yellow River changed its course and wrought hardships in the North China plain. Frontier defenses crumbled, border states reasserted themselves, and the unruly Xiongnu invaded the capital. In indirect criticism of the monarch, officials began to report natural disasters and rebellions. One serious peasant uprising broke out in A.D. 18 in Shandong and was led by the Red Eyebrows, so-called because of that distinguishing feature. Their Daoist tendencies supported the cause with religious connotations. Similar to later major agrarian uprisings that combined economic and religious factors, the Red Eyebrows were the first major Chinese socio-economic and religious group to seize the standard of widespread rebellion. But they lacked the administrative experience and the know-how to replace the government they wished to destroy. It was left to the bureaucrats, the established order, to reinstitute efficient government. In A.D. 23, engulfed by political confusion and problems, Wang Mang was killed by rebels.

The Eastern Han Dynasty (A.D. 23 to 220)

After two years of civil strife, Liu Xiu (Liu Hsiu), related to the former ruling house and cousin of that last emperor, emerged victorious. Reconsolidation proceeded under the Later or Eastern Han. During his rule, A.D. 25-57, Liu Xiu relocated and rebuilt the capital at Luoyang, the former center (Luoyi) of Eastern Zhou power. His restoration stood in Chinese histories as the model of a strong, centralized government reestablished after a period of great rebellion. But because, in this instance, a new family did not found another dynasty and the Liu family simply came back into power, the Han restoration was unique.

Liu Xiu, known by his posthumous title of Guangwudi (Shining Martial Emperor), suppressed domestic revolts and repelled unruly border peoples. He reemphasized the role of scholars and favored Confucianism as the state doctrine. He restored the territorial boundaries to those of the Earlier or Western Han. Northern Vietnam, which formerly had been incorporated as three prefectures of a larger province in South China, was now carved into a separate provincial entity. Contact was made with Japan. In A.D. 57, the first Chinese record on missions from Japan noted that an envoy from there was received by the Chinese emperor at Luoyang and from him was given a gold seal (the like of which was discovered in 1789 on the southern Japanese island of Kyushu), with an inscription that seemed to read "King of Nu of Wa [Vassal of] Han." At that time, in the first century A.D., Japan was a political aggregate of a hundred tribes or primitive states, of which Nu was probably one. The Chinese, with a superior attitude toward things Japanese (as to most things foreign), called the country and people Wa, a pejorative character for dwarf.

Mingdi (Enlightened Emperor), the second monarch of the eastern Han, ruled from A.D. 57 to 75. Under him, Central Asia and the northern barbarians were reconquered essentially by the exploits of one man, Ban Chao (Pan Ch'ao). At this time the Xiongnu forces were, fortunately for the Chinese, in disarray and they surrendered readily. Local politics and local armies helped Ban Chao's cause, and by A.D. 91, after Mingdi's death, the Tarim Basin in Xinjiang was again in Chinese hands. A new emperor conferred on Ban Chao the title of Protector of the Western Regions (*Du Hu*) with headquarters at Qiuzi (Kucha) roughly midway on the northern route around the Taklamakhan desert in the Tarim Basin. By the end of this second period of imperial expansion under the Han, the Chinese had conquered areas as far west as the Caspian Sea. Only Parthia, located in the area of present-day Iran, lay between the westernmost domains of China and Rome. Ban Chao sent a scout to explore a farther route to Dachin, the Chinese designation for the Roman Empire, but the emissary returned after having reached Mesopotamia by the Persian Gulf. After Ban Chao's death in A.D. 102, Chinese power declined in Central Asia.

During the expansive Han dynasty, China was not isolated. Various land trade routes led to countries in the west and south. The most commonly used ones, the silk routes that started at Chang'an or Luoyang, proceeded west to Xinjiang and the Tarim Basin. The western deserts were then skirted by oasis-hopping along the northern or southern fringes. The routes reunited at the far western edge of the basin and continued into Central Asia, or turned south through the Pamir mountain passes into India. A secondary trade route from southwest China crossed the jungles and mountains into Burma and India. A sea route out of central and southern Chinese ports, principally Guangzhou, wove its course along the coast to Southeast Asia, then around the Malayan peninsula into Malacca Strait, and onto India and the Near East.

Via this maritime route, Chinese annals noted in A.D. 12, jugglers from Dachin disembarked in China. In A.D. 132, the king of Java sent tribute, and in A.D. 166 an emissary claiming to have come from Marcus Aurelius, emperor of Rome, arrived at the Chinese capital. International trade by sea or land consisted mainly of luxury items. The Chinese imported precious stones, ivory, wool, linen, glass, and horses. Chinese goods, mainly silk, were desired abroad more than foreign goods were valued in China, not because of any particular prejudice on the part of the Chinese, but because of the greater wealth and availability of domestic goods. This imbalance of trade was to persist into the nineteenth century.

For a century and a half after Mingdi, no emperors of note sat on the Han throne. Despite the lack of strong emperors, the dynasty carried on, although economic and political crises intensified in its final decades. Offices were put up for sale, and families and bureaucrats close to the throne became increasingly influential. Large landholders, including the imperial family, took their land off the tax rolls; the growth of these tax-free estates, a clear and present danger to the Chinese economic structure, presaged troubled times. Many peasants fled south to escape increasing tax burdens. At the time, no one fully realized that part of the economic problem was the fact that the population was growing and that land was filling up. An Earlier Han census of A.D. 2 established China's population as 59.6 million, whereas one in A.D. 105 listed 53.2 million. The decrease should probably be attributed not to a population decline, but to less vigorous government supervision of the tax registers.

Popular rebellions and military insurrections helped to terminate

Han rule. Between 184 and 196, the Daoist-inspired Yellow Turbans, centered in Shandong, plagued the countryside. Their name derived from the yellow bands of cloth they wore in revolt. The rebels believed in superstitious reasoning that yellow, symbolizing the earth, was able to conquer the royal red, the color of fire, which characterized the Han throne. Sichuan province was disrupted by another Daoist group, the Five Pecks of Rice band, whose members paid that quantity of the grain in dues to their leaders. The disparate rebel groups were eventually pacified by Han generals or by warlords operating independently in various regions of China, who themselves became threats to the throne. One general sacked Luoyang itself, destroying valuable records and looting royal tombs.

In the chaos at the end of the Han era, three generals predominated. They founded three states contending for the mandate of heaven: Wei centered at Luoyang, Shu Han at Chengdu in Sichuan, and Wu at present-day Nanjing. None of the three had the ability to reunite China immediately. Instead of the expected political reunion of the country that usually followed the disintegration of a dynasty, China remained divided for over three and a half centuries. After the long combined period of Qin and Han centralized rule, China had become administratively and politically fragmented once again. The Chinese empire seemed to be falling apart as the Roman was to do, never to be reunited.

Han Society

One of the most distinguishing features of Han times was the triumph of Confucianism, after a slow process of growth and modification, as the state political philosophy. What emerged at the end of the Han was an eclectic Confucianism, a philosophical syncretism that differed in some ways from the tenets postulated by the founding fathers in the Later Zhou dynasty. Borrowing appreciably from the Legalists, Han Confucianism stressed efficient authoritarian administration. To appeal to the uneducated masses, it appropriated from Daoism and particularly from the Naturalist school of the Zhou, the popular ideas of *yang* and *yin*, the five elements, concern with signs, portents, unusual natural phenomena, various types of magic, and the search for long life and physical immortality. Some early Confucianists, such as Gungsun Hung and Dung Zhongshu, rose to fame mainly on their manipulation of magical qualities and pseudo-scientific practices.

Intellectual Confucian activity complemented the popular basis and appeals. Scholars recovered the old classics and as many of the earlier writings as possible. In their zealous search for documenting sources, they exercised little philosophic or historical perspective, and they accepted most writings as valid. As they discovered or recreated the ancient texts, they added commentaries and exegeses that were passed onto later scholars. Out of the mass of the previously unorganized literature, Han bureaucrats defined the Five Classics. Official scholarship also spread into lexicography; in the third century B.C., and around A.D. 100, dictionaries were compiled. One of the latter, the *Explanation of Writing* (*Shouwen*), gave pronunciations and 540 radicals arranged over 9,000 characters, some of which, from the Wu area, were polysyllabic. About this time, the first national bibliography listed some 700 works written on wooden tablets and on silk. A 960-volume code of law ran over seven and a half million words.

Confucian scholars received their initial impetus from the Gaozu emperor, who used them in official positions and as tutors to his heir. In 124 B.C. Han Wudi founded an imperial university along Confucianist lines. By 50 B.C., it had 3,000 students and grew in numbers to 50,000 in the Eastern Han era. Confucianist education at government expense attracted a large proportion of the lower bureaucracy. Periodic conferences of scholars determined true interpretations of ancient texts, the descendants of Confucius were honored, and in A.D. 175, the classics were carved on large stone tablets at Luoyang. In part, Confucianism won out by default because the competing doctrines were either too strict or too vague. Confucian ritual appealed to the sense of form and order, and the doctrines enhanced imperial prestige and the role of the educated man. To promote political unity, the emperors pursued cultural uniformity through that philosophy.

Although Confucianism emerged as the leading doctrine, Daoism was not quiescent. Some emperors in official as well as in private life venerated in ritual the Daoist saints. In the Eastern Han, Zhang Daoling, also called Zhang Ling, as the first "pope," was said to have built up an organized Daoist cult. His family successors, governing through a Daoist hierarchy, created in effect a separate state in southwest China that propagated and kept alive much of popular Daoist doctrine. Few philosophers of note emerged in other schools, and independent speculation seemed to fade away.

The Han found its highest intellectual expression in two of China's greatest individual historians, Sima Qian (Ssu-ma Ch'ien) and Ban Gu (Pan Ku). Although not incorporated into the classics, their works were studied, admired, and in part, memorized by generations of Chinese. From early times there had been an appreciation of the art of history, as indicated not only in the *Classic of History* but in the *Spring and Autumn Annals*, two works elevated to the status of classics. The Han historians carried on the tradition and like their anonymous predecessors, considered it the function of history to impart both factual information and moral instruction. The twin traditions of teaching and preaching have persisted into present-day Chinese historiography.

The first great Han historian, Sima Qian, 145?–90 B.C., lived in the Western Han era during Wudi's reign. He compiled the *Historical Records (Shiji)*, a general history of China from ancient times to his day, which had been initiated by his father, Sima Tan (Ssu-ma T'ian). His position as court historian and astrologer gave Sima Qian access to the imperial library. A man of prodigious knowledge and great imagination, he traveled widely throughout the country. In 99 B.C., he defended a general who was in disrepute, and the emperor had the historian castrated, a punishment common to the time. Retiring from court life, Sima Qian, the Chinese Herodotus or father of history, completed his work. The *Historical Records* set the pattern of content, style, and approach for most of the later Chinese histories. His book was written in a succinct prose style without benefit of punctuation and was an extended collation of passages and paraphrases from earlier works. He established a matter-of-fact approach that avoided the dramatic and the vivid and sought the most reliable sources. On questionable points he copied different accounts in parallel columns.

The history contained 110 chapters and 700,000 characters, which in the English language would be considerably longer because of the conciseness of Chinese characters used in classical context. The first dozen chapters of the *Historical Records* contained the basic biographies of the outstanding political personalities from the mythological emperors to Han Wudi. The next ten chapters were devoted mainly to chronological tables of the Zhou feudatories. The third section of eight essays described in topical rather than in chronological fashion such subjects as court ritual, elements of music, calendrical events, aspects of geography, and matters of economics. The ensuing thirty chapters presented more Han and Zhou biographies, including that of Confucius. The concluding seventy chapters, over half the book, arranged further biographies under such rubrics as intellectuals, assassins, and patriots. Accounts of colonies and foreign lands and peoples rounded out this final part of the work.

Within another two centuries, in the Eastern Han during Mingdi's reign, Ban Gu, A.D. 32-92, wrote the second great history with the assistance of other members of his family, a famous one in Chinese letters. His father, Ban Biao (Pan Piao), began the project, and his sister Ban Zhao (Pan Chao), China's first distinguished woman scholar, completed it. His brother Ban Chao was the famous diplomat and explorer. Carrying on where Sima Qian had left off and following his predecessor's pattern, Ban Gu blocked out the *History of the Earlier Han* (*Han Shu*), but he dropped pre-Han sections because he was not concerned with earlier dynasties. His additional essays on law, geomancy, geography, literature, and economic affairs formed a basic source of Han life and culture. The *History of the Earlier Han* evolved into the model for later dynastic histories of China, which concentrated on one period or a subperiod of a particular dynasty.

Early Han literature other than classics and official works exists in fragments of wood manuscripts. One work of seventy-seven strips bound with the original thongs was discovered in a Central Asian outpost. Poetry was composed. The most notable type of the medium was free verse in long lines of irregular meter and rhyme (*fu*). Poems described in rich imagery and great exuberance the capitals and main cities of China, life at the court, imperial activities, and lovely landscapes. They romanticized the themes of love of life and pursuit of pleasure.

The Han took great strides in inventive and technological science. The Chinese first recorded sunspots in 28 B.C. (In Europe Galileo did not discover them until 1613.) They calculated a nine-year elliptical orbit of the moon around the earth (close enough to the actual 8.85 years). An early form of seismograph recorded earthquakes; by 132 B.C., its inventor, also an astronomer, had enumerated 11,520 different stars. The Chinese had sundials and water clocks, divided into 100 or 120 equal parts. They continued to note solar and lunar eclipses. They adopted the official lunar calendar that lasted until 1927, in which the four seasons commenced in the first, fourth, seventh, and tenth moons, the equinoxes noted in the second and eighth, and solstices in the fifth and eleventh. The Eastern Han developed the water-powered mill. As depicted in bas-reliefs in tombs, the horses wore shoulder collars, which increased their efficiency as draft animals (a similar collar was not used in the West for another ten centuries). The Chinese experimented with problem-resistant rice strains, practiced crop rotation, and terraced slopes to grow fruits, vegetables, and bamboo. They developed a technique of iron casting. In A.D. 16, the Chinese recorded a medical dissection, and they described the various uses of valuable herbs. In the first part of the third century A.D., a Daoist prepared a medical manual on the manufacture of drugs, and about the same time, a Chinese translated a Buddhist text that listed 404 diseases.

In an epochal advance, the Western Han developed paper from rags, fibers, or the bark of trees to replace the bulky and unwieldy wooden and bamboo slips. Pure paper, manufactured around A.D. 100, has been discovered in Han outposts in dry Central Asian deserts. As an early form of printing, the classics, engraved on stone, were reproduced on paper by rubbing techniques with ink. Because of natural disasters and civil strife, however, only fragments of the many Han books remain.

The various arts flourished. The Chinese played a variety of musical instruments, including a four-stringed plucked lute (*piba*) that derived from Central Asia and a zither of thirteen strings (*zheng*). Fine pottery glazes were developed and early porcelains fashioned. In tombs, clay figures of people, houses, and household items have been found. Architectural remains are nil, but from literary and pictorial sources, as well as from ground excavations, grandiose palaces, built in the traditional platform, column and beam pattern, can be reconstructed (as have the five adjacent imperial residences of the Western Han emperors in their capital of Chang'an). A few segments of crumbling walls of military outposts in Central Asia attest to the former glory of the dynasty as well as some tombs in North China and Korea that contained funerary objects and artifacts, including jade burial garments of a royal couple.

During the Han, a class of professional painters arose, although not much remains of their work. In bas-reliefs and paintings on tomb walls, on lacquer, on shells, and on tiles are depicted mythological figures, historical incidents, and scenes of daily life. Animal designs in silhouette, a Central Asian importation, were sketched. Artisans wrought bronze mirrors and lacquer work, including cosmetic boxes that have been discovered as far afield as the province of Sichuan. The culinary art gained oranges and nuts, and Zhang Qian brought back alfalfa and grapes from his trips. The Chinese enjoyed falconry, adapted from northern nomads. Other pastimes included archery, juggling, walking on stilts, puppetry, and dancing. Football as a sport was developed for the physical training of soldiers.

The long Han dynasty was a creative one. The Qin laid the imperial foundations, but the Han erected on it an enduring political superstructure with Confucian bureaucrats servicing the royal government. Over the four centuries of Han role, the Chinese achieved political and cultural unity, although at the price of philosophic conformity and orthodoxy. The Chinese way of life radiated into the corners of China proper and peripheral areas. Northern Korea, southern Manchuria, northern Vietnam, and the oases along the silk routes into Central Asia adopted Chinese cultural patterns through force or tactical volition. Official scholarship abounded, as evidenced in the first great individual works of history; inventive technical genius shone; and many arts were developed. The Han fashioned China's first great empire; the Chinese have honored it by identifying themselves with the dynasty.

Chronology

57	First Japanese mission to China
57-75	Rule of Mingdi
102	Death of explorer-diplomat Ban Chao
Late dynasty	Rebellions by Yellow Turbans (184-196); Five Pecks of Rice band
220	Han empire splits up into Three Kingdoms: Wei, Shu Han, and Wu

Chinese Sovereigns:
The Qin and Han Dynasties
(Number of reign names in parentheses)

Qin dynasty:

    Shi Huangdi, 221-210 B.C.

    Er Shi, 209-207

Western Han dynasty:

    Gaozu, 206-195

    Huidi, 194-188

    Luhou, 187-180*

    Wenti, 179-157

    Jingdi, 156-141

    Wudi, 141-87 (11)

    Zhaodi, 86-74**

    Xuandi, 73-49 (7)

    Yuandi, 48-33 (4)

    Chengdi, 32-7 (7)

    Aidi, 6-2 (2)

    Pingdi, 1 B.C.-A.D. 5 (1)

    Rudzu, 6-8 (2)

Interregnum: Xin dynasty:

    Wang Mang, 9-23 (3)

Eastern Han dynasty:

    Kuangwudi, 25-57 (2)

    Mingdi, 58-75 (1)

    Zhangdi, 76-88 (3)

    Houdi, 89-105 (2)

    Shangdi, 106 (1)

Andi, 107-125 (5)***
Shundi, 125-144 (5)
Chungdi, 145 (1)
Zhidi, 146 (1)
Huandi, 147-167 (7)
Lingdi, 168-189 (4)****
Xiandi, 190-220 (3)

*   Empress who dominated two infant emperors, Shaodigung, 187-184, and Shaodihung, 184-180.
**   Succeeded by Liu Ho (personal name), who ruled for 27 days.
***   Succeeded by Shaodi, who ruled for seven months.
**** Succeeded by another Shaodi, who ruled for four and a half months.

12

THE SIX DYNASTIES
(220 to 589)

In the latter decades of the Han dynasty, the usual cyclical symptoms of decline manifested themselves. The terminal years were marked by weak rulers, relatives and eunuchs wielding power, warring generals, factional pressure groups, uprisings, and rebellions. After the long period of Han centralization, political disunity characterized China. Feudalism reappeared, large estates grew, and barter dominated commercial activity. But despite political disorder, Chinese culture did not die out. In the north, it merged with fresh infusions from barbarians and non-Chinese peoples. Population continued to fan out in southward migrations; for the first time in history, the Chinese demographic center shifted from the north to the Yangtze valley.

In this politically divided period, while mixed racial dynasties ruled in the north, purely Chinese monarchs presided over southern kingdoms. Because of regionalism and civil strife, distinctions began to separate northern and southern life. The former was typed as complex, austere, and vigorous; the latter tended to be less complicated and more easygoing. But the ideal of a unified empire never died out, for the Qin and the Han had completed the political task too effectively. The process of reunification was delayed until 589 only because all the pre-Sui rulers, although aspiring to the task, were individually unable to reunite China.

From these turbulent times, certain parallels might be drawn with contemporaneous events in Europe. Alien migrations from Central Asia affected both the Chinese and the Roman empires. In a type of falling domino pattern, restless tribes in the Mongolian area for one reason or another expanded or pushed out neighboring and Central Asian tribes farther south or west. But once established, their overextended desert empires, lacking the political and military cohesiveness to withstand other later onslaughts, fell apart. Much as Byzantium carried on the Latin culture after Rome fell, so did the Chinese states south of the Yangtze, considered as legitimate by Chinese historians, carry on the cultural continuum against the non-Chinese rulers of the north. More-over, in these centuries of political division, a new religion entered each empire. Christianity took over much of the Mediterranean, and Buddhism spread into China from India, although Buddhism histori-cally did not affect China to the same degree that Christianity affected Western civilization.

The term for the Chinese period of political division from A.D. 220 to 589 is Six Dynasties (*Liu Chao*). Out of the welter of petty princi-palities, later Chinese historians sifted what they considered as the legitimate succession of six imperial dynasties: the Wei (or Cao Wei) at Luoyang, 220-265, which was one of the Three Kingdoms into which Han China split up; then the ensuing Jin, 265-420, in both its succes-sive western and eastern branches at Luoyang and Jiankang or Jianye (Nanjing); and finally, the four southern Chinese-ruled dynasties, 420-589, all continuing at Jiankang—the Liu Song, the Southern Qi, the Liang, and the Chen. (An alternative schemata, with a chronological gap, lists the six dynasties as all those with capitals at Jiankang: Wu, Eastern Jin, and the four southern states.)

The Han was replaced by three states known as Three Kingdoms (*San Guo*), which existed from 220 to 265, a romantic time for later Chinese writers. One of the greatest Chinese novels, *Romance of the Three Kingdoms*, composed a thousand years later, idealized this bloody era. The Wei dynasty, also 220 to 265, founded by a Han general of the Cao family, ruled, with four successors, from the erstwhile Han capital of Luoyang over an area roughly comparable to that of the Earlier Zhou. The Wei state was warlike and highly centralized, and in its constant conflicts with neighboring tribes and areas, peasants were impressed into a semimilitary life. The Wei maintained official relations with Central Asian countries; they held the line against incursions from the north; they kept outposts to the east in southern Manchuria and Korea. In 238, a Japanese "empress" dispatched a mission to Luoyang. The Chinese, in turn, sent one of their own officials, bearing numerous gifts; two years later another Chinese envoy reached Japan. A third-century dynastic history contains one of the earliest descriptions of Japan as given by such firsthand Chinese visitors.

The second of the Three Kingdoms, the Shu Han, which lasted from 221 to 264, ruled from Chengdu. It was also founded by a Han general, but since he was directly related to the former imperial Liu family, he appended the name of Han, in an effort to signify orthodoxy to Shu, a former Sichuan kingdom. In the fertile Red Basin, with its underly-ing sandstone and extensive irrigation systems, the state prospered. The prudent kings and ministers did not disturb the leading families, but they shifted peasant populations about freely. It was with this kingdom that the *Romance of the Three Kingdoms* dealt mainly in its narration of imaginary events concerning real military heroes, one of whom became the God of War, Guan Di.

The third state, Wu, 222-280, centered at Jiankang, was founded by the son of a Han official and general. The area had been colonized earlier by people driven from the north. In the southward migration, many of the fleeing pioneers kept up their aristocratic life in the new surroundings. Blocked by the Wei and the Shu Han from expanding northward or westward, the Wu pressed farther south and developed connections with Cambodia, India, and Annam. Histories note that in 226, a merchant from the Near East reached the capital via northern Vietnam. Around 235, embassies arrived from the two early Southeast Asian Indianized kingdoms of Funan in Cambodia and of Lin Yi, also called Champa, in southern Vietnam. Between 245 and 250, two Chinese travelers who visited Cambodia, India, and Ceylon (known as Sri Lanka after 1971), wrote the first reports of India and its cultural world in Chinese history.

The Western Jin, with four monarchs, succeeded the Wei at Luoyang and remained there from 265 to 316. The Jin imposed a brief period of unity in China by conquering the other two of the three kingdoms, but this empire soon fell apart. A branch of the family went south to carry on the legitimate succession at Jiankang as the Eastern Jin, 317-420, with eleven kings. After its demise, more political turmoil created a subperiod that traditional Chinese historians, in their predilection for categorizing and shaping events, labeled the Nanbei Chao (Southern and Northern dynasties), 420-589. The barbarians pressing down conquered the Chinese in the north and set up a series of alien kingdoms. The pendulum was now swinging in favor of the marauding hordes. When China was strong, it contained or pushed back the frontier peoples, but now that China was weak, the stronger barbarians infringed on Chinese sovereignty and territory. (It was rare in time when both China and the barbarian forces were strong concurrently and in a stand-off situation.) The border relationship in power and political affairs between the Chinese *yang* and the barbarian *yin* was constantly in flux.

Under pressure of the aggressive nomads, the Chinese continued to move south. After the Eastern Jin at Jiankang collapsed, other generals founded at the great metropolis the four southern kingdoms of Liu Song, 420-479, with seven rulers; the Southern Qi, 479-502, with five; the Liang, 502-557, essentially a one-man dynasty with three weak short-lived successors; and the Chen, 557-589, with five monarchs. Despite disunity and constricted kingdoms, the rulers retained the pretentious title of emperor, for the idea of Chinese political and cultural unity never faded. But they all failed to restore the unity of the

Han empire. Unity was to come instead from the north in a combination of barbarian and Chinese elements, much as medieval Europe fused cultural Latin and semicivilized Teutonic elements.

Political affairs in the northern non-Chinese-ruled states were even more confused. What the Chinese termed as the Five Barbarians of the fourth century pressed down from the north and west into China proper: two groups of Tibetans; the Xianbi (Hsien-pi), of largely Mongolian extraction; the ever-present Xiongnu; and an affiliated tribe. In time, some of them set up some of the sixteen northern kingdoms (*shiliu guo*), 301-439, that followed the Western Jin in overlapping fashion. The Tuoba (T'o-pa), related to the Xianbi, were the most important tribe of the invading peoples who left a historical imprint. They established first at Datong, and then at Luoyang, their Northern Wei dynasty, 386-584. As the barbarians gradually took over more of North China, they assimilated sinic culture. The Tuoba, who were exposed to peripheral Chinese culture even before they set up their regime in the north, deliberately strove to adopt Chinese ideas and institutions. They outlawed their own language and customs, took Chinese family names, and encouraged intermarriage. They defended Chinese civilization against new incursions from the north. Although some rulers were Confucianist, most subscribed to Buddhism, which was infusing China with cultural vitality during these centuries.

The Northern Wei in history were notable for more than only subscribing to Chinese ways. They continued to use Chinese bureaucrats in civilian posts, but they appropriated the military bureaucratic positions for themselves and effected strong military measures. They built up peasant militias and emphasized military training. They consolidated their kingdom against the other barbarians growing in power along their frontiers, including the newly expanding forces of the sixth-century Turks (*Tujue*), whose empire in the second half of that century stretched from Mongolia to Central Asia.

The Tuoba took equally strong taxation measures, which carried over to later dynasties. To keep land out of large tax-free estates and subject them directly to government taxation, they instituted in 489 the equal-field (*juntian*) system. All able-bodied adult peasants were assigned specific tracts; a man and his wife could jointly hold about nineteen acres. Only a small part of the landholdings, such as plots with trees and shrubbery around houses, was permanently owned by peasants. Most land reverted to the state upon the death of old age of the cultivators. Keeping such arrangements effective necessitated a periodic census and reapportionment of land. The Northern Wei further refined the concept of mutual responsibility in the three-chiefs (*San Zhang*) system. Five families were grouped into a neighborhood (*lin*) under a chief; five neighborhoods into a village (*li*) under a chief; and five villages into an association (*tang*). The Tuoba also promoted Buddhism by artistic means, fashioning some of the finest early Buddhist sculptures. After a flourishing century and a half, the Northern Wei split up two ways into the short-lived Eastern Wei (534-557) and its successor, the Northern Qi (550-557), as well as the Western Wei (534-557) and its successor, the Northern Zhou (557-581), the state which finally reunited China as the Sui dynasty.

Life in the Six Dynasties

Not only in the Northern Wei but throughout China, despite the political turmoil, culture continued to flourish. Although the chaos and change encouraged a widespread pessimism and uncertainty in life, the Chinese revealed a renewed interest in both the natural world and the realm of the spirit. Chinese inventiveness persisted. Paper was now widely used. The wheelbarrow, particularly in South China's hilly and winding narrow paths, came into common use. Water mills were widespread. Suspension bridges were erected, especially across the deep, rushing river courses of southwestern China. Screens, windows, and decorations were fashioned of mica. Flying kites was a popular pastime, and chairs and sedan chairs became widely available. Coal was developed as a fuel and in North China; it was particularly easy to come by because of surface outcroppings.

The sciences flourished. In the mid-third century A.D. one of the greatest Chinese cartographers lived; his maps on wood portrayed grid divisions, orientation, route miles, altitudes, bends, and angles. A botanical book, published around A.D. 300 by a former governor of a southern province, classified four groups of plants into bamboos, herbs, fruit trees, and forest trees. More plants, including bananas, walnuts, and pomegranates, enriched Chinese palates. A book of the late third century A.D. made the first reference to tea, which was also recognized for its therapeutic value. Medicinal studies were written, especially by Buddhists. One third-century missionary from Central Asia listed medicines and cures for physical ailments, such as hot water baths for various disabilities. Another Chinese Buddhist practiced and advocated acupuncture and the examination of the pulse for diagnostic purposes.

In art, there were the beginnings of the great schools of secular painting. Gu Kaizhi (Ku K'ai-chih) 345?-406?, a government official, painted realistic scenes that emphasized figures rather than landscapes. Extant portions of the scroll, "Admonitions of the Instructress at the Palace," attributed to him (although it might have been a later Tang copy), gracefully depict nine scenes of court life illustrated from a poem of the same title. Daoist painters delineated landscapes. Around 500, Xie He (Hsieh Ho) set forth six canons of painting, which were regarded as definitive by later generations. Except for some cave murals, little remains of Buddhist painting, but its sculpture was noteworthy. It existed in aesthetic religious figures in northern Shanxi province and at Longmen near Luoyang. Buddhists also led in music, especially in psalms composed as hymns. As can be seen in paintings, the Chinese continued to play the piba, the clarinet, and the harp, but the emphasis in music was vocal rather than instrumental. A wide range of pottery tomb figurines of human, animal, and architectural representations continued to be fashioned.

Literature was rich in variety and open to the inspiration of Buddhist religious tales and wonder stories. China's greatest calligrapher, Wang Xizhi (Wang Hsi-chih), 321-379, a scholar and an official, was taught by a woman, and specimens of his calligraphy are available today. Much was written on philology and phonology, with characters representing certain sounds. The origin of the four tones in Mandarin is unknown, but they were in evidence by the fifth century. Poetic forms, preoccupied with style, favored stilted and artificial expressions. One of the most important forms was a lyric in five-syllable meters (*shi*), dating from the Later Han and perfected by Gao Zhi (Kao Chih), 192-232. The greatest liner of his time, flexible in style, was Tao Qian (T'ao Ch'ien), known also as Tao Yuangming, 376-427. A scholar–official, he abandoned the bureaucratic life and returned to his home in the south, where he lived the life of a peasant, drank copiously, and wrote Daoist poems and short stories.

Scholarship also flourished despite the political turmoil. In the third century, the earliest critiques of literature appeared. They culminated in the efforts of Liu Xie (Liu Hsieh), who in 480 produced the *Treatise on the Fundamentals of the Literary Art* (*Wenxin diaolong*), in which he discussed some thirty-five forms of literature. A short time later, Xiao Tong (Hsiao Tung), a member of the royal house of Liang, one of the four southern kingdoms, compiled the *Literary Selections* (*Wen xuan*). It is probably China's most famous anthology, and it gathered together three dozen literary compositions. Around 500, the *Thousand-Character Classic* appeared. A unique work later used for instruction in the primary grades, it summarized Chinese history and the Confucian doctrine in 250 lines, each with four characters, none of which is repeated. In 519, a Buddhist monk published the *Lives of Eminent Priests* (*Gaosengchuan*), a compilation of biographies of about five hundred Chinese and foreign monks, including seven self-immolators. (One chapter of one Buddhist text advocated self-immolation as the most commendable human sacrificial act.)

The earliest encyclopedia was compiled in the third century for the first ruler of the Wei dynasty. Now lost, it is said to have run to more than eight million words. The first local district encyclopedia of a sub-provincial administrative unit, a gazetteer of twelve chapters, appeared in the fourth century. It dealt with northern Sichuan and southern Shaanxi, and describes the city of Chengdu, as well as the flora and fauna of the region. Such local histories, now numbering more than 7,500, became valuable regional sources of history to supplement the national dynastic annals.

In philosophic life, Confucianism managed to hold its own, although the classics were subjected to a growing criticism nourished by popular disillusionment. Because Luoyang was the Wei capital, Confucian studies centered there. The rulers tried to bolster the official religion by such projects as carving the history classics on stone at the capital. But few notable orthodox Confucian scholars emerged, and the examination system deteriorated.

Daoism experienced an upsurge, and some philosophers sought to inject new meaning into Confucian texts by using Daoist terminology and concepts. In the third and fourth centuries, there arose a somewhat amorphous neo-Daoist movement that focused on the two chief Daoist classics, the *Daodejing* and the *Zhuangzi*. It interpreted the idea of *wuwei*, not as the traditional inaction or nonexistence, but rather as an absolute metaphysical being that transcended reality. According to this school, the sage was to move in both the internal and external realities; he was not to retreat from society but to participate in it and contribute to human welfare.

The Zhang family papacy in Jiangxi province advanced the popular Daoist aims of happiness, longevity, and wealth with its numerous shrines, spirits, utopias, body exercises, sexual practices, and alchemy, which searched not for wealth, but for immortality. Quacks and credulous believers manufactured pills of immortality. Men of philosophical and literary interests gathered for conviviality and conversation in Daoist associations such as the Seven Sages of the Bamboo Grove and the Eight Understanding Ones, who, being frank hedonists, loved life, drank heavily, and composed poems. Although Confucianism survived, and Daoism in various forms flourished, Buddhism in its introduction, development, and growth made the greatest and the most remarkable strides during the Six Dynasties.

Buddhism

Buddhism was the most fundamental idea or institution imported into China prior to the coming of the modern West. In contrast to the West's imposition of its alien concepts in the unequal treaty settlements of the nineteenth century, Buddhism was not forced on the Chinese, who voluntarily adopted it from India after considerable modification. It provided a major cultural tie between South and East Asia. As the Indians exported the faith to Southeast Asia, so the Chinese in turn sent it onto Korea and Japan. Buddhism became a potent force during its six centuries (the fourth to the ninth) of organized existence before it was relegated to secondary importance in the Chinese religious scene. Millions subscribed to the faith, but no strong Buddhist ecclesiastical structure carried on into modern China, although Buddhism in a variegated form known as Lamaism persisted in Tibet and Mongolia.

The origins of Buddhism lie in India. Its founder, a historical figure, whose traditional dates are given as 567 to 487 B.C., had several designations: the personal names of Siddhartha Gautama, as well as the appellations of Sakyamuni (Sage of the Sakya tribe), and the Buddha (Enlightened One). Born the son and heir of a king of Kapilavasu, a country in what is now southern Nepal, Gautama, who was brought up in luxury and given a good education, married and fathered a son. He brooded continually over the mysteries of human life and the problems of suffering, sickness, calamities, and death.

To find answers to these issues, he renounced his riches and royal succession (a not unheard of practice in ancient India). After subjecting himself to various experiences to find the truth, he eventually reached enlightenment after long meditation under a fig tree. He concluded that life consisted of four truths: that life equaled suffering, that suffering was caused by desire, that to rid oneself of suffering one therefore had to eliminate desire, and that desire was to be eradicated through the eightfold path. The eightfold path consisted of right views, resolve, speech, conduct, livelihood, effort, mindfulness, and concentration. For further guidance, he also gave his disciples ten commandments, similar in nature to those of the Bible. Each believer, he stated, had to find for himself the path to salvation through these precepts that ended in a state of nirvana, the extinction of desire, the annihilation of self.

After the Buddha's death, his disciples propagated the faith which, in time, gave rise to differing interpretations, since the Buddha wrote nothing. To help preserve doctrinal unity, councils were periodically called in India, but by the fourth council, around A.D. 100, two basic branches of Buddhism had developed. The earlier and purer form was termed Hinayana (Xiao cheng), the Lesser Vehicle, because it rejected all later accretions. Its only surviving sect is known as the Theravada. Drawing from the Buddha's sayings and doctrine, it stressed self-salvation. Although this branch had monastic orders, it emphasized the layman's gaining of merit by ritual acts. Hinayana spread from India to Sri Lanka and into the mainland Southeast Asian countries of Burma, Thailand, Cambodia, and Laos.

The later, amended form was Mahayana (Da cheng), the Greater Vehicle, all-inclusive in nature; it posited fundamental differences from Hinayana. First formulated in northern India, it spread via Central Asia to China, Vietnam, Korea, and then Japan. Over the centuries, nebulously and anonymously, it created nonhistorical buddhas (*fo*) in addition to the founder of the faith, who came to be venerated as only one of many. Also worshiped were the compassionate bodhisattvas (*pusa*), beings of wisdom, real and fictional, who postponed salvation, although they were qualified for it, until they could unselfishly save others as well. Moreover, Mahayana replaced the "nothingness" (nirvana) with an afterlife; it developed a concept of a Western paradise with a hierarchy of heavens to reward believers as well as hells to await unbelievers. In this simpler and more understandable form of salvation through faith, with deities represented in vivid pictorial or sculptured forms, Mahayana took hold in China.

Despite basic differences, both major streams of Buddhism adopted similar canonical categories of the *Tripitaka* (*Three Baskets*): that of conduct and rules for monks and nuns; that of discourses, which consisted of the Buddha's sayings, or sutras; and that of supplementary doctrines, which were elaborating works of Buddhist psychology and metaphysics. Although not comparable to a single holy book like the Bible or Koran, the flexible *Tripitaka* embraced Hinayana (in Pali, a vernacular script) and Mahayana (in Sanskrit, a literary script) works. A specific orthodox canon for the *Tripitaka* never crystallized, and country and regional ideas on what to include in it varied greatly. Moreover, neither tradition included an ultimate ecclesiastical authority, such as a pope, to decide on issues of infallibility.

Just when and by what route Buddhism first arrived in China is uncertain. It was probably introduced in the early Christian era as a religion of foreign traders who plied the Central Asian trade routes. Tradition relates that in A.D. 64, Mingdi of the Later or Eastern Han dreamed of a golden statue of a man who was identified as the Buddha. (According to tradition, his skin turned to that color after enlightenment.) Prior to his reign, envoys to Central Asia had seen evidence of Buddhism and also may have imported the religion into China. Historical records, for example, reveal that in 2 B.C., a Chinese envoy heard of the Buddha from barbarians in Central Asia. As early as the first century A.D., Buddhist monks and laymen were living in China.

In A.D. 166, the religion was already propagated in China, possibly through the efforts also of a converted Parthian prince in Central Asia, who with scholars gathered by himself translated Sanskrit Buddhist texts into Chinese. The faith had a following in the capital of Luoyang, where the emperor was a devotee. The site of the White Horse Temple, earliest in China, dates to around this time, near the city. The figures of various buddha types discovered throughout China indicated that the faith had reached the northeast, the lower Yangtze valley, and the southwest.

Pilgrims augmented the spread of Buddhism in China. Of the Indian missionaries traveling to China via land and sea routes, one of the most famous was Dharmaraksha, a great scholar who lived in the latter half of the third century in a famous desert cave-temple complex at Dunhuang and in Luoyang. He is said to have known three dozen languages or dialects and to have translated more than 175 Buddhist sutras. Kumarajiva, 344-413, who lived in Chang'an for nine years, established a bureau that translated almost a hundred religious works. He converted many Chinese, one of whom helped to found the meditative Chan sect. A third great Indian pilgrim and scholar was Bodhidharma, who, in the first half of the sixth century, lived in Nanjing and Luoyang. He also translated many works, and he was one of the contributors to the meditative Chan sect. Tradition relates that while meditating in Luoyang for also nine years gazing at a wall, his legs atrophied.

In turn, the Chinese traveled to India for enlightenment and to collect the true and latest texts. In 259, the first recorded Chinese pilgrim left for Central Asia, where he remained for half a century. Between that time and 790, about two hundred identified persons embarked on similar pilgrimages to the west and south. In 399, Faxian (Fa-hsien), a famous and early pilgrim, took the silk caravan route across the Tarim Basin, crossed the Pamirs, and visited Buddhist centers in India, chiefly in the north Gangetic plain where the faith had taken strong hold. In 414, he returned home via sea by way of Sri Lanka and Southeast Asia with many valuable texts that he translated into Chinese. He also left a diary of his trip, which proved valuable in adding to China's knowledge of Indian, Central Asian, and Southeast Asian life.

In some ways, it was paradoxical that Chinese took to Buddhism, which incorporated certain imported strands of thought antithetical to China's way of life. The Indian doctrine, in its context of growing out of Hinduism and ancient thought there, was otherworldly and mystical, whereas the Chinese were essentially practical and concerned with present society. Indian Buddhist pessimism (one could not improve oneself in this life but only, and hopefully, in the hereafter) was alien to the Chinese optimistic belief that life now was worth living. Unlike the Chinese, Indians were not, in general, history-oriented. Buddhist monks were to maintain celibacy, practice asceticism, and engage in begging, concepts that all ran counter to cherished Chinese social beliefs. Buddhism had to be modified before the Chinese could accept it.

Buddhism was initially embraced by some wealthy, powerful families and rulers in both North and South China, where, in the latter, the faith appealed to the gentlemen, the literati, who engaged in philosophical discourses and pretensions. In a pattern that was the reverse of the spread of Christianity in the Roman Empire, from the common folk up the social ladder, in China not until several centuries later did Buddhism funnel downward into popular acceptance. Buddhist adherents, winning converts by exemplary living and precepts, did not utilize militant tactics in preaching the doctrine. No holy wars marred its spread. In art, Buddhism exercised a powerful aesthetic and intellectual pull with its manifold and visibly portrayed buddhas and bodhisattvas. (How could the Chinese represent in art an impersonal *tian* or a vague *shangdi*?) It introduced more elaborate forms of religious life, literature, astronomy, mathematics, letters, and philosophies, and added some seven thousand new words to Chinese language. Jataka tales, or stories relating to the birth and reincarnations of the Buddha before earthly life, enriched Chinese literature. Early stupas (domelike shrines) were built to commemorate Buddhist sites, but little remains of them.

Moreover, Buddhism seemed to fulfill some basic demands of the Chinese spirit that the existing religious and ethical systems could not meet. Mahayana sects pictured specific afterlife heavens and hells. On the one hand, the doctrine provided a relief from the determinism and rituals of rigid Confucianism; on the other, it was more concrete, vivid, and understandable than nebulous Daoism. Providing a millennium, Buddhism offered a philosophic escape from wars, disunity, and confusion. As the politically fluid times weakened the Chinese social fabric, the foreign faith thrived. Buddhism's adaptability could modify Chinese ways and embrace in its pantheon Chinese traditional cultural heroes and philosophies. The non-Chinese rulers of the northern states, particularly the Northern Wei, with no stake in necessarily preserving Confucianism, also deliberately adopted Buddhism to weaken the opposition.

Considered along with Confucianism and Daoism as one of the three great systems of thought in China, Buddhism flourished during the Six Dynasties and the subsequent Sui and Tang dynasties. The fourth to the ninth centuries constituted the Age of Buddhism in China and in Asia, when there were probably more Buddhists in the world than Christians or Muslims. Buddhism left a definite imprint on China. Influenced by that faith, Daoists built temples and adopted thirty-three heavens and eighteen hells for their highly structured afterlife. Buddhist pilgrims heightened travel between China and the rest of Asia; Buddhism inspired, as it were, the first international wave of student exchanges.

In incorporating the many new ideas into Chinese cultural patterns, the Chinese intellectually neutralized the original doctrine; monastic orders grew, monks married, and Buddhist temples with great riches and extensive lands became grounded in the temporal world. From the mid-ninth century onward, fearing the growth of Buddhist power, Chinese emperors exercised their imperial prerogative of interfering in religion to make it subservient to the state. But because it could be modified, Buddhism survived, and as it added to cultural patterns rather than basically altering or displacing them, it remained the longer on the Chinese scene.

A number of Buddhist Mahayana sects developed in China. All basic theological tenets had derived from India, but the Chinese, with their penchant for arranging and classifying matters, defined certain Buddhist schools. In time, four of these emerged as the more important and influential. Chan, deriving from *dhyana* (meditation) in India and passed onto Japan as Zen, stressed inward enlightenment and a conversion experience to achieve personal salvation. Tiantai (T'ien T'ai), named after a holy mountain in Zhejiang province, was founded by Hui Si (Hui Ssu), died 577, and his disciple, Zhi Yi (Chih I), 531-597, who was an energetic translator, missionary, and builder of monastaries. This school argued that salvation did not result solely from enlightenmemt but from a variety of factors that included study, meditation, ritual, discipline, insight, and clean living.

The Qingtu (Ch'ing T'u) or Pure Land Sect, founded by a former Daoist, Hui Yuan, 333-416, was known also as the Lotus or Amida school. Never prominent in Indian Buddhism, the Amida branch arose by the fifth century A.D. possibly as a solar cult in Central Asia. It stressed the central concept that salvation lay in the Lotus sutra, which emphasized the role of Amitabha (O-mi-to-fo in China, Amida in Japan), a buddha who dwelt in the pure land, the Western paradise. Its adherents believed that through constant invocation of Amida one could be saved. The Zhenyen (Chen-yen) or True Word Sect believed that truth and existence emanated from the Eternal Buddha, Vairocana (Hua-yen in China, Dainichi in Japan), whose ultimate reality was suggested by magic symbols and incantations and revealed in obscure literary works and vivid schematic cosmological drawings (*mandalas*). A bodhisattva that transcended any definite school because of its widespread appeal was Guanyin, the Goddess of Mercy. Originally deriving from the male Hindu god Avalokitesvara, the figure changed sex by the time of its adoption in China (and Japan, where she is known as Kannon).

Over the centuries, the varied appeal of Buddhist sects won many converts. Yet Buddhism eventually lost hold in China. Promising to become a state church during the Six Dynasties, by A.D. 900, it was not of first-rank political or religious strength. The attrition of time and inner decay took their natural toll. Strong Buddhist sects and powerful monasteries became a political threat as potential substates within a state. There was some organized official persecution of the faith, but this was not crucial. Despite the temporizing doctrinal accommodations, Buddhism remained counter to dearly held Chinese social values. In the final analysis, Chinese nativists, including influential Confucian scholars, considered Buddhism a foreign doctrine. It faded as a religious force in Chinese life. But by its persistent and peaceful coexistence with other schools of thought, Buddhism was to add subtle philosophical dimensions to Daoism and Confucianism in subsequent dynasties.

Chronology

192-232	Poet Gao Zhi
220-265	Three Kingdoms; Wei at Luoyang
221-264	Shu Han at Chengdu
222-252	Wu at Jiankang
245-250	Two Chinese emissaries to Cambodia, India, and Sri Lanka; first reports of these areas
265-420	Jin dynasty; Western branch at Luoyang, 265-316; Eastern branch at Jiankang, 316-420
321-379	Calligrapher Wang Xizhi
345?-406?	Painter Gu Kaizhi
376-427	Poet Tao Qian or Tao Yuangming
386-584	Northern Wei, first at Datong, then at Luoyang
420-589	Southern and Northern Kingdoms
420-479	Liu-Song
479-502	Southern Qi
480	Liu Xie's *Treatise on the Fundamentals of Literary Art*
485	Northern Wei well-field system
ca. 500	Art critic Xie He; *Thousand-Character Classic* appears

502-557   Liang
557-589   Chen

Chinese Sovereigns: The Six Dynasties
(Numeral preceding dynasty name indicates
orthodox succession. Numeral following indicates
number of reign names.)

Three Kingdoms:
(1) Wei dynasty:
   Wen Di, 220-226 (1)
   Ming Di, 227-239 (3)
   Zhaolinggung, 240-253 (2)
   Gaogueiching, 254-260 (2)
   Yuangi, 260-265 (2)
Shu Han
   Zhao-Liedi, 221-223 (1)
   Houzhu, 223-264 (4)
Wu
   Dadi, 222-252 (6)
   Houguanhou, 252-257 (3)
   Jingdi, 258-263 (1)
   Guaiminghou, 264-280 (8)
(2) Jin dynasty:
Western
   Wudi, 265-290 (3)
   Huidi, 290-307 (7)
   Huaidi, 307-313 (1)
   Mingdi, 313-316 (1)
Eastern
   Yuandi, 317-323 (3)
   Mingdi, 323-326 (1)
   Chengdi, 326-343 (2)
   Kangdi, 343-345 (1)
   Mudi, 345-362 (2)
   Aidi, 362-366 (2)
   Feidi, 366-371 (1)
   Jian-wendi, 371-373 (1)

 Xiao-wudi, 373-397 (2)
 Andi, 397-419 (3)
 Gungdi, 419-420 (1)
Southern Dynasties:
(3) Liu Song dynasty:
 Wudi, 420-423 (1)
 Feidi, 423-424 (1)
 Wendi, 424-454 (1)
 Xiao-wudi, 454-465 (2)
 Mingdi, 465-473 (2)
 Fei di, 473-477 (1)
 Shundi, 477-479 (1)
(4) Southern Qi dynasty:
 Gaodi, 479-483 (1)
 Wudi, 483-494 (1)
 Mingdi, 494-499 (2)
 Dung-hunhou, 499-501 (1)
 Hodi, 501-502 (1)
(5) Liang dynasty:
 Wudi, 502-550 (7)
 Jian-wendi, 550-552 (1)
 Yuandi, 552-555 (1)
 Qingdi, 555-557 (2)
(6) Chen dynasty:
 Wudi, 557-560 (1)
 Wendi, 560-567 (2)
 Feidi, 567-569 (1)
 Xuandi, 569-583 (1)
 Hou Zhu, 583-589 (2)

The Sixteen Northern Kingdoms (301 to 439)

Shu, 301-347
Earlier Liang, 302-376
Former Zhao, 304-329
Later Zhao, 319-352
Former Yen, 348-370
Former Qin, 352-410

Later Qin, 384-417

Later Liang, 386-404

Later Yen, 386-409

Western Chin, 389-431

Southern Liang, 397-414

Northern Liang, 397-439

Southern Yen, 398-410

Xia, 407-431

Northern Yen, 409-436

Western Liang, 410-423

Chronology: Buddhism

B.C.

567-487	Traditional dates for the Buddha's life

A.D.

64	Mingdi's dream of Buddha statue
ca. 100	Two major branches of Buddhism form in India: Hinayana and Mahayana
166	Buddhism in Luoyang, worshiped by emperor; existence of first temple, White Horse, near city
259	First recorded Chinese Buddhist pilgrim to Central Asia
Latter half, 3rd century	Dharmaraksha at Dunhuang and Luoyang
333-416	Hui Yuan, founder of Chingtu sect
344-413	Kumarajiva; lives in Chang'an for nine years
399-414	Pilgrim Faxian goes to India by land, returns by sea
First half, 6th century	Bodhidharma at Nanjing and Luoyang
531-597	Zhi Yi, Tiantai monk, disciple of Hui Zi
577	Death of Hui Zi, founder of Tiantai school
ca. 900	Buddhism atrophies

A Chinese Mahayana (*Da cheng*)
Buddhist Syllabary
(with Sanskrit names)

Main buddhas (*fo*):

Healing (Bhaisajyaguru): Yao-shi-fo

Historical (Sakyamuni): Shi-jia-fo or Shi-mou-ni

Universal (Vairocana): Pi-lu-fo

Western paradise (Amitabha): O-mi-to-fo

Main bodhisattvas (*pusa*):

Avalokitesvara (*Guanyin*): goddess of mercy; in many representations

Maitreya (*Mi-lo-fo*): present bodhisattva in heaven but will descend as a buddha in world's final days; also known in one variation as the Laughing Buddha

Manjusri (*Wen-shu*): represents wisdom

Samantabhadra (*Pu-kian*): pilgrim associated with the eastern quarter; rides elephant

Some other deities:

Arhats (*lohans*); usually eighteen in number (but with variations in count and identity); holy men, hermits, disciples of the Buddha

Devas (gods): a host of celestial beings, propitious, evil, or in different, including the Four Heavenly Kings (*Si Tian Wang*) of the cardinal points:

Dowen (Kuvera): north, black, autumn, with pearl and snake

Zengjang (Virudhaka): south, red, spring, holds umbrella

Chiguo (Dhritarashtra): east, blue, summer, strums guitar

Guangmu (Virupaksa): west, white, winter, sword in left hand

Miscellany:

Eight holy symbols (*ba-ji-xiang*): conch (call to the sermon); wheel (the sermon); canopy (protection for humans); umbrella (royalty); lotus (purity); jar (wisdom); fish (release from desire); knot (eternal life)

Four mountains (*xi shan*): Jiuhua (Anhui), Omei (Sichuan), Putou (off Zhejiang coast), and Wutai (Shanxi)

Sects (main ones): Qingtu (Pure Land), Tiantai (eclectic), Chan (meditation), Zhenyen (True Word)

Three jewels (*San Bao*): the Buddha, his law, and his monks

Tripitaka (Three baskets): the Buddhist bible; with sutras, or Buddha's sayings (*jing*); the vinaya, or commentaries (*lu*), and abhidharma, or monastic rules (*lun*)

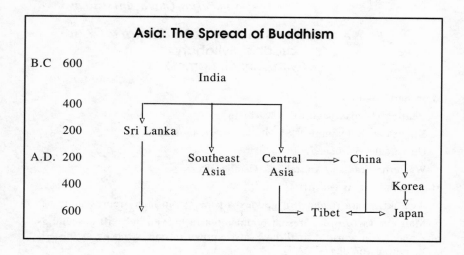

Part Four

IMPERIAL CHINA

Second Phase—589 to 960

In the course of the next four centuries, imperial China experienced a political phase similar to that of its first phase. The country was reunified by the Sui, 589-618, a short-lived dynasty like the Qin. Then the long, glorious Tang dynasty, 618-907, followed, in another era of territorial expansion and cultural activity much like but greater than the Han. After the collapse of the Tang, there once again ensued a period of political division, but this time for only half a century, an epoch designated as the Five Dynasties, until 960. Kingdoms in the north and south competed for ultimate power when the Song, 960-1279, again unified much of China, but on a more constricted scale because of barbarian pressures from and occupation of the north.

13

THE SUI, TANG, AND FIVE DYNASTIES
(589 to 960)

The Sui Dynasty (589 to 618)

Despite political division of centuries, the concept of *tianxia* (all under heaven) proved to be too durable to disregard, and the Sui brought most of China back under the sway of one emperor and one imperial family, the Yang. Regional cultural differences did persist between north and south after the renunciation of the country, but to a lesser degree than those that had existed in the long preceding centuries of political division under the Six Dynasties. In this second phase of empire, originality and creativity were diminished, but the Sui, as did later the Tang, utilized, modified, and strengthened the political, economic, and social institutions bequeathed by the Qin and the Han.

The twenty-nine-year Sui dynasty produced only two important rulers. (The third and last, a child, was on the throne the final dynastic year.) The founder of the new line, whose dynastic name derived from a geographic region, was Yang Jian, known as Wendi (Cultured Emperor), or by his posthumous designation of Gaozu (High Progenitor); in a confusing practice, emperors of different dynasties often received similar titles. He ruled from 589 to 604. Of Chinese stock but married to a Xiongnu, he was an official of the northern Zhou dynasty, the last of the petty northern kingdoms that came into power after the Northern Wei. Starting on the road to power in 581, he deposed a minor on the throne and then conquered the last Chinese dynasty in the south. He located his capital at Daxingcheng (Great Revival City), present-day Xi'an.

An effective administrator, he centralized the operations of government and restored Confucianism to the forefront, with its emphases on stability, ritual, and the importance of the monarch. At the same time, having been reared by a Buddhist nun, he had the scriptures of that faith read daily at court. Recruiting bureaucrats largely from fellow northerners and appointing local officers, he reinstituted the examination system and developed it systematically. He kept the distinction between military and civilian administrators. He abolished the Qin and Han commanderies or provinces and substituted prefectures and counties. For a financial base, he broadened the tax structure of the Northern Wei equal-field system to include all of China. Four public granaries were erected at the capital, and two others at Luoyang.

As was often the case in dynastic cycles, the Sui reached its political apex in the rule of a successor, that of Huangdi's son, Yang Guang, known as Yangdi (Zealous Emperor), 605-617. The son probably committed patricide to ascend the throne. He maintained great royal entourages at his capital and at Luoyang and added a subsidiary political center at Yangzhou, located in the lower Yangtze valley near present-day Nanjing. In the three centers, he erected vast palaces. One of the more extensive imperial grounds at Luoyang contained a park 75 miles in circumference with a 5-mile-long lake. On the water floated real and artificial lotus blooms, and on its shores sixteen villas housed the imperial concubines.

Yangdi built two new extensions to the Great Wall system. The projects consumed great energy and a prodigious number of lives. In the course of one ten-day period in the summer of 607, he put to work a million men, half of whom died or disappeared. The emperor embarked on a similarly ambitious project to extend the Grand Canal system and finished what previous monarchs had begun. His united system enhanced internal transport, supplied North China with rice from the south, carried grain tribute, and supported armies engaged in campaigns against the northern barbarians. By the end of his rule, the network consisted of efficient interlocking canals, commencing in the capital and extending to the Yellow River, then south to the Huai River, to the Yangtze, and onto Hangzhou. A secondary canal route from the Huai and Yellow rivers north to Beijing sustained the Korean campaigns.

A grand total of five and a half million people worked on these various interrelated projects. In some areas, all men between the ages of fifteen and fifty were impressed, and neighborhoods along the canal routes additionally had to contribute a child, or an older man or woman, to augment the imported labor corps. Into modern times, the north-south Grand Canal system with all its tributaries provided effective internal maritime navigation and transportation to augment the natural east-west river systems of China.

Yangdi promoted Chinese military campaigns and diplomatic adventures in peripheral lands. He experienced the usual troubles in the north and west with the barbarians, in whose ranks appeared the Turks as the most troublesome. Fortunately for the Chinese, the Turks were split into two factions, the eastern in Mongolia and the western in the Ili Valley of Central Asia. The emperor's divide-and-rule tactics contained the Turkish princes in the desert oases, although he himself became trapped in a fortress in northern Shanxi by an eastern Turkish faction. Yangdi was rescued by a brilliant young officer, who was later to ascend the throne as the second emperor of the Tang dynasty. The emperor's meddling in Korea's internal affairs aggravated the perennial fighting among the three kingdoms in that country. The Sui's four Korean campaigns from 598 to 614 all proved to be disastrous or inconclusive.

Although the dynasty did not dispatch missions to Japan, that country sent four embassies to the Chinese capital. Around 600, Shotoku Taishi, Japan's first statesman and prince regent in the young state of Yamato, located in the Nara-Kyoto plain, impressed with Sui grandeur, started the first wave of sinicization in Japan by promoting Buddhism and borrowing fundamental Chinese economic, administrative, and political ideas. The Chinese showed more direct interest in Taiwan, which had been known to China since the first century B.C. and had been penetrated as early as A.D. 210. The Sui sent an exploring party in 607 to the nearby island, then called Liu Chiu (a geographic term later applied more specifically to the Ryukyu archipelago to the north). An armed expedition followed in 611, but the inhabitants refused to bow to the Chinese invaders, and they did not pay tribute.

Other lands proved restive. Around 600, a revolt broke out in northern Vietnam. Wendi dispatched one of his generals, who brought back many prisoners, musicians, golden tablets, works of art, and 1,350 Buddhist sutras. In 605, another expedition penetrated farther south into Indochina and conquered Champa and its capital at Indrapura, near the present-day city of Hué, in central Vietnam. Champa paid tribute, and envoys from the southern lands visited the Chinese court until 939. For a time, the Sui received tribute from a state centered at Palembang in southern Sumatra in Indonesia. In 607, a Chinese officer visited the islands of Bali and Lombok off of eastern Java, and in 610, the Indonesians dispatched a mission to China. But the neighbors to the south, geographically remote from northern Chinese capitals, were difficult to govern. And epidemics, including malaria and possibly beriberi, regularly decimated Chinese troops on southern campaigns.

Yangdi reasserted Chinese prestige abroad, but his foreign policies and domestic measures cost the Sui dearly. His measures to end unrest at home and the revolts abroad drained the treasury. In 617, rebels in Yangzhou killed the emperor, then residing in the southern capital. In the ensuing civil war, in which the last monarch, the child Gungdi, was eliminated from the throne, the Sui lost the mandate of heaven to the

Tang. Because he turned out to be a loser and because of his many draconian measures, Yangdi has fared poorly at the hands of Chinese historians, who viewed him as the prototype of the last bad emperor of a dynasty.

The Tang Dynasty (618 to 907)

The Tang dynasty marked another high tide of Chinese politics and culture. It resembled the Han, but it had more of everything. Chinese of later days, and particularly those in the south, designated themselves as the men of Tang in addition to the commonly used term of Han Chinese. Contemporaneous with Charlemagne's empire in Western Europe in the early Middle Ages, the Tang upon its inception embraced an estimated population of 130 million people.

Li Yuan of the family Li was the founder of the dynasty. A general who emerged victorious in succession struggles after the Sui collapse, he was helped by his ambitious second son, Li Shimin, who was to succeed him as monarch. With the aid of the eastern Turks, former enemies but now allies, Li Yuan and his son captured the Sui capital and the father known to annals in a now-familiar posthumous title as Gaozu (Gao Tzu, or High Progenitor) was enthroned as the first of the line. Of aristocratic lineage, the family had intermarried with barbarian families of North China; the founder's mother was non-Chinese. Through his successors, the dynasty continued for three centuries, but out of twenty subsequent rulers, only a few imperial names (including the only reigning empress in Chinese history) were prominent. The dynasty, with its name derived from a geographic region, kept power centered in the Xi'an area and resurrected the former Han capital name of Chang'an. By the end of Gaozu's reign, the country had been pacified, and in 626, the first emperor, in his early sixties, abdicated to his son, who then eliminated two rival brothers in the ensuing struggle for the throne.

Li Shimin, a versatile man, ruled as Taizong (T'ai Tsung, or Grand Ancestor), from 626 to 649. During those twenty-three years, the monarch faced and met the perennial problems of Chinese history. The second emperor reconstituted the central organs of government, subdued the barbarians, rebuilt palaces, constructed more canals, erected public works, and dispatched armies abroad. He surrounded himself with an elaborate hierarchy of court aristocracy that consisted of nine ranks: princes of two classes, dukes of three classes, marquises, counts, viscounts, and barons. All officials of the nine ranks, in junior and senior grades, were appointed directly from the capital and were supported by taxes or lands proportionate to their rank.

The emperor kept the distinction between military and civil officials. He continued the Northern Wei and Sui policies of conscripting peasants as a mass militia to serve in domestic and frontier duty. In the civil service, he maintained the examination system in principle, but he did not hesitate to go outside it to recruit promising men. The bureaucratic examinations were broadened beyond the customary Confucian topics to include history, law, poetry, mathematics, and even aspects of Daoism. An efficient centralized government operated at the capital. The country was divided into ten provinces (*dao*) and in 639, into 358 prefectures (*zhou*) and many more subprefectures (*xian*). Barbarian princes with Chinese titles ruled over nonChinese areas.

Taizong tolerated other philosophies, but he established Confucianism as the state cult. The emperor had temples erected in every *zhou* and *xian*, and he and his court honored Confucius and Confucian scholars of previous dynasties. He further refined the equal-field system and he increased the number of public granaries. He established a system of government education at public expense, whereby prefectures supported preparatory schools and provincial capitals supported colleges. At Chang'an a central university with six affiliated colleges enrolled more than 3,200 students, among them the heirs and children of foreign potentates. Extensive law codes were compiled to cover a multitude of subjects including the rights of foreigners, who were granted a degree of extraterritorial legal freedom. Persons of the same alien nationality were permitted to settle civil disputes according to their law, but Chinese law governed criminal issues, conflicts between differing nationalities, and disputes between Chinese and foreigners. Each national group had a headman responsible for order who received official instructions from the government.

Taizong pursued vigorous foreign policies. In another burst of dynastic imperial power (much like that of the Han), he regained the Tarim Basin from the western Turks with the help of some newfound Central Asian allies, the Uygurs. Part of his success lay in his emphasis on the cavalry. In 630, he conquered the now belligerent eastern Turks and two other frontier groups, the Khitans and the Mongols. Tibet, unified as recently as 607 for the first time, came under Chinese suzerainty, or political influence. Upon request from the Tibetan monarch, the emperor sent a princess to marry him. She carried Chinese culture and Buddhism to the land, also influenced by the Hindu culture of Nepal and India to the south across the Himalayas. Tang contacts extended into northern India. After one Chinese envoy suffered indignities at the hands of a petty king in the Gangetic plain, the Chinese, with Tibetan and Nepalese reinforcements, captured the offending king and brought him in 648 to Chang'an. Chinese Buddhist pilgrims continued to travel to India by land and sea. In the northeast, Taizong did not interfere in Korean affairs, but his successor brought the whole of the peninsula temporarily under Chinese influence.

After Taizong's death and a brief succession struggle, one son, whom historians designated as Gaozong (High Ancestor), reigned from 649 to 683. He performed on a grand scale the traditional imperial sacrifices to heaven and earth, but devout in his Buddhism, he had many monasteries of that faith erected. In his initial years of rule, he maintained aggressive foreign policies. All of Korea came within the sinic fold. Among the three Korean warring kingdoms, China backed Silla, which defeated Paekche and Koguryo in 668, unified Korea, and became a vassal of Tang China. The Chinese presence was felt to the boundaries of India and Central Asia, despite the inroads of the Muslim Arabs. But Chinese rule was tenuous, and by the end of this emperor's reign, much of Korea and Central Asia had reverted to foreign rule.

Gaozong himself came under the influence of an ambitious woman, Wu Hou, who had been his father's concubine. She dominated the monarch, killed his wife, and after his death deposed or eliminated four weak successors. She openly took the reins of government and declared a new dynasty, the Zhou. She exiled members of the imperial family who remained in opposition, and she officiated in person at the elaborate rites and sacrifices. In 690, she assumed the title of Empress Wu and became China's only empress (other strong women ruled the country in fact but not in title). She was strong-willed, competent, energetic, and lusty. She fell in love with a Buddhist monk, and she believed herself to be an incarnation of Maitreya (Mi-lo-fo in Chinese, Miroku in Japan), a bodhisattva in heaven who was to return to the corrupt world as a buddha and reestablish Buddhist truths. Shortly after disaffected court circles forced her out of office in 705, she died at the age of eighty-two.

Within a few years, a grandson of the Empress Wu ascended the throne and ruled from 712 to 756, the longest reign of the Tang dynasty. The young monarch, most commonly known as Xuanzong (Hsüan Tsung, or Mysterious Ancestor), was able, strong, and energetic. Under him, the Tang reached new heights. Confucian doctrine became more entrenched. The provinces increased to fifteen, but in a reversal of centralization, their governors supervised provincial affairs with more autonomy. The world's first newspaper began publication at the imperial court as a gazette. Some of the greatest Chinese poets and painters lived during this reign. In 725, the emperor founded the Hanlin Yuan, an imperial academy of letters at the capital. Originally, it included scholars, musicians, court favorites, and acrobats, but in later centuries it evolved into a highly prestigious literary and scholarly body.

Recording cultural achievements on the one hand, the Tang met a number of reverses, however, in foreign affairs. Large Tang armies, some under non-Chinese leadership, marched into the Tarim Basin and the trans-Pamir areas of Central Asia. In 751, a Chinese army under Gao Xianzhi (Kao Hsien-chih), a Korean general, lost to Arab forces at Talas, north of Fergana in present-day central Russian Asia. This defeat marked the end of Chinese expansion in that area and began five centuries of steadily diminishing Chinese military prestige there, with the Arab conquest of Central Asia and the supplanting of Confucianism by Islam. That same year (751), the southwestern state of Nanzhao in present-day Yunnan province defeated the invading Tang armies. But northern Vietnam remained in the imperial fold, Korea maintained nominal loyalty, and Japan continued to send missions to Chang'an until the mid-ninth century.

A combination of circumstances led to Xuanzong's downfall. In his sixties, he appropriated from one of his sons the beautiful concubine Yang Guifei (Yang Kuei-fei). This imperial romance of youth and age became a popular literary theme, and Yang Guifei was portrayed as the paragon of feminine beauty. She did not possess much political acumen, but she exercised great influence over the aging monarch. Under the powerful patronage of the emperor and the concubine, An Lushan, a young general of barbarian origins, came to control 200,000 border troops. He eventually collided with the emperor, and in 755, he captured the capital. As the court fled south to Sichuan province, imperial troops killed Yang Guifei. In 756, the emperor abdicated, although he lived for another six years, long enough to witness the end of the rebellion. In 757, An Lushan was killed by his own son, who in turn was murdered by a nonChinese rebel.

Tang adherents recaptured the capital, and the dynasty carried on for another century and a half. But times were changing. Never again, under solely indigenous rule, did China attain the territorial limits of the earlier Tang. The alien blood of the founder of the Tang and of its generals played an increasingly important role in Chinese politics. For a time, inertia kept the Tang going despite personal and administrative factors of decay. After An Lushan's revolt, court and factional struggles became intensified. A combination of ineffective kings, strong-willed concubines, powerful eunuchs, and faction-ridden bureaucrats weakened the state. Barbarians raided North China. In 763, when the Tibetans sacked Chang'an, the Tang turned for help to nonChinese sources. The equal-field tax system partially broke down. Population grew, extensive land areas reverted to tax-free estates, and fiscal receipts in grain from peasant cultivators declined.

A few Tang ministers instituted reforms, somewhat belatedly, to shore up economic fortunes. In 780, one of them instituted the double tax, which consolidated the various rural and familial imposts into two levies a year, one collected in the sixth month and the other in the eleventh. To make tax collections easier for the weakened government, assessments were imposed on the actual land areas rather than on the individual owners or cultivators who tilled or occupied the land. The simplified scheme helped to revitalize the Tang, which continued for another century.

The dynasty finally came to an end after a renewed round of revolts, uprisings, and generals warring against each other. Governmental ineptitude and mismanagement at the capital were matched by numerous disturbances in the countryside. Rebels played havoc in rural areas. One of them in the south, Huang Chao, a disgruntled bureaucrat, sacked Guangzhou, marched north to the capital, captured it in 880, and set himself up as emperor. Four years later, the Tang, employing Turkish military leadership, retook Chang'an and slew the pretender. A lieutenant of Huang Chao continued the struggle, however, and in 907, he usurped the throne and established the Later Liang dynasty, which presided over a limited geographical area. Other military leaders repudiated his supremacy in their own domains, and once again competing kingdoms came and went throughout China.

The Five Dynasties (907 to 960)

For five decades after the collapse of the Tang in 907, civil strife divided the empire into small states, some of which in the north were dominated by rulers of alien extraction. Amidst general administrative breakdown and internecine wars, five successive Chinese states, considered legitimate by Chinese historians, carried on in the north, the first two with capitals at Luoyang, while the last three centered at Kaifeng to the east. These small states appropriated pretentious dynastic names to suggest orthodoxy and grandeur. Zu Wen, a lieutenant of Huang Chao and one of the many rebels contending for the throne in the wake of the Tang collapse, established a new dynasty at Luoyang, which he termed the Later Liang. It lasted from 907 to 923, when, rent by internal and external dissensions, it was overthrown by a general of Turkish stock named Li, who established the Later Tang, 923-936.

A second Turkish general, with the aid of mercenary Khitans, who were growing in power to the north, destroyed the Later Tang and founded the Later Jin, 936-947, at Kaifeng. The new capital had better access to riverine and canal transport than Luoyang, but its location in a flat plain was indefensible. A third Turkish general, of the Liu family, then set up the shortest dynasty in Chinese history, the Later Han, 947-951. He forced the Khitans out, but he had less success in perpetuating his line. A general from a family named Guo established the last of the Five Dynasties, the Later Zhou, 951-960. He was a capable administrator and military leader, but neither he nor his weaker successors could reunify China.

Concurrently, ten other kingdoms competed in the struggle to reunite the country. In the south were the Min, 909-944, at Fuzhou on the Taiwan Strait; and the Southern Han, 907-971, at Guangzhou and the West River valley. In the lower Yangtze region were the states of Wu, 902-937, at Yangzhou; Wuhue, 907-978, at Hangzhou; and the Southern Tang, 937-975, at Nanjing. They were powerful patrons of Buddhism. In the middle Yangtze area was the Southern Ping, 907-963, which straddled the broad river. Farther to the southwest was the state of Chu, 927-951, centered at Changsha in Hunan province. In western China were the Earlier Shu, 907-925, and the Later Shu, 934-965, both with their capitals at Chengdu in Sichuan, to which many scholars and poets had fled from Chang'an. Lastly, the Northern Han, 951-979, was located in northern Shanxi province.

Extensive fighting and hard times characterized the Five Dynasties, but China was reunified after only some fifty years, in contrast to the three and a half centuries of political division that had followed the Han disintegration. Never again was mainland China rent into competing regional political units for so long as half a century. Although the Middle Kingdom subsequently experienced chronic warlordism, military regionalism, and foreign domination after the Tang, China coalesced into an indestructible political entity. In peace or war, under native or foreign rule, the vision of unity, *Zhongguo*, was never lost.

Chronology

589-604	Wendi
ca. 600	Mission from Japan's Shotoku Taishi; northern Vietnam revolt
605	Expedition to Champa
609-617	Yangdi
607, 610	Missions to and from Indonesia
607, 611	Expeditions to Taiwan
607	Tibet unified for first time

618	End of Sui dynasty
618-26	Gaozu; abdicates to
626-649	Taizong
630	Eastern Turks, Khitans, Mongols conquered
648	Expedition into northern India
649-683	Gaozong
668	Silla, a Tang vassal, unifies Korea
690-705	Empress Wu Hou on throne
712-756	Xuanzong; abdicates
725	Hanlin Yuan established
751	Fateful Battle of Talas, stops any farther Chinese expansion into Central Asia; Nanzhao defeats Tang armies
755-757	An Lushan rebellion
763	Tibetans sack Chang'an
780	Double tax reforms
880-884	Rebel Huang Zhao in Chang'an
907	End of Tang dynasty

Chinese Sovereigns: The Sui, Tang, and Five Dynasties
(Number of reign names in parentheses)

Sui dynasty:

Wendi, 589-604 (2)

Yangdi, 605-617 (1)

Gungdi 617-618 (1)

Tang dynasty:

Gaozu 618-626 (1)

Taizong 625-649 (1)

Gaozong, 649-683 (14)

Zhongzong, 684 (1)

Empress Wu Hou, 684-705 (13)

Ruizong, under her, 684-90 (2)

Zhongzong, restored, 705-712 (2)

Xuanzong, 712-756 (3)

Suzong, 711-762 (4)

Daizong, 762-779 (3)

Dezong, 779-805

Shunzong, 805 (1)

Xienzong, 805-820 (1)

Muzong, 820-824 (1)

Jingzong, 824-827 (1)

Wenzong, 827-840 (2)

Wuzong, 840-846 (1)

Xiuanzong, 846-859 (1)

Yizong, 859-873 (1)

Xizong, 873-888 (5)

Zhaozhong, 888-904 (6)

Aidi, or Zhaokuan, 904-907 ((1)

Five dynasties:

Later Liang

Taizuu, 907-913 (2)

Modi, 913-923 (3)

Later Tang

Zhuangzong, 923-925 (1)

Mingzong, 926-933 (2)

Mindi, 934-935 (1)

Feidi, 935-936 (1)

Later Jin

Gaozu, 936-943 (1)

Chudi, 943-947 (2)

Later Han

Gaozu, 947-949 (2)

Yindi, 949-951 (1)

Later Zhou

Taizu, 951-953 (1)

Shizong, 954-960 (1)

The Ten Kingdoms

South:

Min, 909-944

Southern Han, 907-971

Lower Yangtze:

Wu, 902-937

Wuhue, 907-978

Southern Tang, 937-975
Middle Yangtze :
Southern Ping, 907-963
Southwest:
Chu, 927-951
West:
Earlier Shu, 907-925
Later Shu, 934-965
North:
Northern Han, 951-979

14

LIFE IN TANG CHINA
(618 to 907)

Life in Tang China, particularly in the course of the earlier, expansive half, was characterized by vitality and variety. As symptomatic of the grandeur of their rule, at their capital of Chang'an, the Tang erected a magnificent walled city from which routes radiated out to all China. The metropolis thronged with Chinese and foreigners. Its estimated population of two million made it probably the largest city in the world at that time. Modern Xi'an is only part of old Chang'an (which the Chinese Communists are excavating). As one of the world's earliest planned urban complexes, the city, laid out in a rectangular plan, measured 5 by 6 miles and covered almost 15,000 acres. In checkerboard fashion, nine streets ran north and south, with the central one 500 feet wide; twelve other major thoroughfares extended east-west. In the north-central quarter rose the walled imperial palace, just above the imperial city, also walled, where the bureaucrats resided. In each of the eastern and western halves of Chang'an was a great government marketplace for the sale and exchange of goods. The rest of the city was divided into 112 rectangular blocks, each block an administrative entry in itself.

Society

At the capital, the central organs operated in a top-heavy system of executive checks and balances. Under the guidance of the emperor, the Imperial Secretariat (*Zhongshusheng*) issued orders. The Imperial Chancellery (*Menxiasheng*) reviewed them, and returned those considered to be in need of revision. The Secretary of State Affairs (*Shangshusheng*) executed the approved orders through the six ministries (*liu bu*), dating back in concept to the Qin and Han dynasties: Civil Affairs or Personnel (*Li Bu*), Revenue (*Hu Bu*), Rites (*Li Bu*, with another character for *li* from that of Civil Affairs), War (*Bing Bu*), Justice or

Punishments (*Xing Bu*), and Public Works (*Gong Bu*). The Secretariat also embraced five directorates (*jian*) and nine courts (*si*) to handle imperial and ceremonial affairs. A Bureau of History (*Lishi Bu*) concerned itself with the writing of dynastic histories. The Board of Censors (*Yu-shi-tai*), a unique feature of Chinese political life, reported directly to the emperor any cases of treason, maladministration, and misgovernment.

In the local government, the three-tiered structure of provinces (*dao*), prefectures (*zhou*), and districts or subprefectures (*xian*, now downgraded to that rank from prefectural status of the Qin and Han with the appearance of the *zhou*) was elaborated. To ensure uniformity of administration, elaborate laws were codified (these were copied in Japan and northern Vietnam). Transport systems were effective. On the main lines of communications emanating from Chang'an, post stations marked 10-mile intervals with hostels and restaurants for travelers with official orders. The militia system continued whereby peacetime farmers transformed into soldiers in time of war. During the reign of Taizong, China had 634 militia units, each under a divisional officer who lived with his men.

Efficient government made necessary a skillful bureaucracy. The government established local and national schools to provide education, essentially of Confucian doctrine and the classics, for public service. There were differing types of examinations. Technical schools provided training in various subjects, such as law, mathematics, and science, but these did not result in appointment to higher offices. Some took tests related to political issues as "budding geniuses" (*ziucai*); others attempted examinations in letters to become, hopefully, "presented scholars" (*jinshi*) to the emperor. The latter degree, because of its all-inclusive literary scope and prestigious nature emerged in time as the most sought-after rank.

Into the early Tang, an aristocratic period, the privileges of nobility survived but by the middle of the dynasty the examination recruiting system helped to fashion an officialdom oriented along orthodox Confucian lines. As a result, China achieved the world's first bureaucracy based on merit; it provided a degree of mobility upward at least in the educational definition. The ruling class performed as a uniform, cohesive corps because its members had all been subjected to the same rigorous procedures before induction into office. But the system had its drawbacks: the stress on education for rule divided Chinese society; orthodoxy and conformity cramped individual thought and expression.

The equal-field system provided the fiscal basis for the early Tang, as it had for its predecessors. Each able-bodied male between the ages of 21 and 59 held the equivalent of 13.7 acres of land, of which only a fifth could be permanently owned. Tillers in other age and sex categories received varying acreage. The purpose of the system was to enable the government to collect taxes directly and expediently, as well as to prevent powerful landowners from building up large tax-free estates.

Tang taxation on the equal-field system was threefold. First, the tax on grain was a required delivery of a fixed amount of unhulled grain. Second, the tax on foodstuffs other than grain and on handicrafts was, for example, in the form of certain lengths of silk or other fibers. Third, a labor tax demanded of able-bodied adults twenty days a year of service to the central state, although the service could be commuted into money or textile equivalents. City people were also taxed; merchants and artisans were subjected to various commercial imposts. To operate effectively, the whole system required thorough and repeated censuses and careful land registries. The government distributed land periodically, but because of population increases and political turmoil, the system broke down. After An Lushan's revolt, the equal-field system disintegrated. Despite government measures, large tax-free estates once again sprouted.

The early Tang improved and elaborated the canal system in order to speed goods and grain taxes to the capital. Continuing to promote copper as a basis for coinage, by 850, the government operated fifty copper mines to produce enough metal to replace earlier types of copper coins. At the time, at least ninety-nine mints annually produced 327,000 thousand-coin strings, each officially weighing 6.4 pounds. The strings had rough equivalents to commodities, such as one ounce of silver, a bolt of silk, a bushel of grain. During the Tang, paper money developed; merchants' receipts for money deposited for safety at provincial offices came to be used as currency called "flying money."

Culture

Tang scholars studied mathematics and astronomy. Daoist alchemists and Buddhist charity organizations investigated materia medica. Gunpowder was used for pyrotechnics. In the course of the dynasty, optical lenses arrived in China, possibly via India. Many new plants added variety to Tang foods: cucumbers, garlic, peas, beans, jasmine, pistachio nuts, pepper, dates, spinach, lettuce, sugar beets, mustard, olives, figs, and almonds. China imported cane sugar from India and learned from Central Asia how to distill wine from grapes. The growing popularity of tea encouraged the further development of the porcelain industry. In 801, one cartographer created a large map, 30 by 33 feet, which represented an area of 10,000 by 11,000 miles. On it, he noted the seven major trade routes to the known Asian world. Paper reached Central Asia through the intermediary of some Chinese who were captured by Arabs in the 751 Battle of Talas; it later spread to Western Asia and eventually to Europe.

Wood-block printing was a significant invention of the Tang. The time was ripe for it because most of the necessary materials were then available. Paper had existed from Han times; ink and the brush had been used since antiquity. Both the examination system and the widespread religious charms and prayer formulas demanded multiple copies of the same text. Printing had precedents in black and white rubbings on paper taken from stone engravings and in imprints made by the large official seals. By the seventh century, full-page wood-block illustrations for texts had evolved. Yet the earliest extant examples of wood-block prints are found, not in China, but in Japan, which had picked up the process. In 770, a Japanese empress had printed a million small Buddhist charms as an act of piety.

The first complete extant Chinese book printed by the wood-block method, dated 868, is a Buddhist sutra, which, discovered at Dunhuang by a British archaeologist, now reposes in the British Museum. The next oldest printed work, dated 877, is a calendar illustrated with twelve animals. Yet not until 883 was the first reference to block printing made in Chinese literature. Later, in the eleventh century, when the Chinese developed movable print, they did not take to it because of its impracticality. It was easy to lose or misplace the small metal or wood plates, each with one of the thousands of characters. Furthermore, because texts tended to be standard and unvarying in content, it was easier to continue to produce them from already cut wood-block prints. At first, Confucian scholars were hostile to the art of printing, which they associated with Buddhist and Daoist inspiration. Only after the Tang did printing come into general use in China, and not until 932 were the Confucian classics printed.

Tang writers produced many scholarly works. Private and imperial libraries were extensive, and a special Tang archival bureau acquired and cataloged books. Printing advanced the compilation and availability of encyclopedias, which were particularly helpful to students preparing for examinations. Many local gazetteers and collections of excerpts from earlier books were issued. After thirty-six years of research, one of the literati, Du Yu, issued in 801 a *Comprehensive Compendium* (*Tungdian*). Another important work, appearing in 961, after the Tang but dealing with its times, was the *Assembled Essentials on the Tang* (*Tang huiyao*), based on earlier compilations. Works like these supplemented the dynastic histories as sources of topical information on Chinese politics, economics, and society. The Confucian scholar Han Yu, 768-824, a statesman, author, and essayist, from his position as head of the Board of Rites, laid the foundations for the later Song neo-Confucianism. He opposed Buddhism as an alien and divisive ideology. In a style much admired for its directness and simplicity, he composed scholarly essays that sought to resurrect the Zhou classics.

The flourishing short story dealt with both religious and everyday topics. Professional storytellers mixed prose and verse, and by the eighth century some of their tales had been written in the vernacular. Drama did not develop, but court jesters produced plays based on short stories, and with time these plays grew longer. The emperor Xuanzong founded the Pear Garden School to train actors and musicians, but during the Tang, drama remained insignificant.

On the other band, poetry (*shi*) reached its height. Several poetic forms were developed with varying rhyme schmes, line lengths, and tonal emphases. One form had five-syllable lines; another had seven-syllable lines. The quartrain was a widely used stanza. Lyrics of popular songs (*ci*) were recited on their own merit, without music. The favorite themes were the emotions aroused by friendship, beautiful landscapes, and war campaigns. Emperors and commoners alike composed poetry, and three Tang poets emerged as the greatest in Chinese poetry.

Li Bai (Li Po), 701-762, was a Daoist, a lover of wine, and a carefree wanderer through several marriages and minor official posts. At different times he had affiliated with such hedonistic groups as the Six Idlers of the Bamboo Brooks and the Eight Immortals of the Wine Cup. In middle life, he returned in Chang'an and knew Emperor Xuanzong. Later, having fallen into disgrace, he returned to his wanderings and died in an eastern province. According to the traditional account, he met his end when, out boating and drunk, he drowned trying to embrace the moon's reflection in the water. In literature, as in life, he sought escape from convention and formality into spontaneous, lyrical, and free dream worlds. His close friend, Du Fu (Tu Fu), 712-770, also a minor official and for a time at the court of the emperor, was a quite different poet. He was idealistic and conscientious. He knew hardship, for the civil wars separated him from his family. Enduring great suffering and reverses of fortune, he depicted adversity and the injustices of life in a stark and moving manner.

Of a later generation, Bai Juyi (Po Chu-I), 772-846, wrote in a simple style akin to the vernacular. He pursued an erratic official career in and out of imperial favor, but as a noted poet (his poetry was printed in his lifetime) he achieved enduring fame that spread to Korea and Japan, where he became the hero of a *Noh* drama. Seldom alluding to the classics or to abstruse literary works, he struck a popular chord. It was said that he was never satisfied with a poem unless an illiterate old country woman could understand it.

Sculpture rose and declined with the fortunes of Buddhism. The Tang added to the cave sculptures at Yungang, Longmen, and Dunhuang. Contrasted with the stiffness of earlier Buddhist icons and imagery, Tang buddhas and bodhisattvas, reflecting prosperous times, were human, intimate, plump, and lifelike. The popular Laughing Buddha was a conventionalized representation of a tenth-century Chinese monk who was supposed to be an incarnation of Maitreya. Other favorite Buddhist-inspired figures were the bodhisattva Guanyin and the buddha Amida. (Guatama Buddha was less likely to appear in Mahayana sculpture than in Hinayana, which revered only the historical Buddha.) The Tang erected monumental figures of beasts along the "spirit paths" near the tombs of emperors and great men. Realistic figurines of horses were derived from bas-reliefs on Taizong's tomb. Other earthenware figures, and small, finely glazed tomb figurines of humans and beasts have survived, mainly in tricolored specimens (*sancai*) of cream, brown, and green hues. A related highly developed craft was that of translucent pottery.

Secular painting flourished, but little remains of Buddhist painting except cave murals at Dunhuang. Texts were printed from wood-blocks, and the earliest surviving example, now in the British Museum, is from the ninth century. Wu Daoxuan (Wu Tao-hsüan), also known as Wu Daozi (Wu Tao-hsi), who died in 792, was China's first great landscape artist. In over three hundred Buddhist and secular frescoes and drawings on silk, none of which survives, he originated the calligraphic brush stroke that came to characterize Chinese painting. Two other famous painters were Han Gan (Han Kan), a painter of horses, and Wang Wei, noted for monochrome landscapes and famous also as an official, physician, Buddhist, and poet. Two schools of style rose in the Tang: a realistic northern school of precision and clarity, and an impressionistic southern school of subdued tones. The publication of the *Record of Famous Paintings of All Periods* (*Lidai minghua ji*) in the mid-ninth century revealed a Chinese antiquarian interest in art.

Tang music used indigenous and Central Asian instruments and eighty-four scales based on seven intervals. The aristocracy enjoyed long operas and orchestrated court music, much of which has been lost. But the adoption of the tradition by imperial Japanese *gagaku* and *bugaku* troupes has made today's derived Tang style probably the oldest authenticated musical tradition in the world.

Religion

In a more formal vein, Confucianism registered marked growth under the Tang. The temples that Taizong ordered erected in every prefecture and district became local literary and scholarly halls of fame. Scholars offered sacrifices to the Confucian founders and possibly borrowing from Buddhist examples, erected Confucian statuary. The classics, receiving renewed emphasis, were engraved on stone for posterity. The examinations based on the doctrine were stressed; tests on other subjects did not lead to top offices.

In the country at large, Daoism with its appeals of mysticism, elixirs, and alchemy remained popular. The imperial house claimed Laozi as an ancestor, and in their private affairs emperors and bureaucrats probably followed Daoist tendencies, but such intangibles are difficult to document. Some state leaders, particularly semibarbarian military generals from border areas, were inclined toward Daoism. The Dao inspired poets and painters, and it offered to everyone an idealistic world as an escape hatch from the troubled times of the later Tang.

Buddhism reached its greatest heights in China during the Tang, after which it began to decline. Xuanzang (Hsuan-tsang), 602-664 (not to be confused with Emperor Xuanzong), was one of the most famous of the Chinese Buddhist pilgrims of the time, who traveled to India in search of the latest texts and doctrines. He was born in Luoyang and raised in a Confucian tradition. At thirteen, he became a convert to Buddhism and entered a monastery. In 629, he embarked for India to visit Buddhist shrines and to study Sanskrit texts. He left the capital secretly because the court, then in an anti-Buddhist phase, had refused him permission to go. Proceeding to Central Asia and India along the branch of the silk route that skirted the northern edge of the Taklamakhan desert in the Tarim Basin, he studied Buddhism in its homeland for fourteen years. He brought back, via the southern silk desert route, buddhist icons and texts. He returned a hero, for Taizong now favored Buddhism. A prodigious scholar and author, Xuanzang translated works twenty-five times the length of the Bible. Two emperors honored his works with prefaces, and upon his death the monk was accorded a state funeral. Like his fifth-century predecessor Faxian, he left a valuable account of his extensive travels.

Another notable pilgrim was Yijing (I-Ching), 634-713, who traveled to and from India via Southeast Asian sea routes. In 671, he sailed from the mouth of the Yangtze for Sumatra, a center of Indian and Buddhist influences in the then-existing Srivijaya empire, where he remained eight months. He proceeded to India, stayed there for fourteen years, 671-685, and returned again via Sumatra, to arrive in China in 689. He gathered disciples to help him and almost immediately went back to Sumatra, finally returning to China for good in 695.

In the second half of the seventh century, some fifty additional pilgrims from China and bordering lands journeyed to South Asia. In turn, Japanese pilgrims traveled to China to study the latest trends in Buddhism. Some stayed for long periods up to thirty years. The Japanese monk Ennin, in China from 838 to 847, left a detailed personal account of Chinese life in the troubled later Tang, when Buddhism was losing ground. By the mid-ninth century, the religion began to slip, partly as a result of fitful but cumulative official attacks, more political than theological, by the court, emperors, and Confucian bureaucrats. Eventually the state won. In 845, the then reigning emperor, a devout Daoist but somewhat insane, destroyed 4,600 temples and secularized most Buddhist monks and nuns. Those who were permitted to remain ecclesiastics were placed under the supervision of the office of foreign affairs. Buddhists from abroad, including Ennin, who recorded these winds of change, were expelled. After the Tang, Buddhism, what was left of it, became thoroughly sinicized.

Buddhism left its imprint in architecture, although few specimens of Tang buildings remain in the homeland. Chinese-inspired Buddhist temples erected in Japan during the seventh and eighth centuries were simpler than those recorded in China, but they expressed similar classic form and balance. Literary descriptions portrayed contemporaneous Chinese palace architecture as vast and lavish, but besides a few brick and stone pagodas, little exists today. The oldest wooden building in China is at the ninth-century Buddhist monastery on Mount Wutai in northern Shanxi province. A stone bridge in adjoining Hebei province, built around 600, is still intact.

Foreign Affairs

During the expansive reigns of the earliest Tang emperors, China enjoyed many contacts with the outside world. In the spirit of cultural tolerance that China displayed in times of political strength, indigenous and foreign ideas were interchanged. Barbarian invasions and Chinese countercampaigns heightened contacts with northern neighbors. Interest in Buddhism brought closer cultural contacts with foreign lands. Interregional Asian trade by sea and land grew beyond that of Han times.

To spur activity in overseas trade, the Chinese built at least ten shipbuilding centers in the lower Yangtze area, which employed 40,000 men. Guangzhou, with its large numbers of foreign residents that included Persians, Arabs, Jews, and Indians, remained important in the southern maritime and land trade routes. In that city, a special government office handled foreign trade, export, collection of duties, and reporting of ship movements. Two other important ports were Yangzhou, the former Sui center near the Yangtze, and Chuanzhou, near present Xiamen (Amoy) on the Taiwan Strait. International trade continued to concentrate on luxuries: exports of silk, porcelains, and spices, and imports of copper, precious stones, and possibly slaves from Africa.

Large numbers of foreigners in China practiced their own faiths, all of which were tolerated by the early Tang. The first reference to Jews in China was by an Arab trader in connection with a domestic revolt in 879 in Guangzhou. Jews had little historical significance, although they persisted in the land into modern times. Manichaeism, a second foreign religion, originated by Mani in Persia in the third century, admitted Persian and Christian influences. Its essential dualism of a continual struggle between good and evil, and between the light and the dark, differed from the *yang-yin* interaction in that the latter sought an accommodating balance. In the years following the sect's first appearance in China, toward the end of the seventh century, its adherents constructed temples at Chang'an, Luoyang, and other main cities. Few Chinese were attracted to the doctrine, but Uygur converts, mainly in Xinjiang, maintained Manichaeism, despite Islamic inroads, into the thirteenth century.

Another Persian creed, Mazdaism or Zoroastrianism, the first foreign religion in point of time to enter China, arrived in the sixth century via land trade routes. Much like its sister faith, it posited an endless conflict between the forces of good and evil. Restricted largely to Persian merchants and refugees, the faith died out in China after ninth-century persecutions. Also present in China was an early variation of Christianity called Nestorianism. The sect was founded in 411 by Nestorius, who was read out of the Roman church for his heresy by claiming that the divine and the human were two disparate strains, rather than a unified one, in Jesus. Despite disapproval from the papacy, this variant became the prevailing Christian creed in the Middle East, Central Asia, and India. Its first missionary settled in Chang'an in 635. The doctrine won a considerable following, mainly of foreigners, for a few centuries. A Nestorian tablet dated 781 was discovered near Xi'an. Finally, Islam flourished in the southeastern coastal cities and in the northwest. At Guangzhou, the large Muslim community enjoyed its own government responsible to Koranic law. Eventually, the faith weakened in South China, but it peacefully won millions of converts among the Uygurs and other minority groups over time in the northwest after the eighth-century Arab conquests in Central Asia, from where the faith trickled into western China and there supplanted Buddhism.

In the secular realm, because of either direct conquest or imitation, the Tang culturally influenced peripheral areas. Central Asia was once again brought into the Chinese fold, and holdings in southern Manchuria were consolidated. Tang emperors neatly defined four protectorates surrounding the Middle Kingdom (known also as *An*, country of peace): Anxi to the west, Andung to the east, Anbei to the north, and Annam to the south. (The derived name Annam, or central Vietnam, has persisted to this day from the Chinese origin.) Monarchs of border states copied Tang political centralization.

In the seventh century, under Chinese influence, the first Tibetan government arose. Around 740, in Yunnan, Nanzhao was founded by native Thais, who imported Tang ideas. Pohai, a barbarian kingdom in southeastern Manchuria from 713 to 926, adopted some Tang offices. In 668, after Silla unification, Korea resembled a type of Chinese state on a small scale. Taiwan at this time remained outside the Chinese sphere of influence, but Japan from the seventh to the ninth centuries succumbed to waves of sinicization. For the moment, in the East Asian world, Chinese *yang* exercise political paramountcy over foreign *yin*.

Perspective

Despite territorial grandeur and periodic governmental efficiency, the Tang dynasty demonstrated no striking political originality. Perhaps none was called for, since the Chinese by this time had fashioned an adequately working political system. Emperors and bureaucrats made maximum use of existing administrative procedures. They institutionalized the examination system, largely according to Confucian tenets, and with the equal-field system, they breathed new life into the tax structure. Buddhism reached its heyday and then entered its decline. Poetry and painting rose to unparalleled heights.

The Tang, particularly in the course of the reign of Xuanzong, noted a turning point in Chinese history. During its earlier decades, the dynasty resembled in many ways the preceding ones, while the latter decades helped to set the stage for a somewhat different China of the succeeding dynasties. Prior to the mid-eighth century, the Chinese maintained their military strength and vitality on the mainland, although they suffered from chronic barbarian inroads in the northern and northwestern parts of the realm. After that point in time, the Chinese orientation shifted perceptibly away from the military vigor they had earlier exercised to one of such weakness that two alien dynasties, the Mongol and the Manchu, were later to impose their rule over the whole country.

Moreover, before 750, the Chinese internally had emphasized barter trade in commercial matters, weighted the rural economy and life at the center of their culture, and were taxed on a per capita basis. In subsequent periods, they developed more emphasis on a money economy, experienced the rapid growth of cities not only as governmental centers but as economic and cultural entities, and broadened the tax base. With the institution of the double tax policy, which relied on taxation by land area rather than by individual ownership or occupation, the system of modern Chinese landlordism was confirmed. During and after the Tang, the Chinese engaged more extensively in foreign trade, noted a turning point in Buddhism, and commenced a trend toward landscape painting, for which their artists are so justly renowned.

Before this watershed in time, China's ruling class was principally an aristocracy of birth and wealth based on land or rank. North China constituted the geographic and cultural center of the country; capitals were located mainly on the Yellow River plain. Now, Central and South China were growing in geographic and demographic importance, and Chinese capitals permanently moved eastward. During the Tang, with a fresh impetus given Confucianism, the rising bureaucratic class of scholar-gentry, recruited primarily through examinations, now entrenched in political life, began to gain most of their income from officeholding rather than from landed estates. By the subsequent Song era, they had displaced the aristocrats. Moreover, philosophic trends in the state doctrine were set into motion that culminated in the formulation of neo-Confucianism during the Song, the last major phase of the doctrine to be formulated in imperial China. In short, early modern China was emerging.

Chronology

6th century	Mazdaism or Zoroastrianism enters China
602-664	Buddhist Xuanzang; pilgrimage to India, 629-643
634-713	Buddhist pilgrim Yijing
635	First Nestorian missionary in Chang'an
668	Unification of Korea by Silla, which follows the Tang model

end of 7th century	Manichaeism appears in China
701-762	Poet Li Bai
712-770	Poet Du Fu
713-926	State of Pohai in Southeast Manchuria
ca. 740	State of Nanzhou founded in Yunnan province
ca. 750	During Xuanzong's reign, the genesis of modern China
751	Battle of Talas; defeated Chinese bring paper to West via victorious Arabs
768-824	Confucian essayist Han Yu
770	Earliest extant example anywhere of wood-block printing, in Japan
772-846	Poet Bai Juyi
781	Xi'an Nestorian tablet
792	Death of painter Wu Daoxuan (Wu Daozi)
8th century onwards	Islam trickles into West China
801	Large map of China created; Du Yu and *Comprehensive Compendium*
838-847	Japanese Buddhist pilgrim Ennin in China
845	First imperial persecution of Buddhism
by 850	Government operating fifty copper mines; money economy noticeable
868	Earliest extant Chinese book printed by wood-block method
879	First reference to Jews in China
883	First Chinese reference to wood-block printing

Part Five

IMPERIAL CHINA

Third Phase—960 to 1644

The third phase of the imperial period experienced a repeated cycle of native and foreign rule. The Song dynasty, 960-1279, in two political phases, presided first from a northern capital, then from a southern one, a departure from the precedent set with earlier west-east centers. Foreign conquerors impinged more and more on North China until the Mongols established their sovereignty, 1279-1368, over the whole country, the first alien conquest of all China. In part, because of institutional weakness, their empire lasted less than a century and was replaced by the nativistic Ming dynasty, 1368-1644. Once again, the indigenous line weakened over the centuries and China fell finally under another non-Chinese people, the Manchus, who were the last of the imperial, and two dozen traditional, dynasties.

15

THE SONG DYNASTY
(960 to 1279)

In 960, when the Song (a name also taken from a geographical region) reunified the Yangtze valley and South China, large areas of North China remained in the hands of alien rulers. During the course of the dynasty, China progressively weakened and shrank territorially because of the continued and expanding pressures from barbarian tribes to the north. The Song, like the Zhou and the Han, was divided into two successive parts (but indicating now a different pattern of location). The Northern Song, 960-1127, with nine emperors, ruled from Kaifeng, the capital of the last three of the Five Dynasties, whereas the Southern Song, 1127-1279, also with nine monarchs, settled in Hangzhou. None of the eighteen monarchs, however, excepting the founder, and possibly the last of the Northern Song line, was particularly noteworthy. Political life continued as usual, but China experienced a commercial revolution through growing urbanization and a cultural renaissance noted for simple but beautiful glazed porcelain, and probably the finest painting in Chinese history—dreamy, impressionistic landscapes. Moreover, by the twelfth century, neo-Confucianism had stamped its features on the seventeen-centuries-old philosophy, which endured without further substantial modification into the twentieth century.

A scholarly military man, Zhao Kuangyin (Chao K'uang-yin), founded the Song. He was the chief general of the Later Zhou, which was the last of the northern kingdoms in the Five Dynasties period. He had acted as regent for the monarch's son. He fought and temporarily subdued the warlike Khitan and then, supported by his military followers, seized the throne. During his reign as Taizu (T'ai Tsu, or Grand Progenitor), 960-976, he regained Central and South China, crushing all but two states by the time he died. The southwestern state of Nanzhao still held off the Chinese. Because of contemporaneous political uncertainties in China, Annam earlier, in 939, had seceded after a thousand years of Chinese rule. As the founder of a dynasty, Taizu followed the usual policy of fostering Confucianism and education as all as the examination system. He centralized bureaucracy and made a deliberate attempt to consolidate as many organs of government as possible under his personal jurisdiction a trend that made the imperial position even more autocratic. The three-tiered Tang system of provinces, prefectures, and subprefectures continued. To ensure conformity, the emperor instituted severe criminal codes, and he personally judged all sentences of capital punishment. He was succeeded by his brother, Taizong (T'ai Tsung, or Grand Ancestor), 976-997, who effectively continued the process of political centralization, although he was yet not able to regain all former Chinese territory. After him, the Northern Song line deteriorated; none of the later monarchs displayed much political acumen or administrative ability. The next last of the anorthern line, Huizong (Hui Tsung, or Excellent Ancestor), 1101-1126, was an enthusiastic patron of the arts, an artist, a calligrapher, and a poet.

The chief problem, which the Northern Song emperors had met unsuccessfully, was the perennial one of barbarian pressures from the north and northwest. At this time, three particularly strong groups were expanding. First, there were the Khitan, nomadic cattle breeders, who established an empire called Liao, 907-1125, centered in Inner Mongolia and Manchuria. Not containing their efforts there, they pushed south of the Great Wall into North China, and in 946, were at the walls of Kaifeng. In that broad region, including the North China plain and the Beijing area which was then called Yen (a designation from Late Zhou times), the dynasty maintained five different capitals, one of which was Beijing. Unlike the earlier Tuoba of the Northern Wei, who adopted Chinese culture eagerly, the Khitan endeavored to preserve their own identity and stave off sinicization (although they adopted a Chinese-type dynastic name). Nobles who studied Chinese or took the civil service examinations were punished. The Khitan extracted tribute from the Song and treated other tribes as vassals. At its height, Liao stretched from the Yellow Sea to Central Asia, but internal divisions and external pressures doomed the temporary empire. The Khitan name survived as Khitai, the Russian term for China, and anglicized as Cathay, the European term (after Marco Polo) for China or, more precisely, for the traditional cultural and political heartland of North China.

The Jurchen (Juchen) were a second important group. They originated in Manchuria and were vassals of the Khitan, but in alliance with the Song, they eventually forced the Khitan out into Central Asia. But this time, the Chinese policy of allying itself with one barbarian group to rid the country of another did not pay off. After the common enemy was dispatched, the Jurchen refused to leave Chinese soil and instead drove the Song farther south. The new conquerors supplanted the Liao dynasty with one of their own, the Jin, 1125-1230, which governed Manchuria and North China, again from Beijing. They soon came to a cultural accommodation with the Chinese.

Another group, the Tangut of Tibetan extraction, established in Ningxia in northwestern China the state of Xixia (Hsi Hsia), 1030-1230, and similarly adopted Chinese customs. They held off their eastern neighbors, but Genghis Khan conquered both the Tangut and the Jurchen around 1230 and began the Mongol rise to power in China.

In the midst of declining Chinese fortunes, the able but dogmatic Wang Anshi (Wang An-shih), 1021-1086, the chief Song councillor, tried to refurbish the economy and bolster the shrinking empire militarily against the northern invaders. He proposed comprehensive reform measures to keep the state viable. In some of his proposals, Wang Anshi was an innovator, but he remained within the Confucianist political mainstream that emphasized tradition, precedent, and appeal to age. Born into the official-scholar class, he had survived the examination system and had no wish to revolt against the classics; on the contrary, he cited them as sanctions for his proposals.

Wang Anshi's program was wide-ranging. Some aspects of its were unique, others were not. To promote utilitarian education, he set up a network of public schools in prefectures and districts, and drafted some of the examination questions himself. To sustain agriculture as the mainstay of state economy, he adopted, as had earlier emperors, state monopolies in commerce, erected ever-normal granaries, and continued the equal-field system to keep lands on tax rolls. He initiated a program of farm credit to extend loans to peasants in the planting season. Expanding economic and financial schemes beyond the agrarian field, he imposed taxes on all types of property and substituted an additional graduated tax for labor conscription. He created a state budget to save and to record expenses, an unusual move, for Chinese political thought did not encompass the concept of fiscal accountability by the government. He instituted compulsory military service, with families providing able-bodied men for frontier and local forces. Families in border areas also kept horses for use by the state, which paid for the provisions. He revived the Northern Wei three chiefs system, which were collective units that guaranteed military quotas imposed by the central government.

Wang Anshi's ideas met widespread opposition. They were too broad and some too revolutionary to be fully implemented, although later emperors, without success, tried to effect his program in whole or in part. The Legalist rule by force, rather than by Confucian good example, particularly alienated bureaucrats and wealthy citizens. Conditions worsened, but the reformer left his stamp on Chinese history as a member of a continuing public-spirited minority who were concerned with necessary and practical political and economic experimentation. The reforms were probably intended to promote state strength more than popular welfare for its own sake, but innovators like Wang Anshi, from time to time in other dynasties, shook up the traditionalist Confucian bureaucratic apparatus with new ideas.

Within five decades after the minister's death, the Song fled south. The unruly Jurchen, former allies of the Chinese, raided Kaifeng and captured Huizong and 3,000 members of his court. A young prince and the rest of the aristocracy escaped south to Hangzhou, then called Lin'an (Temporary Peace), on the West Lake in the lower Yangtze Valley. (Marco Polo, who visited it after the fall of the Song, described it as the finest city in the world.) The Jurchen crossed the Yangtze and took several cities south of the river, but eventually they withdrew. The Huai River, between the Yellow River and the Yangtze, became the tenuous boundary between northern barbarians and southern Chinese.

To forestall further depredations, the Southern Song, as had their predecessors, adopted a policy of accommodation. One general, Yo Fei, advocated resistance and invasion of enemy territory to capture Beijing, but the appeasement faction, led by minister Chin Guei, prevailed, with the result that the Southern Song paid the Jurchen an annual tribute of 500,000 units, half in silver and half in silk. Eventually, the Mongols conquered the Jurchen and the other northern tribes. Pushing south in force, the Mongols also defeated the last of the Song in 1279 in a naval engagement off the modern Portuguese colony of Macau, near Hong Kong.

Militarily weak but culturally brilliant, the Song maintained in Central and South China the political institutions that previously had existed in all of China. The examination system, based on Confucian tenets and dating in concept from the early Han, now became entrenched. As a result, political life became increasingly bureaucratic. As in Tang times, examinations were conducted in many subjects, such as law, economics, history, and the sciences, but those leading to the highest rewards stressed a knowledge of the classics. At first, the government administered the tests irregularly, but after 1065, they were given triennially. The overall process involved three steps. At the first rung, the prefectural level, only up to ten percent of the candidates passed. The few who were successful were then examined at the capital in a second round, where again an average of only a tenth qualified for the final palace examination, which weeded out more and ranked the remaining officials.

From 997 to 1124, an average of some two hundred men annually were recruited into the civil service through the examination system, and they filled about half the official positions. The other offices were replenished by direct appointment, purchase, or other methods, but the most distinguished positions were reached through the orthodox path of examination. Rivalries developed between those who passed the tests and those who gained entry by other means, among the various bureaucratic factions from different regions of the country, and between the conservatives and the reformers. Bitterness grew and times worsened, but despite factionalism the best talent entered government service. Although most officials were educated in government schools, Buddhist, Daoists, and Confucians sponsored over a hundred private academies, usually located in quiet country spots.

The Song, like the Tang, continued to base taxes on landholding rather than on individuals in order to prevent consolidation of huge tax-free estates. But growing population, shrinking territory, and restricted agricultural production reduced tax yields. China had more mouths to feed and less grain for the government. While revenues fell off, military expenditures rose. The Song devoted up to eighty percent of government expenses to military affairs, yet they were not successful in war. The tribute to the Jurchen involved not only commodities but great sums as well, and the inefficient mercenary standing armies recruited from lower social echelons of society drained the treasury. Meanwhile, the cost of maintaining an expanding civil bureaucracy also went up.

In the eleventh century, the government matched rising obligations by minting more currency. Annual production maximums went up to 1,830,000 strings of a thousand coppers each, much more than the average annual Tang production. Although rarely used in small-scale transactions, silver ingots and gold dust changed hands in heavy-volume trade. Barter continued in rural trade, but money was demanded in urban transactions. Paper money, developed in Tang times, circulated widely. Banks, exacting a three percent service charge, held savings and issued certificates of deposit. The Song tried to exert the usual government controls over commercial activity, but interregional domestic trade outpaced the restrictions. Grouped by localities or streets, there sprang up trade guilds and merchant associations called *hang* (or *hong* in South China, where they later were intermediaries in the trade with the West). The guild headman was responsible for taxes and held liable for the collective conduct of the members.

Guangzhou, on the south coast, was the center of overseas trade, much of which was in alien hands, notably the Muslims. Persians and Arabs dominated trade with the southern regions, Koreans with the northeast. Overseas trade was concentrated at the designated foreign quarters in official ports, where customs duties, a major source of government revenue, were collected. The government put the squeeze on all merchants and foreigners with taxes of ten to twenty percent on sales of commodities, which continued to consist of luxury goods. Traders voyaged, on round trips, sometimes as long as two years, as far abroad as the east African coast and the Persian Gulf.

In society, the nobility disappeared as a class, and the aristocracy of the Six Dynasties and the Tang merged with the new scholar-gentry bureaucracy. The sources of wealth and social prestige were no longer principally derived from rank, title, or military strength, but from officeholding and prerogatives of education. City folk, although a minority, dominated Chinese society from these times. By 1100, the populations of at least five cities had exceeded one million. The most important cities were Luoyang, Kaifeng, Chengdu, Yangzhou, Hangzhou, nearby Ningbo on the sea, Chuanzhou, and Guangzhou. There the arts flourished, and the well-to-do enjoyed luxurious amusement quarters, tea shops, restaurants, and wine shops. The rich took concubines, and for what were considered erotic connotations, the upper classes imposed on their women the uniquely Chinese practice of foot binding.

A wide range of innovations improved life in the Song. Chairs at home and sedan chairs for travel came into general use. By 1119, the compass had been introduced. By 1274, the Chinese had developed, or borrowed from Central Asia, the abacus for reckoning purposes, but adapted the concept of zero from India. They practiced inoculation against smallpox and alleviated leprosy with chaulmoogra oil derived from the seeds of an East Indian tree. Their crossbreeding of rice probably doubled China's crop, so that the food supply kept up with the growing population. Tea drinking spread north, where aliens adopted it. Botanical encyclopedias and other books described cultivation of fruits, including citrus fruits. Although firecrackers had existed since the sixth century A.D., the Chinese, by 1161, were using gunpowder in military projectiles, including hand grenades. Blocked by barbarians on land, the Song turned to the sea and developed seagoing junks, including a navy of twenty squadrons and over 50,000 men.

Song arts were varied. Multistoried pagodas, utilizing brick or colored glazed tiles, were built. At Kaifeng, Li Jieh (Li Chieh), an architect who died in 1110, composed a basic illustrated text that explained how to build many kinds of structures from differing materials. With Buddhism ebbing, Song sculpture declined. Moreover, the practice of burying tomb figurines with the wealthy also went into disuse after 1000, and that rich archaeological source for artifacts on Chinese life dried up. For use in daily life, Song artisans created beautiful monochrome and multicolored porcelains, celadon, and crackleware. With their interest in antiquity, artists also fashioned some of their ceramics on Song prototypes.

Landscape and nature painting reached a new height. The southern topography lent itself to impressionistic scenes on silk or paper. Although most painting was related to secular themes, the dreamy landscapes were stimulated also by Daoism and the meditative Chan Buddhist sect. Its appeal was partly a result of the times to withdraw inward spiritually in response to the military ineffectuality of the times. According to the microcosmic theory of painting, landscapes represented nature as a whole, and even a bamboo or a plum splay was a small world unto itself. The lovely scrolls, usually in monochrome, subordinated man to his environment with a minimum of detail. Ma Yuan and Xia Guei (Hsia Kuei) of the Southern Song were famous for landscapes, including those of West Lake.

The intellectual Song produced some notable essayists, historians, and philosophers. From the wood-block printing presses flowed classics, dynastic histories, encyclopedias, and other scholarly works, some of which have survived. (Extant whole books date back only to the Song.) The versatile Su Shi (Su Dungpo), 1037-1101, was a bureaucrat, scholar, essayist, poet, art critic, and engineer. Ouyang Xiu (Ouyang Hsiu), 1007-1072, president of the Board of War, wrote a history of the Five Dynasties and another on the Tang. Sima Guang (Ssu-ma Kuang), 1019-1086, working with three collaborators over two decades, published the *Comprehensive Mirror for Aid in Government* (*Zishi Tongjian*), a well-written exhaustive history of China from 403 B.C. to A.D. 959 that drew on 322 sources. As the title implied, its thesis was that emperors could avoid mistakes by studying how great men surmounted obstacles. The important historical contribution was subsequently reworked by two other scholars of the Southern Song period.

Although some pilgrims still went to India, Buddhism continued to atrophy, for its homeland now lay in the hands of Muslim rulers. Chan Buddhism persisted with some vitality in South China, but by the time of the Song, the Chinese had wrung out of Buddhism most of what they had wanted, which was essentially emotional satisfaction. Between 972 and 983, Buddhists in Sichuan published a *Tripitaka* of 5,048 volumes, a work so valuable that it was exported to Korea and Japan. In 1019, Daoists presented the throne with 466 cases of documents containing 4,656 rolls with the essence of their doctrine.

Capitalizing on previous trends and borrowing from other philosophies, the amended doctrine of neo-Confucianism came to full bloom in the Southern Song, although it was not entirely the creation of the Song. They took from Daoism the belief in a first principle that permeated the universe and manifested itself in nature. From Buddhism, especially from the Chan variant, they borrowed the practice of a period of long meditation followed by sudden enlightenment, and contemporaneous disciples gave it a renewed emphasis on native traditions and past eras.

The last and greatest teacher of neo-Confucianism was Zhu Xi (Chu Hsi), 1130-1200, who advocated Confucianism in its pristine form: the hierarchical five relationships, the rule of government by virtue, and the importance of an educated bureaucracy. But familiar with Daoism, Buddhism, and other schools of thought, the Song philosopher emphasized universal reason and the duty of the scholar to investigate it. He made much of the investigative spirit, not in the modern scientific sense of examining phenomena, but rather in the sense of probing the mind, ethics, and the Confucian doctrine.

Neo-Confucianism fashioned a dualism of the principle (*li*) and matter (*chi*) in which the principle expressed itself. Zhu Xi claimed that the *li* of man's nature was good, but the *chi* distorted it. Corrective measures were possible through the practice of reverence (*jing*) and sincerity (*cheng*). The philosopher settled the long-standing conflict over the nature of man in favor of Mengzi, who deemed that man was essentially good, rather than Xunxi, who thought man unethical. Zhu Xi included the work attributed to Mengzi in his recommended *Four Books (Shu)*: *Mengzi*, the *Analects*, the *Great Learning* and the *Doctrines of the Mean*, the latter two being selections from the *Classic of Rites*. Subsequently, the examination system admitted only orthodox neo-Confucianism as defined by the scholar-gentry who ran the state.

By the end of the Song in the thirteenth century, China had achieved a high degree of cultural cohesiveness that persisted into modern times. The countervailing, balanced Chinese social, political, and economic sectors operated fairly harmoniously within their geographic and territorial confines. Pax Sinica descended upon the country, and China enjoyed, as a whole, relative stability over eight centuries until the advent of the modern West. China's cultural or historical uniqueness may in retrospect have seemed tragic, because China could not adequately resist the later onslaughts of and by the Occident in the nineteenth century. But, on the other hand, it did create an extended era of peace and relative prosperity, a major accomplishment for any country to record at any time in history.

Chronology

907-1125	Alien Liao dynasty
939	Annam throws off Chinese rule of a thousand years
960-1127	Northern Song at Kaifeng
960-976	Rule of first emperor, Taizu
1007-1072	Historian Ouyang Xiu
1007-1086	Historian Sima Guang
1021-1081	Statesman and reformer Wang Anshi
1030-1230	State of Xixia
1037-1101	Versatile Su Shi (Su Dongpu)
1065	Examinations begin to be administered triennially
1101-1126	Rule of next to the last emperor of Northern Song, Huizong, an aesthetic
1110	Death of architect Li Jieh
1119	Compass in use
1125-1230	Alien Jin dynasty
1127-1279	Southern Song at Hangzhou
1130-1200	Neo-Confucianist Zhu Zi
1161	Chinese using gunpowder in military projectiles

Chinese Sovereigns: The Song Dynasty
(number of reign names in parentheses)

Northern Song dynasty:

> Taizu, 960-976 (3)
>
> Taizong, 976-998 (5)
>
> Zhenzong, 998 -1023 (5)
>
> Renzong, 1023-1064 (9)
>
> Yingzong, 1064-1068 (1)
>
> Shenzong, 1068-1086 (2)
>
> Zhezong, 1086-1101 (3)
>
> Huizong, 1101-1126 (6)
>
> Chinzong, 1126-1127 (1)

Southern Song dynasty:

> Gaozong, 1127-1163 (2)

Xiaozong, 1163-1190 (3)

Guangzong, 1190-1195 (1)

Ningzong, 1195-1225 (4)

Lizong, 1225-1265 (8)

Duzong, 1265-1275 (1)

Gungzong, 1275-1276 (1)

Duanzong, 1276-1278 (1)

Dibing, 1278-1279 (1)

16

THE YUAN DYNASTY
(1279 to 1368)

Culminating the long history of the waxing and waning of alien power on its peripheries, China was finally and amazingly conquered and ruled by the Mongols, a small group, probably only a twenty-fifth to one-tenth of the Chinese population of the time. In their conquest, they utilized the latest military technology, principally a mobile cavalry. Climatic and geographic factors rather than fanatical religious crusades probably drove the hordes southward. Central Asia may have been drying up; the aggravated weather and agricultural conditions led to chronic instability for the pastoral nomadic people. At the same time, various dynamic leaders mustered political authority among the clans and confederations. The growth in the barbarian *yin* matched the deterioration of the Chinese *yang*. An agriculturally rich and militarily weak China offered a great temptation.

This foreign power started in Mongolia and North China under Temuchin known to history as Genghis (spelled variously) Khan, the Illustrious Ruler, 1167?-1227. Little is known of his early life but, in 1204, he emerged as overlord of all Mongolia. Two years later, a great convocation at the capital of Karakorum confirmed his supreme position. He campaigned against the Jurchen, the Tangut, and peoples farther to the west. On the open plains of North China, his horsemen encountered little opposition, but besieged walled cities, in positional warfare, put up stiff resistance. In 1215, Beijing, then called Zhongdu by the Jurchen, fell, but only after traitors had admitted Genghis's forces, whereupon the barbarians looted the capital and massacred the inhabitants. Genghis was eventually killed without having conquered all of North China, but at the time of his death, half of the Eurasian heartland had fallen under his sway.

The effective Mongol military machine was organized on a decimal system divided into units of tens, hundreds, and thousands. Upon Genghis's death, the total strength of the Mongol army was 129,000, a huge number by nomadic standards. At their greatest strength, the military forces probably reached a quarter of a million. The Great Khan enjoyed a personal bodyguard of eighty men, who eventually grew to an elite corps of 10,000, recruited from sons of clan leaders and nobility. Both leaders and men were fiercely disciplined. Trained in the saddle from boyhood, they operated in coordinated and long-ranging campaigns. (In Hungary, Mongol horsemen once covered 270 miles in three days.) They developed an effective signal system that involved lanterns, smoke, and colored pennants. Spies operated in the cities and countryside to spread rumors and divide inhabitants. Troops lived off the land by plundering and looting, and their bloody campaigns enhanced their notoriety as the "yellow peril."

Upon Genghis's death, his empire fell apart into four khanates ruled by his three sons and a grandson. Batu, the grandson, succeeded to the Khanate of the Golden Horde, in Persia, the lower Volga, and Central Russian Asia. Chaghadai established himself in Afghanistan and the Tarim Basin; Tului, in northeastern Asia; and Ogodai, at Karakorum. Ogodai reopened hostilities against the Chinese in the north, fought down to the Yellow River, and penetrated Sichuan. He conquered the alien rulers in North China, but farther south, he met more resistance.

Kublai Khan

The Southern Song put up a stiff fight, and it took the Mongols half a century to absorb the rest of China. Chinese resistance, plus the hilly and wet terrain that hindered cavalry movements, held off the Mongols until the grandson of Genghis, Kublai (spelled variously) Khan, defeated the last Song in 1279 (a traditional date for commencing the Yuan dynasty). As the greatest of the Mongol line in China, Kublai, upon advice of Chinese courtiers, had earlier appropriated not only the title of Grand Khan but the dynastic name of Yuan (First Beginning or Origin, from the *Classic of Change*) to ensure orthodoxy. Ruling at Beijing from 1264 to 1294, he adopted a Chinese style as emperor. Despite the accommodating imperial manner, the Chinese, particularly in the south, who were not used to alien overlords, disliked the new barbarian line. But since it governed all of China, its emperors could not be ignored and thus, were listed in the indigenous annals, in the absence of any competing legitimate Chinese faction, such as the successor dynasty to the Song.

Kublai not only gained Chinese territory but ambitiously extended it into peripheral areas. In the south, the Mongols conquered Nanzhao and pushed the Thai population south via various funneling riverine routes. One stream of these migrating people established the foundation of modern-day Thailand. The racially related Shans moved into upper Burma, while the Laos went south into the country that now bears their name. But the Mongols also penetrated farther into Southeast Asia, which received the brunt of several waves of land and sea invasions. Four expeditions invaded Vietnam; five penetrated Burma, twice proceeding south of Mandalay. Envoys traveled to Sri Lanka and south India by sea. By the 1280s, ten states of South and Southeast Asia were sending tribute to the capital. Troops were never dispatched to Thailand, but tribute came from there for a time. In 1292, a Mongol fleet attacked East Java without success, and an attempt to subdue the Ryukyus failed when the leader of the expedition died. Everywhere, heat, disease, long distance, and logistical problems took their toll of the invaders. The wide-ranging expeditions did not establish Mongol power in other lands, and tributary relations proved short-lived. But the Mongols shook up East and Southeast Asia, impelled migrations, and indirectly contributed to political changes and ethnic admixtures in neighboring lands.

Kublai also turned his attention to Japan. For an invasion of that country in 1274, he assembled in Korea a fleet of one hundred fifty vessels manned by unenthusiastic Korean and Chinese subjects. The flotilla landed that November in Hakata Bay (now Fukuoka) in Kyushu, across the Tsushima Straits from Korea. The local Japanese repelled the invaders in a day's fighting. A storm, unusual for that time of the year, forced the fleet, after suffering losses, to withdraw.

The Mongol emperor, concentrating on the subjugation of South China, postponed the conquest of Japan for some years. Then, in 1279, he ordered four shipbuilding centers to provide six hundred ships within two years for a renewed effort. Two fleets assembled on schedule, one in Korea and another in southeastern China. In the summer of 1281, they again rendezvoused in Hakata Bay. The Japanese, who had expected a return engagement, once more put up stiff resistance. After several months of inconclusive fighting, a hurricane, more normal for that time of the year, drove the invaders into retreat. The Japanese maintained defenses for two more decades, but the Mongols never returned. Although both times Japanese bravery held off the mainlanders, the Japanese traditionally have ascribed their victory to the *kamikaze* (divine winds) that blew the invaders away.

Kublai, in policies reminiscent of those practiced during the early Tang, employed able men of all nationalities and listened with an open mind to various philosophies. Marco Polo became one of many foreign officials, some of whom rose to be governors of provinces. Kublai discontinued the civil service examinations in order to draw on able Chinese and non-Chinese who might not have passed the Confucian-oriented tests. He hired foreign contingents for Mongol armies, but he forbade Chinese civilians to carry arms and confiscated those which they already had.

He streamlined the bureaucracy by consolidating its ministries into four: Finance, Justice, War, and Rites. For greater governmental efficiency, four years after the commencement of his reign in 1260, he moved the capital from Karakorum, in Mongolia, to Beijing, which he renamed Khanbaliq (Cambaluc in European literature). The Chinese called the city Dadu (Tatu). Shangdu (Xanadu) in eastern Mongolia, north of the Great Wall but near Beijing, became the summer residence. Over the following three decades, an Arab architect rebuilt Beijing and constructed great palaces and extensive parks.

Although his mother was a Nestorian, Kublai combined animism and Lamaism and officially supported several creeds. He honored Confucianism and the family of Confucius. On the condition that they pray on his behalf, he exempted from taxation Daoist and Buddhist monks, Muslim leaders, and Nestorian priests. At times, he became annoyed with the Daoists for threatening the peace of the land by their antagonism to Buddhists; but he nevertheless confirmed the Daoist pope in office. Nestorian Christianity reappeared and Roman Catholicism penetrated China during the Yuan, although both later died out with the Mongol decline for lack of native converts. Islam survived in the northwest because of geographic contiguity with Muslim-populated areas of Central Asia.

The Mongols adopted some Chinese ways and rejected others in order to govern China and keep power in Mongol hands. They accepted Confucian ideology and bureaucratic political life as the bases of the state, but they differed from the Chinese in language, customs, costumes, and food habits. They lacked surnames, a truly barbarian attribute as far as the family conscious Chinese were concerned. Chinese historians portrayed their alien masters as filthy boors, savages, drunkards, and culturally backward.

Nevertheless, under alien rule, cultural and literary activity continued to broaden, especially the novel and the drama (171 extant plays date from this period). Almost all playwrights were from the north, and most of them resided in the capital. The seventy-eight-year suspension of examinations encouraged drama because unemployed, educated officials now turned their literary talents to the stage. An imperial geography of a thousand chapters, written in 1303, was the largest on the subject, the study of which was encouraged by Kublai who sent a mission to locate the source of the Yellow River. Because of the close ties in religion and culture between Mongols and Tibetans (Kublai Khan sent troops into Tibet), many Tibetan maps and books were also translated into Chinese. Mongols erected magnificent buildings in Beijing, the imperial capital. Muslim mosques, of which the earliest dated one is 1258, were built, complete with Chinese and Arabic inscriptions. Persian designs and decorations crept into Chinese ceramic, bronze, and plastic arts. Song-inspired landscape painting predominated, but not without Persian influence. Mongol artists emphasized the horse and Lamaistic Buddhist themes in their works.

Other Foreigners in China

China and Europe entered another era of cultural and commercial exchange, for, as during the Tang, secure land routes promoted trade and travel. Before the Yuan dynasty, few foreigners in China were European. Chinese international relations developed a new dimension when, from the mid-thirteenth century onward, Europeans began to arrive in China, first as individuals and then as representatives of the emerging Western European nation-states. There were several reasons for European interest in China in the late Middle Ages. In an age during which Rome exerted great power, the Catholic Church recognized a new opportunity to carry Christianity to the pagans. Moreover, somewhat unrealistically, the princes of Christendom sought alliances with the distant non-Christian Mongol powers against the common enemy in between, the Muslims of Central Asia and the Near East. Riches also drew Europeans eastward. The Crusades had inspired the desire for new goods, luxuries, and spices, which arrived in Europe but at high Arabian, Egyptian, or Italian prices. Western Europeans wanted new and direct sea routes to the East, although they also followed the relatively safe but long land routes through the Mongol-dominated empire.

The earliest Europeans to penetrate China were friars and traders, some of whom left fascinating accounts of their journeys to the distant eastern land. John of Plano Carpini, an Italian Franciscan and the first ambassador from the Roman Catholic Church to the East, traveled in Asia from 1245 to 1247. From Pope Innocent IV he brought a letter urging conversion of the Great Khan Guyug at Karakorum. Instead of accepting the faith, the Khan suggested that the pope come to him and pay homage. On his return, the monk wrote a *History of the Mongols.* Louis IX of France sent Andrew of Longmeau to seek an alliance against the Muslims, but the Mongols rebuffed the emissary in 1249. The monarch later sent a Flemish Franciscan, William of Rubruck, on a similar mission from 1252 to 1255. He was similarly received in Mongolia and met other Europeans at Karakorum. He never actually reached China proper, but he recorded what he had learned, hearsay, about the Middle Kingdom.

The Polo family of Venice were the first Western merchants of note to reach China. From 1260 to 1269, the brothers Nicolo and Maffeo Polo traveled on business to Asia. Kublai received them in Beijing. The Polos returned to Europe with letters from the Khan to the pope requesting that a hundred scholarly missionaries be despatched to the Mongol capital. On their return to China, the men took along Nicolo's son Marco, who was about seventeen years old when they left Venice in 1271. The papacy sent two Dominicans with them, but the monks proved to be fainthearted and returned to Europe before the journey was well underway. During their seventeen years in China, 1275 to 1292, all three Polos were in the service of the Mongols, whom they served well, as did many other foreigners. Marco returned home via Southeast Asia in rags, but he was rich, for he had sewn many precious stones into his tattered clothes to mislead thieves.

Back home, he was caught up in the wars among the Italian city-states, and when Genoa defeated Venice in 1298, he landed in jail. He dictated his *Description of the World* to a fellow prisoner about his adventures in China and the East. His book gave the West its first detailed account of China, and it was the first European history to mention Japan (*Zipango*), although he had not visited the country. Marco Polo did not know the Chinese language, only some Mongol. He omitted from his story, perhaps because he took them for granted, any details about well-known phenomena such as the Great Wall, tea drinking, foot binding, or printing. The book, widely read in Europe, was printed in many editions and languages. Although the Venetian is famous in the West, the Chinese histories never mentioned him.

Other foreigners, both Christian and Muslim, followed. John of Monte Corvino, an Italian Franciscan, arrived in Beijing in 1294 and established the foundations of Catholicism in China. By the time he died at the capital in 1338, he had made about 30,000 converts. The pope appointed him archbishop of Cambaluc and sent him assistants. One of them, Odoric of Pordenone, also an Italian Franciscan, traveled by way of Southeast Asia and South China, stayed in Beijing three years, and returned to Padua via Central Asia in 1330. A decade later, John of Marignolli journeyed via Central Asian routes to Beijing, where he gave the Khan a large horse. The monk returned to Avignon in 1353 by way of Xiamen (Amoy), a port in South China, and India. He was the last medieval Roman Catholic missionary to penetrate China.

When the Mongol cause collapsed, the Catholic church in China also went under because the ensuing Ming dynasty enforced policies of nativism. Of the Muslim travelers to China, the Arab Ibn Battuta, who was in China around 1342, left the most detailed and balanced account of Chinese life. His narratives contributed greatly to the growing body of information on China available to the West, much of which was devoted to exotic and supposedly peculiar Oriental customs. In Rabban Sauma, a Nestorian monk, the Mongols had a counterpart to these European travelers and records. Sauma, accompanied by a disciple, went to Mesopotamia and Europe, by way of Constantinople, in 1287, to seek Christian help against Islam. He met the pope in Rome and several potentates in France, but he returned home empty-handed save for various religious relics that he had collected in the Holy Land.

Decline of the Dynasty

Eventually the Mongols lost their grip on their expansive empire in China and Central Asia. None of Kublai's eight successors in Beijing approached his capability. Cultural differences, great distances, and the difficulty of communication wore down the political structure. After a century or so in China, the Mongols, a minority, although trying to preserve their cultural identity, assimilated the customs of their numerous subjects and lost their own distinctive stamp.

For seventy-five years after Kublai, the line held on at Beijing as the government fell apart and the ruling line at Khanbaliq lost vigor; the last monarch ascended the throne as a boy. The adverse personal and administrative factors of the usual syndrome of dynastic decline emerged: famines, uncontrolled floods, excessive taxation, and revolts. Rebellions led by the Red Turbans, the military arm of White Lotus Society, a group from Song times, broke out in South China and in the lower Yangtze valley and spread north. The rebels compounded agrarian distress with Buddhist heresies and prophesied the impending arrival of Maitreya and the millennium. But, as usual, with peasant revolts even into the twentieth century, the rebellious chiefs did not unite in common campaigns against the Mongols, who might otherwise have fallen earlier. It required a single strong native Chinese general to end the alien dynasty.

The Yuan, the first foreign dynasty to rule all of China, constituted an interim between the Song and the Ming. The process of acculturation favored the Chinese because the country was too large for Mongol absorption of the host people. Despite the far-flung empire and the presence of foreigners during these years, Mongol China underwent no basic changes in its way of life. No new major religion or philosophy took hold. No innovative political, economic, or social institution entered the imperial framework. Contact with foreigners did not stimulate the Chinese to cultural heights, and in reaction after the Mongol expulsion, the Chinese later turned to their pre-Mongol heritage, to Ming nativism, and eventual stagnation. China was not to experience foreign invasion again until the arrival in force of the Manchus, several centuries later.

Chronology

1167?-1127	Genghis Khan
1206	Genghis confirmed as Great Khan at Karakorum
1215	Jurchen capital of Zhongdu (Beijing) falls to Mongols
1245-1247	Italian Franciscan John of Plano Carpini to China
1249	Andrew of Longmeau in Karakorum
1252-1255	Flemish Franciscan William of Rubruck to China
1260-1269	Nicolo and Maffeo Polo's first trip to China
1264-1294	Kublai Khan rules from Khanbaliq (Beijing)
1274, 1281	Invasions of Japan
1275-1292	Polos (with Nicolo's son Marco) again in China
1279	Kublai Khan defeats last of Southern Song; beginning of Yuan dynasty
1294-1338	Italian Franciscan John of Monte Corvino in Khanbaliq
1327-1330	Italian Franciscan Odoric of Pordenone to China
ca. 1342	Arab traveler Ibn Battuta in China
1353	John of Marignolli returns to Avignon after China trip
1368	End of Yuan

Chinese Sovereigns: The Yuan Dynasty
(Number of reign names in parentheses)

Shizu (Kublai Khan), 1279-1294 (1)

Zhengzong, 1295-1307 (2)

Wuzong, 1308-1311 (1)

Renzong, 1312-1320 (2)

Yingzong, 1321-1323 (1)

Tai-ding-di, 1324-1327 (1)

Mingzong, 1328-1329 (1)

Wenzong, 1330-1332 (1)

Shundi, 1333-1368 (3)

17

THE MING DYNASTY

(1368 to 1644)

The new rulers appropriated the name *Ming* (Bright). An archetype of Chinese dynasties, the Ming, of the Zhu family, brought peace, prosperity, stability, and the stereotyped image of a traditional China ruled by scholar-gentry on neo-Confucian principles. In these years of rule, 1368 to 1644, the territorial limits of China did not grow, but the population rose from about 60 million to 108 million, because of a concurrent increase in food production.

During the breakup of the Mongol empire, with the attendant rebellions, many factions contended for power, the strongest of whom eventually founded the Ming dynasty. He was Zhu Yuanzhang (Chu Yüan-chang), born of peasant parents. At the age of seventeen, an orphan without means of support, he entered a Buddhist monastery and became a monk. After seven years, he gave up monastic life and became a soldier in the forces of an anti-Mongol leader in Anhui province in the lower Yangtze. His military ability attracted the attention of his commander, who promoted him rapidly. In 1356, he captured Nanjing, and in this regional base of power, he established himself as the Duke of Wu, a title derived from the old kingdom of that name. After defeating his rivals, he drove the Mongols out of Dadu (Beijing) by 1368, when the dynasty was officially established. It took several more years to push the enemy completely out of China. Court officials designated the successful contender as the Hungwu (Great Military Power) emperor. The use now of a single reign name for the full period of rule rather than several titles, or even a posthumous title, set a precedent for later emperors.

Zhu was able and bright, but cruel. With his grotesque snoutlike nose, annals informally referred to him as the "pig emperor." After consolidation at home, he turned to Chinese interests abroad. He took defensive coastal measures against the Japanese pirates ravaging the China coast. Ming troops held the line against Tamerlane (Timur the

Lame), a descendant in the Mongol line in Samarkand in Central Asia. After the Chinese monarch died in 1398, Tamerlane planned an invasion of China when he himself died in 1405.

In internal administration Hungwu displayed little originality. In a reaction against foreign importations and Mongol innovations, he re-emphasized tradition. He restored many time-honored Chinese institutions, but he set up his capital at Nanjing, in the heart of the country he knew best. There, he erected magnificent buildings and enclosed the city with 20 miles of walls 60 feet high. This was probably the largest and grandest project of its kind in the world at the time. He replaced the centuries-old premiership with a cabinet, or Grand Secretariat, and reinstated the civil service examinations for government offices. He organized Buddhist monks into a hierarchy to facilitate state control and at the same time, strengthened Confucianism, primarily by building a system of Confucian schools throughout the country.

Upon the emperor's death in 1398, civil war broke out for several years between the grandson placed on the throne and the fourth son (out of the twenty-six of the late monarch), who ruled as the Prince of Yen in the Beijing area. After destructive fighting in North China, the latter assumed the throne as Yongle (Yung Lo, or Perpetual Happiness), the most important of sixteen dynastic sovereigns (one ruled in two separate periods with different reign names). Yongle's reign, 1403 to 1424, marked the height of Chinese power. He moved the capital back to Dadu, renamed Beijing, which was in a better location than Nanjing for defense of the empire against the northern barbarians. He rebuilt the city on its Mongol foundations, and his palaces and many other structures of the time are still standing. Yongle effected policies usually associated with strong monarchs: the improvement of public works, such as the Grand Canal, the administration of Confucian examinations, and the movement of populations for colonization or reclamation of areas laid waste by war. In a notable program of foreign expansion, Yongle pushed into Mongolia and established diplomatic relations in Japan with the shoguns (military governors) who, as advisers to the emperor, were the indirect rulers of that country. He dispatched expeditions into Annam and Burma.

His most prominent international activity was the maritime penetration of Southeast and South Asia. In an unusual outburst of energy, he and his successor sent admiral Zheng He (Cheng Ho) of Mongol-Arab origins (and castrated at the age of ten) on several long and costly naval expeditions to distant lands. The undertakings were occasioned for several possible reasons. The monarch, fearful that his disenthroned nephew was still alive, wanted to track the rival down and eliminate him. He was also probably searching for allies to help ward off future Mongol invasions, since the enemy still hovered on China's northern border. Most likely, he wished to promote Chinese prestige abroad through normal trade and tribute relations with southern and western lands through sea trade routes, as alternative land passages which were now blocked by enemies. Whatever the imperial motivation was, in 1405, the first fleet of 63 junks manned by some 27,870 seamen under Zheng He sailed south on a two-year expedition. The admiral brought back to China the ruling prince of Palembang in South Sumatra. On the third voyage, he returned with the king of Ceylon, who had put up strong resistance.

From these expeditions the Chinese learned much about international sea routes, foreign harbors, and distant customs. By 1415, sixteen states, including Arabian principalities as far away as Aden and Hormuz, were sending tribute to Beijing. In colorful processions to the capital, envoys brought exotic gifts and animals. During these expeditions, Chinese maritime technology was advanced. The highly developed junk (the origin of the word is unclear) appeared ungainly as it hugged the coastal lanes, but in open seas, it could travel up to six knots. The junks, with various amenities and public rooms for passengers, were quite comfortable for their time. Some of the larger vessels contained up to four decks.

The Ming expeditions, seven between 1405 and 1431, ceased abruptly because of several considerations. The costs of the voyages were high, the bureaucrats resented eunuch leadership, and the more immediate Mongol menace remained on China's northern borders. After Yongle's reign, Ming foreign relations went downhill; Japanese piratical raids intensified. Foreign marauders burned the port of Ningbo, and despite Chinese precautions, they raided the Yangtze River cities, besieged Nanjing, and held sway over Taiwan. In a return to isolationist policies, the emperors forbade Chinese ships or nationals to sail beyond coastal waters and made coastal defense a primary military policy.

Although Chinese international prestige declined, domestic policies were consolidated. When, in 1421, Yongle started to rebuild Beijing, he adopted city plans more extensive than those of the Mongols. As his predecessor had done in Nanjing, the emperor surrounded his capital with massive city walls forty feet high and fourteen miles in circumference. The city was laid out in the form of a square with nine gates, each protected by a secondary gate. At its center was the Imperial City, which was another walled square area with a five-mile perimeter, where the bureaucrats lived. Within the Imperial City was the Forbidden City, where the imperial family resided in sumptuous palaces surrounded, yet again, by high, red walls and moats of about two miles in circumference. The rebuilt Beijing was a symbol of Ming monumentality and symmetry. (The Manchus later developed the city to the south of the

Ming Imperial City. Today, Beijing has architectural residues of the Mongol, Ming, Manchu, Nationalist, and Communist regimes.)

Life In Ming China

The capital visibly symbolized Ming rule, which grew more despotic in nature over the years. Many governmental powers personally were concentrated in the person of the emperor, the culmination of trends begun in the Song and augmented in the Mongol. Because the preceding Mongols were alien conquerors, their state bureaucracy had required vigorous arbitrary control and direct executive action at the top. The first Ming rulers themselves appropriated strong tactics and concentrations of power. To this end, in order to enhance the role of the emperor, the Ming abolished the position of prime minister and made other chief posts, in effect, advisory. A strong ruler heading a strong centralized political institution meant efficiency at best or tyranny at worst.

The Ming refined the tripartite system of government: the civilian bureaucracy, the military, and the censorate. A civilian officialdom returned to the traditional Six Ministries (Liu Bu) and restored to normal the number from the four of Mongol times: Revenue, War, Justice, Rites, Public Works, and Civil Office. The centralized military hierarchy paralleled the civilian. The Board of Censors reported on the conduct of official affairs. The censors, usually young officials of low rank drawn from the general civil bureaucracy, served in the provinces on one-year tours of duty and investigated the conduct of justice and ceremonies. They reported directly to the throne, but their powers were limited, for their total duration in office was nine years or less. Upon the completion of the special duty, they returned to regular civil bureaucratic jobs without the protection of immunity or tenure.

Local administration became more complex with the increase in population. The Ming divided China into fifteen provinces, headed by rotating governors who did not, however, serve in their home province, in accordance with the law of avoidance. Circuit officials acted as police and supervisors of monopolies. Country administrative units were reorganized into four levels. The provinces (*sheng*) were divided into 159 prefectures (*fu*), 234 subprefectures (*zhou*), and 1,171 districts or counties (*xian*). The government inaugurated the *lijia* system, in which representatives of family groups were designated to preserve order, collect taxes, and recruit labor for public works. The Ming also drew up comprehensive codes of criminal and administrative law.

To ensure effective tax collection, the Ming continued the detailed official registers of land and population. According to land registers dated 1383, China had the equivalent of 129 million acres under cultivation, much less than the arable land now. In a variation of the Tang-instituted double tax, the government imposed the important autumn grain tax on rice and a summer tax, mainly on winter crops harvested in early summer. The nonagrarian taxes were on silver, silk, produce other than grain, and labor service. To effect a workable tax structure in the last century of the Ming, harried provincial authorities resorted to the single whip system (*yitiaobian*) of taxation, whereby all the various types of imposts were combined into one or several collections, payable in silver.

New crops continued to enter China. Cotton was one. At first, farmers were reluctant to raise it, but the government coerced them to include the plant as a secondary crop. Official edicts ordered peasants in districts considered agriculturally favorable to it to deliver annually a certain quota of cotton in lieu of a head tax. Because of this official encouragement of the crop, Ming China became one of the world's great cotton-producing areas, as it is today. Maize or Indian corn was another. After making its way from the Western Hemisphere through Spain and the Arabs in the Near East, it became widely cultivated in China. The sweet potato and the peanut arrived from the New World, possibly by way of the Philippines. These crops, grown in soil of low fertility, added variety and nutrition to Chinese diets, especially in the south. Indirectly through commercial avenues at Manila, or via Japan and Korea, tobacco reached South and North China. Officials opposed its introduction and the Ming prohibited its cultivation and use, subject to severe penalties, but to little effect.

Other new imports included a different type of coin. From the Western Hemisphere came the Spanish silver peso, minted in Central and South America. In coastal southeastern Chinese ports, the wide use of the imported dollars via the Philippines eventually displaced the local currency so thoroughly that even in the twentieth century, under the Republic of China, the standard Chinese unit, although minted in China from indigenous silver, was popularly referred to as the Mexican dollar. Another import was eyeglasses. As early as the Tang, optical lenses had been imported; during the Song these were adapted as magnifying lenses. But not until the Ming did the Chinese wear eyeglasses, which came from Europe via Southeast Asia. Chinese scholars took to them, and eventually eyeglasses became part of the stereotype of the literati with their Mandarin gown, straggly beard, and long fingernails.

The Ming constructed bridges, temples, and pagodas. Their emperors seemed obsessed with wall-building, especially with the Great Wall, most of which existent dates from this era. With the ebbing of Buddhism, sculpture was minimal. Near the capital are tombs of most of the Ming monarchs, with spirit paths guarded by great animal and human sculptures, among the few remnants of that art in the round. On pottery and porcelain forms, artisans produced polychrome patterns as well as the blue and white for which the Ming became famous. Ceramics were produced in many sites, but the center was Jingdezhen (Ching-te-chen) in Jiangxi province, a town that derived its name from a Song reign period (1004-1008). That locality contained all the minerals necessary for the manufacture of porcelain, including kaolin, a white clay that could be fired under high pressure. Song tradition persisted in watercolor painting, especially landscapes, although as the dynasty progressed, ornateness set in. The first emperor established at Nanjing the academy of painting, which in the course of the dynasty codified theories of painting and rules of aesthetics in such books as the *Mustard Seed Garden Painting Manual (Jieziyuan huazhuan)*.

By the advent of the Ming dynasty, the educational and examination system operated in government schools on district, local, and prefectural levels. The schools taught the Confucian classics, although without organized facilities or regular curricula, and they held periodic local examinations. The advanced government schools for bureaucrats at the capital were crowned by the Hanlin Yuan, by now a national imperial institution of arts and letters. Under patronage of high officials or of rich merchants, about three hundred private academies brought together scholars and students, who received free maintenance and tuition. They published scholarly works, compilations, and encyclopedias, and they stored the wooden printing blocks on the academy's premises. A unique primer, widely used in elementary instruction, was the thirteenth-century *Three-Character Classic (Sanzi jing)*, a summary of basic knowledge in 356 alternatively rhyming lines, each with three characters.

The Ming bureaucratic examination system continued (and into the Qing), with variations, the three-tiered Song structure. After preliminary examinations in district towns, the first level of tests took place at the prefectural capital in two out of every three years. The successful candidate received the lowest principal degree of "budding genius" (*xiucai*) and was permitted certain privileges, among them exemptions from performing menial jobs and liability to the labor tax. But he could not vegetate in office; he had to advance higher or take periodic examinations, usually every three years. At the second rung of the ladder, provincial examinations were conducted every third year, again after preliminary tests. The successful candidate became a "recommended man" (*juren*), eligible to compete on the countrywide level. The third-rank examinations were given at the capital again every three years.

If he passed these, the candidate now became a "presented scholar" (*jinshi*) and was subject to a highest examination conducted in the imperial presence. If successful at this highest level, he received an official rank and post. An average of two hundred eighty applicants annually made the grade in this final round.

The system recruited the best literary and scholarly minds. To ensure proportional geographical representation, provincial and district quotas were set. Candidates did not need recommendations, and their names were withheld from the examiners. But there were weaknesses in the system. The tests dealt mainly with the classics, and they adhered to a rigid form and style. Some questions called for eight-legged essays (*baigu wenzhuang*) with answers organized under eight main topics, using no more than seven hundred characters, and written in prescribed style. Some bureaucrats did not take the examinations because they were imperial favorites or had purchased their offices, a practice that tended to increase toward the ends of dynasties when emperors needed more revenue.

The dynasty produced one noted philosopher, Wang Yangming, 1472-1529. He came from a family of scholars, passed the examinations, and became a bureaucrat, but one with a curious and incisive mind. Opposing the Zhu Xi school, he taught that the search for truth lay within one's self through intuition, examination of conscience, and sudden illumination. He adhered to many traditional Confucian ideas but was influenced by the emphasis in Chan Buddhism on intuition and meditation. Wang Yangming's thought became the vogue in Japan, where he was known as Oyomei.

In China, Wang's school remained a minority one, for the state-sponsored neo-Confucianism was too firmly entrenched. The Confucian classics enjoyed general acceptance, although in a growing critical spirit, one scholar boldly declared that parts of the *Classic of History* were spurious. The greatest Ming scholarship proceeded along other intellectual lines. Retired scholars and officials compiled geographies and valuable gazetteers, which gave detailed information on the economic, social, and political life of the authors's local areas. In one noteworthy endeavor, two botanists spent eighteen years compiling works on herbs. One medical scholar described more than eight thousand prescriptions and classified about nine hundred vegetables and a thousand animal and mineral drugs in sixty-two categories. This work went through fourteen editions and became a standard reference in Japan. At least three illustrated encyclopedias were compiled during the Ming. A 1615 dictionary listed 33,179 characters under 214 radicals, an arrangement used today. Yongle ordered a vast compendium of works and excerpts from the mass of Chinese literature. The endeavor, *Encyclopedia of the Yongle Period* (*Yongle dadian*), involved

2,180 scholars, who eventually turned out 11,095 volumes with 22,877 chapters. The cost of printing was prohibitive, so the imperial treasury never printed the entire collection, most of which remained in manuscript form, and only 869 volumes can be accounted for now.

The novel flourished in Ming China. The most popular stories, which had been developing over the centuries in one form or another, assumed their final shapes. Four novels were particularly prominent. The *Romance of the Three Kingdoms (Sanguozhi yanyi)*, a long historical novel attributed to Lo Guanzhong (Lo Kuan-chung), a writer of the late fourteenth century, was set in the time of political division and civil war among the three kingdoms of the third century A.D. The second, translated variously as *All Men Are Brothers* or *The Water Margin (Shuihuzhuan)*, originated in legends about a minor bandit named Song Jiang, who lived around 1120 in the Song dynasty. With three dozen cohorts, he maintained a lair in the great marshes in western Shandong near the juncture of the Yellow River and the Grand Canal. In later times, professional storytellers celebrated the exploits of the band in narratives, put partly to music. As Yuan playwrights developed the theme, the bandits became Robin Hood-like characters, and their number grew to 108. Its final form, as the novel fashioned by Ming authors, became popular with the large literate, but non-Confucian, audience.

A third work, the *Golden Lotus (Jin Ping Mei)*, China's first great realistic novel, borrowed its central character, Ximen Qing, from a chapter of *All Men Are Brothers*. This non-Confucian novel describes the pursuit of pleasure in everyday urban life and convincingly treats the women characters as individuals. *Monkey*, or the *Record of a Journey to the west (Xiyou ji)*, the work of a single author, Wu Chengen, 1500?-1580, is the absorbing story of an omnicompetent monkey who overcame great obstacles while escorting the great Buddhist pilgrim Xuanzang on his travels to the Western lands.

Foreign Affairs

Although weakened, the Ming perfected the tribute system. When he assumed the throne, Hungwu endeavored to reestablish the Confucian concept of the superior Chinese state in foreign affairs by dispatching envoys to neighboring states to announce his succession as the Son of Heaven. The theory considered the Middle Kingdom as the center of the universe with the emperor of China heading the political world order. Other states fitted in only as defined by the Chinese. The tribute system was a misnomer, for it involved much more than the presentation of gifts and the performance of the *kowtow*. It embraced all aspects of interstate relations, such as the regulation of trade, the exchange of ambassadors, and the conduct of diplomacy. In return for gifts brought to them, the Chinese often gave costlier presents in return. In a regularized system of diplomacy, "vassal" kings were given official patents of appointments and were confirmed by the emperor. Passport tallies kept tabs on the officials coming and going through designated ports. The tribute system, a nonaggresive form of imperialism, was essentially a policy of pacification through the exchange of gifts. The Chinese did not always fight to maintain their privileges; in fact, the Ming could ill afford to.

Although some Asian states sent tribute to China, the arrangement had little appeal to Westerners, who had begun to appear under official aegis in China. Now on a national basis under the protection of their country's gunboats, traders and missionaries came in renewed waves to seek commerce, profits, and converts. The Portuguese were first in point of time. In 1514, they landed on Lintin Island, located in the mouth of the river leading to Guangzhou. Three years later, the first official Portuguese mission, headed by Tomas Pires, arrived in the southern port, where it was well received. It was granted permission to proceed to Beijing, but no sooner had Pires arrived at the northern capital than he was hustled back to Guangzhou and imprisoned because of his haughty demeanor and impossible demands for trade. Driven out of the city, the Portuguese developed trading posts at Ningbo and Xiamen, but the Ming continued to consider them as insolent people.

The Portuguese made little dent in China, and for this they had mainly themselves to blame. They did obtain, however, the post of Macau in 1557 as a leasehold in return for their aid against the pirates ravaging the coast. The small uninviting peninsula off the mainland across the wide river mouth from what was later to become Hong Kong quickly became the jumping-off point for Westerners visiting China. The court disliked the foreign traders, but because Beijing was far from Guangzhou and the southern interests, it did not always assert its authority. For their part, the southern merchants welcomed foreign trade but not necessarily foreign customs and ideas. Conflicting interests arose: Beijing against Guangzhou, Chinese against Westerners.

Similarly, the Ming kept the missionaries at bay, although the Jesuits eventually received permission to proceed to Beijing. The order, associated with the Portuguese national interest, came early to China. It emphasized education and scholarship, trained its missionaries in the Chinese language, and selected a small but highly qualified band to propagate the faith. Francis Xavier, one of the missionaries, proceeded to Macao via the Portuguese outposts of Goa in India and Malacca in Southeast Asia. He spent some years in Japan and then

returned to Guangzhou, trying in vain to penetrate the Chinese mainland. He died in 1552 on an island near Macau, and his remains were
taken back to Goa.

Another Jesuit, Matteo Ricci, an Italian student of mathematics and
astronomy, had more luck. In 1582, he arrived at Macau via the usual
route of Goa. To ingratiate himself, he at first wore the habits of a
Buddhist monk and when this failed to gain his entry, he later dressed
as a Chinese Confucian scholar. In 1601, he received permission to
reside and preach in the capital, where he converted some eminent
officials and where he remained until his death in 1610. The secular
knowledge of the Jesuit held more appeal than the religious message
to the Chinese, who expressed interest in Western science and scholarship. Ricci prepared a map of the world, where he tactfully placed
China at the center. Reacting to their favorable reception in China, the
Jesuits described China to Europeans as a land of wise philosopher-
kings.

The Spanish, a second national European interest in East Asia,
showed little desire for trading or establishing mission posts in China.
The governors-general in Manila directed their main efforts to internal
exploitation, colonization, and conversion of the Philippine islands.
Chinese middlemen in the Philippine capital grew in economic wealth
and status in trade between Manila and the south China ports despite
occasional massacres of Chinese in the Spanish colony.

The Dutch were not successful in establishing toeholds in China. In
1604 and 1607, they requested permission to open trade at Guangzhou,
but the Chinese denied them access, probably at the instigation of their
European enemies, the Portuguese. In retaliation, the Dutch attacked
Macau unsuccessfully in 1622 and then moved to the Pescadores Islands off Taiwan to carry on further campaigns against the Portuguese.
They traded with the Chinese until two years later, when they retired
farther east to the island of Taiwan itself and established a trading post
and fort known as Zelandia Castel. After the pirate Koxinga (Zheng
Chenggung, or Cheng-kung) drove them out in 1662, the Dutch concentrated on trade efforts in Japan and Indonesia.

The Russians tried unsuccessfully in 1567 and 1619 to reach the
Ming court from northern Chinese border areas, as did the British from
the southern. The latter were the last major European power to arrive
in China, but they left the deepest imprint. In 1635, the first English
vessel reached Guangzhou; two years later, it was followed by a squad-
ron of English vessels commanded by Captain John Weddell. The
Chinese tried to thwart the British desire to trade by military force, but
the four tiny British ships easily blasted their way past Chinese forts
on the Guangzhou delta. When these ships returned to London, their

men carried evaluations of the Chinese that were not so laudatory as those of the Jesuits. This disparaging attitude became a portent of events to come.

Decline of the Dynasty

With the initial arrival of the Westerners, the Ming was already in its last decades, marked as usual by weak rulers, administrative abuses, revolts, and economic distress. Eunuchs increased their control of state affairs to such an extent that many officials resigned. Court favorites and members of the imperial family built up great estates; one prince owned 250,000 acres of land. In desperation, peasants driven from the land formed discontented bands that survived on brigandage and plunder. The Chinese became divided among themselves, and opportunists fought out succession disputes. In North China; Wu Sanguei (Wu San-kuei), a general seeking aid against a rival who held Beijing, made an alliance with the growing Manchu forces in Manchuria. After the Chinese rival had been vanquished, the foreign troops, upon request, refused to leave. Instead, the Manchus descended upon all China.

With internal peace and little interest in experimentation, the Ming registered the height of Chinese culturalism and unity in a prosperous realm; the tribute system enhanced ethnocentric traits. Much attention was still given by the Ming to the Mongols and central Asian tribes on the northern and northwestern borders, but the ocean contacts, however temporary, forecast the events of the future. Powerful Western forces began to encroach upon China from the south and by sea, and their presence in China was later to initiate the wrenching process of unwanted modernization.

Chronology

1368-1398	Rule of Emperor Hungwu, founder of Ming dynasty, in Nanjing
late 14th century	Novelist Lo Guanzheng, *Romance of the Three Kingdoms*
1403-1425	Rule of Yongle, moves capital to Beijing
1405-1431	Seven sea expeditions under Zheng He
1472-1529	Philosopher Wang Yangming
1500?-1580	Novelist Wu Chengen, *Monkey*
1514	First Portuguese on South China coast
1517	Unsuccessful Portuguese mission under Tomas Pires to Beijing

1552	Jesuit Francis Xavier dies off Macau
1557	Portuguese receive Macau as leasehold in perpetuity
1567	First unsuccessful Russian attempt to reach the Ming court
1601-1610	Jesuit Matteo Ricci in Beijing
1619	Second unsuccessful Russian attempt to reach the Ming court
1624-1662	Dutch on Taiwan
1635	First British vessel at Guangzhou
1637	British expedition under Captain John Weddell, using force, reaches Guangzhou
1644	End of Ming dynasty

Chinese Sovereigns: The Ming Dynasty

Hongwu, 1368-1399

Jianwen, 1399-1402

Yongle, 1403-1425

Hongxi, 1425-1426

Xuande, 1426-1436

Zhengtong, 1436-1450

Jingtai, 1450-1457

Tianshun (the restored Zhengtong), 1457-1465

Chenghua, 1465-1488

Hongshi, 1488-1506

Zhengde, 1506-1522

Jiajing, 1522-1567

Longqing, 1567-1572

Wanli, 1572-1620

Taichang, 1620

Tianqi, 1620-1627

Chongzhen, 1627-1645

The Ming, discarding the centuries-old custom of designating emperors in historical annals by their posthumous or temple names, used and equated (and the Qing followed) one reign name with one imperial rule. (The reign name was adopted on the first New Year's day after the accession to power).

Part Six

IMPERIAL CHINA

Fourth Phase—1644 to 1912

Like the earlier Mongols, the Manchu, or Qing, line with its emperors, consolidated its political hold over all of China. It ruled over the greatest extent of territory of any dynasty save that of the Mongols. Both dynasties had strong leaders who unified home territory before subjugating a weaker China. But the Manchus involved themselves more than the Mongols did with Chinese life and customs. In part because of this immersion, they ruled longer. Their emperors kept the Confucian bureaucracy and structure of state. But one problem with which they coped unsuccessfully was the persistent growth of Western powers, which by 1844 had imposed the first treaty settlement. This commenced the disintegration of the Chinese empire, which finally collapsed in 1912.

18

THE QING DYNASTY
(1644 to 1844)

The Manchus came from Jurchen tribes, like those who had plagued the northern Song. Rising in central and southern Manchuria, the Manchus by the early seventeenth century had perfected an efficient military organization. They possessed a script derived from Mongolia. They had an effective leader in Nurhachi (1559-1626), the founder of the Manchu state. He followed in the tradition of Genghis Khan in a rise to power through consolidation of clans and tribes. In 1616, he proclaimed himself khan and appropriated the dynastic title of the Later Jin, to denote Jurchen descent. Establishing his capital at Shenyang (known to the Manchus as Mukden), he used Chinese captives and residents as advisers. Adopting Confucianism, he won the tacit support of Chinese in Manchuria, where three million of them gave him their loyalty.

The Manchu line after Nurhachi fortunately had a succession of capable men to consolidate the kingdom. Abahai (1592-1643), the eighth son of the founder of the line, assumed the throne upon his father's death. He took the term Manchu (of obscure origin) to supersede the Jurchen appellation. In 1636, at the capital, he proclaimed the Qing (Pure) dynasty. Under his guidance, the Manchus conquered Inner Mongolia and temporarily subjugated Korea. They prepared for the conquest of North China, where troops broke through the Great Wall and knocked at the gates of Beijing. Next on the Manchu throne was Fulin, a young son of Abahai, a boy of nine who benefited from a strong regency under his uncle Dorgon. The regent ruled the Manchu kingdom until his death in 1651, by which time the Manchus were securely ensconced in Beijing with the transferred throne under Shunzhi (1644-1661).

Strong men continued in imperial position. Kangxi (K'ang-hsi), 1661-1722, second ruler of the dynasty in Beijing, was one of China's greatest emperors. Also initially ruling through a regency, at fifteen, he broke its power and appropriated political control. A man of great physical energy and intellectual ability, he loved the outdoor life and traveled extensively throughout his empire. Although originating nothing new in statecraft, he reinvigorated the political structure. He promoted the well-being of his subjects. He initiated public works, encouraged literature and the arts, subsidized scholarship, financed new editions of the classics, and composed short moral maxims. On his death, his son, the Yongzheng (Yung-cheng) emperor, ascended the throne for twelve years (1723-1735).

More noteworthy was Kangxi's grandson, the Qianlong (Ch'ien-lung) emperor, (1736-1796). He achieved a long life and carried China to another height of political power at home and abroad. He rounded out the boundaries of China and extended military campaigns into Central Asia, Tibet, Nepal, and Burma. At home, through a policy of censorship, he tried to eliminate antidynastic literature. Yet he was interested in other types of learning, and he authorized the compilation of encyclopedias. Like his grandfather, he was a patron of the arts and letters. He achieved domestic order in China, which noted phenomenal increases in wealth and population, from around 110 million at the beginning of his rule to triple that number at its conclusion. In 1796, the emperor abdicated, not wishing to reign longer than his famous grandfather. Three years later, he died. (In an amazing record, only three men ruled China for 135 years.)

It took a century for the initial Manchu emperors to consolidate China's borders. Taiwan came into the territorial fold and was eventually incorporated as part of coastal Fujian province. Inner Mongolia, already under Manchu domination, was supervised by a Superintendency of Dependencies (*Li-fan yuan*), first in Shenyang and later in Beijing. Xinjiang proved harder to assimilate. In the 1670s, Galdan, one of many rebels there, with Tibetan support, conquered the Tarim Basin oases and pushed on toward Beijing, but he was defeated in the Gobi. In Xinjiang itself fighting continued sporadically for another century, but eventually it became the New Dominion in the Manchu empire. The Qing also interfered in Tibetan affairs. They conducted three interventions there between 1720 and 1820, after which garrisons and advisers were permanently stationed at Lhasa, the capital. Under Chinese domination, the Dalai Lama and Panchen Lama, as spiritual and secular descendants of Buddhist deities, presided over the Tibetan Buddhist theocracy. From Tibet, Qianlong sent forces across the Himalayas into Nepal to pacify the Gurkhas, who were forced to recognize Chinese suzerainty.

Along the Burma border, wars also broke out. Despite the indecisive campaigns, the Burmese king sent periodic tribute to Beijing. Annamese rulers received investiture from the Chinese capital. Although Qing rule did not effectively embrace other areas of Southeast Asia, Chinese cultural influence and physical presence manifested themselves in peripheral countries. Into the newly established Southeast Asian colonies emigrated Chinese, mainly from the economically marginal southeastern coastal areas. Abroad, Chinese quarters grew in the chief cities. Commercial relations were maintained with Western colonizers, who used them to promote trade interests in China. Chinese junks, as well as Western ships, carried products to South China ports, where other Chinese merchants, the *hong*, processed the merchandise.

Despite border successes, by 1800, the Manchu dynasty registered aspects of cyclical decline. Favorites amassed fortunes, bureaucrats became corrupt, and revolts broke out. The White Lotus group rampaged in the central Yangtze area, while other secret societies conducted anti-Manchu campaigns elsewhere. Following the abdication of Qianlong came weak successors, Jiaqing (Chia-ch'ing), 1796-1820, and Daoguang (Tao kuang, 1821-1850). It was during the reign of the latter that matters came to head with the West.

In Manchu cultural life, little was new or striking. In Beijing, emperors erected more palaces (replacing those of the Mongol and the Ming) that remain to this day. Ceramic forms copied earlier models, although the Kangxi and Qianlong periods were noteworthy in both monochrome and polychrome specimens. In painting, there was imitation of previous masterpieces. Poetry and prose evidenced a commonplace inspiration. There was one outstanding novel, *Dream of the Red Chamber* (*Hongloumen*) by Cao Xueqin (Ts'ao Hsüeh-ch'in), known also as Cao Zhan (Ts'ao Chan), ca. 1715-1763, an autobiographical account in a riches-to-rags theme of a merchant family dealing in silk. Buddhism had long since, in the post-Tang period, become ossified in religious or cultural inspiration.

In philosophy, the school of Han Learning (Han Xue) sought to return to the original classics of the Han rather than analyze the works as transmitted by the Later Song neo-Confucianists. Another school termed Statecraft, in anti-Manchu statements, sought reasons for Chinese weakness and political decline. These stemmed, in part, they argued, from inbred attitudes and mistaken neo-Confucian concentration on human nature rather than on solving practical affairs of state.

During Qing rule, the Chinese noted an increased use of land devoted to food crops, which helped to sustain the population increase. The Chinese imported a variety of plants, some from the New World, including potatoes, squash, and varieties of beans. The deleterious opium was also imported, chiefly from India. Imperial decrees forbade the sale or importation of opium, but despite the bans, the drug was brought into the land by Western firms, which took over the profitable trade. The importation of opium was the immediate cause of the first war between China and Western powers.

The West in China

European and later American interests in China had been chiefly commercial in nature, but religious groups were also present. The Jesuit Ricci's successors, especially Adam Schall and Ferdinand Verbiest, carried on in the capital from Ming times. During most of Kangxi's reign, the emperor displayed a spirit of toleration toward them and other orders. But theological squabbles among the alien resident missionaries vitiated the cause. In the Rites Controversy (1628-1742), semantic debates ranged over appropriate Biblical translations, among others, of God and Jesus Christ. Kangxi sided with the more tolerant Jesuits, and papal missions and others who held a contrary view were expelled by the Chinese emperor, who had the final word in any debate on any subject. Qianlong continued the strong policy of suppression. Catholic missions atrophied in China, not only because of hard-hitting Chinese policies, but also because of conditions in Europe. The Jesuit order was proscribed by Pope Clement XIV in 1773, and the French Revolution and a secularist climate of opinion distracted from the evangelical spirit of missionary endeavor.

As missions declined in China, trade with the West increased. Economically self-sufficient, China, like India and southeast Asian lands, did not need Western products. By the nineteenth century, the Chinese desired from abroad only a few commodities (opium, furs, and certain foodstuffs). The Western merchants wanted tea and silk, the two traditional Chinese exports, on which they made great profits back home. Southern Chinese merchants cooperated with Western traders because they also profited from commerce. They often disregarded Beijing's orders regulating international commerce. At Macau, the Portuguese at first enjoyed a monopoly of trade. Other Western nationalities arrived, but in the ensuing centuries, the English East India Company, expanding from its Indian base of operations, overtook the Portuguese and all the others to become preeminent in the South China trade.

Because of official policy, trade was confined in the south to Macau and Guangzhou. In the latter port, Beijing sought to control foreign trade through the appointment of specific hongs, banded together into a co-hong or guild, to handle commercial matters with aliens. The monopolistic system was regarded as an inequity by Westerners, who desired more flexible trade arrangements. In the so-called Canton trade, foreigners were confined in residence and business activity to a suburb (Shameen), although their ships discharged cargoes farther downstream at the Whampoa Island anchorage. They had to conduct operations through the merchants or hongs, assigned to them. Each nationality was responsible to a certain hong who in turn was responsible to the *hoppo*, or customs superintendent, for Guangdong province, of which Guanzhou was the capital. Western merchants chafed under these limitations. But the Chinese made the rules, and if the aliens desired to trade, as they did for profit, they had to meet inequities.

Russia was the only Western state to penetrate China by land from the north and into the capital, the focus of power. As early as 1656, a mission from the czar had arrived in Beijing for purposes of trade, but it met with no success. Subsequent missions were similarly unsuccessful, and occasional warfare erupted along the long border. In 1689, a treaty at the border town of Nerchinsk settled Sino-Russian differences. It was the first treaty (in Latin) between China and a Western state, and it was an agreement concluded between equals rather than one forced on China. The articles defined mutual boundaries, regulated commerce, and provided for extradition. Over the ensuing century, other agreements, including that of Kiakhta (1728), further refined the nature of bilateral relations.

In the south, basic issues, besides trade matters, separated the Westerners and the Chinese. The Westerners advanced the notion of sovereign equality of nationals; the Chinese kept up tributary relations and termed Westerners as barbarians, even in official correspondence. Western law guaranteed individual rights; Chinese jurisprudence posited group responsibility for individual wrongdoing. Westerners wanted fully publicized, low, and regularized tariffs; the Chinese imposed secret, ad hoc, quixotic rates. Westerners objected to dealing only with the hong merchants; the Chinese refused to widen trade contacts. Western life and residence were restricted to Macau in the winter months and Shameen in the summers. The Chinese intended to keep it that way, although Western merchants sought year-round residence at Shameen.

Western traders became increasingly restive. Although the English spearheaded the Western cause in the Canton trade, they made little headway with the Chinese rulers. In contrast to its contemporaneous successes in India, the English East India Company made little gain in expanding China operations. In 1787, it designated Lieutenant Colonel

Charles Cathcart as a special envoy to Beijing to negotiate for improvements in trade conditions, but he died before reaching the capital. Five years later, Lord George Macartney was named chief of another mission which reached Beijing, but he was also unsuccessful. In 1816, the English dispatched Lord Amherst, whose failure at the capital was more resounding than Macartney's. In 1834, the year after the monopolistic hold of the company was abolished and English overseas trade was thrown open to any private enterprise, Lord Napier went to Guangzhou as the first Superintendent of British Trade to represent all British firms. He was similarly instructed to obtain concessions, but he never managed to depart Guangzhou for Beijing.

Like the British and other Europeans, the Americans desired additional rights in China, including rights equal to any which might be granted to any other third party. This oft-enunciated plank of the Open Door policy (equal commercial rights for all in a foreign country) was as old as American presence in Asia. In 1784, the first American ship, the *Empress of China*, sailed for Guangzhou from New York with a heterogeneous cargo, including furs. Other vessels soon followed. To regularize trade, resident American trading firms were soon established in Guangzhou. In 1787, Samuel Shaw was appointed American consul resident at Guangzhou. As the first official U.S. representative in China, Shaw administered estates of Americans who died there, disciplined mutinous sailors, and left an informative diary reporting some of his problems of office. Mission work augmented trade concerns. In 1829, the first Protestants arrived at Guangzhou, and other missionaries, including more Catholics, soon followed. American naval vessels sailed upstream to Guangzhou to remind the Chinese of the presence of an American iron fist in a velvet glove, a tactic the British were similarly pursuing.

The issue of opium triggered the first conflict. In 1839, Commissioner Lin Zexu (Lin Tse-hsü) arrived in Guangzhou from Beijing to deal with the matter. He compelled Westerners to deliver their opium stocks, which were then mixed with salt, lime, and water, and dumped into the river. Protesting, the English retired to regroup forces in the nearby uninhabited island of Hong Kong. Conflict shortly thereafter erupted between the English and Chinese, but war was never formally declared. Chinese forces were defeated by English in lopsided campaigns, mainly on water, in South and Central China. In August 1842, a peace treaty was signed on the deck of the *Cornwallis*, a English warship anchored off Nanjing on the Yangtze River.

The terms of the Treaty of Nanjing generally reflected immediate British and overall Western objectives in China. Five ports—Guangzhou, Xiamen (Amoy), Fuzhou, Ningbo, and Shanghai—all south of the Yangtze, were now opened to English trade. In these ports, the English could station a superintendent of trade or consular officer and were granted rights in leased settlements or concessions (not necessarily cessions) where they might reside. In Guangzhou, the monopolistic co-hong was abolished and there, as well as in the other ports, the British could trade with whomever Chinese they wished. English-Chinese official intercourse was placed on a plane of diplomatic equality. Reflecting the mid-nineteenth century English free-trade philosophy, the treaty terms fixed the tariff at a low five percent ad valorem (cost of goods). Losers in the war, the Chinese paid an indemnity the equivalent of $21 million. They also ceded Hong Kong in perpetuity to the English. The treaty mentioned nothing about opium, other than payment ($6 million of the overall indemnity) for the confiscated lot.

In October 1843, in the supplementary Treaty of the Bogue (the mouth of the Pearl River), the English elaborated commercial terms and received extraterritoriality in criminal cases. According to this principle of international law, foreigners in a country were tried according to their own law codes by their own judges. This second treaty also delineated the most-favored-nation clause, in which a concession extended to one foreign power could be requested by all others. (In effect, all nations would be most-favored.)

Four months after the Treaty of Nanjing was signed, President John Tyler of the United States requested from Congress authority to send an emissary to China to conclude a similar treaty. With congressional approval, the post was conferred on Caleb Cushing of Massachusetts, a member of the House Committee of Foreign Affairs and a friend of the president. In February 1844, Cushing arrived in Macau, where the Chinese stalled him off. He then threatened to proceed directly to Beijing to negotiate the treaty. The threat resulted in Chinese signature of a treaty, known after his name (or the Wangxia Treaty, after a Macau suburb where it was concluded). Its terms followed in general those of the two English agreements (without any territorial cession), but the American version extended extraterritoriality to include civil as well as criminal cases.

Last of the major parties, the French concluded the Whampoa Treaty of 1844 along similar lines. With subsequent revisions, the treaties in the aggregate provided the legal basis for Western rights in China over the following century. Their all-encompassing terms included the opening of ports, regularizing of commercial representation, grants of leaseholds in concessions for residential purposes, territorial cessions, payment of indemnities, tariff controls, extraterritoriality in both civil and criminal cases, and freedom of worship. As a result of the first treaty settlement (1842-1844), Western presence came to the coastal provinces of China south of the Yangtze. But with it came concurrent increasing problems for the Chinese and Manchus. There was now no containing the alien threat.

Chronology

1559-1626	Nurhachi at Shenyang
1592-1643	Abahai
1628-1742	Rites Controversy
1644-1661	Emperor Shunzhi; capital relocated to Beijing
1656	Unsuccessful Russian mission to Beijing
1661-1722	Emperor Kangxi
1689	Chinese-Russian Treaty of Nerchinsk
ca. 1715-1763	Novelist Cao Xueqin
1720-1820	Three Qing interventions in Tibet
1723-1735	Emperor Yongzheng
1728	Chinese-Russian Treaty of Kiakhta
1736-1796	Emperor Qianlong
1784	First American ship, *Empress of China*, to China
1787	Cathcart mission
1792	Macartney mission to Beijing
1796-1820	Emperor Jiaqing
1816	Amherst mission
1821-1850	Emperor Daoguang
1829	First Protestant missionaries arrive in China
1834	Lord Napier, first Superintendent of British Trade at Guangzhou
1833-1842	Opium War; Treaty of Nanjing
1842-1844	First Treaty Settlement
1843	Chinese-British Treaty of the Bogue
1844	Chinese-American Cushing (or Wangxia) Treaty; Chinese-French Treaty of Whampoa

Chinese Sovereigns: The Qing Dynasty

Shunzhi, 1644-1661

Kangxi, 1661-1722

Yongzheng, 1723-1735
Qianlong, 1736-1796
Jiaqing, 1796-1820
Daoguang, 1821-1850
Xianfeng, 1851-1861
Tongzhu, 1862-1874
Guangxu, 1875-1908
Xuangtong, 1908-1912

19

CHINA AND THE WEST

(1844 to 1912)

As a result of the first treaty settlement of the 1840s, Westerners acquired toehold bases along coastal South China. They expanded out from these areas, to receive more rights and privileges over the ensuing decades. Through subsequent treaty provisions, they penetrated all of China. Manchu rulers and Chinese intellectuals varied in reaction to Western encroachments. Some accommodated themselves; others compromised with foreign ideas; some ignored the alien presence. Those who favored Westernization were themselves divided as to what to adopt and how to adopt fresh ideologies and institutions. Thus China was modernized in a wrenching process that involved disintegrating Manchus, divided Chinese, and forceful Westerners.

As a result of the first treaty settlement, foreigners flocked to the open ports. Traders and missionaries came there to reside. Few Chinese or treaty-port Westerners knew the language of the other party, and a type of "pidgin," or corrupt, English arose as a medium of communication. Scholars of China were rare, although an American Protestant, S. Wells Williams, compiled a dictionary and the first general account of China available to Americans, *The Middle Kingdom* (1848). In the midst of minimal contact, misunderstandings arose at all levels. In the wake of the treaties and enforced foreign presence, some Chinese sought ways to graft onto Chinese life some of the more desirable imported concepts. Some in the south continued, in the earlier tradition of the Manchu School of Statecraft, to examine what caused Chinese weaknesses and seek ways to invigorate decaying institutions. Lin Zexu authored a book on maritime history that included updated naval tactics. But the official line generally subscribed to by the Manchus was to minimalize relations to strict interpretations of treaty settlement terms. The situation simmered along until the outbreak of the Taiping (Heavenly Peace) Rebellion.

Lasting over two decades, this rebellion, was a major event of nineteenth-century Chinese history. Because of it, at least 20 million persons perished directly or indirectly. Its leader was Hung Xiuquan (Hung Hsiu-ch'uan), 1814-1864. A peasant who belonged to the minority group called the Hakka, he was a poor student who failed the traditional Confucian examinations repeatedly. Converted in Guangzhou to Christianity, he began to preach his own brand and attracted a following. He predicted a millennium for China in which he would rule the state in good Confucian hierarchy with Christ as the Heavenly Elder Brother. Amassing followers in the south, in the early 1850s, he moved up to the Yangtze valley. In addition to the planned overthrow of Manchu rule, he promised land redistribution to peasants and other social reforms, including the outlawing of opium and foot binding. Westerners, initially sympathetic to the movement, withdrew moral support because of its violence and its perversion of Christian theology. Hung died and with no successors but divided leadership, the rebellion faded by 1865. As a typical Chinese agrarian-religious revolt, the uprising unfolded according to historical form. But the Taiping phenomenon was also revolutionary because it was spawned, in part, by modern factors, including the humiliation of China by Western powers and the introduction of Christian ideas.

The Taiping threat was the greatest of many mid-century rebellions. Bandit groups roamed at will throughout the land. The Nien groups in North China were particularly destructive. Two serious Muslim revolts occurred, one in the south and another in the west.

In the midst of internal strife, the Manchus faced renewed Western aggression. In 1856, war once more erupted between Beijing and the English, now allied with the French. The immediate causes for war were the British charges that the Chinese had poisoned Hong Kong bread and had boarded a British-owned ship, the *Arrow*, in Guangzhou, where its cargo was confiscated. The French excuse for war was the murder of a French priest in South China, far outside treaty-stipulated boundaries of residence. Although invited to join as allies, the Russians and the Americans stayed on the sidelines. The conflict was easily won by the British and French. They retook Guangzhou, pushed into North China, and occupied Tianjin. Treaties there were once again negotiated with the Chinese. But before ratifications could be exchanged, fighting again broke out, and English-French forces moved on Beijing, where they burned the Summer Palace as a punitive move.

The second settlement (1858-1860) consisted of a series of new treaties. Because of the most-favored-nation clauses, the Americans and Russians in later treaties received similar rights. The Tianjin treaties (as they were collectively called) with the English and French ceded a part of Kowloon, opposite Hong Kong, to the English in perpetuity. New indemnities were imposed. The Chinese were to create a foreign affairs bureau and permit alien diplomatic residence in Beijing. The term barbarian was dropped in official communications. For trade and residence, the treaties added ten more ports (four on the Yangtze, two on Taiwan; one each in Manchuria, Shandong, Guangdong, and Hainan Island). The supplementary treaty of Beijing in turn opened Tianjin to trade. The Yangtze was made accessible to Western merchant ships. Foreigners were allowed to travel in the interior, and missionaries received added protection. Tariff schedules were revised, and the opium trade, instead of being abolished, was legalized.

Russia, through two special treaties, received additional consideration. In the Aigun Treaty of 1858, China ceded to Russia the territory north of the Amur River to the watershed but kept joint occupation of the territory east of the Ussuri River, in Siberia. Two years later, Russia received full title to the latter territory, known as the Maritime province. Manchu rulers, through pledges of aid, concluded these treaties because Russia had promised them help against British and French forces. But the Russians never aided the Chinese; instead, Anglo-French forces occupied the capital. The Chinese lost all around. Without committing any manpower, Russia won out. Yet several times again in the later decades, the hard-pressed Chinese turned to the Russians for help.

The Taiping Rebellion and the second treaty settlement spurred at Beijing a program of limited reform known as the Tongzhi (T'ung-chih) Restoration, termed after the reign name of the Manchu emperor (1861-1874). Some new leadership emerged in this interim. Prince Gung, a man in his late twenties, stayed behind to negotiate with the Western powers after the court fled south in 1898, to avoid the advancing Anglo-French expedition. A few Chinese generals also rose to prominence through platforms of reforms and efficiency. Of these, probably the most important was Zeng Guofan (Tseng Kuo-fan), 1811-1872. In the process of defeating the Taiping, he organized the first modern army in China. His tactics of restoration were to reestablish civilian morale, reinstitute the examination system, rebuild libraries, and return pacified areas to normalcy. Li Hungzhang (Li Hung-chang), 1823-1901, his disciple, operated in the Shanghai area, where he established arsenals. He also founded a Chinese navigation company, a coal mine, and a textile mill. Developing into a statesman-diplomat, he later negotiated for China some of its chief treaties.

With a few top men promoting some Westernization, Beijing embarked on a limited reform program under the Tongzhi emperor. It restored peace and order by quelling not only the Taiping, but also the Nien and the Muslims. In the latter campaigns, Zuo Zongtang (Tso Tsung-t'ang), another strong Chinese general in the employ of the Manchus, was particularly effective. The Manchu government also reduced the land tax, initiated a more effective collection, instituted economy measures at court, and sent the first Chinese abroad to learn various technological skills. The conduct of foreign relations was modernized with the establishment of the Zongli (Tsungli) Yamen, an office to deal with the West. The Tongzhi measures also included the modernization of the military, the promotion of industry, and the construction of short railroad and telegraph lines.

Some of the court protested even a limited program of modernization. Heading the opposition was Cixi (Tz'u-hsi, the empress dowager), who in effect, directed the political fortunes of China from the mid-1870s until her death in 1908. A Manchu concubine of the emperor, she presented him with a son who became the Tongzhi emperor. Throughout the period of his minority, she was the actual ruler of China. When he died the year after attaining majority, the empress chose as his successor a nephew four years of age, known as the Guangzu (Kuang-hsu) emperor, 1875-1908. In 1884, she ousted Prince Gung and his clique. She misappropriated naval funds and used them to rebuild the Summer Palace. She had little concept of important state matters and underestimated the strength of the West.

Meanwhile, Western rights proliferated. As a result of the terms of the second treaty settlement, foreigners were now residing in Beijing, along the China coast from Guangzhou to Manchuria, and in the interior. Commercial and missionary interests expanded. Unique among the treaty ports, Shanghai grew phenomenally. There, foreign settlements and concessions burgeoned. Chinese studied at home and abroad. The Zongli Yamen founded a College of Foreign Studies to train young diplomats. Founded in 1854, the Qing Imperial Maritime Customs in these decades grew into an international bureaucracy with branches in all the treaty ports where customs duties were efficiently collected. (The monies collected not only helped to secure the payment of Chinese treaty indemnities, but supported official modernizing projects.) Presiding over the institution for years was the capable Britisher Robert Hart. In 1877, the first resident Chinese minister abroad took up his post in London. Within two years, other diplomatic posts were established in the United States, Japan, and Western Europe. Chinese students went to the United States, England, and France. Other Chinese who went abroad were the work emigrants and coolies (unskilled laborers), who fanned out over Southeast Asia and countries farther afield, including the United States.

By the end of the century, foreign interests in China had expanded further. In 1870, the French, as a result of mission persecution in the north, retaliated with extensive diplomatic demands. In the south, they clashed with the Chinese over Vietnam. In 1885, with Li Hungzhang as negotiator, a treaty was concluded which ended Chinese suzerainty there. After a member of the British consular service was murdered in Southwest China, the Zhefoo Convention of 1876 gave the English, in addition to the usual indemnity and apology, more open ports on the Yangtze and an official residence in Yunnan province in the southwest. In 1887, after annexing the last of Burma, the English eliminated Chinese political influence there. That same year, the Portuguese received in perpetuity Macau, a colony they had leased since the mid-sixteenth century, Meanwhile, Russia in the 1881 Treaty of St. Petersburg, had settled western China borders, established consulates in Turkestan and Mongolia, and received permission to trade in border areas without the payment of duties.

The United States also escalated interests. After the first treaty settlement, in 1845, representatives in Guangzhou were upgraded from consuls to commissioners. In 1857, the rank again jumped to that of envoy extraordinary and minister, with residence at Beijing. The most famous name in Chinese-American diplomatic relations of these years was that of Anson Burlingame, whom President Abraham Lincoln sent to the Chinese capital (1862-1867). Counseling restraint in Western demands on the Chinese, he won favor in the host country. Upon his resignation from the U.S. diplomatic service, Beijing in turn requested his services to negotiate new and more equitable Western treaties for China.

In 1868, Burlingame, in Washington, concluded a treaty with Secretary of State William Seward. The agreement provided for Chinese sovereignty in treaty ports over areas not already ceded, granted the right to station Chinese consuls in American ports, and extended reciprocal freedom of religion. Its terms provided for immigration of coolie labor into the United States. The provisions stipulated the most-favored-nation treatment for Americans in China and for Chinese in the United States, except for naturalization for citizenship. They proclaimed equal educational opportunity and reconfirmed American noninterference in Chinese affairs. Burlingame proceeded to European capitals in an attempt to wring similar concessions of equality for the Chinese government, but he died before completing his task.

Japan concurrently advanced interests in China and peripheral areas. In 1894, war broke out over Chinese and Japanese rights in Korea, where both neighbors had long historic affiliations. The conflict was short-lived and one-sided. The modernized Japanese fleet and troops easily defeated the Chinese. The next year, a treaty concluded at Shimonoseki in Japan imposed harsh terms on the Chinese. Among then, China renounced its suzerainty in Korea, recognized Korean independence, paid an indemnity, and opened four new treaty ports to Japan (which, through the most-favored-nation status, became available to the other powers). China ceded to Japan the Liaodong peninsula in southern Manchuria, Taiwan, and the Pescadores, an island group off Taiwan. But within a week after the treaty was signed, Russia, France, and Germany, in the so-called Triple Intervention, forced Japan to return the Liaodong peninsula to China because it threatened sea approaches to Beijing. The Japanese, bowing to a superior force, complied, but received an additional indemnity from China for the territory lost.

Some Chinese in the post-Tongzhi period continued to opt for modernization. Zuo Zongtang and Zhang Zhidong (Chang Chih-tung), 1837-1909, another bureaucrat, showed interest in constructing railroads financed by consortiums, or groups of foreign powers. But while China needed general reorganization on a broad basis, the measures taken tended to be piecemeal, halting, and ineffective. Kang Yuwei, 1858-1927, was one of the few Chinese who came to grips with the problem of total modernization. A scholar in the traditional Confucian system, he studied Western subjects and wrote several books, including *Confucius as a Reformer (Kungzi Gaizhi Kao)* and the *Book of the Great Unity (Da Tung Shu)*, in which he envisioned universalism and social harmony as China's contribution to world civilization.

Kang's ideas soon reached the youthful Guangzu emperor who, during a temporary retirement of the dowager empress, called in the philosopher to effect reforms. In the spring of 1898, during the so-called Hundred Days of Reform, Kang Yuwei drafted edicts which rained down upon the country from Beijing. A multitude of measures were promulgated relating to constitutional monarchy, education, literacy, industrialization, military training, formulation of a budget, and the abolition of the banners (the traditional Manchu military units). Factionalism split the court, and the Old Buddha, as the dowager empress was informally known, came out of retirement to reassume command. Yuan Shikai (Yüan Shih-k'ai), 1859-1916, the commander of the only modernized army in the Beijing area, sided with the conservatives rather than with the reformers, whose programs were abruptly squelched. Kang escaped with his life, and the reforms ground to a halt.

As a result of China's weakness after the Sino-Japanese War, Westerners moved in to demand additional rights. Foreign powers sought to obtain additional cessions of territory and to create spheres of influence in the third treaty settlement (1895-1898). They forced loans on the hapless Chinese and practiced financial imperialism. In the south, the French asked for railway and mine concessions, and the adjustment of the northern Vietnam border in their favor. The Germans procured Giaozhou (Kiaochow) Bay in Shandong with the port of Qingdao (Tsingtao) under a ninety-nine-year lease. The English, concentrating in the rich and vast Yangtze valley, extracted other economic concessions. In 1898, they obtained the New Territories, extending behind Kowloon, opposite Hong Kong, on the mainland, on a ninety-nine-year lease.

The Russians, at the coronation of the czar at St. Petersburg in 1896, persuaded Li Hungzhang to sign a fifteen-year treaty of alliance directed against Japan. They also received the right to construct the Chinese Eastern Railway across northern Manchuria as a shortcut to Vladivostok for the trans-Siberian railroad. In 1898, in the Liaodong peninsula, from which they had just three years earlier helped to eject the Japanese, they now received twenty-five-year leases for Lushun (Port Arthur) and Dalian (Dairen); both ports are collectively known as Luda. The Russians also built the South Manchurian Railway, a southern spur from the Chinese Eastern Railway, to link up with the newly acquired coastal leaseholds.

As the dismemberment of China proceeded, the United States, concerned for its own rights and for those remaining to the Chinese, reformulated the Open Door policy. In September and November 1899, Secretary of State John Hay instructed American ambassadors in the chief European capitals and Japan to seek economic assurances from their accredited governments that they would freeze the spheres of influences, apply the Chinese treaty tariff equally in all spheres, and charge equal harbor and railway costs. Foreign replies gave only conditional acceptances at best.

After the third treaty settlement (1895-1898) and with growing Chinese unrest, in 1900-1901, the Boxer Uprising broke out in North China. An offshoot of an eighteenth-century secret society, the Boxers (so-called because of their clenched fist signal) initially revolted against the Manchus, but Cixi redirected their energies against the foreigners. Encouraged by the dowager empress and court conservatives, they besieged the capital's Legation Quarter, where the foreign diplomats lived and worked. They killed several diplomats and a number of missionaries and desecrated foreign cemeteries. In the course of the rebellion, in July 1900, Secretary of State Hay in Washington once again circularized another round of Open Door notes, this time more political than economic in substance, in ten European capitals and Tokyo, giving the official U.S. position. American policy was to preserve Chinese territorial and administrative integrity, while at the same time to seek peace, protect treaty rights, and adhere to international law. More immediate American aims were to rescue Americans in danger, protect American lives and property, and stop the spread of disorder.

The Hay notes did not prevent American military intervention in

China. American troops participated in the joint allied action to lift the siege in Beijing (a rare use of force in China not only by Americans, but in concert with others). The city was finally taken, looted, and burned as the court temporarily relocated in Xi'an. In 1901, China signed with the Western powers the Boxer Protocol, the last extensive group of demands imposed on imperial China. China tendered apologies to those countries whose ministers had been murdered, and erected monuments in the foreign cemeteries that had been desecrated. To undercut the Confucian basis of Chinese political life, the allies demanded the suspension of civil service examinations for five years in all places where foreigners had been manhandled or killed. The Chinese government posted edicts in all district towns discouraging antiforeign activities. The Zongli Yamen was transformed into a fullfledged Ministry of Foreign Affairs. China was prohibited from manufacturing munitions. A total indemnity the equivalent of $333.9 million was paid to thirteen powers. (In 1924, the United States returned its unused share of $12.5 million, or half of the total received, to be used for Chinese education.) The powers occupied strategic posts in North China and moved the Legation Quarter in Beijing to a better defensive location. Using the protocol as a cover to improve commercial relations, the foreign states amended the existing treaties of commerce and navigation in their favor.

China emerged from the Boxer experience with an increased debt, in greater humiliation and in effect, a subject nation. Large-scale contingents of foreign troops were stationed in the country. Following the Russo-Japanese War of 1904-1905, China, although not a belligerent, had to acquiesce in Japan's assumption of Russian rights, railroads, and ports in southern Manchuria, including the Liaodong peninsula (all Chinese territory), where concessions once again changed hands. The Boxer Protocol and subsequent allied moves impressed on some Chinese more than ever the urgency of creating a strong China. To carry on the work initiated by Zeng Guofan, Zuo Zongtang, Li Hungzhang, and Kang Yuwei, other reformers came to the fore. Among their ranks was Liang Chichao (Liang Ch'i-ch'ao), 1873-1929, who came into prominence during the Hundred Days of Reform. A pupil of Kang Yuwei, he advocated nationalism but in moderate guise. A leading editor and journalist, he was influential until around 1905, when his peaceful evolutionary tactics lost favor among the more militant revolutionary-minded youth.

Some Chinese wanted to take direct action in the political arena. Of these, the most prominent was Sun Yat-sen, 1866-1925, called the father of the modern Chinese political revolution. A southerner, he traveled widely in his country and abroad to obtain financial and personal backing for his programs. His original revolutionary organization was the Prosper China Society (*Xingzonghui* or *Hsing Chung Hui*), active for a decade, 1894-1905, whose aim was to establish a republic. He then created another society, the League of Common Alliance (*Tongmenghui*). The League's political manifesto and early publications embraced the Three People's Principles (*Sanmin Zhuyi*) : people's rule (nationalism), people's authority (democracy), and people's livelihood (socialism). He also outlined the three stages in the revolutionary process to achieve these ends: the first one of military control; the second one of political tutelage; and the final one of democratic, constitutional government. These ideas were elaborated in his books and subscribed to by the later Nationalist government of Chiang Kai-shek.

As the revolutionaries embarked on extremism, the Manchus effected last-minute reforms. In 1905, the civil service examinations, already suspended, were abolished. In effect over some two millennia, the Confucian-based political system came to a sudden end with nothing viable to replace it. The dowager empress also ordered the provincial governors to modernize their troops. Some concessions were made toward representative government. In 1906, an edict pledged the formation of a constitutional monarchy. Three years later, after the dowager empress's death, provincial assemblies were elected by a limited franchise with high property qualifications. The assemblies governed, but they displayed an independence of mind. In a second step, in 1910, a national assembly was formed. Also not docile, it openly discussed in Beijing the political issues of the day.

The last-minute Manchu reform program helped to terminate dynastic rule rather than to prolong it. The program did not satisfy the Chinese revolutionaries. On October 10, 1911, in Wuhan, the militant League of Common Alliance precipitated an uprising, which spread to other cities and provinces to become national in movement. (The date—Double Ten—was later appropriated by the Nationalists as a national holiday to commemorate the start of the Chinese Revolution.) Before the end of the year, a Nationalist council representing revolutionaries assembled at Nanjing and elected Sun Yat-sen as provisional president of the Republic of China. Yuan Shikai tried to save the situation for the dynasty, but the Manchu days were numbered. On February 12, 1912, the throne was abdicated on behalf of the six-year-old emperor Xuantong (Hsüan-tung, or Aisin Gioro Pu Yi by his Manchu name). Yuan then threw his military support behind the revolutionaries. Sun bowed out of office as Yuan stepped in to replace him as president of the fledgling republic. Thus ended abruptly and simultaneously the long-standing Chinese imperial structure as well as the even more ancient royal family cycles of China's two dozen dynasties. The first half of the twentieth century was to consume Chinese energies in the quest for a modern, independent, and viable state.

Chronology

1811-1872	Zeng Guofan (Tseng Kuo-fan)
1812-1885	Zuo Zongtang (Tso Tsung-t'ang)
1814-1864	Taiping leader Hung Xiuquan (Hung Hsiu-ch'uan)
1823-1901	Li Hungzhang (Li Hung-chang)
1837-1909	Zhang Zhidong (Chang Chih-tung)
1845	American consuls in Guangzhou upgraded to commissioners in China
1848	S. Wells Williams publishes first general American work on China
early 1850s-1865	Taiping rebellion
1854	Imperial Maritime Customs founded
1856-1860	Anglo-French conflict with China; Tianjin and Beijing treaties
1857	American commissioner rank upgraded to minister
1858, 1860	Chinese-Russian treaties relating to Siberian territories
1858-1860	Second Treaty Settlement
1858-1927	Kang Yuwei
1859-1916	Yuan Shikai (Yüan Shih-k'ai)
1861-1874	The Tongzhi (T'ung-chih) emperor
1862-1867	Anson Burlingame, U.S. Minister to China
1866-1925	Sun Yat-sen
1868	Burlingame Treaty signed in Washington, D.C.
mid-1870s-1908	Dowager empress Cixi (Tz'u-hsi) directs China's political fortunes
1873-1929	Liang Chichao (Liang Ch'i-ch'ao)
1875-1908	The emperor Guangzu (Kuang-hsu)
1876	Chinese-British convention of Zhefoo (Chefoo)
1877	First resident Chinese minister in London
1881	Chinese-Russian Treaty of St. Petersburg
1885	Chinese-French treaty on Vietnam
1887	British eliminate Chinese presence in Burma; Portugese receive Macau as colony

1894-1895	Sino-Japanese war; Treaty of Shimonoseki
1894-1905	Sun Yat-sen's Prosper China Society
1895-1898	Third Treaty Settlement
1896	Chinese-Russian-15 year treaty of alliance; Chinese Eastern Railway established
1898	Spring: Hundred Days of Reform; Russia receives rights on Liaodong peninsula
1899	September and November: first round of Hay Open Door notes
1900	July: second round of Open Door notes
1900-1901	Boxer Uprising; Protocol
1904-1905	Russo-Japanese War; Japan receives Russian rights in Liaodong peninsula
1905	Sun Yat-sen forms League of Common Alliance; civil service exams abolished
1908-1912	The boy emperor Xuantong (Hsüan-tung)
1909	Provincial assemblies meet
1910	National assembly formed
1911	October 10: outbreak in Wuhan of Chinese Revolution; national day for Republic of China
1912	February 12: abdication of last emperor, young Xuantong; empire and royal dynasties end; Yuan Shikai becomes president of the Republic of China

Part Seven

MODERN CHINA

1912 to Present

In the course of the twentieth century, modern China experienced profound changes. Out of the disintegration of the imperial structure came several contenders for political power. Initially centered in Beijing and later in Nanjing, the government of the Republic of China, in the years 1912 to 1937, as successor to the Manchu regime, was, in fact, only a hollow shell. It exerted only a limited jurisdiction, and because of this, the years were strife-filled, since no effective national political structure replaced the vacuum lost by the sudden demise of the late empire. Regionalism increased; economic distress compounded; Western and Japanese political demands continued to compromise Chinese sovereignty. Philosophies from left and right competed for the ideological mantle of Sun Yat-sen, although all indigenous parties had common goals of reunification of China and the termination of the unequal treaties. Despite manifold problems, the growth of Chinese nationalism during this period was significant in both its positive pro-China stance and its negative antiforeign expression.

In 1937, after absorbing Manchuria, Japan initiated its attempted subjugation of China proper. Within a year and a half, it succeeded in absorbing most of the rich coastal areas, with important urban centers, into its territorial sphere. The alien thrust resulted in temporary, but wary, cooperation between the Nationalists in the Republic of China under Chiang Kai-shek and the main opposition leader, the emerging Communist leader, Mao Zedong, in North China. After the Japanese surrender in 1945, the uneasy Chinese coalition fell apart, and in the course of the four-year postwar civil strife, the Communists emerged victorious by 1949. The Republic of China relocated on Taiwan while the People's Republic of China firmed its regime at Beijing over the Chinese mainland.

20

FERMENT

(1912 to 1937)

Domestic and Foreign Affairs (1912 to 1924)

The Republic of China began in 1912 with Yuan Shikai as president in Beijing. Essentially a military regime, and the one recognized by foreign powers, it claimed to speak for the whole country, although it was effective only in North China. After Yuan's death in 1916, other presidents and prime ministers came and went in rapid succession at the capital. In opposition to the northern republic was a rival party and government centered in the south, the Guomindang (Kuomintang, the National People's Party), Sun Yat-sen's third political party, founded in 1912. Moreover, throughout the land, there were warlords who set up their independent military entities that were based generally on provincial strength. They played an important role in modern Chinese history, but they lacked any appealing or popular ideological foundations.

In World War I, Japan once again entered a weak and politically divided China. Allying itself with the West, Japan appropriated German rights in China. These were concentrated mainly in Shandong province, with the newly built port city of Qingdao (Tsingtao), its surrounding territory, railroads, and economic concessions. Going further, the Japanese, in 1915, at a time when world attention was riveted on the European war, pressed on Yuan Shikai's government the Twenty-One Demands. In these the Japanese sought permanent possession of the German rights in the temporarily occupied Shandong, the extension of southern Manchurian leaseholds and acquisitions, more economic concessions in the central Yangtze valley, the nonalienation of territory along coastal China opposite Taiwan (which, as noted, Japan acquired in 1895), and various miscellaneous privileges and rights, such as joint Sino-Japanese ventures in administration and military affairs. After these terms leaked out, Secretary of State William Jennings Bryan

273

of Woodrow Wilson's administration informed China and Japan that the United States would not recognize any agreement that impaired American treaty rights in China. The Japanese backtracked on some demands, and the Chinese acquired greater national consciousness and more distrust of their Asian neighbors.

The Republic of China also joined the Allied wartime cause but it played only a negligible role in World War I. At the peace conference at Versailles, the Chinese wanted to terminate the unequal treaties, but they met with little success. The Japanese kept Shandong rights, and overall Western privileges were not terminated. After learning of the diplomatic defeats, on May 4, 1919, several thousand Chinese students demonstrated in Beijing. They directed their particular ire against the Japanese, and they held anti-Japanese rallies. Student unrest spread throughout the county and extended to the treaty ports, where Japanese goods were boycotted. The May Fourth movement remained significant in modern Chinese history, in part because groups, including merchants and laborers, not historically noted for political activism, participated in issues of the day. Non-Marxists agreed that the outburst was the first strong indication of a broadly based Chinese nationalism. Chinese Communists interpreted the phenomenon as the genesis of their movement.

By 1919, Communist doctrine had entered China in both Marxist and Leninist garb. From Marxism, the Chinese Communists adopted such scientific socialist theories as an economic interpretation of history that emphasized control of modes of production through five stages of history (primitive, slave, feudal, capitalist, and socialist) and class struggles. Leninism's legacy was as profound. It emphasized the importance of Communist parties as the vanguard of the political revolution in hastening the socialist (read Communist) millennium. It dwelt on the negative aspects of imperialism and predicted its inevitable downfall. After 1919, Russians representing both the new Soviet state and the Communist International (Comintern) went to China is search of converts. Some Chinese, essentially in Beijing, formed study groups and were won over. In July 1921, the first congress of the Chinese Communist Party, with representatives from already-formed provincial cells, convened at Shanghai. Twelve delegates and Maring (or Sneevliet) from Moscow were in attendance. Chen Duxiu (Ch'en Tuhsiu), a scholar from Beijing National University, although not present, was elected secretary-general. Among the original founders of the party was Mao Zedong (Mao Tse-tung). The party affiliated itself with the Comintern.

The following year, party members were authorized as individuals to join the Guomindang, which the Russians realized was the most potent force for change and reunification at the time. Adolf Joffe was dispatched to China to initiate Soviet cooperation with Chinese Nationalists. At Shanghai, in 1923, he signed an agreement with Sun Yatsen in which the Russians agreed to provide help in reorganizing the Guomindang into a tightly knit party structure but without the communist ideology. Reorganized the next year, the Guomindang spearheaded a movement to oust the warlords, replace the Republic at Beijing, and eject the Western presence. Michael Borodin (born Grusenberg) became the most prominent of the civilian Russian advisers. General Galens (born Vassily Bleucher) was the principal military adviser. Under Russian guidance, the Guomindang army was also reconstructed with young Chiang Kai-shek as the chief Chinese general. As president of the newly established military academy at Whampoa, he brought in his former classmates and built up in traditional personalized Chinese style a group of army leaders loyal to him. Soviet advisers resented this competition in leadership, but they could do little about it. Coalescing several groups, the Whampoa Military Academy grew, and the Guomindang extended its influence in the south.

After helping to found the Chinese Communist Party and to reshape the Guomindang, the Russians proceeded to reestablish diplomatic relations (ruptured by the 1917 revolution) with the Republic of China in Beijing. In 1924, Leo Karakhan of the Soviet Foreign Office went to China to negotiate a definitive agreement. The new agreement canceled or replaced some former treaties, stipulated that the Soviet Union was not to engage in subversive activities in China, recognized Outer Mongolia as an integral part of China, and ended some Russian rights in China. It kept, however, a joint Sino-Russian management of important Manchurian railroads.

Unity and Division (1924 to 1927)

The first united front, 1924-1927, was a period of nominal cooperation among the Guomindang, the Chinese Communist Party, and the Soviets. Despite their common aims, the disparate groups competed for overall power. The Guomindang itself was rent with factions, and Chiang had a difficult task to keep the party viable after 1925, when Sun Yat-sen died. Military cliques worked at cross purposes with civilians, who themselves were split into left- and right-wing groups. The liberals wanted a greater degree of unity with the Communists and emphasis on land and social reforms, while the party conservatives wanted less or none of this. The most important of the non-Communist Guomindang left faction was Wang Jingwei (Wang Ching-wei), a rival of Chiang's, to whom Sun Yat-sen had dictated his will shortly before his death and who cast himself in the role of Sun's successor. After a jockeying of forces, Chiang slowly improved his position in the party and with the Communists. He planned a move north to subdue recalcitrant warlords and conquer Beijing.

In the summer of 1926, the campaign to reunify China under the Guomindang commenced its northward march in two columns. One, with Chiang, moved up in a flank with most of his army and the civilian right-wing Guomindang faction. The other, proceeding up the more interior left route, coalesced Russians, Chinese Communists, and the Guomindang's liberals. Some warlords in the south capitulated as the columns progressed northward in two wings. The English, impressed with newfound Guomindang strength, promised to give up certain rights and privileges. Converging on initial success, the Chinese cause then divided. Upon reaching the Yangtze River valley at disparate middle and delta points, the columns refused to unite. For added strength, Chiang at Nanjing turned to the Chinese business leaders in nearby Shanghai and to Western powers. He calmed the antiforeign spirit that had earlier surged once again from an incident of the year before (1925), when Chinese police under British command had fired on demonstrating Chinese students and workers in Shanghai (the May 25 incident).

The left wing, centered at Hankou as part of a sprawling industrial complex, endeavored to effect socialist doctrines in the urban setting. It also provoked antiforeign incidents, such as those which broke out in Nanjing in March 1927, and which brought allied gunboats, including Americans, to the scene. Chiang settled the Western claims, and the next month, in Shanghai, he conducted a violent anti-Communist purge. Now that he was securely in control of Guomindang's right wing, Chiang's next step was to reassume control of the whole party. In this move, he was aided fortuitously by swift-moving events in Hankou. There, the non-Communist left faction of the Guomindang under Wang Jingwei on its own initiative had expelled the Soviets and the Chinese Communists because it had taken issue with their too drastic land reform measures and attempted nationalization of Hankou industries. Non-Communist left-wing leaders, moreover, feared that Chinese sovereignty might be subordinated to foreign interests, a possibility indicated in Stalin's communications to Chinese Communists working at Hankou along with the Soviets.

The departure of the Soviets, who returned home, and of the Chinese Communists, who went underground, eased the path for Guomindang reunification under Chiang. In January 1928, he was confirmed as commander-in-chief of the army and chairman of the party's Central Executive Committee (positions held until his death in 1975). With South and Central China partially reunited, Chiang then continued his march northward to subdue Beijing and the northern warlords, who paid him token allegiance. The seat of the Republic of China was then relocated to Nanjing and the former northern capital was renamed Beiping (Northern peace). Chiang considered that he had now implemented Sun Yat-sen's first stage of the Chinese revolution, that of reunification by military means.

Chinese peripheral land borders in those years were caught up in developments that affected the Chinese scene. In Manchuria, the warlord Zhang Zuolin (Chang Tso-lin, or the Old Marshal) operated independently of both the earlier Beijing regime and then the Guomindang, but in home territory he met rising Japanese military pressures. In the Liaodong peninsula, where they had appropriated Russian economic rights in 1905, the Japanese had built up their security forces over the years into a veritable army. The Japanese, watching Chiang Kai-shek's move north and fearing a rapprochement between Chiang and the Old Marshal, in 1928 eliminated the latter and hoped that his son, Zhang Xueliang (Chang Hsüeh-liang), the Young Marshal, would be more amenable to their ends. To the west, in Xinjiang, with the outbreak of the Chinese revolution, the Chinese political grip became progressively weaker. Warlords there also acted independently, or gave their allegiance to Chinese and Soviet interests as they saw fit.

In 1911, in Mongolia, with the end of Manchu control there, the Hutukhtu, the religious head of Mongolia, was proclaimed chief of an independent Mongolian state. Czarist Russia recognized the new regime and dispatched arms. The Mongolian political position remained precarious because, in 1913, Russia had signed a treaty with the new Republic of China that recognized the latter's suzerainty, while safeguarding Russian rights. In June 1915, Russia convened at Kiakhta a conference of the three involved parties that in effect transferred Mongolia into a joint Sino-Russian protectorate. With the subsequent Soviet consolidation of Siberia, in 1921, a revolutionary government spearheaded by the newly created Mongolian (Communist) People's Revolutionary Party, came into power at Urga, the capital, later renamed Ulan Bator (Red Hero). In 1924, it proclaimed the Mongolian People's Republic, the world's second-oldest Communist state. But, as noted, in a Sino-Soviet treaty concluded that same year in Beijing, the Soviet Union recognized Mongolia as an integral party of China. Over the years, under Marshal Choibalsan, a Stalin-like dictator, the Mongolian People's Republic pursued the Communist path under Soviet aegis. With Chinese attention diverted elsewhere, the country was absorbed into the Soviet fold.

Right and Left (1927 to 1937)

Now relocated at Nanjing, the Republic of China under the Guomindang, popularly called the Nationalist government, functioned and received international recognition. The United States recognized Chiang's government by concluding a treaty of commerce in July 1928. But the Republic was far from unifying China because Nationalist power was still based primarily in the lower Yangtze valley. In North China and Manchuria, as well as in some southern provinces and the west, warlords continued to rule independently. Guomindang factional struggles persisted. Personal rivalries continued among Nationalist leaders who were subordinate to Chiang. At Nanjing, Wang Jingwei remained at the head of the left-wing faction, which urged more rapid policies toward representative government, while the right wing wanted the consolidation of national power as the first order of priority.

Over the years, despite obstacles, the Guomindang effected Sun's second period, that of political tutelage. In the Nationalist structure, party, army, and government positions were interlaced. Chiang presided over all three components in top but complementary offices. The Organic Law of 1928 created the national bureaucratic structure, but it did not provide for mass participation. Attempts were made to promulgate provisional constitutions, but these were curtailed by Japanese invasions of northern and central China in the mid-1930s. In 1930, the Guomindang formulated a basic land rent law stipulating that rent was not to exceed 37.5 percent of the value of the main crop. The Nationalist government recorded limited gains in establishing banks and a managed currency, improving transportation lines, and developing postal services.

In foreign affairs, the Nationalists concentrated their efforts on the rights recovery program that aimed at the termination of the unequal treaties with the west. Rebuffed at Versailles, the Chinese met with some later success. In 1928, they regained tariff rights, and in the following year, they put into effect a native import tariff schedule, their first since 1843. At the Washington Naval Conference (1921-1922), the signatories agreed to relinquish their post offices on Chinese soil. In the ensuing years, some leaseholds were terminated, but the powers remained in Shanghai, the most important and populous treaty city.

The Boxer indemnities were, for the most part, remitted, and the chief powers used the payments mainly for Chinese educational purposes, as had the United States. Little headway was made on abolishing extraterritoriality. (Not until 1943, in the midst of World War II, did the United States surrender that right in China, ninety-nine years after it had acquired it.)

Chiang and the Guomindang were also concerned with the growth of the Chinese Communist movement. After its expulsion in July 1927 from the Guomindang left wing at Hankou, the Chinese Communist Party reorganized itself on Comintern orders. It created a scapegoat in Chen Duxiu, who was later expelled from the party for a variety of alleged ideological crimes. The party subscribed to Stalin's line that despite failures, the Chinese revolution was entering a higher phase, one that was to be marked by insurrections and communes. In the face of overwhelming odds, the Chinese Communists, between late 1927 and 1930, embarked on a series of rural and urban uprisings, all disastrous to them. While blame for failures was fixed on other Chinese Communists (Stalin was never criticized), some went to the Soviet Union for reindoctrination, but Mao Zedong, in home territory, slowly and surely started his climb to the top.

From central Hunan province, Mao, born in 1893, in his youth had turned to communism. He helped to initiate the Chinese Communist Party, and he built up the Hunan provincial cell. During the first united front, he worked in the executive committee of both Communist and Guomindang parties. After the split-up in 1927, he directed political efforts in his home province toward the peasants, his main force for the Chinese revolution. Over the years, he consolidated his gains and attracted others to him, including Zhu De (Chu Teh), a military commander, who, on August 1, 1927, defected with some of his troops from the Nanchang branch of the Whampoa Military Academy. (The Chinese Communists mark the day as the establishment of their People's Liberation Army.) Maoism, in early form, emerged in the mountains of southwestern China, where it benefited from peasant support, Red Army strength, and a territorial base in a well-protected mountainous strategic location but with assured food supplies.

In November 1931, Mao proclaimed the Chinese Soviet Republic (known as the Ruijin Republic after the town in which it was proclaimed, or the Jiangxi Republic after the province). There, the Chinese Soviet issued its own constitution and laws. It received no substantial foreign aid, and no foreign advisers or personnel were present to perform major advisory roles. Alarmed by the growth of the Communist movement in the south, Chiang dispatched expeditions there.

Applying ever-increasing pressures through blockades, histroops ringed the Communist stronghold. Holding out for some time, the Chinese Communists then decided, either on Moscow's prodding or on their own initiative, to evacuate and reestablish a new base of power to the north in the Yan'an area of Shaanxi province, closer to Mongolia and Soviet territory and where another Communist center was also located.

The Long March was an epic in Chinese Communist history. In October 1934, in several columns and groups (and from other Communist pockets in China), they broke through the Guomindang encirclement and trekked their way toward the Yan'an region. Over the ensuing year, the main bulk proceeded by circuitous routes through western and northern China. Initially numbering some eighty thousand, the marchers lived off the countryside. They forayed through a dozen provinces and across mountain ranges. They fought major battles with opposition forces, usually local provincial warlords. Along the routes, the soldiers continually propagandized the peasants.

When they finally arrived and took command from the local Yan'an faction in late 1935, the Communist movement had been considerably weakened. Perhaps only a quarter survived the ordeal. (Along the way, many valuable records had to be jettisoned, and documentation from the early days of the party is scarce.) But the Long March strengthened Mao's position. On the way, in January 1935, at a conference of party leaders in Zunyi (Tsunyi) in Guizhou province, and in the absence of any Soviet advisers, he was formally elected chairman of the Central Committee (a position retained until his death in 1976). Simultaneously, Chiang's hand was also strengthened by the Long March because in its course, local warlords and provincial armies assumed much of the brunt of the fighting against the communists. By simultaneously weakening the non-Communist opposition, the Guomindang gained greater control of southern and central China.

Eventually the Chinese Communist factions coalesced and created the Yan'an Border Government (1935-1949). Under Mao, with little or no outside aid, they initiated new tactics and revived old ones. Under pressures generated by Japanese expansion and Guomindang containment, the Yan'an government assumed form. Mao was the chief power in the one-party government. His tactics were to harness peasant discontent and promise much to most groups, including those with grievances in the class struggles as defined by Marxist-Leninism. As in the south, his regime in the north emphasized the role of the peasant and his participation in decision-making village councils. Cadres of workers and activists pushing party aims were also organized. They accompanied Red Army units into "liberated" villages and indoctrinated the peasants. They initiated the administration of newly incorporated territory, proclaimed land reforms, and effected redistribution programs. They eliminated the age-old curse of foot binding and promoted education programs and literacy.

China and Japan (1931 to 1937)

As the Communists entrenched themselves in the north and Chiang consolidated their power in central China, the Japanese in Manchuria were expanding their base of operations. Aided by developments in Japan that were leading to fascism and militarism, they were ready to take over the land. After an incident on September 18, 1931, in which train tracks were blown up near Shenyang (Mukden), their Manchurian capital (an incident, it turned out later, that they themselves had created), they forced Zhang Xueliang and his army to evacuate into North China near the Communist base. The Japanese then established the puppet state of Manchukuo under the young last emperor of China, Pu Yi. From there they pushed toward and across the Great Wall. Chiang, more concerned in containing the Chinese Communists and involved in closer and more immediate problems in central and southern China, could not stem the Japanese advance in the northeast, where the invaders also set up puppet regimes.

The Japanese presence on the Asian mainland left repercussions on the Chinese scene. The two chief domestic parties initiated moves toward a second united front, this time not directed against internal enemies but to contain the growing foreign menace. As early as 1932, the Chinese Communists from the Ruijin Republic had declared war on Japan, and they appealed for cooperation against enemy encroachments in Manchuria. From Yan'an four years later, they reiterated the appeal, now backed by Soviet support. The Comintern line had opted for the united front tactic in order to stop the rise of Hitler in Germany and of fascism in Japan, both threats to the Soviet state. Chiang, at the time, did not go along with the priority of stemming Japanese advances, for he put the containment of the "cancer" of domestic communism as a more urgent goal. To this end, he urged Zhang Xueliang's troops in North China to help eradicate the Communist neighbor. The warlord demurred; he assigned a greater priority to taking action against the foreign enemy who had displaced him from his home base. In December 1936, Chiang flew to Xi'an, near the Communist stronghold, to persuade the reluctant Zhang to change his mind. Instead, the warlord placed him under arrest. The Chinese Communists (possibly on Moscow orders) acted as mediators. The triangular talks resulted in Chiang's release and warlord declarations pledging support to the Guomindang in the foreground of another united front directed against the Japanese.

By 1937, China verged on a second united front. But the political pattern was not so clear cut. The Guomindang and Chinese Communists continued to compete for overall power and international recognition; warlords were yet sprinkled throughout the country. Each protagonist had his own disparate prescription for national salvation. Negligible third parties advanced some liberal and centrist programs, but these left little impact in the times. With China divided, it seemed peculiar that the two main rival factions would again fashion a united front, this time to contain Japanese advances. But such was the case that year. Modern Chinese political history has been documented by surprising twists and turns.

Chronology

1912-1916	Yuan Shikai president of the Republic of China (ROC)
1912-present	Guomindang
1915	Twenty-One Demands
1919	Versailles Treaty; May 4 Movement
1921	July: Chinese Communist Party formed
1923	Sun-Joffe agreement
1924-1927	First united front
1924	Chinese-Soviet treaty; Mongolian People's Republic established
1925	Death of Sun Yat-sen; May 25 incident
1926-1927	Northern Expedition
1927	March: antiforeign incidents; April: Chiang Kai-shek cracks down on Shanghai Communists; left-wing Guomindang expels Commmunists and Soviets; party reunified; August 1: defection of General Zu De to Communist cause
1928	Chiang as commander-in-chief of the army and chairman of party's Central Executive Committee; capital of ROC relocated by Chiang at Nanjing; Organic Law; July: US–ROC treaty of commerce; ROC regains tariff rights
1930	Land rent control law
1931	September 18: Shenyang (Mukden) incident; November: Ruijin (or Jiangxi) Chinese Republic proclaimed
1931-1932	Japanese takeover of Manchuria (Manchukuo)

1934-1935	Long March
1935	Mao Zedong elected chairman of Central Committee
1935-1949	Yan'an Border Government
1936	December: Xi'an kidnapping incident
1937	Second united front formed

21

CONFLICT

(1937 to 1949)

Two Chinas

Under a militaristic government and with a highly industrialized economy, Japan prepared for war. Hastened by the turn of events in China that led to the formation of a united front, the Japanese embarked on their conquest of that country. In an incident on July 7, 1937, at the Marco Polo Bridge (Luguoqiao) near Beijing, Japanese forces exchanged shots with the Chinese. In the tense situation, aggravations were compounded. Although the Chinese government apologized, the Japanese proceeded to occupy North China. After making initial gains, they encountered Communist forces, who put up formidable resistance. As a result, much of northwestern China (at least that area west of the Yellow River bend) stayed in Chinese, but Chinese Communist, hands. Simultaneously, the Japanese came in force to protect their extensive Shanghai interests and pushed the Chinese army out of central coastal areas. Campaigns moved up the Yangtze, but before the fall of Nanjing, the capital, Chiang Kai-shek had evacuated to Chongqing (Chungking), up in the river gorges where he was safe from surface attacks (but not immune from continual Japanese aerial bombings). Also moving up southern river valleys, the Japanese occupied strategic cities and coastal areas in South China. Between mid-1937 and late 1938, the Japanese had gained most of coastal and central China, the richest part of the country. After 1941, they acquired little additional territory.

Occupied China was only one area, although a major one, of the Chinese political scene. Searching for a national figure to head a puppet Republic of China at Nanjing, the Japanese obtained the services of Wang Jingwei, who defected from the Guomindang. Under him, a government was declared at Nanjing in March 1940 and recognized by the Axis powers. Economic reorganization accompanied political control in occupied China, and Japanese companies and corporations took over the economic sector. Cultural redirection was also ordered. Farther inland from Chongqing, Chiang, after 1938, ruled over what was called Free China. Numerous Chinese evacuated to the interior, and schools and offices were reestablished in new rural locations in western and southwestern provinces. But much of northwestern China remained in the Communist's hands. Centered at Yan'an, the Communists maintained guerrilla warfare behind Japanese lines. On the fringes of the country, independent warlords continued to operate. They ruled over some border provinces in a high-handed manner.

In the course of the undeclared war, the Guomindang and the Communists took some measures, at least on paper, of political and military cooperation to implement the second united front. In March 1938, Chiang formed a People's Political Council, consisting of two hundred members appointed from various political organs, including Communists and third parties, as an advisory body. The council was not effective. Military clashes between the Communists and Nationalists continued even behind Japanese lines. The most critical one occurred in January 1941, where in the lower Yangtze valley the Communist Fourth Route Army, disobeying Chiang's orders for frontal suicidal attacks on Japanese troops, were set upon from the rear by Nationalist forces. This clash strained even the nominal cooperation of the second united front.

In China, Japanese expansion impinged on Western treaty rights, particularly those of the English, who retained extensive economic interests in occupied China. Their subjects were maltreated and suffered indignities. As it had done on previous occasions, the United States protested infringement of its rights, individual and collective, in China. Washington participated in collective security measures to restore peace on the Asian mainland, such as the 1937 Brussels Conference called by Belgium but not attended by Japan. Although not a member of the League of Nations, the United States cooperated unofficially with the Lytton Commission (to investigate the Mukden incident) on which it had an observer. It also extended supplies and loans to Chiang and applied economic sanctions against Japan.

After Pearl Harbor and subsequent declarations of war between China and Japan, the Republic of China became one of the Allies, but in wartime Chongqing, the Nationalist government had to wrestle with numerous problems. Leadership was aging, and no new blood replenished the ranks. Cabinets were reconstituted, but the same men occupied different positions over time. The situation necessitated military priorities, but it was difficult to sustain in the technologically backward areas of mountainous southwestern China an infrastructure, including industry to support a modern war machine. Moreover, with the scarcity of consumer goods and the excess printing of currency, inflation became rampant. The usual charges of graft and corruption were hurled at the government.

Guomindang politics increasingly centered on Chiang Kai-shek, whose monolithic titles included Generalissimo of the Army, President of the Government (after 1943), Chairman of the Executive Yuan, and Chairman of the party's Central Executive Committee. In 1943, he wrote two books whose theses essentially blamed Westerners for China's basic ills. *China's Economic Theory* stressed the traditional Chinese official policy of state control over economic life, emphasized industrial goals, but paid little attention to pressing agricultural problems. *China's Destiny* marked the end of a century of unequal treaties, which the work indicated had caused China's humiliation and distressing conditions.

While the Guomindang, as a siege government, held out in the interior, the Communists expanded in the northwest. Recouping from losses incurred during the Long March, party membership grew phenomenally. By 1945, according to Mao Zedong himself, it had skyrocketed to 1.2 million. Through guerrilla activities, the party expanded its territorial hold behind Japanese lines in North China. In the midst of membership and territorial gains for the Communists, Mao reinforced his top party position by composing definitive literature. In these war years, he devoted much time to studying Marxism-Leninism-Stalinism. Among his most important works were two composed in late 1939 and early 1940. The earlier one, entitled *The Chinese Revolution and the Chinese Communist Party,* developed the two aspects of the political revolution: an internal one that set the masses against the feudal rulers and an external one that pitted the Chinese nation against the imperialists. Mao's later work, *On New Democracy,* outlined two stages to realize the goals of the Chinese revolution. The first temporary period was to be marked by a coalition government, Communists and others, after which, in the second and final stage, the party would lead the nation into socialism.

By 1945, these and other basic volumes of Mao had defined and refined his ideology. They were significant because his thought and programs were to carry over as guidelines for the Communist state which came to rule all of mainland China after 1949. While Mao wrote, he tightened control ever the party structure throughout the war years. He pursued rectification programs and reindoctrination measures, the most important of which was the *zheng feng* (correct the wind) program in 1942 and 1943. By the end of World War II, communism in China had become Chinese to the core, and Maoism was grafted onto Marxism and Leninism as party dogma.

International Diplomacy

Events after Pearl Harbor complicated the international scene as it related to China. Most of the wartime Allied conferences concerned Europe and Japan, but two especially affected China. In late 1943, at Cairo, Chiang Kai-shek, Franklin Roosevelt, and Winston Churchill (Joseph Stalin was not present because the Soviet Union was not in conflict with Japan at the time) convened to discuss postwar Pacific problems. In the Cairo Declaration of December 1, the three leaders promised the return of all territories that Japan had "stolen" from China to the Republic of China, and that these territories would specifically include Manchuria, Taiwan, and the Pescadores.

The Yalta Conference, held in the Crimea in February 1945, was attended by Roosevelt, Churchill, and Stalin. In order to involve the Soviet Union in the final campaigns against Japan and to save American lives in the projected invasion of that island country, Roosevelt in a secret protocol with the Soviets promised to restore certain pre-1904 rights they had enjoyed in Manchuria. Among these rights were preeminent interests in Dalien (Dairen) and Lushun (Port Arthur), and the management of Manchurian railroads. Chiang was not informed of the terms for four months and then only by the next U.S. president, Harry S. Truman. Chiang reluctantly sent his foreign minister to Moscow in August 1945 to confirm details of a treaty.

In wartime China, diplomatic representatives of Roosevelt and Truman sought to sustain Chiang's claim as the leading and legitimate Chinese government. No official aid was channeled to Yan'an, whereas, in the course of World War II, the Guomindang received some $1.5 billion worth of grants and loans from Washington. Subsequent to the outbreak of the Pacific war, several military missions went to China to coordinate Chinese and Allied efforts against Japan. But as the war entered its final phases, China was bypassed. Japan was eventually defeated not from the mainland, but by sea and island campaigns in central and southern Pacific island chains. As was the case in international conferences, so in military strategy; China, at war with Japan the longest of any party, was relegated to a final subordinate role.

Concerned with the necessity of immediate victory against Japan, and anticipating political problems that could result from a divided China, the United States endeavored to cement the second united front. Roosevelt dispatched several civilian missions to Chongqing to heal Chinese political breaches. In late 1944, General Patrick Hurley, the American ambassador, endeavored to unify Nationalist and Communist military and political stands. At first welcomed by both factions, he commuted between Chongqing and Yan'an. But claiming obstruction from Department of State representatives in the field, he cut short in a huff his difficult mediating task. Hurley left in late 1945, but Americans were now all the more committed to the China problem. The requested American intercession soon turned into Chinese charges of unwanted intervention.

By the end of World War II in August 1945, political and military affairs in China were confusing. As stipulated in the Yalta Agreement, the Soviets entered the Pacific war in its final week against Japan and occupied Manchuria to accept the Japanese surrender. They received back their old rights. In North China, the Communists were extended and growing in numbers, yet the Nationalists remained the stronger of the two main Chinese domestic factions. They received international diplomatic recognition (even from the Soviets) and had the military advantages. Their troops reoccupied the important coastal cities (with American help) after the Japanese surrender on August 15, 1945. In contrast, the Communists had no sea coast, limited agricultural lands, few industrial complexes, a mediocre air force, tenuous logistical lines, and little Soviet support or aid (until the Soviets evacuated most of Manchuria by spring, 1946, and left behind Japanese war booty to them). Yet in the course of the next few years, Mao Zedong emerged victorious on the Chinese mainland.

With the surrender of the Japanese, Nationalists and Communists jockeyed for mastery of the mainland. Warlords were gradually eliminated or absorbed into one camp or the other. But despite the fighting, negotiations continued, particularly after the Sino-Soviet treaty of August 1945, in which the Soviets continued aid and recognition to Nationalist China and left the Chinese Communists out on a limb. Later that month, Mao himself came to Chongqing through the good offices of Ambassador Hurley, but the fragile united front remained a touch-and-go situation. After Hurley resigned, General George Marshall arrived in December 1945 as President Truman's special envoy with instructions that reiterated long-time U.S. policies toward China. These included the desirability of establishing a strong, united, and democratic China, previously required to help defeat Japan, but now essential to maintain peace and advance the cause of the United Nations, according to official U.S. reasoning. A strong China could be achieved only with the cessation of civil war. To help end the conflict, a national conference of all major political elements was to convene.

In January 1946, soon after Marshall's arrival, the Political Consultative Conference met in Chongqing. It firmed three basic agreements. In a military truce both sides were to freeze troops in their respective occupied areas, which were to be policed by truce teams, each consisting of a Nationalist, a Communist, and an American officer. A second agreement, political in nature, concerned the division of territory between the Nationalists and Communists, an elected legislature, and the creation of a forty-man State Council with membership divided between twenty for the Guomindang and twenty for all other parties. A third agreement sought the integration of Communist armies into the Nationalist Chinese military command. The three agreements soon broke down, for neither Chinese party wanted to implement effective cooperation.

Under some American prodding, the Nationalists effected limited reforms. In November 1946, a constituent assembly convened in Nanjing, but Communist delegates refused to attend. Under Chiang's guidance, the assembly adopted a constitution that called for a parliamentary system with a cabinet responsible to an elected legislature. Two subsequent elections were conducted in Nationalist-held territory, one to reelect Chiang president, and the other to form a unicameral legislative body. Few third parties cooperated, the Communists did not participate, and the Guomindang dominated the electoral processes. Despite drawbacks, the constitution, effected in 1948, theoretically ended Sun Yat-sen's second stage of political tutelage and ushered in the third and last stage, that of democracy and constitutionalism.

Over the months, Marshall experienced an increasingly difficult time in reconciling obstructionist Nationalist and Communist aims, and he departed in January 1947. The following month, the Nationalists expelled the Communists from Nanjing, once again the capital site. Full-scale civil war erupted. American aid to Nationalist China after the Marshall mission reflected more the domestic American political scene than developments in China. (As it was, the United States extended some $2 billion in aid between August 1945, and early 1948 to the Nationalists.) After the Communists and Nationalists openly split, the Guomindang continued to face spiraling economic and political problems. Inflation continued, the national budget was hopelessly imbalanced, civilian morale declined, and corruption was evident. With growing expenses, the Nanjing government had fewer sources of revenue. The government embarked on a widespread policy of the nationalization of industry. Key plants were appropriated as government monopolies by leading officials and their families.

Last-minute Guomindang political reforms proved too late and too little. The campaigns for the mastery of mainland China mounted in Communist favor. When Manchuria fell to the Communists late in 1948, the Nationalist house on the mainland collapsed like a stack of cards. In Manchuria, the Nationalists fought a stationary war from city bastions, while the Communists, aided by Soviet-left munitions, captured the countryside. Growing Communist strength isolated Nationalist troops, who eventually withdrew to Mukden, which was captured in November 1948. The Nationalist position in North China was no longer tenable. Beijing soon fell. The Communists consolidated their gains in the North China plain. In late 1948 and early 1949, they confronted the Nationalists in a massive pitched battle at Xuzhou (Hsuchow), between the Yellow River and the Yangtze. Each side threw in a million troops, but superior mobile Communist strategy helped to turn the tide in their favor. As a result of increasing Communist military successes, Mao announced to Chiang surrender terms, which were comprehensive. Chiang asked Western powers for aid, but none came. He then temporarily retired from the presidency, while the Communists crossed the Yangtze in April 1949 and spread south. Chiang soon returned to the presidency, but the Guomindang was eventually forced to evacuate to Taiwan, where on December 8, 1949, the Republic of China was set up in exile.

As the Nationalist cause collapsed, the Communists busily organized their political and ideological machines. Mao promoted conferences of various kinds, including all-China students', women's, and youth assemblies. In June 1949, the party convened a preparatory committee to create the Chinese People's Political Consultative Conference as a multiparty and interclass organ to establish a base for the new China. In September, in Beijing, the conference adopted an Organic Law and a Common Program, which became the administrative structure and philosophy for the Central People's Government of the People's Republic of China, proclaimed on October 1, 1949. Two months before Chiang had evacuated to Taiwan, the Communist regime had been established in Beijing, once again renamed the northern Capital.

The victory of the Chinese Communists encompassed military organization, strategy, and tactics. It was a total approach, one in which political, social, economic, and military matters were interrelated. The Communists were never voted into power, nor were the Nationalists voted out. Continuing in the traditional manner of establishing new dynasties, the Chinese people were never consulted on the issues or the choices.

The Republic of China (Since 1949)

As a result of wartime and postwar developments, Taiwan reverted to the Chinese fold. The Cairo Declaration restored Taiwan and the Pescadores to the Republic of China, but this statement, as a declaration of intent, did not constitute a legal transfer of title, which was the concern of a peace treaty. General Douglas MacArthur's order of August 15, 1945 (authorized by the Allied powers) bestowed upon Chiang Kai-shek control of Taiwan and the Pescadores in order to accept the surrender of Japanese forces. Nationalist generals and armies occupied the islands and the capital of Taipei. An initial period of harsh rule culminated in massacres in March 1947, which decimated local Taiwanese leadership. In late 1949, Chiang Kai-shek arrived to set up a government in exile, which eventually included some two million military and Guomindang members who had escaped the Communist regime on the mainland.

The U.S. policy of wait-until-the-dust-settles, previously pursued on the mainland after the Marshall mission, carried over to the Republic of China in Taiwan. In January 1950, both Secretary of State Dean Acheson and President Truman indicated that Taiwan was not considered an essential link in the western Pacific defense perimeter from Japan to the Philippines. But with the outbreak of the Korean War five months later, Taiwan catapulted into a prominent place in defense arrangements. On June 27, Truman ordered the Seventh Fleet into the Taiwan Strait, not only to prevent a Communist attack on the island, but to deter any Nationalist ambitions to return to the mainland, which had been Chiang Kai-shek's primary aim. Concerned with the possible spread of Communist military activity in East Asia generally and with a possible renewed outbreak of the Chinese civil war in extended territorial areas, Truman made this drastic decision. In effect this resulted in a two-China political policy for the United States and complicated Asian international relations for decades.

After the outbreak of the Korean War, American military and economic aid flowed to the island. In May 1951, a military advisory group was established in Taipei. In December 1954, a mutual defense treaty was concluded between the Republic of China and the United States. Under terms of the treaty, in the event of an armed attack in the western Pacific against their territories, each party undertook to act in accordance with the constitutional processes of their countries. For Chiang, the pertinent territories were defined as Taiwan and the Pescadores. In another note, the Nationalists pledged not to launch attacks on the mainland without American consent. The Nationalist-held offshore islands of Quemoy, opposite the Chinese Communist port of Xiamen, and Matsu, opposite Fuzhou, were not governed by these agreements.

As other military priorities emerged in Asia, and as the Taiwanese economy improved, American aid programs slowed down. Between 1951 and 1961, a total of approximately $1.3 billion and $2.7 billion of economic and military aid respectively had been extended. In 1961, the economic programs were terminated, although some funds and surplus food arrangements remained in the pipeline for several years. After 1979, when the United States terminated its diplomatic recognition of the Republic of China and transferred it to the People's Republic of China in Beijing, the American military and diplomatic presence in Taiwan deescalated.

The Nationalists operated on Taiwan with a national structure to implement provincial-sized duties. The political organization was three-tiered in nature, consisting of national, provincial, and local governments. The defiant Guomindang Party ruled the island according to the constitution adopted in 1946 in Nanjing (and effected two years later). Initially elected for six-year terms, National Assembly members sat indefinitely because of the emergency. As a center of power, the president was similarly elected for a six-year term with the possibility of a second; Chiang Kai-shek was reelected in 1954 and kept the office until his death in 1975.

After three years, his older son, Chiang Ching-kuo, assumed the presidency as well as the chairmanship of the Guomindang, until his death in 1988. Vice President Lee Teng-hui then moved into these two top positions, the first native Taiwanese to occupy them. In 1993, Lien Chan, who headed the provincial government, similarly became the first native politician to become prime minister.

The traditional five *yuan*, or boards, continued to operate—the executive, legislative, judicial, control, and examination boards. The provincial capital was located at Taichung on the west coast. This level of government was concerned with matters of taxation, education, social welfare, and implementation of land reforms. At the local level, district magistrates operated, as did mayors and urban legislative councils elected by the people. In this lowest rank of the political hierarchy, native Taiwanese participated, but by the 1990s, as mainlanders died off, they came to constitute the majority of Guomindang members and moved up into higher offices.

In economic life, agriculture was important; two-thirds of national income and 90 percent of foreign exchange derived from it. Rice and sugarcane accounted for half the agricultural production. Lumber was an important commodity for export. The Taipei regime embarked on a series of land reform acts. In 1949, it put into effect measures (on the books since 1930) that limited rents to 37.5 percent of the main crop and guaranteed tenants security of tenure. Two years later, the government began the sale of public lands. In 1953, it placed ceilings on landholdings of 3 hectares (about 7.4 acres). In part, because of such measures, four out of five peasant families came to own their own land, a remarkable percentage in Asian agrarian life.

Improvements were also noted in industry. In 1949, the island was predominantly agricultural with little industry. Over the years, the industrial sector was developed. By 1952, industry had recovered to prewar levels, and then doubled in the ensuing decade. Food processing was Taiwan's leading industry, with sugar refining, pineapple canning, and tea packing among the other most important activities. Textile mills, aluminum plants, power projects, and fertilizer factories were established. In the early 1950s, three-fifths of industry was state-owned, but within a decade, the private sector of the economy accounted for that ratio. Favorable investment laws attracted overseas Chinese and foreign capital. Taiwan embarked on the usual economic development, with four-year plans. Worldwide non-Communist foreign trade markets opened, one with Japan accounting for one third of Taiwan's exports. Because of the conditions favoring expansion, including a great emphasis in electronics and the service sector, Taiwan into the 1990s registered phenomenal economic growth, to amass almost $80 billion in foreign exchange reserves, an outstanding figure for any Asian country, much less one of small size (like West Virginia) and modest population (20 million).

After 1949, although the Republic of China was recognized as the leading government of China by half the United Nations membership, the question of Chinese representation came up perennially for debate in General Assembly sessions. The charter of the United Nations named the Republic of China as one of the five permanent Security Council members with power of the veto; additionally, its representatives sat on the specialized commissions and agencies. With the consolidation of the Chinese Communist movement on the mainland, another contender appeared for the China seat. The General Assembly annually debated the problem. Solutions that advocated the seating of both Chinas in the United Nations organs or the admission of Taiwan as a separate state appeared unacceptable to Taipei (and to Beijing).

Over the decades, as more nations came to recognize the People's Republic, the trend shifted toward seating that government in the United Nations, which was accomplished in 1971. Within five years, the number of countries recognizing Taipei as the spokesman for all China dwindled to twenty-seven. President Richard Nixon's surprise visit to the People's Republic in February 1972 heralded an American shift of policy that culminated in President Jimmy Carter's administration on New Year's Day, 1979, with statements of mutual diplomatic recognition between Washington and Beijing. Between Chinese factions themselves, relations began to thaw. From the 1980s, individuals from Taiwan were permitted to visit the mainland; trade contacts soon followed. But as long as the bitter heritage of China's civil war years remained, the domestic and international status of Taiwan would remain a problem.

Chronology

1937	July 7: Marco Polo Bridge incident; Brussels Conference
1937-1938	Japan occupies north, central, and south coastal Chinese areas
1939-1940	Mao Zedong authors works on China's revolution
1940	March: Puppet Republic of China at Nanjing
1941	January: Fourth Route Army incident
1941-1945	Pacific war
1942-1943	*Zheng feng* program at Yan'an
1943	Chiang Kai-shek authors two books on China's problems; December 1: Cairo Conference declaration
1944-1945	Ambassador Patrick Hurley attempts reconciliation moves
1945	February: Yalta Conference; August: Sino-Soviet treaty
1945	Chinese control returns to Taiwan
1945-1947	Marshall mission
1947-1949	Renewed civil war
1948	November: Communists capture Mukden
1949	Fall of mainland to Communists. October 1: People's Republic of China proclaimed
1949	December: Chiang Kai-shek, military, and Guomindang arrive in Taiwan
1950	Korean War erupts; United States has a two-China policy
1954	U.S.–Republic of China mutual defense treaty (to 1979)
1971	People's Republic of China replaces Republic of China for China seat in the United Nations
1975	Death of Chiang Kai-shek
1978-1988	Chiang Ching-kuo, president of Republic of China
1979	January 1: United States switches diplomatic recognition to People's Republic
1988	Taiwanese Lee Teng-hui becomes president
1993	Taiwanese Lien Chan becomes prime minister

22

PEOPLE'S REPUBLIC OF CHINA

(Since 1949)

Mao's China (1949 to 1976)

Until his death in 1976, Mao Zedong remained at the helm of the People's Republic of China. During the first years of his rule (1949-1958), national consolidation proceeded and basic development programs were initiated, for the country had been wracked by civil and foreign wars since the 1920s. By the mid-1950s, the government felt confident enough to establish solid foundations of state in both the political and the economic spheres. After defining the basic outline of state policy, in the course of the next years (1958-1966) the Chinese Communists began to experiment with more revolutionary goals. They formulated grandiose sweeping plans for further change, such as the people's militia, agricultural communes, and the Great Leap Forward in industry. In Mao's final decade (1966-1976), the country descended into turmoil with the Great Proletarian Cultural Revolution and its unsettling aftermath. Over the decades, foreign affairs reflected the shifts in domestic policies, but as a world political power, the People's Republic could not be ignored in international council.

During the first five years (1949-1954), the People's Republic structure was based on the 1949 Organic Law, formulated by the Chinese People's Political Consultative Conference. This called for a Government Council, State Administrative Council, and a People's Revolutionary Military Council. China was divided into six regional administrations. The Common Program, or temporary constitution, outlined basic rights and duties of citizens. In late 1952, after a national census to determine the population in China (583 million), elections were held for the First National People's Congress. Six million were elected to village, town, and municipal congresses and councils. The elected officers in the lowest tier then elected from their ranks 16,807 deputies to the provincial congresses, who in turn elected 1,226 delegates to the National People's Congress at Beijing. Reflecting a Marxist orientation, the Election Law of 1953, through a process of ideological gerrymandering, heavily favored urban and industrial areas over the rural areas in representation.

In September 1954, the First National People's Congress met in Beijing. It approved the new constitution promulgated by party leaders that created new government organs and elective offices of government. The constitution outlined the general principles of the road to socialism, described the organizational framework of the new state structure, and noted fundamental rights and duties of citizens. It disregarded the principle of the separation of powers, never strong in China. The rights of citizens were hedged by many stipulations. The National People's Congress also elected the main officials of the national apparatus, including Mao as the country's president (or chairman, who nominated the prime minister or premier), the vice presidents, and cabinet-rank members.

The State Council was designated as the highest executive and administrative organ. Premier Zhou Enlai (Chou En-lai), a long-time party member, headed the body, which supervised day-to-day operations of the vast bureaucracy and implemented party and government directives. Other government organs included the Supreme State Conference, the Supreme People's Court, and the Supreme People's Procuratorate (the justice department). China was divided into twenty-one provinces, two special municipalities (Beijing and Shanghai; Tianjin was added later), and five autonomous regions. The provinces, with varying numbers of county, subcounty, and village units, were all under the direct supervision of the central government.

Behind the government was the Communist Party structure built on Leninist lines, a state within a state, with little relation or resemblance to Western-type political parties. Top party members were also at the helm of government and military affairs; the offices were interlarded. At the apex of power was the party chairman, presiding over the Standing Committee (a half dozen members); Mao had held supreme position since 1935 on the Long March. Then came the Politburo, composed of some two dozen members, and the Central Committee of around a hundred. These made decisions when the National Party Congress was not in sessions (only several weeks annually). The party structure also embraced the Central Control Committee, a secretariat, various departments, and regional bureaus. At lower levels were provincial and local congresses as well as cells on farms, in factories, and in schools. Each echelon elected members to the next higher rank.

The military arm augmented party control. All formal military organizations in China were infiltrated on every level by party members, who acted as political commissars with ranks equivalent to their counterpart military colleagues. The most important overall military unit, the People's Liberation Army (PLA), comprised the army, navy, air force, and supporting service troops. With a total of around three million, it ranked as the third largest military establishment in the world (after the Russian Federation and the United States).

To ensure further control over the population of mainland China, the Communists created mass organizations and institutions based on occupation, religion, and country or regional friendship interests. Other party control organs included the uniformed police, the secret police, and the People's Procurator General's Office that enforced laws and policies. In working through all these bureaus, the Chinese Communists drew a fine line between coercion and persuasion. On a mass basis, the Chinese performed their appointed tasks by rote as directed from above. To counteract flagging revolutionary spirits, the regime stirred up the people through the promotion of various slogans and campaigns. In the early 1950s, the party embarked on the 3-anti campaign aimed against party sluggards, and the 5-anti campaign against bureaucrats and the middle class. The Chinese conducted hate-America campaigns during the Korean War. They promoted their versions of model men and women, who tended to be dedicated but stereotyped party figures.

The role of agriculture was most vital. Mao and other leaders faced agricultural problems with practical solutions and Marxist dogma. Drawing upon Ruijin and Yan'an experiments, Mao categorized five rural classes: the landlord, the rich peasant, the middle peasant, the poor peasant, and the tenant. An individual's status depended on the amount of land and tools he owned and the degree to which he exploited or was exploited by others. The first three classes lost land, which was distributed among the latter two classes. These programs of land redistribution, often bloody, were effected in the first three years (1949-1952) of the Communist regime. Between 1952 and 1955, it then exhorted farmers to join together in mutual aid teams and agricultural producer cooperatives. In 1955, Mao announced the second phase of the land program, that of collectives. Over the next three years, collectivization, which made land and tools the communal property of a collective (private peasant groups), became the key word in agrarian policy. Beijing also had developed experimental state farms, although most of the collectives at this time were private.

Despite the importance of agriculture, the Chinese Communists emphasized industry, commerce, and transport in economic planning. In the early years, factories were rehabilitated and confiscated from former Nationalist owners, counterrevolutionaries, and foreigners. Private firms were converted to state-owned enterprises. With the inception of the first five-year plan (1953-1957), emphasis was placed on industrial development. The industrial labor task force was recruited from off the land and paid in a wage-unit system or a commodity-equivalent practice, in which amounts of food and money were paid according to the type of job and hardship involved. The state controlled commerce, as it did industrial development. All important facets of domestic and international trade and commerce were placed under national direction. The regime manipulated goods and prices through various control schemes of rationing, compulsory buying, and allocation priorities. The Chinese Communists utilized great masses of people (and the People's Liberation Army) on public works projects and communication systems. They did not rely only on traditional waterways but extended roads, railroads, and the domestic air system.

In social matters, the Chinese Communists capitalized on and hastened modernization trends. The Marriage Law of 1950 made consent mandatory to contract, a provision already stated when the Nationalists formulated the 1931 civil code. Again, building on precedent, the Chinese Communists effected certain reforms in the language to simplify its written and oral variants. In health programs, they showed concern for public welfare and made headway against traditional diseases. Religion continued to be deemphasized. Confucianism was dead, and Daoism was dying. Buddhism remained weak as an organized force, but Islam, associated with substantial minority groups, held its own in the border areas as a religious and political entity. The Christian churches were nationalized.

The Chinese Communist leadership emphasized the necessity of education to create literate masses. The formal educational structure embraced kindergarten, primary grades, junior and senior middle (high) schools, and higher education. In the curriculum, the Communists emphasized a blend of physical and mental work, a revolutionary concept in Chinese thought. Postgraduate schools existed, and scientific organizations conducted advanced research. Despite the emphasis on education, the role of the intellectual was uncomfortable. For one to be both "red" and "expert" proved trying. An ideological lid was placed on intellectual activity although, in 1957, Mao permitted a brief period of relaxation known as the "let the hundred flowers bloom" period, during the contemporaneous de-Stalinization period in the Soviet Union.

He also set the orthodox line of socialist realism in literary and artistic works, which called for unity of art and politics, of life and ideology. To promote these ends, the regime utilized all media for popular dissemination of propaganda and culture. Official newspapers with the party line blanketed China. The *Renmin ribao (People's Daily)*, was the mouthpiece of party and government, while other official organs had their journals. The film industry was centralized, television stations were established, and regional networks spread out from the capital. Short-wave services were maintained that beamed programs particularly to overseas Chinese,

In foreign policy, Chinese national and ideological attitudes kept up with the changing international environment. A Ministry of Foreign Affairs existed at the capital and dozens of embassies were established abroad. Augmenting the formal diplomatic machinery were political, economic, and cultural ties that Beijing participated in with communist and noncommunist countries, recognized or not. The People's Republic refused to sit in any world organs or committees in which Nationalist China was represented (an attitude reciprocated by the Republic of China). Foreign economic relations were formulated. Through extended trade and aid programs, Beijing sought ties with over a hundred countries. For the first decade or so after 1949, up to three-fourths and more of total trade was conducted with the Soviet bloc.

The Soviet Union recognized the People's Republic of China on October 1, 1949, that day it was proclaimed in Beijing. Early the next year, the initial framework of Sino-Soviet relations was set in agreements signed in Moscow, where Mao had gone in his first recorded trip outside China. The most important of these was the thirty-year treaty of friendship, whose major clause related to military cooperation. A second document promised up to $300 million in loans to the Chinese for industrial projects. A third agreement related to the Manchurian railways and ports (Dalian and Lushun), all of which were to be evacuated upon the conclusion of a Japanese peace treaty, but no later than 1952. (The Chinese later requested Soviet presence in Lushun until 1955 because of the Korean War.) A fourth exchange of notes reaffirmed the independent status of the Mongolian People's Republic. A final agreement (terminated in 1954) established joint-stock companies in Xinjiang to exploit oil and nonferrous metals. It also outlined routes for airways between Beijing and central Russian Asian cities.

While Stalin was alive, the alliance seemed to operate smoothly. In late 1952, the Soviets agreed to underwrite more projects. The following September, after the Korean armistice and the death of Stalin, another technical assistance program was announced. Under new leadership, the Soviets paid more attention to their Chinese partner, who assumed greater independence and initiative in international communism. Mao continued his ideological and international rise to power in bloc politics, and the Chinese participated in Eastern European affairs.

The Soviets provided more economic programs, and more top Soviets came to Beijing, but despite visitations and aid programs, as the 1950s progressed, stresses developed in Sino-Soviet relations.

Among noncommunist nations in Asia, Japan remained a prime consideration in Chinese Communist policy. With the recovery of Japanese independence in 1952, various issues arose and were settled between the two countries. Tens of thousands of Japanese residents in China and prisoners of war still on the mainland were repatriated. Several fishing conventions were concluded. Trade agreements were initiated (although Japan still diplomatically recognized Taiwan). Among other noncommunist East Asian entities, Hong Kong had an anomalous position. Although it was Chinese territory, Beijing made no immediate territorial demands, because the port was a great foreign exchange earner for the mainland. Chinese Communists sold foodstuffs to the colony, which was also the transmitter of remittances from overseas Chinese to families back home on the mainland. They also tolerated, in Portuguese hands, the enclave of Macau. With South Korea, there were no relations.

In Southeast and South Asia, Chinese Communist objectives related principally to securing frontiers and border areas. Beijing aspired to include states in these regions within its sphere of political influence through the creation of friendly, or at least nonhostile, states. Southeast Asians reacted variously to their Chinese neighbor. Some states chose to align themselves with the West through military pacts; others preferred nonalignment and acted independently. In South Asia, the Beijing government developed official, formal, and diplomatic relations with Sri Lanka, Afghanistan, Pakistan, Nepal, and India. The Chinese proved themselves accommodating to small powers, such as Nepal and Afghanistan, in the conclusion of treaties of friendship and boundary matters as well as to large nations, such as Pakistan. But China developed differences with India. Border issues were the most acerbating ones, and the Chinese related them to their conquest and occupation of neighboring restive Tibet.

Toward the United States, the Chinese Communists almost from the inception of their regime displayed hostility, an attitude that Americans reciprocated. Beijing put out continual propaganda aimed at the United States, its allies, and their interests. Its attitude was shaped by several factors: American bases ringing the land, ideological dogma that precluded peaceful coexistence with capitalist countries, and the security desire to eliminate or to lessen the American presence, at least in East Asia. The People's Republic used American actions as catharsis for tensions within the country as well.

The confrontations were broken by a few thaws, such as the Korean truce talks (1951-1953) where both parties were represented, and the Bandung Conference (1955) of Asian and African nations at which Zhou Enlai claimed that China was ready to negotiate with the United States over Asian tensions. The Americans picked up the cue, and bilateral talks resulted sporadically over the years, first at Geneva at the consular level, and later at Warsaw at an ambassadorial level. Issues of discussions at the meetings included the return of American and Chinese civilians detained in the other's country; alleged territorial violations by American aircraft and vessels into Chinese air space and territorial waters (set at twelve miles); U.S. trade embargoes; and the position of Taiwan and the offshore islands of Quemoy and Matsu in diplomatic and defense arrangements of the United States.

At the end of the first decade of existence of the People's Republic, between late 1958 and early 1959, its constituency elected the Second National People's Congress. Liu Shaoqi (Liu Shao-ch'i), a party man of long standing, was elected the new chairman or president of the People's Republic after Mao bowed out. In late 1964, the third round of elections took place. By this time, the number of deputies to the National People's Congress more than doubled to 3,040. Inasmuch as the National People's Congresses met infrequently, the elected standing committees (like the party's counterpart, but much larger in membership) took care of governmental affairs. Delayed by internal events, the fourth national elections were postponed until 1975.

At this time, in military affairs, China proceeded along various lines. It built up the People's Liberation Army, but in 1958, the people's militia was created, in effect, to transform every able-bodied adult into a part-time soldier. These millions augmented the professional army not only as a paramilitary force, but also as a huge pool of available labor. Although Mao continued to emphasize the importance of manpower in military might, his regime developed nuclear weapons. In this second decade, Communist China entered the atomic age. It had the requisite engineers and research physicists, some of whom had trained in the United States. In October 1957, a Sino-Soviet agreement was concluded to provide China with a sample atomic bomb and data on its manufacture, but two years later, the Soviets tore up the agreement. On its own, Beijing proceeded with experiments and tests began in the Lop Nor area of desolate Xinjiang. On October 16, 1964, China joined the exclusive nuclear club with the explosion of its first nuclear device, the equivalent of 20 kilotons (20,000 tons of TNT). Within the next three years, half a dozen other experimental detonations took place, including a hydrogen explosion in mid-June 1976. Around 1958, a short-range missile development program, utilizing ground-to-air missiles, was begun. The implication of nuclear energy and its potential military uses by Beijing were not lost on neighboring Asians.

Toward the end of the first decade, in economic life, agricultural policy also tightened when in 1958, collectives merged into communes. These were multipurpose administration units created to manage interrelated agricultural, industrial, commercial, social, and military affairs. Generally, the communes were formed from the preexisting boundaries of a district or a group of villages. (Mao also tried to introduce urban communes in the cities, each to cover a certain number of blocks.) But because of climatic and administrative setbacks in the 1960s, many communes broke down into the smaller and more efficient component parts of production brigades and teams.

Experimentation also proceeded in industry. The Great Leap Forward of 1958 coincided with the commencement of the second five-year plan. But because of ever-ambitious planing and poor harvests over a three-year period (1959-1961), adjustments had to be made. Heavy industrial priorities gave way to light industry, and as a whole, industry was sidetracked to favor agricultural priorities. The fits and starts in general economic planning in the aftermath of the second plan revealed adverse conditions. The third plan, first broached in 1963, dropped out of sight for three years, was briefly resurrected in 1966, and then was again lost from public view. A fourth plan was initiated in 1971.

Another economic difficulty that the Chinese faced was the overriding one of population growth. As the 1970s approached, the mainland was inhabited by more than 750 million Chinese, with an annual increase rate of some three percent, a high one in a populous country. The Chinese Communists reacted variously to the dangers of overpopulation. Marxism stressed labor as the chief source of national wealth, an argument which seemed to justify a great labor force to guarantee economic development. But China had to face reality; it had limitations of land and food on which to support a burgeoning population. Top party leaders came out quietly in the late 1950s for birth control projects, which were advocated more openly later as problems persisted. Among other measures the regime promoted and advocated were late marriages and the happiness of the small family.

In foreign affairs, despite sporadic Sino-American talks, mutual distrust continued. Yet winds of change blew in the course of Chinese Communist relations with other countries. One of the most conspicuous trends after 1958 was the open eruption of Sino-Soviet differences. As revealed in the Chinese version of the story, these developed as early as Nikita Khrushchev's 1956 de-Stalinization speech at the Twentieth Soviet Party Congress in Moscow. Yet the next year, Mao went a second time to Moscow to help celebrate the fortieth anniversary of the Russian revolution. There he signed the Moscow Declaration that admitted the possibility of differing roads to socialism. Two years later, however, he publicly questioned the propriety of the Khrushchev-Eisenhower communiqué that pinned hopes of peace on peaceful coexistence of communism and capitalism.

Late in 1959, more fuel was added to the fire, when in the course of Himalayan border warfare between China and India, the Soviet Union remained neutral instead of supporting a fraternal socialist country. The following year, Soviet technicians began to leave China in large numbers. The 1960 Moscow statement issued by Communist leaders contained no reference to the Soviet Union as the head of the socialist camp. The Chinese subsequently elaborated their side of the argument in ideological, political, military, and economic issues. They also raised the racial issue and branded Soviet leaders in the aggressive role of a superior nation lording over inferior ones. They claimed that mutual boundaries were inequitable and sought revisions of the long borders. Fighting periodically erupted along the Manchurian front as the various Sino-Soviet issues simmered.

After various programs over the years in which Mao sought to mold the allround socialist man who was, at once, a peasant, worker, intellectual, and military figure, another paroxysm of zeal resulted in the Great Proletarian Cultural Revolution, at its height from 1966 to 1969. This probably originated from a combination of factors that stemmed from interparty power struggles and ideological differences in which Mao found himself outmaneuvered. In the course of these years, top party heads, including Liu Shaoqi, lost office, while factions around Mao swirled in and out of favor. Formal party operations were undercut by such temporary but publicized organs as the Red Guards and revolutionary committees. Party purges, although not bloody, were extensive. The repercussions of uncertainty and extremism were reflected in economic life and the educational field. Students were exiled to the provinces to perform manual labor. Many schools at all levels shut down or were oriented solely toward current political lines. In the name of eradicating old ways and customs, the Red Guards went on rampages and destroyed much property and valuable historic artifacts and buildings. As the Chinese themselves later said, these were the lost years.

Mao continued as top man, but new groups, including some different names, emerged. Into the mid-1970s, key figures came and went. Lin Biao, successor designate to Mao after Liu's fall from grace, disappeared in a plane crash after allegedly trying to usurp power. In 1976, both Zhu De, the founder of the army, and Prime Minister Zhou Enlai died, after which the moderate Hua Guofeng assumed the premiership. In July, Chinese experienced a terrible earthquake centered in Tangshan, a city of a million northeast of Beijing, an omen that presaged more misfortunes to come. Within two months, in September, Mao himself, in ill health, having given up functions of state, died in seclusion.

In foreign affairs, as relations soured with the Soviet Union, the Chinese Communists turned to other directions. Despite political differences, Japan became the largest noncommunist trading partner of the People's Republic. In Southeast Asia, the escalation of the Indo-Chinese war in the latter half of the 1960s saw Chinese involvement with military aid to Hanoi and presence at negotiating tables. Prior to 1965, Chinese ties had been quite close with the Indonesian Communist Party, while Beijing followed the underground activities of Communist parties in other lands and encouraged at least a pro-Beijing, as against a pro-Moscow, orientation. Border disputes with India after 1958 acerbated feelings with that country, but they drew Pakistan closer to China.

In the 1970s, China maintained diplomatic relations with most Western European counties. London early on recognized Beijing, which accepted the recognition but kept relations at a secondary level, with an exchange of chargés d'affaires rather than ambassadors. Despite Chinese disapproval of the historic English imperialistic record in China, Beijing, especially after open differences with the Soviets, turned to London for trade and commerce and invited British scientists and teachers to China. There the British sometimes represented American interests.

Despite the earlier lack of formal diplomatic ties with other Western European nations and with the white Commonwealth countries (Canada, Australia, and New Zealand), the People's Republic concluded trade agreements with their governments and business concerns. It sought to develop diplomatic, political, and commercial relations along with the Middle Eastern, Arab-African, and Sub-Saharan countries in Africa. Beijing was interested in trade contacts, particularly in the acquisition of crude oil stocks.

It sought support for causes in international organs. It endeavored through long-running programs and almost insuperable obstacles to compete with Soviet and American influence in some underdeveloped countries. It fished in muddied political waters to extend its national and communist policies, promoting, to the concern of some established indigenous regimes, the export of revolution. The Chinese allied themselves with Middle Eastern and African guerrilla movements for national liberation, as well as with other causes, and they recognized governments dedicated to eradicating colonialism and neocolonialism. They sought common cause with those African and Middle Eastern peoples who eschewed Western military pacts and promoted the goal of self-determination. They expanded trade with Latin American countries, although it was as yet on a small scale.

The prospect of improving relations between the United States and the People's Republic was complex and multifaceted. In the United States, individual proposals called for the development of trade and exchanges and contacts along various lines. Although the prospects for increased mutual understanding appeared involved, in the early 1970s, fresh approaches and reexamination of existing issues were indicated. American passports were validated for travel to mainland China, which was selectively issuing visas for travelers. The Nixon administration (1969-1974) relaxed restrictions on trade with Beijing and permitted Americans to purchase Communist-made goods. The American public debated China policies, although the Chinese Communists remained more inflexible in their responses. The bamboo curtain opened partially in early 1971 when an American ping-pong team was permitted to enter China for a week; selected American journalists and scientists were similarly allowed visits.

After a mission to Beijing in July 1971, by President Nixon's adviser on security matters, the Chinese Communists extended, and Nixon accepted, an invitation to visit the People's Republic, which materialized the following February. The visit precipitated a visible swing by uncommitted countries toward formal diplomatic relations with the People's Republic, as well as with the establishment of liaison offices in Beijing and Washington. President Gerald Ford journeyed to Beijing in 1975 in one of several moves toward the normalization of relations, while more states recognized the regime in the changing international environment.

China After Mao (Since 1976)

After Mao's death, Hua Guofeng, already the prime minister (having assumed the post in early 1976 after Zhou Enlai's demise), also took on the position as party chairman. A compromise candidate, he had the unenviable task of trying to continue Mao's revolution yet endeavor to harness radical elements, the most notorious of whom was the Gang of Four headed by Mao's widow, Jiang Qing (Chiang Ch'ing), and her accomplices. Moreover, the economic sector faced aggravated problems of inflation and fiscal deficits that were not satisfactorily addressed. Deng Xiaoping (Teng Hsiao-p'ing), a long-time party member, twice disgraced (1966 and 1976), in and out of Mao's shadow, came to contest leadership with his appeals to pragmatism ("seek truth with facts") and a moderate approach to issues.

By the early 1980s, his faction had eased Hua and his supporters out of leadership positions. Deng's two protégés came into power: Hu Yaobang (Hu Yao-pang), as party chairman (1981-1987), and Zhao Ziyang (Chao Tzu-yang) as prime minister (1980-1987), who then replaced Hua as chairman (1987-1989). Interparty power and ideological struggles continued and Deng's men were turned out of office by hardliner Li Peng as prime minister (1987) and Jiang Zemin (Chang Tze-min) as party chairman (1989). Deng himself held only a vice chairman position in the party, as well as the position of chief of the Military Affairs Commission, but he was tacitly accepted as the party's de facto leader into the 1990s. In 1993, the National People's Congress dutifully elected Jiang, apparently Deng's groomed successor, also as president of the People's Republic.

Deng advanced the Four Modernizations: agriculture, industry, science and technology, and defense; under this slogan he implemented some changes. In agriculture, the communes were dismantled and the responsibility system was inaugurated; farmland was recollectivized; fiscal and crop accountability was transferred from central decision-making and local party planning authorities to individual families, who, through the incentive system, could dispose and sell much of their own produce. Over the years, farm incentives grew unevenly but in some areas spectacularly, and according to the new agrarian slogan, to be rich was glorious.

In industry, local entrepreneurs, replacing centralized planning agencies, developed profit retention enterprises that emphasized consumer goods products. Foreign trade was encouraged. For the first time, the government sought joint ventures and direct capital investments. Special economic zones, with various incentives to lure foreign money, were set up in coastal cities traditionally associated with overseas trade. (Hong Kong capital was particularly quick to seize the economic opportunity; its funds flowed into mainland projects, especially into those of the neighboring province, Guangdong.) A burgeoning population and growing industrial base gave rise to problems of environmental pollution. An expanding infrastructure made demands on natural resources to tap potential sources of energy. A public outcry particularly arose when the government announced plans to build a multipurpose dam, the world's largest, on the scenic Three Gorge pass of the mid-Yangtze River, which would inundate spectacular scenery and flood riverside communities.

In the science and technology field, the Chinese Academy of Sciences was injected with new life and urged cooperation among ministers. Under the State Council, the S & T Leading Group, cutting across traditional vertical ministerial structures, integrated research of a multitude of agencies and sought as well more links between research and production. In defense, a professional military establishment was projected. Old generals retired; more than a hundred were given sinecure positions in the newly created Control Advisory Commission. The army's eleven military regions were reduced to seven. Into the 1990s, despite the disappearance of traditional enemies, Chinese budgets increased expenditures for defense and the projected military power for possible deployment beyond the country's shores. Two flash points were of particular concern. In Xinjiang, potential problems existed with minority Muslim groups affiliated in race and religion to those across the border in several contiguous areas of the Russian Federation. In the South China Sea, China contested the sovereignty claims of several other countries over the Paracel Islands and the Spratly Islands and sought to enforce its position with military actions.

The government bureaucratic structure continued to operate at four levels. Elections proceeded for local, county (and city), provincial (28), and countrywide (National People's Congress) organs. The officially controlled media channeled party lines to the public who in turn were encouraged to submit criticism, some of which turned out to be unwelcome. With the appearance of a degree of economic liberalism, intellectuals hoped for a concurrent easing of political strictures. In the winter of 1978-79, in Beijing, there sprouted a Democracy Wall on which were plastered broadsheets (a traditional Chinese medium of expression protest) commenting on party and government shortcomings. One critic went so far as to advocate democracy as the Fifth Modernization, after which the wall prematurely ended.

Over the decade of the 1980s, intellectual alienation from officialdom escalated, to reach its climax at the Tian'anmen Square incident of June 4, 1989. Coinciding with Soviet Party Chairman Mikhail Gorbachev's official visit to China, in the spotlight of international television cameras, Beijing students, restive under an accumulation of academic gripes and criticism of party corruption and inefficiency, had set up a tent city in the central square. Demonstrations remained peaceful, but aged party spokesmen, after initial indecision, called in the military to dispense forcibly the students whom the leaders, cemented in historical attitudes, perceived as threats to their personal survival and to the Communist cause. While the peasants—the majority of China—went about their accustomed ways, savoring their material benefits, the urban intellectuals became even more estranged from the political status quo. Deng and others continued to differentiate between economic liberalism and political pluralism. The former was advocated; the latter was repressed, for it could destablize the country, the argument went. Where in the Western historical tradition the two reforms could proceed hand-in-hand, China (not unique here) judged them to be incompatible.

In foreign affairs, despite a hard attitude on the human rights issue, the People's Republic broadened its diplomatic and other relations. In a treaty with the British, Hong Kong was to revert to Chinese administration in 1997; the Portuguese colony of Macau was similarly to return by the turn of the century. Beijing dealt with both Koreas; regimes of the North and South were separately admitted as United Nations members. Japan moved to accelerate trade ties when Emperor Akihito visited China in late 1992. Chinese leadership moved toward rapprochement with Vietnam after the Soviets withdrew military and economic aid programs in the late 1980s. Soviet withdrawal also augured Beijing's escalated cooperation in resolving the muddled Cambodian political situation. With other Southeast and South Asian countries, including India, formal relations continued. Ties with the rest of the world, excepting the United States, seemed more remote. During the Persian Gulf war of early 1991, Beijing remained on the sidelines. The demise of the Soviet Union eased border and security problems along China's periphery.

With mutual Sino-American diplomatic relations established on January 1, 1979, in the Carter administration, relations become both more intimate and more stressful. Deng Xiaoping paid a visit to the United States, followed by a stream of over 10,000 Chinese students and technicians to study in the United States (the number continued to climb). Over 300,000 American tourists traveled annually to mainland China, spending welcome hard currency, to visit publicized and mostly well-known historic sites. Washington extended some military aid and technological expertise to Beijing, but after the Tian'anmen Square incident (and reported suppressive moves in Tibet), the U.S. Congress, in opposition to a more liberally minded President George Bush, and later President Bill Clinton, sought to end the annual renewals of China's most-favored-nation status in mutual trade. With the collapse of the Cold War by 1990, and its blow to international socialism, the People's Republic could no longer count on its leverage in the three-way Sino-Soviet-American power play. International issues could now be focused more on bilateral considerations.

Faced with a plethora of domestic and foreign considerations, Beijing pursued its own policies and goals, some flexible, some nonnegotiable. The initial leadership was disappearing; the post-Mao succession was strained. But after a generation, the regime was firmly entrenched on the Chinese mainland, resolving dissent at home and enjoying respectability abroad, recognized by some hundred countries and represented in the United Nations and all its councils. As dynastic heirs to the ancient, imperial, and modern eras in ongoing Chinese history, the People's Republic of China laid claim to legitimacy, to pursuing and to fulfilling the reality of one China, *Zhongguo,* the Middle Kingdom.

Chronology

1949	Temporary Organic Law and Common Program. October 1: People's Republic of China established
1950	3-anti- and 5-anti- campaigns; Marriage Law; Sino-Soviet agreements
1951-1953	Korean War and truce talks
1953-1957	First five-year plan
1954	First National People's Congress establishes foundations of state
1955	Agrarian collectives formed; Afro-Asian Bandung conference in Indonesia; Sino-American talks commence
1957	"Let the hundred flowers bloom" period
1958	People's militia; agricultural communes; Great Leap Forward; beginning of deteriorating Sino-Soviet ties
1959	Indian border wars
1964	People's Republic detonates first nuclear explosive
1966-1969	Height of Great Proletarian Cultural Revolution
1972	President Richard Nixon visits the People's Republic (February)
1976	Deaths of General Zhu De, Prime Minister Zhou Enlai, Mao Zedong (September 6)
1978	Deng Xiaoping emerges as top party man; Four Modernizations
1979	Sino-American diplomatic relations established (January 1)
1989	Soviet Party Chairman Mikhail Gorbachev's visit; Tian'anmen Square incident (June 4)
1992	Japanese Emperor Akihito visits China
1997	Hong Kong reverts to Chinese administration, Macau by turn of century

BIBLIOGRAPHY

Contents

General/Reference/Source

Area Handbook Series. China: A Country Study. 4th ed., Washington, D.C., 1988.

Cambridge Encyclopedia of China. 2nd ed., Cambridge, 1991.

Couling, Samuel. *Encyclopedia Sinica.* London, reprint 1964 (1917).

De Bary, William T., and others, eds. *Sources of Chinese Tradition.* New York, 1960; edition in paperback, 2 vols., 1964.

Gentzler, J. Mason. *A Syllabus of Chinese Civilization.* 2nd ed., New York, 1972.

Hermann, A.A.L. *Historical and Commercial Atlas of China.* Taipei, reprint 1966 (1936).

Hu Chang-tu and others. *China: Its People, Its Society, Its Culture.* New Haven, 1960.

Hucker, Charles O. *China: A Critical Bibliography.* Tucson, 1962.

Journal of Asian Studies. Ann Arbor, quarterly, 1956-current. And annual bibliographic issue.

MacNair, Harley F., ed. *China.* Berkeley, 1946.

Mathews Chinese English Dictionary. Cambridge, reprint 1944 (1931) and index, 1947.

Moule, A.C. *The Rulers of China 221 B.C.-A.D. 1949.* London, 1957.

ONeill, Hugh D. *Companion to Chinese History.* New York, 1987, paper.

History: General

Beasley, W.G., and E.G. Pulleyblank, eds. *Historians of China and Japan.* London, 1961.

Cambridge History of China. Denis Twitchett and John K. Fairbank, gen. eds. fifteen projected volumes.

1. *China and Han Empires, 221 B.C.-A.D. 220.*1986.

3. *Sui and Tang China, 589-906.*Part I.1978.

7. *Ming dynasty, 1368-1644.* Part I. 1988.

10. *Late Ching, 1800-1911.* Part I. 1978.

11. *Late Ching, 1800-1911*. Part II. 1980.

12. *Republican China, 1912-1949*. Part I. 1983.

13. *Republican China, 1912-1949*. Part II. 1986.

14. *People's Republic of China*, Part I. *1949-1965*. 1987.

15. *People's Republic of China*, Part II. *1966-1982*. 1991.

Fairbank, John K. *China*. Boston, 1973, chapters from 2 vol. set of *East Asia: Tradition and Transformation*.

————. *China: A New History*. Cambridge, 1992.

Fitzgerald, Charles P. *China: A Short Cultural History*. 3rd ed., London, 1965.

Gardner, Charles S. *Chinese Traditional Historiography*. Cambridge, 1961.

Goodrich, L. Carrington. *A Short History of the Chinese People*. 4th ed., New York, 1964.

Granet, Marcel. *Chinese Civilization*. London, 1910.

Huang, Ray C. *China: A Macro-History*. Armonk, N.Y., 1989.

Hucker, Charles O. *China's Imperial Past*. Stanford 1975.

Latourette, Kenneth S. *The Chinese: Their History and Culture*. 4th ed., New York, 1964.

Li, Dun J. *The Ageless Chinese*. New York, 1975.

Meskill, John, ed. *Introduction to Chinese Civilization*. Lexington Mass., 1973.

Wilkinson, Endymion. *The History of Imperial China, A Research Guide*. Cambridge, 1975, paper.

Ancient China: (Prehistory to 221 B.C.)

Chang Kwang-Chih. *The Archaeology of Ancient China*. Rev. ed., New Haven, 1968.

Cheng Te-Kun. *Archaeology in China*. Vol. I. *Prehistoric China*. And supplement. Cambridge, 1966; Vol. II. *Shang China*. 1960; Vol. III. *Chou China*. 1963.

Creel, Herrlee G. *The Birth of China*. New York, 1937.

Ho Ping-ti. *The Cradle of the East*. Hong Kong, 1975.

Hsu Cho-yin. *Ancient China in Transition: An Analysis of Social Mobility, 722-222 B.C.* Stanford, 1965.

Levenson, Joseph R., and Franz Schurmann. *China: An Interpretative History from the Beginnings to the Fall of Han*. Berkeley, 1969.

Li Chi. *The Beginnings of Chinese Civilization*. Seattle, 1957.

————. *The Formation of the Chinese People Republic*. Cambridge, 1928.

Watson, William. *Early Civilization of China*. New York, 1966.

Imperial China: First Phase (221 B.C.–A.D. 589)

Bielenstein, Hans. *The Restoration of the Han Dynasty*. Stockholm, 1953.

Bodde, Derk. *China's First Unifier*. Leiden, 1918. About Li Si (Li Ssu).

————. *Statesman, Patriot and General in Ancient China*. New Haven, 1940.

Chu Tung-tsu. *Han Social Structure*. Seattle, 1972.

Dubs, Homer H., trans. *The History of the Former Han Dynasty, by Pan Ku*. 2 vols., Baltimore, 1938, 1944; vol. 3., London, 1955.

Hirth, F. *China and the Roman Orient*. New York, reprint 1939 (1885).

Loewe, Michael. *Everyday Life in Early Imperial China*. New York, 1968.

Pirazzoli-ttSerstevens, Michele. *The Han Dynasty*. Janet Seligman trans. New York, 1982.

Swann, Nancy Lee, trans. *Food and Money in Ancient China, by Pan-Ku*. Princeton, 1950.

————. *Pan Chao, The Foremost Woman of China*. New York, 1932.

Teggart, Frederick J. *Rome and China*. Berkeley, 1939.

Watson, Burton, trans. *Records of the Grand Historian of China*. 2 vols. New York, 1962. About Ssu-ma Chien.

————. *Ssu-ma Chien, Grand Historian of China*. New York, 1958.

Yu Ting-shih. *Trade and Expansion in Han China*. Berkeley, 1967.

Imperial China: Second Phase (589–960)

Bingham, Woodbridge. *The Founding of the Tiang Dynasty.* Baltimore, 1941.

Eberhard, W. *Conquerors and Rulers.* Leiden, 1952.

Fitzgerald, C.P. *The Empress Wu.* London, 1956.

————. *Son of Heaven: A Biography of Li Shih-min, Founder of the Tang Dynasty.* Cambridge, 1933.

Pulleybank, Edwin G. *The Background of the Rebellion of An Lu-shan.* Oxford, 1955.

Twichett, Dennis. *Financial Administration under the Tang Dynasty.* 2nd ed., Cambridge, 1971.

Schafer, Edward H. *The Golden Peaches of Samarkand.* Berkeley, 1963.

————. *The Vermillion Bird.* Berkeley, 1967.

Wright, Arthur F. *The Sui Dynasty.* New York, 1978.

————, and Dennis Twitchett, ed. *Perspectives on the Tang.* New Haven, 1973.

Imperial China: Third Phase (960–1644)

Song:

Gernet, Jacques. *Daily Life in China on the Eve of the Mongol Invasion, 1250-1276.* H.M. Wright trans. New York, 1902.

Hirth, F., and W.W. Rockhill. *Chau Ju-kua.* St. Petersburg, 1912.

Kracke, E. A., Jr. *Civil Service in Early Sung China, 960-1067.* Cambridge, 1953.

Liu, James T. C. *Reform in Sung China, Wang An-shih, 1021-1086, and His New Policies.* Cambridge, 1959.

Wittfogel, Karl A. and Feng Chie-sheng. *History of Chinese Society: Liao (907-1125).* Philadelphia, 1949, paper.

Yuan:

Hart, Henry H. *Venetian Adventurer.* Stanford, 1942. Marco Polo.

Martin, Henry D. *The Rise of Chingis Khan and His Conquest of North China.* Baltimore, 1950.

Schumann, Herbert F. *Economic Structure of the Yuan Dynasty.* Cambridge, 1956.

Ming:

Boxer, Charles R., ed. *South China in the Sixteenth Century.* London, 1953.

De Bary, William Theodore, ed. *Self and Society in Ming Thought.* New York, 1970.

Gallagher, L.J. *China in the Sixteenth Century: The Journal of Matthew Ricci.* New York, 1953.

Goodrich, L. Carrington, ed. *Dictionary of Ming Biography, 1368-1644.* New York, 1976.

Ho Ping-ti. *The Ladder of Success in Imperial China.* New York, 1962.

Hucker, Charles O. *The Censorial System of Ming China.* Stanford, 1966.

————., ed. *Chinese Government in Ming Times.* New York, 1969.

————. *The Traditional Chinese State in Ming Times, 1368-1644.* Tucson, 1961.

Spence, Jonathan. *The Memory Palace of Matteo Ricci.* New York, 1984, paper.

Wang I-t'ung. *Offical Relations between China and Japan, 1368-1549.* Cambridge, 1953.

Imperial China: Fourth Phase (1644–1912)

Qing Domestic Affairs:

Cameron, Meribeth E. *The Reform Movement in China, 1898-1912.* Stanford, 1931.

Ch'en, Jerome. *Yuan Shih-k'ai, 1859-1916.* 2nd ed., Stanford, 1972.

Franke, Wolfgang. *The Reform and Abolition of the Traditional Chinese Examination System.* Cambridge, 1961.

Hummel, Arthur W., ed. *Eminent Chinese of the Ch'ing Period.* 2 vols., Washington, D.C., 1943-1944.

Levenson, Joseph R. *Liang Ch'-ch'ao and the Mind of Modern China.* Cambridge, 1955.

Michael, Franz. *The Origin of Manchu Rule in China.* Baltimore, 1942.

———. *The Taiping Rebellion: History and Documents.* 3 vols., Seattle, 1966.

Powell, Ralph L. *The Rise of Chinese Military Power.* Princeton, 1955.

Purcell, Victor. *The Boxer Uprising: A Background Study.* Cambridge, 1963.

Spence, Jonathan. *Emperor of China: Self Portrait of K'ang-hsi.* New York, 1974.

———. *The Death of Woman Wang.* New York, 1978.

Tan, Chester C. *The Boxer Catastrophe.* New York, 1955.

Wright, March C., ed. *China in Revolution: The First Phase, 1900-1913.* New Haven, 1968.

———. *The Last Stand of Chinese Conservativism: The T'ung-Chih Restoration, 1862-1874.* Stanford, 1957.

Qing Foreign Affairs:

Fairbank, John K. *Trade and Diplomacy on the China Coast: The Opening of the Treaty Ports, 1842-1854.* Cambridge, 1964.

Hsü, Immanuel C.Y. *China's Entrance into the Family of Nations: The Diplomatic Phase, 1858–1880.* Cambridge, 1960.

Morse, Hosea B. *The Chronicles of the East India Company Trading to China, 1635-1834.* 4 vols., Taipei, reprint 1966 (1926). Supplementary volume, 1929.

———. *International Relations of the Chinese Empire.* 3 vols., Taipei, reprint, nd. (1910-1918).

———. *The Trade and Administration of China.* Rev. ed., Shanghai, 1913.

Pritchard, Earl H. *Anglo-Chinese Relations During the Seventeenth and Eighteenth Centuries.* Urbana, Ill., 1930.

Wakeman, Frederic, Jr. *Strangers at the Gate: Social Disorder in South China, 1839-1861*. Berkeley, 1966.

Waley, Arthur. *The Opium War through Chinese Eyes*. London, 1958.

Modern China (Since 1949)

General:

Fairbank, John K. *The Great Chinese Revolution, 1800-1985*. New York, 1986.

Franke, Wolfgang. *A Century of Chinese Revolution, 1851-1949*. New York, 1970, paper.

Hsü, Immanuel C.Y. *The Rise of Modern China*. 3rd ed., New York, 1983.

MacNair, Harley F. *Modern Chinese History: Selected Readings*. Shanghai, 1933.

Spence, Jonathan. *The Gate of Heavenly Peace: The Chinese and Their Revolution, 1895-1980*. New York, 1981.

————. *The Search for Modern China*. New York, 1990.

Teng Ssu-yu and John K. Fairbank, eds. *China's Response to the West*. Cambridge, 1961.

Republic (1912-1949)—Domestic Affairs:

Bianco, Lucien. *Origins of the Chinese Revolution, 1915-1949*. Muriel Bell trans. Stanford, 1971.

Boorman, Howard L., ed. *Biographical Dictionary of the Republic of China*. 4 vols., New York, 1967-1971.

Chen, Stephen, and Robert Payne. *Sun Yat-sen: A Portrait*. New York, 1946.

Chiang Kai-shek. *China's Destiny and Chinese Economic Theory*. Authorized translation by Wang Chuang-huai, New York, 1947. Unauthorized by Philip Jaffe, New York, 1947.

————. *Soviet Russia in China: A Summing Up at Seventy*. New York, 1957, Abridged reissue, 1966.

Chow Tse-tung. *May Fourth Movement*. Cambridge, 1960.

Clubb, O. Edmund. *20th Century China*. 2nd ed., New York, 1972.

Fitzgerald, Charles P. *Revolution in China*. London, 1952. Reissued as *The Birth Of Communist China*. New York, 1964.

Isaccs, Harold R. *The Tragedy of the Chinese Revolution*. Rev. ed., Stanford, 1961.

Liu, F. F. *A Military History of Modern China, 1924-1949*. London, 1956.

Sun Yat-sen. *Fundamentals of National Reconstruction*. Taipei, 1953.

————. *San Min Chu I*. Frank L. Prince trans. Nanking, 1947.

White, Theodore, and Anallee Jacob. *Thunder Out of China*. New York, 1946.

Young, Arthur N. *China's Wartime Finance and Inflation, 1937-1945*. Cambridge, 1965.

Republic (1912-1949)—Foreign Affairs:

Bassett, R. *Democracy and Foreign Policy: A Case History, the Sino-Japanese Dispute, 1931-1933*. London, 1953.

Fishel, W.R. *The End of Exterritoriality in China*. Berkeley, 1952.

Jones, Francis C. *Manchuria Since 1931*. London, 1949.

La Fargue, Thomas E. *China and the World War*. Stanford, 1937.

Pollard, Robert T. *China's Foreign Relations, 1917-1930*. New York, 1932.

Whiting, Allen. *Soviet Policies in China, 1917-1924*. New York, 1954.

Wilbur, C. Martin, and Julia Lien-ying How. *Documents on Communism, Nationalism and Soviet Advisors in China, 1918-1927*. New York, 1956.

Young, Arthur N. *China and the Helping Hand, 1937-1945*. Cambridge, 1963.

Communism—General/Source/Background:

Barnett, A. Doak. *China on the Eve of Communist Takeover*. New York, 1965.

Brandt, Conrad. *Stalin's Failure in China, 1924-1927*. Cambridge, 1958.

————, and others. *A Documentary History of Chinese Communism*. Cambridge, 1952.

Chen, Jerome. *Mao and the Chinese Revolution*. London, 1965.

Cole, Allan B. *Forty Years of Chinese Communism: Selected Readings with Commentary*. Washington, D.C., 1962, paper.

Compton, Boyd. *Mao's China: Party Reform Documents, 1942-1944*. Seattle, 1952.

Houn, Franklin W. A. *Short History of Chinese Communism*. Updated ed., Englewood Cliffs NJ, 1973.

Johnson, Chalmers. *Peasant Nationalism and Communist Power: The Emergence of Revolutionary China, 1937-1945*. Stanford, 1962.

Klein, Donald W., and Anne D. Clark, eds. *Biographical Dictionary of Chinese Communism, 1921-1965*. 2 vols., Cambridge, 1971.

Mao Zedong (Mao Tse-tung). *Selected Works of Mao Tse-tung*. 4 vols., Peking, 1961-1965.Vol. V, 1977.

Meisner, Maurice. *Li Ta-chao and the Origins of Chinese Marxism*. Cambridge, 1967.

North, Robert. *Moscow and the Chinese Communists*. 2nd ed., Stanford, 1963.

Schwartz, Benjmin. *Chinese Communism and the Rise of Mao*. Cambridge, 1951. Reissued, 1964.

Snow, Edgar. *Red Star Over China*. New York, 1938.

Uhalley, Stephen, Jr. *History of the Chinese Communist Party*. Stanford, 1988, paper.

People's Republic of China:

Barnett, A. Doak. *Communist China and Asia*. New York, 1960.

Camilleri, Joseph. *Chinese Foreign Policy*. Seattle, 1980.

China Quarterly, London, 1960-.

Griffith, Samuel B. *The Chinese People's Liberation Army*. New York, 1967.

Halperin, Morton H. *China and the Bomb*. New York, 1965.

Hinton, Harold. *Communist China in World Politics*. Boston, MA, 1966.

Lewis, John W. *Leadership in Communist China*. Ithaca, N.Y., 1963.

MacFarquhar, Roderick. *The Hundred Flowers Campaign and the Chinese Intellectuals*. New York, 1961.

North, Robert. *The Foreign Relations of China*. 3rd ed., Belmont, Calif., 1978, paper.

People's Republic publications in the English language including the New China News Agency press releases, miscellaneous publications of the Beijing Foreign Language Press, the weekly *Beijing Review*, and the monthlies *China Today* and *China Pictorial*.

Salisbury, Harrison. *The New Emperors: China and the Era of Mao and Deng*. Boston MA, 1992.

Schram, Stuart R. *Mao Tse-tung*. New York, 1960.

————. *The Political Thought of Mao Tse-tung*. New York, 1963.

Schurmann, Franz. *Ideology and Organization in Communist China*. Berkeley, 1966.

Schwartz, Benjamin I. *Communism and China: Ideology in Flux*. Cambridge, 1968.

Snow, Edgar. *The Other Side of the River*. New York, 1962.

Tang, Peter. *Communist China Today*. 2 vols., rev. ed., New York, 1961.

Treadgold, Donald W., ed. *Soviet and Chinese Communism*. Seattle, WA, 1966.

U.S. Consulate General, Hong Kong. Communist China's press translations: Survey of China Mainland Press, Extracts from China Mainland Publications, Selections from China Mainland Magazines, Current Background.

Wu Yuan-li. *The Economy of Communist China: An Introduction*. New York, 1965.

Zagoria, Donald S. *The Sino-Soviet Conflict, 1956-1961*. Princeton, 1964.

Topical

Philosophy/Religion/Mythology:

Broomhall, Marshall. *Islam in China*. London, reprint 1966 (1910).

Chan Wing-tsit, trans. *A Source Book in Chinese Philosophy*. Princeton, 1963.

Creel, Herrlee G. *Chinese Thought from Confucius to Mao Tse-tung*. New York, 1953.

———. *Confucius and the Chinese Way*. New York, 1949

———. *Confucius: The Man and the Myth*. New York, 1949

Christie, Anthony. *Chinese Mythology*. London, 1968.

Eberhard, Wolfram. *A Dictionary of Chinese Symbols*. G.L. Campbell trans. London, 1988, paper.

Fairbank, John K., ed. *Chinese Thought and Institutions*. Chicago, 1957.

Fung Yu-lan. *A Short History of Chinese Philosophy*. New York, 1960.

Latourette, Kenneth S. *A History of Christian Missions in China*. New York, 1929.

Levenson, Joseph R. *Confucian China and Its Modern Fate*. Berkeley, 1968.

Nivison, David S., and Arthur Wright, eds. *Confucianism in Action*. Stanford, 1959.

Waley, Arthur. *The Analects of Confucius*. New York, 1939.

———. *The Way and Its Power*. London, 1942.

Ware, James R. *The Sayings of Mencius*. New York, 1960, paper.

Watson, Burton. *The Complete Works of Chuang Tzu*. New York, 1968.

Welch, Holmes. *The Parting of the Way: Lao Tzu and the Taoist Movement*. Boston, 1957.

Werner, E.T.C. *A Dictionary of Chinese Mythology*. New York, 1961.

Wilhelm, Richard. German trans. *The I Ching or Book of Changes*. Rendered into English by Cary F. Baynes. 2 vols., New York, 1955.

Williams, C.A. *Outline of Chinese Symbolism and Art Motives.* 3rd. rev. ed., Rutland Vt., 1984 (1941).

Wright, Arthur, ed. *The Confucian Persuasion.* Stanford, 1960.

————. *Confucianism and Chinese Civilization.* New York, 1964.

————, ed. *Studies in Chinese Thought.* Chicago, 1953.

————, and Denis Twitchet, eds. *Confucian Personalities.* Stanford, 1962.

Buddhism:

Ch'en, Kenneth. *Buddhism in China: A Historical Survey.* Princeton, 1964.

————. *The Chinese Transformation of Buddhism.* Princeton, 1973, paper.

Eliot, Sir Charles. *Hinduism and Buddhism: An Historical Sketch.* 3 vols., London, reprint 1954 (1921).

Fa Hsien. *A Record of Buddhist Kingdoms.* Peking, 1957. James Legge trans. New York, reprint 1965 (1886).

Hsüan-tsang. *Buddhist Records of the Western World.* Samuel Beal trans, Delhi, reprint 1981 (1884).

————. *On Yuan Chuang's Travels in India, 629-645.* Thomas Watters trans. 2 vols., Taipei, reprint 1975 (1904).

I-ching. *A Record of the Buddhist Religion* , J. Takakusu trans. Taipei, reprint 1970 (1896).

Prip-Moller, J. *Chinese Buddhist Monasteries.* 2nd ed., Hong Kong, 1967 (1937).

Reischauer, Edwin O., trans. *Ennin's Diary.* New York, 1955.

————. *Ennin's Travels in T'ang China.* New York, 1955.

Waley, Arthur. *The Real Tripitaka.* London, 1952.

Whitefield, Roderick. *The Art of Central Asia.* 3 vols., Tokyo, 1982-1985. Vols 1 and 2: *Paintings from Dunhuang*; Vol 3: *Textile, Sculpture and Other Arts.* The Stein Collection in the British Museum.

————., and Anne Farrer. *Caves of the Thousand Buddhas.* London, 1990.

Wright, Arthur. *Buddhism in Chinese History.* Stanford, 1959.

Zucher, E. *The Buddhist Conquest of China.* 2 vols., Leiden, 1959.

Literature:

All Men Are Brothers. Pearl Buck trans. 2 vols., New York, 1937.

Buck, Pearl. *The Good Earth.* New York, 1931.

Carter, Thomas F. *The Invention of Printing in China and Its Spread Westward.* Rev. ed., L. Carrington Goodrich. New York, 1955.

Chen Shou-yi. *Chinese Literature: A Historical Introduction.* New York, 1961.

Dream of the Red Chamber. Chi-chen Wang trans., Garden City, N.Y., 1929.

The Golden Lotus (Chin Ping Mei). Arthur Waley, intro. 2 vols., New York, 1940.

Hightower, James R. *Topics in Chinese Literature.* Cambridge, 1953, paper.

Hsia, C. T. *A History of Modern Chinese Fiction.* 2nd ed., New Haven, 1971.

Hsu Kai-yu, ed. and trans. *Twentieth Century Chinese Poetry: An Anthology.* Garden City, N.Y., 1963.

Lau Shaw. *Rickshaw Boy.* New York, 1945.

Monkey. Arthur Waley trans. New York, 1943.

Romance of the Three Kingdoms. C. H. Brewitt-Taylor trans. 2 vols., Rutland, Vt., reprint 1959 (1925).

Tsien Tsuen-Hsuin. *Written on Bamboo and Silk: The Beginnings of Chinese Books and Inscriptions.* Chicago, 1962.

Waley, Arthur. *The Life and Times of Po Chü-I, 772-846 A.D.* New York, 1949.

———. *One Hundred and Seventy Chinese Poems.* London, 1939.

———. *The Poetry and Career of Li Po, 701-762.* New York, 1950.

Watson, Burton. *Chinese Lyricism: Shihi Poetry from the Second to the Twelfth Centuries.* New York, 1971.

Society and Politics:

Ayscough, Florence. *A Chinese Mirror*. London, 1925.

———. *Chinese Women Yesterday and Today*. Boston, 1937.

Balazs, E. *Chinese Civilization and Bureaucracy*. New Haven, 1964.

Bodde, Derk, ed. *Essays on Chinese Civilization*. Princeton, 1981, paper.

Dawson, Raymond. *The Legacy of China*. Oxford, 1964.

Ho Ping-ti. *The Ladder of Success in Imperial China: Aspects of Social Mobility, 1361-1911*. New York, 1962.

Loewe, Michael. *Imperial China*. New York, 1966.

Lin Yu-tang. *My Country and My People*. New York, 1939.

Schwartz, Benjamin, ed. *Chinese Reaction to Imported Ideas*. New York, 1951.

Economics and Geography:

Buck, John L. *Land Utilization in China*. Shanghai, 1937.

Cressey, George B. *China's Geographic Foundations*. New York, 1934.

———. *Land of 500 Million*. New York, 1955.

Fei Hsiao-t'ung. *Peasant Life in China*. London, 1939.

Ho ping-ti. *Studies on the Population of China, 1368-1953*. Cambridge, 1959.

Morse, Hoses B. *The Guilds of China*. Shanghai, 1932.

United Kingdom, Naval Intelligence Division. *China Proper*. 3 vols., London, 1949.

Winfield, Gerald F. *China, The Land and The People*. New York, 1950.

Science and Technology:

Needham, Joseph. *Science and Civilisation in China* series. Cambridge, several dozen volumes projected.

I. *Introductory Orientation*, 1954.

II. *History of Scientific Thought*, 1962.

III. *Mathematics and the Science of the Heavens and the Earth*, 1959.

IV. *Physics and Physical Technology:* 1. *Physics*, 1962. 2. *Mechanical Engineering*, 1965. 3. *Civil Engineering and Nautics*, 1971.

V. *Chemistry and Chemical Technology*: 1. Tsien Tsuen-Hsuin. *Paper and Printing*, 1985. 2. *Spagyrical Discovery and Invention: Magisteries of Gold and Immortality*, 1974. 3. *Spagyrical Discovery and Invention: Historical Survey from Cinnabar Elixirs to Synthetic Insulin*, 1976. 4. *Spagyrical Discovery and Invention: Apparatus Theories and Gifts*, 1980; 5. *Spagyrical Discovery and Invention: Physiological Alchemy*, 1983; 7. *Military Technology: the Gunpowder Epic*, 1986; 9. Kuhn Dieter. *Textile Technology: Spinning and Reeling*, 1988.

VI. *Biology and Biological Technology:* 1. *Botany*, 1986. Franceaca Bray, *Agriculture*, 1984.

Ronan, Colin A. *The Shorter Science and Civilisation in China.*

I. Volumes I and II of the Major Series, 1978.

II. Volume III and a Section of Volume IV, part 1 of the Major Series, 1981.

III. Section of Volume IV, Part I and a Section Volume VI, part 3 of the Major Series, 1989.

Temple, Robert. *The Genius of China.* New York, 1986.

Art—General:

Arts of Asia. Hong Kong. Every two months. 1971-.

Asian Art. Washington, D.C.: Arthur Sackler Gallery, Smithsonian Institution. Quarterly, 1987-1993. Then titled *Asian Art and Culture*. Thrice yearly, 1994- .

Grousset, Rene. *Chinese Art and Culture.* New York, 1959.

———. *The Civilizations of the East.* Vol. 3: *China.* New York, 1934.

The Horizon Book of the Arts of China. New York, 1969.

National Palace Museum. *Masterpieces of Chinese Art . . .* , 25 vols., Taipei, 1969-1974.

Orientations. Hong Kong Monthly, 1979-.

Sickman, Laurence, and Alexander Soper. *The Art and Architecture of China.* 3rd ed., Baltimore, 1971.

Siren, Osvald. *A History of Early Chinese Art.* Vols. I and II: *Prehistoric and Pre-Han Period,* 2 vols. in 1, New York reprint 1970 (1930); Vols. III and IV: *Sculpture and Architecture,* 2 vols. in 1, New York reprint 1970 (1930).

Smith, Bradley, and Wang-go Weng. *China: A History in Art.* New York, 1972.

Sullivan, Michael. *A Short History of Chinese Art.* Berkeley, 1967.

Universe Books. *Chinese Art.* 4 vols., New York, 1963-1966.

Watson, William. *Art of Dynastic China.* New York, 1981.

Willetts, William. *Foundations of Chinese Art.* London, 1965.

Williams, C.S.S. *Outlines of Chinese Symbolism and Art Motives.* 3rd rev. ed., Rutland Vt., reprint 1974 (1941).

Art—Specific:

Beurdeley, Cecile and Michael. *A Connoiseur's Guide to Chinese Ceramics.* Kathrine Watson trans. New York, 1974.

Binobi. *Costumes of the Minority Peoples of China.* Np, nd.

Deydier, Christian. *Chinese Bronzes.* New York, 1980.

Goodrich, L. Carrington, and Nigel Cameron. *China as Seen by Photographers and Travelers, 1860-1912.* New York, 1989.

Hyman, Virginia D., and William C.C. Hu. *Carpets of China and Its Border Regions.* Ann Arbor, Mich., 1982.

Jenyns, Soame. *A Background to Chinese Painting.* New York, 1972, paper.

Liang Ssu-ch'eng. *A Pictorial History of Chinese Architecture.* Wilma Fairbank ed. Cambridge, 1984.

Liu, Laurence. *Chinese Architecture.* New York, 1989.

Luo Zewen and others. *The Great Wall.* London, 1981.

Mao Yi-shen. *Bridges in China Old and New.* Peking, 1978.

National Minority Costume in China. Hong Kong, 1985.

Nott, Stanby Charles. *Chinese Jade Throughout the Ages.* Rutland Vt., 1962.

Paludan, Ann. *The Imperial Ming Tombs.* New Haven, 1981.

Rowell, Galen. *Mountains of the Middle Kingdom.* San Francisco, 1983.

Siren, Osvald. *Chinese Painting: Leading Masters and Principles.* 7 vols., New York, reprint 1973 (1956).

————. *Chinese Sculpture.* 4 vols in 2. New York, reprint 1970 (1925).

————. *Gardens of China.* New York, 1949.

————. *The Imperial Palaces of Peking.* New York, reprint 1976 (1926).

Waley, Arthur. *An Introuction to the Study of Chinese Painting.* London, 1923.

Border Areas/Foreign Relations:

Bagchi, Prabodhi C. *India and China: A Thousand Years of Cultural Relations.* 2nd ed., New York, 1951.

Boulnois, Luce. *The Silk Road.* New York, 1966.

Chen, Jack. *The Sinkiang Story.* New York, 1977.

Clyde, Paul H. *International Rivalries in Manchuria, 1689-1922.* Columbus, Ohio, 1928.

Fairbank, Joseph K., ed. *The Chinese World Order.* Cambridge, 1968.

Grousset, Rene. *The Empire of the Steppes.* Naomi Walford trans. New Brunswick, N.J., 1970.

Hudson, Geoffrey. *Europe and China: A Survey of Their Relations from the Earliest Times to 1880.* London, 1931.

Lattimore, Owen. *Inner Asian Frontiers of China.* 2nd ed., New York, 1962.

————, and Eleanor, eds. *Silk, Spices, and Empire.* New York, 1968.

Rupen, Robert. *How Mongolia is Really Ruled.* Stanford, 1979, paper.

Sinor, Denis, ed. *Cambridge History of Early Inner Asia.* Cambridge, 1990.

Spence, Jonathan. *The China Helpers.* London, 1969.

Wei, Henry. *China and Soviet Russia*. Princeton, 1956,

Whiting, Allen S., and General Sheng Shih-ts'ai. *Sinkiang: Pawn or Pivot*. East Lansing, Mich., 1951

Tibet:

Avedon, John F. *In Exile from the Land of the Snows*. London, 1985.

Batchelor, Stephen. *The Tibet Guide*. London, 1987.

Beckwith, Christopher I. *The Tibetian Empire in Central Asia*. Princeton, 1987.

Bell, Charles. *The People of Tibet*. Oxford, 1928.

———. *The Religion of Tibet*. Oxford, 1931.

Dowman, Keith. *The Power-Places of Tibet: The Pilgrim's Guide*. London, 1988, paper.

Fourteenth Dalai Lama. *My Land and My People*. New York, 1977.

Hopkirk, Peter. *Trespassers on the Roof of the World: The Race for Lhasa*. Oxford, 1982, paper.

Pal, Pratapaditya. *Art of Tibet*. Los Angeles 1983.

Rinchen, Dolma Taring. *Daughter of Tibet*. London, 1987.

Richardson, Hugh E. *Tibet and its History*. Boulder, Colo., 1984.

Snellgrove, David, and Hugh Richardson. *A Cultural History of Tibet*. Boston, 1986.

Tucci, Guiseppe. *The Religions of Tibet*. London, 1980.

———. *Tibet: Land of Snows*. J.D. Stapleton Drive trans. 2nd ed., Calcutta, 1973.

———. *To Lhasa and Beyond*. London, reprint 1985 (1949).

Travelers/Archaeologists:

Andrews, Roy Chapman. *Across Mongolian Plains*. New York, 1921.

———. *On the Trail of Ancient Man*. New York, 1926.

Hedin, Sven. *Across the Gobi Desert*. New York, 1933.

———. *Central Asia and Tibet*. 2 vols., London, 1930.

————. *My Life as an Explorer.* Garden City, N.Y., 1925.

————. *Overland to India.* 2 vols., London, 1910.

————. *Through Asia.* 2 vols., New York, 1899.

————. *Trans-Himalaya.* 2 vols., New York, 1909.

Hopkirk, Peter. *Foreign Devils on the Silk Road.* London, 1980.

Mirsky, Jeannette. *Great Chinese Travelers.* London, 1965.

————. *Sir Aurel Stein.* Chicago, 1977.

Stein, Sir Aurel. *Innermost Asia.* 5 vols., New Delhi, reprint 1981.

————. *Ancient Khotan.* 2 vols in 1. New York, reprint 1975 (1907).

————. *On Ancient Central Asian Tracks.* Taipei, reprint 1982 (1933).

————. *Ruins of Desert Cathay.* 2 vols., New York, reprint 1968 (1912).

————. *Serindia.* 5 vols., Delhi, reprint 1980 (1921).

von Le Coq, Albert. *Buried Treasures of Chinese Turkestan.* Hong Kong, 1855, paper.

Yule, Sir Henry, and Henri Cordier. *Cathay and the Way Thither.* 2 vols., Taipei, reprint 1966.

China and the United States

General/Sinologues:

Cohen, Warren I. *America's Response to China.* 3rd ed., New York, 1990, paper.

Dennett, Tyler. *Americans in Eastern Asia.* New York, reprint 1941, (1922). Chapters on China.

Dulles, Foster. *The Old China Trade.* New York, reprint 1970 (1930).

Evans, Paul W. *John Fairbank and the American Understanding of Modern China.* New York, 1988.

Fairbank, John K. *Chinabound.* New York, 1982.

————. *The United States and China.* 4th ed., Cambridge, 1979.

Griswold, A. Whitney. *The Far Eastern Policy of the United States.* New York, 1938.

Liu Kwang-ching. *Americans and Chinese: A Historical Essay and a Bibliography.* Cambridge, 1963.

Spence, Jonathan D. *Chinese Roundabout.* New York, 1992.

Stuart, John L. *Fifty Years in China.* New York, 1954. Missionary, educator, diplomat.

Williams, Frederick. *A History of China.* New York, 1897. Son of S. Wells Williams.

Williams, S. Wells. *The Middle Kingdom.* 2 vols., New York, 1848; rev. ed, 1883.

Pre-twentieth Century:

Abeel, David. *Residence in China.* New York, 1834. Early missionary.

Danton, George H. *The Cultural Contacts of the United States and China.* New York, 1931.

Dulles, Foster Rhea. *The Old China Trade.* New York, reprint 1970 (1930).

Griffin, Eldon. *Clippers and Consuls.* Taipai, reprint 1972 (1938).

Hunt, Michael E. *The Making of a Special Relationship: The United States and China to 1914.* New York, 1983, paper.

La Fargue, Thomas E. *China's First Hundred.* Pullman, Wash., 1942.

Latourette, Kenneth S. *The History of Early Relations between the United States and China, 1784-1844.* New York, reprint 1964 (1917).

Ledyard, John. *Memoirs of the Life and Travels.* Jared Sparks ed. London, 1828. First recorded American in China.

Lubbock, Basil. *The China Clippers.* Boston, 1914.

Shaw, Samuel. *Journals.* Josiah Quincy ed. Taipei, reprint 1968 (1847). First American consul in Canton.

Smith, Arthur H. *Chinese Characteristics.* New York, 1894. Missionary.

Tamarin, Alfred, and Shirley Glubok. *Voyaging to Cathay: Americans in the China Trade.* New York, 1970.

Williams, Frederick W. *Anson Burlingame and the First Chinese Mission to Foreign Powers.* New York, 1912.

Yung Wing. *My Life in China and America.* New York, 1909. Headed first Chinese student group.

Twentieth Century:

Borg, Dorothy. *American Policy and the Chinese Revolution, 1925-1928.* New York, 1947.

————. *The United States of the Far Eastern Crisis of 1933-1938.* Cambridge, 1964.

Dulles, Foster Rhea. *American Policy Toward Communist China, 1949-1969.* New York, 1972.

Feis, Herbert. *The China Triangle.* Princeton, 1953.

Kahn, E.J., Jr. *The China Hands: America's Foreign Service Officers and What Befell Them.* New York, 1975.

Reinsch, Paul. S. *An American Diplomat in China.* Taipei, reprint 1967 (1922).

Schaller, Michael. *The U.S. Crusade in China, 1938-1945.* New York, 1979.

————. *The United States and China in the Twentieth Century.* New York, 1980, paper.

Shewmaker, Kenneth E. *Americans and Chinese Communists, 1927-1945.* Ithaca, 1971.

Stilwell, General Joseph W. *Papers.* Theodore E. White ed. New York, 1948.

Stimson, Henry L. *Far Eastern Crisis.* New York, 1936. Secretary of State.

Tong Te-kong. *United States Diplomacy in China, 1844-60.* Seattle, 1964.

Tuchman, Barbara W. *Stilwell and the American Experience in China, 1911-45.* New York, 1977.

U.S. Department of State. *Papers Relating to the Foreign Relations of the United States.* Volumes on China.

————. *United States Relations with China, with Special Reference to the Period 1944-1949*. Washington, D.C., 1949. The White Paper.

Varg, Paul A. *Missionaries, Chinese, and Diplomats: The American Protestant Missionary Movement in China, 1890-1952*. Princeton, 1958.

INDEX

Titles of books and proper nouns are usually entered in their English equivalents. Chinese names are listed in pinyin (most followed by the Wade-Giles equivalents in parentheses) except those associated with the Republic of China, which adheres to the latter system. Honorifics, except for imperial connotation, are generally omitted. Where English variations exist in spelling names, the simplest version is accepted (i.e., Kublai Khan). China's relations with foreign countries are listed under the latter, including England and the United States. Macau substitutes for Macao; the more commonly used Burma and Ceylon for Myanmar and Sri Lanka.

ABOUT THE AUTHOR

Milton W. Meyer, professor emeritus of history at California State University at Los Angeles, is the author of many volumes relating to Asia, including *Japan: A Concise History* and *South Asia: A Short History of the Subcontinent*. Both are available from Rowman & Littlefield and Littlefield Adams Quality Paperbacks.